60

FARRAR
STRAUS
GIROUX

ALSO BY ALAN TRACHTENBERG

Shades of Hiawatha:
Staging Indians, Making Americans, 1880–1930

Reading American Photographs:
Images as History, Mathew Brady to Walker Evans

The Incorporation of America:
Culture and Society in the Gilded Age

Brooklyn Bridge:
Fact and Symbol

LINCOLN'S SMILE
AND OTHER ENIGMAS

Lincoln's Smile
and Other Enigmas

ALAN TRACHTENBERG

Hill and Wang

A division of Farrar, Straus and Giroux

New York

Hill and Wang
A division of Farrar, Straus and Giroux
19 Union Square West, New York 10003

Grateful acknowledgment is made for permission to reprint "Mule Team and Poster" from *Collected Poems* by Donald Justice, copyright © 2004 by Donald Justice. Used by permission of Alfred A. Knopf, a division of Random House, Inc.

Library of Congress Cataloging-in-Publication Data
Trachtenberg, Alan.
    Lincoln's smile and other enigmas / Alan Trachtenberg.— 1st ed.
        p.   cm.
    Includes bibliographical references and index.
    ISBN-13: 978-0-8090-4297-5 (hardcover : alk. paper)
    ISBN-10: 0-8090-4297-5 (hardcover : alk. paper)
        1. United States—Civilization. 2. Photography—United States—
History. 3. American literature—History and criticism. I. Title.

E169.1.T7215 2007
973—dc22

                                                        2006043920

Designed by Jonathan D. Lippincott

www.fsgbooks.com

1   3   5   7   9   10   8   6   4   2

In memory of my brother, William Trachtenberg
1 September 1934–9 January 2006

A book in itself is a symbolic act of synthesis. The writer of the book is in a personal situation involving a myriad of different factors. His own particular combination is unique—and the book that has engrossed him is the summing-up of this unique combination. But though his situation is unique, it is in many ways like the situation of other people. Hence, their modes of summing-up will manifest patterns that correspond with his.

—Kenneth Burke

Contents

PREFACE

I composed the essays gathered here over some forty years for diverse occasions and purposes. Some were lectures that segued into essays, others were written as articles for journals or contributions to books, still others were introductions or catalog essays. All but two have previously been published, and all are reproduced in their original versions except for minor adjustments. The original source or occasion for each is indicated. Although I have put the essays in roughly chronological order, there's no narrative of origins intended or commentary on each piece's place within my work. The essays stand on their own; there's no buttress of a larger story within which they fit as structural parts.

No larger story, at least not in any overt sense. It would be disingenuous to deny general principles at work in my choices here, not to say in the original composition or construction of each essay. Each on its own should evoke a horizon of general concerns of which it is a specific instance. They are all in some manner studies of *cultural* phenomena within the United States in the nineteenth and twentieth centuries, *American* studies; and they deal with expressive artifacts in the media of literature, photography, and material objects (a bridge, a building, cities as such). In Parts Two and Three, the essays on specific works by specific artists adduce a context in social and cultural history. Although not tightly focused in either urban or photographic or literary studies, these selected essays, if they fulfill my hopes, will cumulatively contribute a measure of historicist and formal analysis to these fields.

I retrieve these essays not to make some grand point but only to give them a chance to live again, to find new vitality in new juxtapositions, to achieve a second life. My hope is that each essay may generate new meanings as parts of a new whole. I have arranged them in roughly the order they were composed, and also roughly in the chronological order of their subjects, to suggest change over time in actual history and in my thinking about the various topics. I also want to give prominence to various dialectical relations within the historical process, between texts and contexts of social experience, between authors (producers) and audiences (consumers).

The essays in Part One, set primarily in the antebellum decades, derive chiefly from the photographic studies that have occupied a large part of my attention over the years. The daguerreotype looms large here, and Hawthorne's *The House of the Seven Gables* is one pole of the dialogic relation implicit in all of this section's essays between image and word or, as in the title of Chapter 5, photography as symbolic history. This section bears kinship with my *Reading American Photographs* (1989). Part Two belongs principally (though not exclusively) to the post–Civil War decades known as the Gilded Age and shares concerns with my *Brooklyn Bridge: Fact and Symbol* (1965) and *The Incorporation of America* (1982). The materials are mainly literary and urban, and I include my discussions of the meanings evolved in the dialogue between urban artifacts like the Brooklyn Bridge and Chicago's Auditorium Building and the general culture. Part Three moves into the twentieth century and returns to photography, expanding it to include cinema and continuing the exploration of the relation between images and words in the form of stories and "phototexts."

What the essays have in common, then, is that they deal with verbal or visual artifacts that express the mingling of individual and collective consciousness at particular moments of U.S. history. Such artifacts can be usefully called cultural texts, which register structures of meaning and feeling shared by most members of the society, though not without significant conflict and disagreement over meanings and applications. As the book's title implies, cultural texts can also be enigmatic, something puzzling, obscure, riddlelike. Certain forms of culture or collective consciousness put questions to those who live within them, questions whose answers are normally taken for granted at a level of behavior so deep that we are hardly aware of the enigmas buried in them. To call this or that familiar picture or habitual action or ritual saying enigmatic is to acknowledge and recover something uncertain, unfamiliar, and strange, something hidden and reified—turned as if to stone—within the practical normalcy of everyday existence. Approaching the commonplace and the familiar as if it were strange and enigmatic is to melt its protective stonelike armature, to reveal the provisional and arbitrary character of all human constructions. As a heuristic, the concept of enigma makes us aware of the role of interrogation we typically ignore by taking it for granted. "Every man's condition is a solution in hieroglyphic to those inquiries he would put," Emerson wrote. "Let us interrogate the great apparition [by this he means "nature," all that is the "NOT ME," including art] that shines so peacefully around us." The aim of interrogation is to dispel the apparition of tranquillity and to reveal how unsettled, how agitated with unanswered questions, is our common life.

Enigma, hieroglyph, apparition: these are some of the tropes or metaphors by which we name not so much things themselves but our awareness of the opacity of things and their meanings. We can add to this list Constance Rourke's "vagary," a term that captures a sense of capriciousness, eccentricity, and extravagance that cannot readily be pinned down. Vagary calls up frolic and prank, any "departure or straying from the ordered, regular, or usual course of conduct, decorum, or propriety" (OED). Humor, Rourke wrote, "is a lawless element, full of surprises." The "American vagaries" Rourke studied with her contagious enjoyment and gratitude are vernacular expressions of the shared everyday life of local and regional groups in the United States, expressions that qualify as native folk culture. High culture is symmetrical, revered as pristine. The divagating character of the vagarious, like the self-questioning character of the enigmatic, gives off for Rourke an authentic aroma of earth and sweat, the true character of the national experience, the people's experience, of the United States.

Vagary and enigma also convey something inherent about the act of criticism, its need to break through appearances to reach fundamental meanings, even as it recognizes that what looks fundamental may in all likelihood be revealed as delusion, conceit, another riddle wrapped in an enigma. Modern criticism subjects all that exists to the corrosive power of reason in the hope of solving the riddle, defeating the enigma, capturing and holding the vagaries under the glass of analysis and deconstruction. Is that a smile half playing on the sad lips of Abraham Lincoln in the last photograph of him taken by Alexander Gardner in Washington shortly before or just after his Second Inaugural Address in March 1865? The speech concludes with the famous lines of offered conciliation, which Lincoln may well have realized would hardly suffice to dispel the bitterness of defeat or the arrogance of victory: "With malice toward none; with charity for all . . ." If it is a smile, what does it signify? The question beguiles us. Does the smile imply that Lincoln's war-weary face hides a secret, an undisclosed meaning? Whatever else it may mean, the smile (if that's what it is) is an artifact of the camera. How does our knowledge of the procedures and the semiotic logic of photography mediate our interpretation of this face that photography has made so familiar? Only by responding to it as an enigma might we recover its life as a trace of an instant in the life of Lincoln, and its secondary life as cultural meaning. I explore such questions in Chapter 4, an essay that exemplifies interrogation of enigmas as cultural criticism.

If pressed to say what these essays are cumulatively about, I'd confess that they aspire to the kind of historical criticism practiced by Constance Rourke and her generation—Randolph Bourne, Van Wyck Brooks, Waldo Frank, Lewis Mumford, William Carlos Williams, Paul Rosenfeld. These early twentieth-century "critics of culture" and left-wing intellectuals were influenced by the Progressive and socialist movements and inspired, as Casey Blake has shown, by promise of a "beloved community" in place of the competitive strife of daily existence. Their works in the 1910s and 1920s laid a foundation for the academic field of American studies that appeared in the 1930s and took hold in the 1950s. Not coincidentally, they were the first American intellectuals to recognize photography as a serious medium of personal and cultural expression. Other influences are obviously evident in these essays: Walter Benjamin and Roland Barthes, for instance, on photography and material culture, Raymond Williams on literature and cultural history, to name the most obvious. But my indebtedness—and the indebtedness of the entire "movement" known as American studies—to these early pioneers in cultural studies deserves remembering and honoring for a legacy especially as it fades from view.

Rourke's *American Humor* has been one of the most durable of responses to Van Wyck Brooks's call for a "usable past," a new heritage in opposition to the complacent aestheticism of "the genteel tradition." But Rourke dissociated herself from two of Brooks's precepts: that America has "had no cumulative culture" and that "the spiritual welfare of this country depends altogether upon the fate of its creative minds." Brooks thought the American cultural tradition was impoverished, in need of regeneration from above by liberated artists and intellectuals. Evoking vagaries, full of surprises, Rourke took Brooks's high-flown motives down a peg or two. In place of impoverishment she showed the indebtedness of major writers from Emerson to Henry James and contemporaries like Frost and Eliot to the bursting, lawless energies of the vernacular comedy of everyday life in America. Even as she accepted the cultural mission of inventing a "usable past," Rourke revised Brooks's view that America's national culture was undernourished, puritanical, chauvinistic, given to celebration of violent individualism, and crippled by antagonistic separation between "highbrow" and "lowbrow." With the broad scholarship in folk life at her command, Rourke demonstrated that "high" art in the United States has always been nurtured by roots in folk cultures.

A woman of the cultural left, modernist rather than antiquarian in her tastes, a friendly critic of 1930s Marxism, an anti-Fascist activist in the years before her early death in 1942, Rourke pledged herself to the goals of democratic cultural criticism. Americans, she wrote, "do not have that strong and natural association with evidences of the past which is still commonplace in other countries." By evidence she meant not only verbal culture but also things, sounds, tales, songs, furniture, paintings and photographs, theater and dance. When she died at the age of fifty-six she was at work on a projected three-volume "history of

American culture"—"evidence of enough native culture to convert a generation of disenchanted artists," as Joan Rubin has written. In a review of the posthumous collection of her work edited by Van Wyck Brooks as *The Roots of American Culture*, Alfred Kazin wrote: "She sought what so many modern Americans have lost, what so many Europeans have established as the first principle of a human existence—the sense of locality, the simple happiness of belonging to a particular culture."

What Rourke and her colleagues sought was a *nation*, an America rooted in particular places, languages, ethnicities, ways of life: America not as a single dominating culture but as a medley of cultures, a harmonious multiplicity of cultures. The word "culture," itself containing a multiplicity of meanings, as Raymond Williams showed in *Culture and Society*, arose in England in response to industrialization; the word came to stand for communal traditions and patterns of behavior and feeling, relations between natural and man-made places that undergo rapid change with the rise of industrial capitalism. Culture came to mean a whole way of life, something that might offer a model for newly formed communal relations imagined by socialist critics of the ferociously selfish and destructive capitalist order. It is what Van Wyck Brooks called "a living culture," which he imagined still survived "everywhere in Europe, in spite of the industrialization of society."

For Brooks this beguiling image of an organic culture projected an image of "nation"—"a living, homogeneous entity, with its own faith and consciousness of self." The vision of a culture both organic and national lay at the base of the idea of an emergent democratic America Brooks shared with Rourke and others of their generation. But the vision foundered in contradiction. America's entry into World War I represented, as Randolph Bourne saw more clearly than others, a fateful step toward imperialism, away from the democratic ethos the critics had assumed as foundational to "our America." Mass immigration and cultural multiplicity had created millions of acculturated city dwellers who had only the poisonous distractions of patriotic fervor and debased commercial culture to prop up their lost sense of identity and of belonging somewhere.

In its origins, the academic field of American studies took from Emerson, Whitman, Brooks, and their followers the idea of America as a yet unrealized ideal, an idea necessary as motive and goal to the practice of historical cultural criticism. "The meal in the firkin; the milk in the pan; the ballad in the street; the news of the boat; the glance of the eye; the form and gait of the body," Emerson wrote in 1837; "show me the ultimate reason of these matters . . . and the world no longer lies a dull miscellany and lumber-room, but has form and order." Through an art of the common, the familiar, the low, and indeed the enigmatic, Emerson believed that "a nation of men will for the first time exist, because each believes himself inspired by the Divine Soul which also inspires all men." This was echoed by Van Wyck Brooks eighty years later: "As soon as the foundations of our life have been reconstructed and made solid on the basis of our own experience, all these extraneous, ill-regulated forces will rally about their newly found center; they will fit in, each where it belongs, contributing to the essential architecture of our life. Then, and only then, shall we cease to be a blind, selfish, disorderly people; we shall become a luminous people, dwelling in the light and sharing our light."

Whitman understood the stakes in this exceptionalist view of the nation to be fateful. In *Democratic Vistas* (1870) he wrote that America and democracy are "convertible terms," or had better be. Otherwise, America is a failed idea, "the most tremendous failure of time," "merely a passing gleam." Following Whitman, Rourke wanted to contribute to the conversion of America into democracy by recovering vagaries of native cultures scorned by the genteel guardians of high culture. The enemy were those who denied that the United States could achieve a discrete cultural nationality on the basis of its native arts and habits. After World War II, in the years of the Cold War, American Studies more or less adopted the same position, with the query "What is American?" as a core, defining issue.

Recently the field has experienced an almost 180-degree reversal on this score. The day has long past when any hint of national celebration has appeared in discourse associated with American studies. To the contrary, the concept of nation has been virtually exorcised as incongruous in an age of globalism. To confine a field of studies to the boundaries of a nation-state has come to seem deliberate blindness. Leading questions now are likely to be about the global menace of the

American military and economic hegemony, the rhetorical conflation of America and democracy as a disguise for imperial intentions and practices. The quest for cultural nationality has been almost entirely surpassed by a quest for transnational and postnational identities and prospects. That American studies faces an uncertain future is a sign of the faded status of the early twentieth-century "critics of culture," since Americanist critics give so little credibility to Whitman's aporia about the convertibility of America and democracy, its having been debased by being used so cynically in U.S. foreign policy.

The notion of interchangeability of the terms "democracy" and "America" mystifies both terms, removes them from actual histories of struggle and conflict, and makes racism, sexism, and economic exploitation seem aberrations rather than structural features of a harshly divided society. To view the United States in a secular way, as a society torn by conflicting interests, pulled apart by struggles over power and wealth, divided by color and gender and social class as much as by region and ethnic distinctiveness, its history shaped more by commodity production and the degradation of labor than by sacral ideals, continually restructured by the privileged to maintain and reproduce privilege—to view it in such a way cannot but jolt the tradition in which the name America was once considered a precondition for cultural democracy.

And the idea of the United States as a singular, coherent nationality based, as Lincoln believed, on universal principles as articulated in the opening lines of the Declaration of Independence, now faces an impasse. It is worth recalling the alternative Randolph Bourne posed in his famous essay of 1916, "Trans-National America." Bourne urged that we think again "of what Americanism may rightly mean." "No intense nationalism of the European plan can be ours," he wrote, and proposed "a new and more adventurous ideal: Do we not see how the national colonies in America, deriving power from the deep cultural heart of Europe and yet living here in mutual toleration, freed from the age-long tangles of races, creeds, and dynasties, may work out a federated ideal?" Colonies of difference, vagarious and enigmatic to each other, "live here inextricably mingled, yet not homogeneous. They merge but they do not fuse." Their lesson is that "we shall have to give up the search for our native 'American' culture."

Bourne proposed to embrace these multiple cultural languages, the heteroglossia of the practical democracy of American streets. His late essays on "war and the intellectuals" implicitly asked whether it was enough for cultural criticism to study culture alone. "The cultural question," wrote John Dewey, "is a political and economic one before it is a definitely cultural one." Historical cultural criticism can desanctify the terms "culture," "democracy," and "America," freeing them from their reified state, flushing out the enigmas and vagaries hidden within their apparently normal and familiar meanings, submitting them to rigorous social and political scrutiny. The essays presented here track the cultural question as it fluctuates among the diverse texts and images that comprise America's collective life. Vision is the core theme: powers of vision and visions of power to light a way ahead. "In a dark time," wrote Theodore Roethke, "the eye begins to see."

PART ONE

ONE

MIRROR IN THE MARKETPLACE

American Responses to the Daguerreotype, 1839–51

I

IN the salon of a Broadway hotel on December 4, 1839, the first French daguerreotypes made their initial New World appearance. In the preceding months American examples of the fledgling art of picturing had already been seen in New York shop windows, but here were specimens from the hand of the inventor and master himself, Louis-Jacques-Mandé Daguerre, offered to the public by his ingratiating agent François Gouraud. With impeccable credentials as "friend and pupil of Mr. Daguerre," Gouraud announced his "charge of introducing to the New World the perfect knowledge of the marvelous process of drawing, which fame has already made known to you under the name of 'The Daguerreotype.'" Already known by name, the curious objects with their flickering images of Parisian boulevards and monuments nevertheless challenged the credulity of the select audience. Seeking an appropriate language to describe "their exquisite perfection [that] transcends the bounds of sober belief," Lewis Gaylord Clark, patrician editor of *The Knickerbocker*, struck upon a perfect solution from the apparatus of everyday life—a looking glass:

Let us endeavor to convey to the reader an impression of their character. Let him suppose himself standing in the middle of

First published in *The Daguerreotype: A Sesquicentennial Celebration*, edited by John Wood (Iowa City: University of Iowa Press, 1989), pp. 60–71.

Broadway, with a looking-glass held perpendicular in his hand, in which is reflected the street, with all that therein is, for two or three miles, taking in the haziest distance. Then let him take the glass into the house, and find the impression of the entire view, in the softest light and shade, visibly retained upon its surface. This is the Daguerreotype! . . . There is not an object even the most minute embraced in that wide scope, which was not in the original; and it is impossible that one should have been omitted. Think of that!

Like Plato's whirling mirror, Clark's panorama of Broadway beguiles the mind with flashing images of the real. Of course, Plato's conundrum of appearance and reality, in which the mirror induces a kind of inebriation in the deceptive pleasure of mere illusion, is hardly the case here; Clark's mirror stands simply and unambiguously for exactitude, and the author's quite anti-Platonic awe at imitation itself: "Think of that!"

Exuberant awe and fascination prevailed at the inauguration of photography in America, as it did everywhere in Europe. Here was proof again, like lithography, the steam engine, the railroad, of an age of "progress," of enlightened reason prevailing over dark superstition, and science over magic. But the chorus of celebration was not without its discordant notes. The very wonder excited by first sight of the new objects occasionally harbored a more reserved, disbelieving response, such as we hear from Philip Hone, another visitor to Gouraud's exhibition, who included among his words of praise in his diary this flickering hint of uncertainty: "One may almost be excused for disbelieving it without seeing the very process by which it is created. It appears to me a confusion of the very elements of nature." This note of discomfort, quickly muffled in Hone's hymn of celebration, finds an answering echo in the reaction of Phoebe in Hawthorne's *The House of the Seven Gables* (1851): "I don't much like pictures of that sort,—they are so hard and stern; besides dodging away from the eye, and trying to escape altogether." Phoebe's unease invokes a little-regarded moment in the early career of photography in America, a moment of shudder, suspicion, and refusal. "I don't wish to see it any more," she cries. To be sure, most Americans proved eager enough not only to see but to possess a specimen of the new art, and a thriving trade in daguerrean images developed rapidly. Photography fit so neatly the rhetoric of the "technological sublime" common in the age of steam in America, how are we to understand the few but insinuating signs of a countervailing response?

For the cultural historian such rifts within the linguistic environment of a technological innovation provide telling signs of an uneven process of change. In regard to photography, the process of acclimatization was neither as spontaneous nor as unequivocal as is often assumed. The compacted overlay of implication within the language of response can help us reconstruct and understand a climate of mind within which photography achieved its initial cultural identity in America. Language in its figurative uses especially—images, allusions, metaphors—preserves nuances of meaning that can be read as indices to the cultural effects of historical change. The figures by which people represent new phenomena to themselves and each other is especially valuable to the historian, for by such language the new is brought into relation with the old and the familiar—in Emerson's words, is perceived "to be only a new version of our familiar experience." By familiarizing new objects, tropes such as Clark's mirror on Broadway serve as more than descriptive terms; they signify an entire process of ingesting new experiences, making a place for them within existing systems of thought and feeling, and in the process modifying old structures in ways only a sensitive attention to language can reveal. Particularly apt and promising for close attention, then, is the metaphor of the photograph as mirror, especially as Clark imagines it: a mirror in the New World marketplace of Broadway.

II

"Talk no more of 'holding the mirror up to nature'—she will hold it up to herself, and present you with a copy of her countenance for a penny." Thus exclaimed N. P. Willis in the *Corsair*, April 13, 1839, the first published news of photography in the American press. He had not set eyes on an actual specimen, had only read William Henry Fox Talbot's account of his experiments in the English *Literary Gazette* (February 2, 1839), but instantly imagined the medium as a kind of mirror press by which nature imprints itself as a cheap picture. Seizing the Englishman's remark that the invention would abridge "the labor of the artist in copying natural objects," and that "by means of this contrivance, it is not the artist who makes the picture, but the picture which makes *itself*," Willis calls up a scene of panic among displaced craftsmen: "Steel engravers, copper engravers, and etchers, drink up your aquafortis, and die! There is an end of your black art—'Othello's occupation gone.' The real black art of true magic arises and cries avaunt. . . . The Daguerreoscope* and the Photogenic revolutions are to keep you all down, ye painters, engravers, and, alas! the harmless race, the sketchers."

The cleverness of the conceit was not entirely a joking matter. New York in the winter and spring of 1839 still felt the worst effects of the catastrophic Panic of 1837: financial collapse, ruinous defaults and bankruptcies, uncontrollable deflation, and an economic slowdown of an order never before experienced in the United States. Over the next ten years, virtually until the discovery of California gold in 1849, the city remained gripped by unemployment, rising pauperism and homelessness, sporadic riots, and an increase in violent crime. In light of what one writer in 1843 called "these Jeremiad times," in which "only the *beggars* and the *takers of likenesses by daguerreotype*" can survive, Willis's "real black art" reveals a distinct social meaning.

Among the early writers on the new medium, mostly gentlemen scientists and artists like Samuel F. B. Morse, Willis is virtually alone in imaging the situation from the point of view of practicing draftsmen, engravers, and printers. The depressed condition in fact created a favorable climate for the commercial development of portrait daguerreotypy. To set up on one's own required only a minor outlay of capital and small expenses, and thus photography could take up some of the slack among unemployed craftsmen. Not that he himself refers

---

*It remains unclear how Willis came upon this misnomer, which implies that he had already heard of Daguerre even before the New York *Observer* published Samuel F. B. Morse's eyewitness account of Daguerre's invention in a letter from Paris.

explicitly to the hard times visible on the streets of New York, but his imaginary scene of discarded craftsmen, their "occupation gone," serves as a sharp reminder that photography appeared in America in the midst of the first modern depression and mass unemployment, the first signal of an unstable economic system keyed to the mysterious vagaries of capital, of money. It seemed to many at the time that blame for the depression lay at the hands of private banks and their issuance of paper money not backed by specie, a practice that encouraged unrestrained speculation. While this is difficult to prove, it is not improbable that loss of the authority of printed money and the consequent widespread perception of instability in society's basic token of exchange affected the reception of photography, a new technique that itself threatened, as Willis foresaw, to destabilize the entire craft of picture making and, not least, to deflate another kind of standard currency: the representational value of handcrafted pictures.

Willis imagines further ambiguities and encroachments in the realm of daily life.

> What would you say to looking in a mirror and having the image fastened!! As one looks sometimes, it is really quite frightful to think of it; but such a thing is possible—nay, it is probable—no, it is certain. What will become of the poor thieves, when they shall see handed in as evidence against them their own portraits, taken by the room in which they stole, and in the very act of stealing! What wonderful discoveries is this wonderful discovery destined to discover! The telescope is rather an unfair telltale; but now every thing and every body may have to encounter his double every where, most inconveniently, and every one become his own caricaturist.

Beneath the witticism lies a vein of serious contemporary worry, the telling linkage of anxiety over losing one's "image" by stealth and one's property by theft. The doubled fear results in a paradoxical predicament: what the magic mirror seems to offer on one hand—security of possessions through an invisible system of surveillance—it removes on the other—the security of self-possession, the danger of appearing in public as a caricature of oneself. Owners and thieves stand equally naked, undefended, against the scrutiny of a newly ubiquitous social eye, a gaze belonging to an invisible body; the implacable mirror is simply immanent, part of the room. Thus the inconvenient "double" is itself doubled, representing two apparently distinct but distinctly connected objects of anxiety: personal goods and public "image." Are owner and thief, then, two sides of the same self? Willis seems to grasp, at least in the unconscious vibrations of his language, that he stands at the threshold of a major turn in culture, toward a condition in which mechanically reproduced self-images will emerge as a new form of marketable, and thus vulnerable, personal property.

This is not to claim any special prescience in Willis but to identify implicit concerns and fears betrayed by the linguistic resources that lay ready at hand to a Broadway writer in 1839. In the following years numerous writers will include, in their list of "applications" of photography, protection against crime both by direct surveillance (anticipating the autoptic functions of the camera) and by physiognomic identification of criminality, or revelation of "character" through "image." Willis's fantasy of self-indicting thieves in the night, slight as it is, can be seen as answering to the sort of tense nervousness in middle-class New York we detect by noticing what lies on either side of Philip Hone's diary entry about his visit to the Gouraud exhibition. His glowing account of the French daguerreotypes appears between two entries of disturbing acts of violence. The first tells of drunken street brawls and stabbings, "some even in Broadway," signs that "the city is infested by gangs of hardened wretches, born in the haunts of infamy"; the second, of "a most outrageous revolt" of tenants near Albany, "of a piece with the vile disorganizing spirit which overspreads the land like a cloud." The social turmoil within which photography appeared in America, and the perceptions of crisis among the earliest elite patrons of the new medium, could hardly be made more graphic than this location within the private discourse of his diary of Hone's appreciation of "one of the wonders of modern times."

Even more graphic and dire are scenes depicted in a slim novel by Augustine Joseph Hockey Duganne, published in Philadelphia in 1846 by G. B. Zieber, suggestively titled *The Daguerreotype Miniature; or, Life in the Empire City.* The earliest appearance of photography in American fiction, this otherwise unremarkable pulp fiction puts into dramatic motion many of the covert concerns and perceptions dashed off in Willis's brief essay. By plot and theme the story belongs to the genre of "city mystery" popularized in the 1840s by the labor radical George Lippard. A country lad appears on Broadway and falls into the clutches of two confidence men who scheme against his life as well as the inheritance of which he himself is ignorant. While their elaborate plans proceed, the innocent hero wanders among the "gorgeous" shop window displays of Broadway and falls in love with a daguerreotype portrait he sees in the window of the "Plumbe National Daguerrian Gallery" at Broadway and Murray streets (an actual place; indeed Duganne dedicates the book to "Professor Plumbe"), recognizing it as the very image of the beautiful young lady he had glimpsed his first day on Broadway, when he risked his life to stop the runaway horses of her carriage. He procures a copy of the daguerreotype in exchange for allowing Plumbe to take his own likeness and wears it in his bosom as an amulet; indeed it proves its magical powers in the end by deflecting a knife blade aimed at his heart by one of the villainous crew and leads him to marriage with the appreciative young heiress.

But the plot alone provides only a fraction of the interest of the tale. *Life in the Empire City*, which takes place chiefly on Broadway, appears as a never-ceasing drama of *eyes*, of watching, observing, gazing. The plot itself centers on acts of deception, of false identity, disguise, and betrayal; its villains are gamblers, speculators, conniving lawyers— a predictable Jacksonian cast of enemies of republican virtue. Duganne opens the narrative upon the "river of life" of Broadway, in which the crowds go about their business mindless of a certain set of "men with cunning eyes . . . watchful and observing, glancing at each and all." They are all "robbers," though "some were called merchants, bankers, brokers, aldermen, judges, lawyers, and gentlemen—others were designated as speculators, sportsmen, bloods, and beggars." What they have in common is a certain kind of eye, "in the expression of which were cunning, and uncharitableness, and cruelty, and deceit." The text overflows with terms of seeing: "survey," "glance," "gaze," "observe," "view," "detect," "penetrate," "look," "behold," "inspect," "stare," "scrutinize," "appear," and "disappear." Moreover, a number of reflective surfaces—the large plate windows of a saloon, the waters on the bay, the gloss and glitter of the arch—confidence man's sartorial splendor, and not least, the eyes in which the united lovers at the end "beheld . . . the light of first love"—provide a mise-en-scène of glinting mirror effects. A paradoxical place of heightened visibility and counterfeit appearances, Duganne's Broadway resembles a hall of mirrors, where selves encounter each other as images, as doubles, and "robbers" disguised as respectable men of business lie spying on unaware victims.

And in the midst of Broadway, at the still center of this swirling spectacle, Duganne inserts a picture gallery. The very site of both image making and exhibition, it is a place above the street where "ladies and their attendant gentlemen" "promenaded the floor, or paused admiringly beneath some elegant frame." Duganne's description of the actual Plumbe gallery corresponds strikingly with a newspaper account by Walt Whitman in the Brooklyn *Eagle* in the same year: "The crowds continually coming and going—the fashionable belle, the many distinguished men. . . . What a spectacle! In whatever direction you turn your peering gaze, you see naught but human faces! There they stretch, from floor to ceiling—hundreds of them. Ah! what tales might those pictures tell if their mute lips had the power of speech!"

The pictures, mainly of the famed and celebrated, engage Whitman in speechless conversation, their silence together with their vividness "creating the impression of an immense Phantom concourse—speechless and motionless, but yet *realities*. You are indeed in a new world—a peopled world, though mute as the grave." A "new world" of images conveying a new order of reality: Whitman thus discovers in Plumbe's gallery of daguerreotype portraits unsuspected powers in the eyesight alone. The eye, he writes, "has a sort of magnetism. . . . An electrical chain seems to vibrate, as it were, between our brains and him or her preserved there so well. . . . Time, space, both are annihilated, and we identify the semblance with the reality."

Duganne evokes a similar mystic sense of the gallery as a new kind of electrical power which "chain[s] the attention of the passer-by." Its function in the tale, moreover, is not merely to embellish the story with a contemporary reference or to provide the deus ex machina to resolve the plot—the physical daguerreotype that saves the hero's life. More than this, the gallery holds the key to the symbolic action of the melodrama, for it holds up a mirror of truth in the place of deception. It provides images that counteract those of the street: portraits of "statesmen, the renowned soldiers, the distinguished _literateurs_ [_sic_] of the country, [who] looked down, life-like, from their frames." With its irresistibly compelling pictures of presidents, governors, poets, and preachers, "Lecturers, Lions, Ladies and Learned Men," the gallery was "a perfect study of character." In a world of rogues and false seemers, the gallery above yet within Broadway offers itself as a paragon of character, a mirror of what ought to be as perceived in the faithful representation of the best that is—what a few years later, following Plumbe's lead, Mathew Brady will call his "Gallery of Illustrious Americans." Just as the hero assures his own salvation by fixing "indelibly within my bosom" the "image" of his love, so citizens can save themselves and their city by gazing on these still, magical images. Thus the "daguerreotype miniature" represents more than an incident and a device of plot but a pedagogy, a kind of "mirror of magistrates," to "the life of the empire city."

Duganne's fiction alludes to a cultural program for photography already established in public discourse by 1846. The photograph represents a different kind of image from that which catches the eye in the crowded flux of the street, and in its difference lies a hope for control, for a moral pedagogy from above: a teaching by images of the virtues missing on city streets and in shops and halls of public office. In the same year an article in the _Christian Watchman_ spoke of daguerreotypes as "indices of human character," providing "so many exponential signs of disposition, desire, character," and thus accomplishing "a great revolution in the morals" of portraiture. Unlike a hand-drawn or painted portrait, most likely designed to flatter, the daguerreotype offers a genuine mediation of a living presence, thus making it possible for the moral leadership of the society to make itself felt as immediate experience. In a world where money transactions prevail, where the marketplace and competitive individualism encourage a traffic in false images, the emerging discourse implied, the daguerreotype portrait offers an especially potent corrective. For it too belongs to the market; it competes as image with image, as true image driving out false. The quasi-magical mirror of the daguerreotype miniature seemed to offer, then, an amulet against the menace hidden within the Broadway spectacle, the threat of counterfeit transactions at the market center of the Empire City.

III

Within the overt appropriation of the mirror image as an emblem of security, a paragon of character, a pedagogy of republican virtue lay less hopeful, more murky implications in the new technology of picturing. Variants of the mirror image—from exactitude to enchantment, from accuracy to necromancy—disclose a fascination that cannot be explained by reference to rational political motive alone. Like Willis's "the real black art of true magic arises and cries avaunt," Phoebe's turning away from the shadowy image as if it possessed a will or spirit of its own revives ancient taboos against graven images and likenesses, against icons, simulacra, imitations—any reproduction of the world's appearances. It may be that reproduction as such excites subliminal unease, as Jean Baudrillard writes in *Simulations*, for "it makes something fundamental vacillate." A closer look at uses of the mirror metaphor offers some clues to its staying power.

The trope seems to have, for example, a basis in physical fact. As an object the daguerreotype indeed resembles a looking glass, the image floating on the surface of a silver-plated copper sheet burnished to a bright mirror effect. By a mere shift of optical focus from the image to the ground upon which the image appears, beholders have a personal hand mirror, their own mutable reflections mingling with the primary image. The result is a doubling of image upon image: the beholder's fluxional image superimposed upon the fixed daguerrean image, most commonly a portrait of someone known to the viewer. The effect is apparitional: at the merest tilt of the plate the photographic image flickers away, fades into a shadowed negative of itself entangled in the living image of the beholder. The primary image comes to seem evanescent, suspended in a depthless medium. Moreover, as in actual mirrors the daguerrean portrait appears reversed right to left, thus allowing the sitter viewing his own finished image the curious experience of catching sight of himself in the past, as if in a mirror-once-removed, coexisting with one's present and immediate mirror image.

But by themselves literal associations only partially explain the pervasiveness and power of the mirror metaphor. In its semantic depths lay resources answerable to needs less articulate than those of physical description, or of the cultural needs to which the emulatory theory of the daguerrean portrait responds. By tradition a paradoxical symbol both of the mind's encyclopedic capacity to depict the sensible world (Plato's whirling mirror) and of the mind's severe and fatal confinement to its own self-image (the Narcissus myth), the looking-glass image was at the same time a folklore motif of wizardry, black magic, occult divination, forbidden encounters with the dead or absent, and it projected alternative, elusive, and contradictory interpretations upon the new mode of picturing by light. Standing at once for truth and deception, the trope of photograph-as-mirror returned to its users their own confusions and incomprehension, a modern version of old suspicions aroused by images and icons. No matter how well intentioned as a term of praise, "mirror" transfers to the photograph the duplicity traditionally suspected of pictures and picture makers.

Of course, no more need be made of such figures than to take them as a sign of linguistic resourcefulness before the unfamiliar. But their persistence into the first decade and beyond of American photography, particularly in popular fiction and verse, suggests something more complex and revealing: oblique or unconscious recognitions of an uncanny and possibly disruptive power in the new medium of mechanical reproduction. In popular fiction of the 1840s and 1850s, daguerreotype likenesses appear not only as amulets but also as objects of unique obsession, as if they were living presences. In sentimental and celebratory verse they are indeed living spirits, animated shadows, or souls of the dead. Most often they appear in Gothic settings of preternatural fantasy, wrapped in the same cloth of motifs and imagery examined by Otto Rank in his study of the "doppelgänger" and by Freud in "The Uncanny."

Like Freud's "uncanny," which arises out of a relation between the familiar and the unfamiliar, the *heimlich* and the *unheimlich*, animistic descriptions of the photograph often arise in an "enlightened," even scientific and technical, discourse in which the invention of photography represents a major event in the progressive liberation of mankind from superstition, magic, and mental tyranny. Animism may seem a minor note within the rhetoric of "progress" that greeted photography, but its effect is acute. The coexistence of discourses suggests that the process of assimilation of photography within the broader culture shaped itself as a dialectic between familiarizing and defamiliarizing languages, between images of science and images of magic. Writers employed the rhetoric of enlightenment to make a home for the new medium and its unfamiliar images within a familiar ideology, just as practitioners tried by a steady current of "improvements" to make the image seem familiar as "fine art." At the same time, and often in the very same pages of journals, other writings reveled in uncanny sensations that, as Freud observed, arise when something novel comes to seem already known, "once very familiar." It is the meeting again, unexpectedly, of "something familiar and old-established in the mind that has been estranged only by the process of repression."

One of Freud's major examples is the recurrence of an emotion associated with "the old, animistic conception of the universe," which supposed that "the world was peopled with spirits of human beings." Thus animistic tropes in written accounts of photography can be taken as a return, at the site of an image, of guilty, repressed beliefs in the old animistic universe expelled by Christianity, reason, and science. Uncanny sensations such as Phoebe experiences would thus represent the unconscious recurrence, charged with guilt, of the long-repressed belief and feeling that likenesses—shadows as well as reflections in mirror surfaces—are detached portions of living creatures, their soul or spirit. Freud's insight into the way the psyche allows itself the pleasurable terrors of the uncanny in order to reinforce its defensive repressions helps us to better understand the function of figures of black magic as reinforcement of the authority of "reason." It suggests that the progressivist view of the origin and development of photography allowed space for "irrational" figurations as a way of reinforcing itself, confirming its own authority to speak for the future of the medium, especially its application to the fine-art genre of portraiture.

The social history of the medium supports this supposition. While commercial practitioners in the early 1840s were often transient entrepreneurs and itinerants, photographic communities began to consolidate in the major cities, and by the beginning of the 1850s a distinct "profession" emerged, complete with national journals, associations, competitions, and awards. A key element in this process was a differentiation between the "mechanics" (including the practical science) and the "art" (including the theoretical science) of photography, as well as between "cheap" and "artistic" pictures.* The early journals took as their major cause the need for theoretically knowledgeable and artistically cultivated practice as the prerequisite for professional status. The mix of articles of history, science, and art, chronicling the history of research leading to photography and combining theoretical discussion of the nature of light and optics with arguments for the fine-art possibilities within the medium, conveys the ambition for the public acceptance of commercial photography as a *serious* and not merely a marketplace endeavor.

Henry Snelling, founder and editor of the *Photographic Art Journal*, titled his lead editorial in the first issue, January 1851, "The Art of Photography":

At the present day it [photography] is viewed, too much, in the light of a mere mechanical occupation to arrive at any high

---

*Insight into the competitive framework within which this distinction appeared can be gleaned from the following double-entry meditation on the trade by the publisher S. D. Humphrey in his *Daguerreian Journal* 1 (1850): 49: "We find 71 rooms in this city, devoted solely to this art; independent of the many stores and manufactories engaged in the making and selling of the materials. In these rooms there are in all 127 operators, including the proprietors and persons engaged in the Galleries, also 11 ladies and 46 boys. We find the amount of rent paid by these artists to be $25,550 per year. Let us allow $10 per week for the 127 operators; this is certainly a very low estimate, we find the amount $1,270 per week, or calculating 52 weeks per year, the result is $66,040. For the 11 ladies engaged, we estimate $5 per week, making $2,860 per year. The 46 boys, at $1 per week, $2,392. Thus we find the total amount necessary to defray the above expenses to be $92,842, per annum. It is seen by the above that we make no estimate of the materials used (such as plates, cases, and chemicals,) . . . , and we forbear to make any estimate of this last, as many artists are now taking pictures at such reduced rates." Humphrey also forbears citing gross intake, but is patently alarmed at the price-cutting tactics of "cheap" competitors.

degree of excellence. In too many instances men enter into it because they can get nothing else to do; without the least appreciation of its merits as an art of exquisite refinement, without the taste to guide them, and without the love and ambition to study more than its practical application, neglecting the sciences intimately connected with it, and leaving entirely out of the question those of drawing, painting, and sculpture, sister arts, a knowledge of which must tend to elevate the taste and direct the operator into the more classical and elegant walks of his profession.

The initial step in the walk toward "profession" is clearly to promulgate standards of excellence. Too many practitioners lack essential qualifications of theory and sensibility. The scene surveyed by Snelling has its beginnings in the economic depression of the late 1830s and 1840s, when to set up as a daguerreotypist seemed relatively free of risk, requiring minimum capital and mechanical skills. While what Snelling most deplores is ignorance of the finer points of the craft and crass commercial motives, he also wants to dispel an aura of quackery and the hint of sorcery clinging to the medium. Robert Taft notes that the earliest photographers, often local blacksmiths, cobblers, dentists, and watchmakers with an eye to expanding their income, "made their work appear mysterious, especially those in smaller towns: that is, they imposed themselves as magicians," a deception made credible by the darkened closet into which the daguerreotypist slipped to prepare and develop his mysterious plates.

In the 1840s the popular press had made much of the perils of having a daguerrean likeness taken, a running comedy in which the humor cuts both ways, toward the primitive devices of the medium and toward the wounded vanity of a public increasingly aware (and the new medium fostered this to an incalculable extent) of "image," of social self-presentation. Shadows were a particular blight. " 'Can't you take me a likeness without these dark places?' asks a lady who sees, with surprise, a dirty mark under her nose, around her eyes, under her chin, or on the side of her cheek. 'There is nothing like this on my face.' " T. S. Arthur, who recounts this misreading of the image in a humorous essay in 1849 in *Godey's Lady's Book*, also tells of a farmer so frightened by the photographer's preparations that he "dashed down stairs as if a legion of evil spirits were after him," and of sitters who suffer the "illusion that the instrument exercises a kind of magnetic attraction, and many good ladies actually feel their eyes 'drawn' toward the lens while the operation is in progress!"

Thus tremors of apprehension, of the "uncanny," survive the humor, a strong enough hint for us to venture that by knowledge of science and art Snelling meant precisely the skills to produce an image so true to conventions of flattering portraiture as to be free of disturbing traces of the unfamiliar, the *unheimlich*. The onus for producing a "true" picture lies with the photographer, his sensibility, his cultivation. The alternative would be surrender to the mechanical apparatus, to the camera as automaton—another image, mirrorlike, steeped in the "uncanny." The lesson of those early grim images in which sitters cannot recognize themselves as they imagine themselves to be is that "no one can be a successful Daguerreotypist unless he is an artist, as well as a manipulator."

Snelling argues obsessively in the early years of the journal that professional status for commercial photographers requires that they take their lead from the fine arts, which themselves in just these years developed distinct institutions, schools, art unions and associations. Everything depended on how the photographer saw himself: artist or mere technician, creator or mere manipulator. Snelling supports his defense of photography as a potential fine art by drawing on the rhetoric of progress and enlightenment that ruled public discourse in America. He enlists photography in the master plot of "progress": the struggle between light and darkness, science and the black arts, reason and barbarism. "The faculty of language," he writes, voicing the commonplace middle-class ideology, "has gradually worked a most wonderful change in the relations between man and all other created things," letting loose "a flood of intellectual light" that washes away "old established opinions and theories" and establishes "others more truthful, more natural, and more intrinsically valuable." A key event is the defeat of superstition: "those things which once appeared . . . marvellous are no longer so, but the mere effects of natural causes." Thus the "progress of knowledge" leads "from the barbarism of former ages to the present civilized state." And from the same civilizing process behind the Copernican revolution and the discovery of the invariable laws of physics, "the photographic art was brought to light." "At once the cynosure of all observers" for the "beauty of its conception, and the importance to which it must ultimately arrive in the world of art," the universal enthusiasm at its birth gave rise "to a class of artists who must one day become as famous as the great masters of painting." Guided by art, photography will inevitably advance toward the goal of the perfectly realized resemblance, as it has already progressed from the "mere half distinct development of the daguerreotype plate" to "the full drawn, bold and clear impressions" of recent improved processes. Thus, as Snelling wrote in the opening number of the journal in 1851, in the not far distant future "our best Daguerreotypists will wonder how they could, for so long a time, be content with the specimens of their art they now put forth, as much as they do at this day at the shadows of six and eight years ago."

IV

To illuminate the shadows, to dispel the aura of sorcery and deception, to exorcise demons still haunting the medium: these motives Snelling shared with the photographic community emerging in the 1850s. Yet, like ghosts and blurs and other inexplicable appearances that frequently marred the most carefully executed of pictures, those demons refused to disperse; they continued to assert themselves in the very diction representing the medium in popular expressions. The term "shadows" may, for example, represent the primitive state of "half indistinct" images, but in the common coin of daguerrean lingo other meanings survived. "Take the shadow ere the substance fade," the popular slogan of daguerreotypists, calls up the notion of shadow as soul, as animate extension, double, and immortal part of self. Of course, such figures of speech had long lost original force, diluted of any distinct supernaturalism. But is it only fanciful to suggest that just as, according to Freud, experiences of the uncanny in tales such as E. T. A. Hoffmann's "The Sandman" represent a recurrence of repressed psychic anxiety (chiefly about castration), so the reappearance within the public discourse of photography of a diction of shadows and shades, spirit lands, mirrored doubles, represents the return of a barely repressed animism comparable to (surely a sign of the same development) the eruption of Gothicism at the height of the age of "enlightenment," "reason," and "revolution"? That in the daguerrean period photography rejuvenated a debased diction of light and shadow, reinvested it with new anxieties provoked by mechanical images of automatic reproduction, the evocation of the visible from the invisible, but just as surely in response to rapidly changing social relations, the displacement of an older system of propertied wealth and deference by an urban market economy of money and its deceptions?

No matter how conventional and formulaic, how drained of literal belief, magical and animistic figures of speech signify strains, tensions, and fears within the culture. Why, for instance, so widespread an association between daguerreotypes and death? Providing a lasting image of departed "loved ones" was among the very first possibilities imagined for the medium. "Take the shadow ere the substance fade": the very taking of a likeness, fixing a transient appearance of flesh as an image, evoked death, cessation, ultimate fixity.

> Here is a genial, smiling, energetic face, full of sunny strength, intelligence, integrity, good humor; but it lies imprisoned in baleful shades, as of the Valley of Death; seems smiling on me as if in mockery. Doesn't know me, friend? I am dead, thou seeist, and distant, and forever hidden from thee; I belong already to the Eternities, and thou recognizest me not! On the whole it is the strangest feeling that I have. . . .

Thus Thomas Carlyle writes to Ralph Waldo Emerson about a daguerreotype likeness of his American friend, and goes on to request that "you get us by the earliest opportunity some living pictorial sketch, chalk-drawing or the like, from a trustworthy hand." A poem by Mrs. G. H. Putnam published by Snelling in 1851, "On Seeing a Daguerreotype Portrait," more literally associates death with the unique look of the daguerrean image:

> What means this vain, incessant strife,
>   To hide thyself in fitful gleams—
> Now standing like a thing of life?
>   Then fading like a poet's dreams.

The flickering that disturbs Carlyle becomes an emblem of the passage between "thing of life" and "dreams," between life and death. The poem goes on to say that the daguerreotype's "visioned form" is like "a fiction," or a trace that "memory leaves / Upon the tablets of the mind," or the "flitting of a thought" that rises from "secret depths" and is quickly "vanished" by "reason sage." It is precisely this tendency toward unfixing itself in the mind, seeming familiar and unfamiliar at once, that gives the image its uncanny power to evoke death. Thus its "semblance" is "airy," "it speaks of forms in spirit land," of "that better state, / Where sin and sorrow never come," and promises that "those we love / . . . Shall wear those well known forms above."

The easy absorption of daguerreotypes into sentimental thanatoptic diction may say more about sentimentalism than about the medium, but it tells of a cultural association of photography with death that we cannot discount as mere convention. In addition to sublimating natural fear of death, consolatory verses appearing in the early photographic journals in the 1850s address more public concerns, at a time of economic recovery but increased agitation over slavery, about the death of leaders and heroes, the "fathers" of the republic. Caleb Lyon's "Stanzas, Suggested by a Visit to Brady's Portrait Gallery" invokes the "soul-lit shadows now around," the pictures of "illustrious Americans" Brady and other leading photographers exhibited like charms on their gallery walls: "They who armies nobly led, / They who make a nation's glory / While they're living—when they're dead, / Landmarks for our country's future." After reciting the names of Brady's pantheon—Taylor, Jackson, Frémont, Houston, Webster, Clay, Audubon, Bryant—the poet concludes:

Like a spirit land of shadows
  They in silence on me gaze,
And I feel my heart is beating
  With the pulse of other days;
And I ask what great magician
  Conjured forms like these afar?
Echo answers, 'tis the sunshine,
  By its alchymist Daguerre.

The rhyme breezes through figures of magic, alchemy, and conjuring spirits without blinking, but even the doggerel conveys an authentic wish that photography preserve not only the appearance but also the actual presence of authoritative fathers so badly wanted by a generation bereft of the moral guidance of the founders.

No surprise, then, that for all his enlightened rationalism, Snelling indulged himself in sentimental verse, let alone Gothic tales in the German manner of E. T. A. Hoffmann. In at least two striking instances he opened the pages of his journal to unadulterated fictions of the uncanny. One is an actual tale by Hoffmann, "The Empty House"; the other, in the same mode but in a manner close to Poe, "The Magnetic Daguerreotypes." Identified only as "A German Tale," without mention of the author, "The Empty House" (1817) bears many similarities to "The Sandman" (1815–16), upon which Freud bases his discussion of "the uncanny." Ambiguity of perception lies at the heart of both tales: in "The Empty House," apparitional visual experiences produce strange "indescribable" feelings of "delightful horror," "at once uneasy and delightful," "full of anxiety and ardent longing." In both tales optical devices, possibly magical, magnify the ambiguity of the visible and heighten anxiety: Nathanael's pocket telescope in "The Sandman," Theodore's opera glasses and pocket mirror in "The Empty House." Powerful erotic feelings affect the bedeviled heroes in both tales, and wizard figures with green catlike eyes appear in both, imagoes of the wicked father. And by use of skeptical, disbelieving characters who insist the hero can free himself from his morbid obsessions, each tale leads the reader to the unanswerable question: are the uncanny experiences self-willed delusions, signs of the hero's mental derangement, or the product of an external cause such as black magic, or both?

The presence of the pocket mirror, so like a daguerreotype in size and intimacy, probably accounts for Snelling's publication of "The Empty House," which he ran serially in four successive numbers. Not only is Theodore able, as he discovers accidentally and not with unalloyed pleasure, to conjure in his mirror the image of the mysterious lady at the window of the empty house—it is never clear whether she is an apparition of the young Edwina, the ancient witch in the seductive form of the young woman, or a painted portrait!—but the mirror also induces in him a strange fixation. While using it to make himself inconspicuous when observing the tantalizing image in the window, Theodore suddenly feels paralyzed as if in a "waking dream." A clue to the mirror's power appears in the confession he then makes, "with shame," that he thought at once of a story told by his nurse when she found him "staring at the large mirror in my father's room." His nurse warned him that "if children looked into the glass at night, a strange ugly face would peep out, and that the children's eyes would at once become fixed." Naturally he could not resist looking, and saw "hideous fiery eyes sparkling in the glass, and fell down senseless."

"The Sandman" concludes with Nathanael's destruction, a victim of his obsession with "the uncanny." Theodore survives, however, aided by a doctor who helps him recognize "the deeper connection between all these strange things." His survival, and the apparent victory of rational explanation, may also account for the story's appearance in Snelling's journal—an example, we might put it, of the mirror image purged of its diabolism. But the tale can be taken as well as an explanation of the persistence of an animistic aura in the daguerreotype. For an "empty house" actually housing strange creatures, including a lascivious witch, translates easily into the unconscious itself—"the dark, mysterious region which is the home of our spirit," in the words of one of Theodore's learned friends. This same "physician" explains that dreams, with their "extraordinary peculiarity" to deposit in the waking mind "dim recollections" that make strangers seem "so astoundingly familiar to me," dispose certain persons vulnerable to influence by "some external psychical principle," "a magnetic relation" that one mind might exert over another. Thus the tale might be read as teaching that animistic representations of the daguerreotype derive finally from propensities within human consciousness itself, from the "empty house" we people with ghosts and wizards and seductive ladies who in the moment of the first embrace draw back the mask to disclose the rotting flesh.

Was it part of Snelling's program to insinuate magic in order to purge it by a kind of homeopathy, a therapeutic reading? "The Magnetic Daguerreotypes," which appeared two years earlier, reprinted from the New York *Sunday Courier*, speaks more directly to the uncanny effects of the photographic image as a *living* presence. Also set in Germany, the tale has a narrator—nameless until the final paragraph—who visits the studio of Professor Ariovistus Dunkelheim (the first name signifies prophetic eyes; the last, dark home) with his betrothed, the lovely Elora, to have likenesses taken by the professor's new process. The sitters place themselves each before a highly polished plate of steel, "a perfect mirror," and by "electro-galvanic" or "magnetic" action their likenesses are fixed instantaneously. That night the narrator learns that the portrait of his beloved, upon which he gazes with mounting desire, is "a faithful mirror of the absent Elora's features," an animate picture in which he sees her as she is at the moment (asleep in bed, as it happens). "How superior to the cold, ghastly, shadowy immobility of the mere daguerreotype, were these living portraits of Dunkelheim's."

The pleasure is short-lived, however, for the narrator remembers that Dunkelheim himself had retained copies of both images, and even now, with his "bottle-green eyes" and his diabolic look of "critical penetration," might be enjoying the look of desire on his face, able to "watch every change in the expression of my face, to read my every thought, as in an open book." He feels himself "forever subject to an excruciating moral espionage! to be denied for life, the security and luxury of privacy," particularly as he grows more excited with "a fever of impatient love" and continues "to gaze and gaze with an intense and burning ardor" on Elora's living portrait. He informs Elora of their predicament ("A detested stranger can, at will, become a witness of our most rapturous moments, our most secret delights, our—") and pledges to regain the copies or to slay their tormentor. Dunkelheim eludes his grasp; they marry after all, "but a spectre haunted us. . . . Night and day, his terrible green eyes were upon us." The hero resumes his pursuit, destroys the fiend, and recovers the telltale plates. " 'Henceforth we are at least our own masters,' cries Elora, 'and not puppets, acting for the amusement of a detestable old necromancer!' " Still, the "cold green eyes" of Dunkelheim return at times to "haunt our fancies."

Only at the very end does the narrator reveal his own name, and we grasp at once the reason for his withholding it until now: Ernest Darkman. The correspondence, slant as it is, of Darkman to Dunkelheim adds a hint of a familial (and oedipal) conflict between hero and villain to the tale's already strained eroticism and prurience. The network of echoes, doublings, parallels through which the tale works toward the frisson of its final revelation serves as a charged setting for its theme of visibility, the fears it raises, in order homeopathically to expel them, of the camera as an all-seeing eye, a disembodied invasive gaze in a system of scrutiny extending through the bedroom into the mind and soul. In this most stunning instance in the early literature of the photograph as mirror we have a graphic diagnostic chart, as it were, of premonitions that among the many ways life would never again be the same after photography, the transformation of self into an object of surveillance as well as an image for manipulation and consumption by others might be the most consequential.

Thus we see that Clark's mirror on Broadway hid within its shadowed depths a far less simple, more troubled—and thereby far richer and more challenging—cultural response to the photograph than we have yet recognized. In part the conflicted structure of response I have described reflects divisions in the early social practices of the medium, including the quite early application of the daguerreotype to the study of criminality. The largest significance of the pattern lies, however, in the ambivalence it represents within the dominant middle-class acceptance of the medium—an ambivalence that suggests a pervasive insecurity about newly gained property and status within a rapidly changing social and political order. Particularly, the homeopathic process of evoking fear in order to allay it that appears in the professionalizing rhetoric of early commercial photography provides a not-inconsiderable clue to forces shaping a modern culture within the passages of antebellum American society.

TWO

MUTE ROMANCE

Stories of a Daguerreotype

IN 1870, more than a decade after it had been replaced by the paper print as the most popular form of photography in America, one of the early masters of the daguerreotype lamented its demise. It has been "laid aside," complained Montgomery P. Simons of Philadelphia, "as an unfashionable thing," its name "like a dead language, never spoken, and seldom written." A frequent author of incisive and often barbed and witty little essays in the photographic press, Simons recounted in an article in 1874 how more than thirty years before, "curiosity" had led him to "the mystic establishment of Mr. [Robert] Cornelius [one of the earliest Philadelphia daguerreoptypists] to see these marvelous mirrors of nature." He wrote: "The first one I took in my hand had an electric effect on me (I certainly felt the thrill of the current), and now really believe that I was art-struck forthwith." It was the thrill of witnessing the making of an image "without hands or pencil. . . . It seemed to me the very height of jugglery throwing likenesses from the face catching them upon polished plates." Enthralled by the illusion of a living face, the young man stood awed by the artistry required to gain this effect. It was "no ordinary skill" or "ordinary taste" that produced such effects. "The sun, although an in-

First published as "Reading Lessons: Stories of a Daguerreotype," *Nineteenth-Century Contexts* 22, no. 4 (2001): 537–57.

Figure 1 Montgomery P. Simons, "Man and Wife" (Dr. and Mrs. Thomas Epps Wilson), ca. 1848. (The Nelson-Atkins Museum of Art, Kansas City, Missouri. Gift of Hallmark Cards, Inc., PS.551.002.98)

dispensable agent, has no more to do with making a daguerreotype than it has with writing a book. Both can be done by candle light."

Fond of embellishing his essays with analogies between language (writing and speech) and photography, Simons followed convention in this regard. "So life-like they almost speak" was a common term of praise and of daguerreotypists' self-advertisements, and it was often applied lavishly to Simons's portraits, many of which earned prizes in competitions and enthusiastic notice in the press. The conventional trope of the living and speaking picture was not merely an article of belief among daguerrean artists and their more cultivated clients and admirers. It was also a principle of differentiation by which the emerging profession of daguerreotype artists in the early 1850s asserted the superiority of their work, grounded in good science as much as fine artistic taste, to the quick, cheap, and careless work of a rising horde of "dollar" practitioners. In the face of competition that the more serious daguerreotypists worried might demean the craft while also depressing the market, they reached back to the old classical tradition of the life-like imitation (late Roman portrait sculpture, for example), and drew also from the revival of the trope of the living picture in the uncanny simulacra (paintings and statues) of Romantic Gothic literature. In a fanciful bagatelle Simons published in 1852, "A Chapter on the Daguerrean Art, and Its Professors, of the Dollar Notoriety," we hear of "these disciples of Daguerre" who "attach the names of sitters to their production, that they may be more easily recognized by their friends." In their "grab game" these cut-rate charlatans produce "caricatures," while the "genuine article" identifies itself without an attached name. The "genuine" comes to life with imagined speech.

The trope of the transparent, living picture served to bolster a fine-art ideology, which emerged as a strategic move within the competitive wars between "cheap" and "fine" daguerreotype portraits in the early 1850s, especially in the larger cities. The better-known daguerreotypists identified themselves with the tradition of what Simons named as the "rich spirited gems of the old masters." The "old masters" (Rembrandt and Rubens were most frequently named) were the guardian angels of "taste," the kind of fine taste violated by the cheaper, less skillful daguerrean entrepreneurs. The upholders of "taste" among the daguerreans saw themselves, with considerable justification, as defenders of true value and worth against the invasion of mechanization and commercialism into the realm of the aesthetic, especially embattled because of their own implication in a process of mechanical reproduction. They stressed the difficulty of the process and the agency of the operator-artist, against the quick-shot routine of the Broadway fast-picture shops.

The issues at stake were not exclusively commercial or aesthetic. There was an important political edge to the campaign to "improve" the "taste" of the daguerrean trade. Simons saw the improvement of "public taste" as a solemn duty. Described in his obituary in 1877 as a

"staunch republican," Simons, like Mathew Brady and other prominent daguerrean artists, seems to have aligned "taste" and "art" with
transparency (sincerity, honesty, allegiance to "truth") as civic virtues.
In the following passage from an essay he wrote in 1852, we see that Simons's republicanism is continuous with his daguerreotypy, that to see
(and to reproduce what is seen in a true image) in a "true light" is as
much a political as an aesthetic act, an act in defense of the republic.

> We are aware that our endeavors to hold these cadets in the art
> up to public gaze, that they may be seen in their true light, may,
> by some, be misconstrued into envy on our part, and by exciting
> public sympathies, increase the evil which we are trying to
> abate. But, however deplorable such a result would be, the task
> had to be performed.—For we should hold the man guilty in-
> deed, who would sit in silence, and see the community in which
> he resides deluded by impostors. But our object must not be
> mistaken. Our intention is not to abuse, but rather to convince
> these mercenary operators that they have either mistaken their
> profession, or have most shamefully neglected to give it that at-
> tention and careful study which it requires, and improving the
> public taste, force this conviction upon them.

Like Holgrave's in Hawthorne's *The House of the Seven Gables*, Simons's
commitments to taste, to truth, to the republic, and to living daguerrean portraits are of one piece.

A particular example of Simons's "life-like" pictures offers, because
of a richness of contextual materials, a unique opportunity to delve
further into the workings of the trope of the living picture, or, to put it
differently, to ask how a photographic (in this case daguerrean) text
might be read (or listened to) as a message from a specific history. What
does it take to release a voice from a photograph? In this case considerable historical information helps us construct a context of social, familial, and personal history. But is enough really enough, or perhaps too
much?

The prevailing historicism in textual criticism argues that context
provides not merely clues to meaning but also determinants of mean-

ing. In regard to images context is assumed to be a final arbiter, in the sense that one must always go outside the image, to a caption or other information, in order to discover the "truth" of the image. The image is assumed to be a supplement, an addendum, in transparent relation to a historical referent. Yet photographic images are also taken to be opaque and dumb, merely *there*, a reflex of an occasion whose adequacy as explanation is never reliable. Between the two cases, the image as transparent sign of a knowable history, and the image as an opacity bearing a physical (as trace) but no logical relation to its putative history, there would seem to lie an impasse. We can restate the question by saying that the role of photographs in the interpretation of history and the role of history in the interpretation of photographs pose mutual problems. What follows is an effort to demonstrate possibilities and difficulties that lie within the mutuality of textual (in regard to images) and historical interpretation.

In 1853, while working in Richmond, Virginia, where he had relocated in 1851 and would remain until 1856, Simons undertook a remarkable collaborative project conceived explicitly as a test of the trope of the animate picture. With two other young men of the city, the artist William Hubbard and a brilliant, eccentric young man of wealth, Mann Satterwaite Valentine II, he executed a series of some thirty daguerreotypes intended to depict not persons but states of mind and feeling. The idea was Valentine's, who commissioned the collaboration to further his interests in art, science, archaeology, and metaphysics. What does it look like to be in a state of rage, of inspiration, of scorn and hate, of desire? What is the look of having a thought, of being at attention, or in admiration? Verbal descriptions of such states of mind and feeling by the eighteenth-century French physiognomist Charles Le Brun would provide captions: e.g., "Anger. The effects of anger show its nature. The eyebrows become red and enflamed; the eyeball is staring and sparkling; the eyebrows sometimes elevated, and sometimes drawn low; the forehead is very much wrinkled."

Valentine noted such "passions" in a diary entry for January 2, 1853: "This day sat to M. P. Simons for daguerreotypes picturing the Passions. They are as follows: What excites these passions?" Then follows a list of eighteen terms, from "Love" to "Jealousy" to "Terror" to

"Weeping." Simons photographed Valentine and Hubbard performing each of these states. In a scrawled note Valentine indicates that he was moved "to possess myself of a key to the passions," and that Hubbard had "fallen upon a beautiful system," presumably based on Le Brun's physiognomy, for achieving accurate images. The results, it appears, were not fully satisfactory. A note by Valentine describes "faults" in the depictions, or rather, in the performances before the camera. "Horror. Mouth too much opened, brow not knitted at all, head too much up-turned. . . . Terror—Head too much uplifted, muscles not correct."

A group of extraordinary (and sometimes amusing) images survives this metaphysical experiment, undertaken by the performers with somber earnestness. What Simons thought of the game is hard to know, but it is not unlikely that his daguerrean intuition would say: "But these are pictures of real people, not abstract passions. And it's all too apparent that they are only playing at feeling certain things. In the end the pictures show not 'passions' but Valentine and Hubbard put-ting on faces before a camera." Relevant to this supposition is a frolic-some essay Simons published in 1873 called "A few thoughts Suggested on Looking over my Photographic Album." "It seems as if one could imagine," he wrote, "by seeing a photograph, the very thoughts of the sitter. To the close observer the expression reveals hidden secrets. The 'photograph,' as has been said to its credit, 'is a tell-tale.' " The essay describes typical sitters, a doctor, a mechanic, a mother, and infers thoughts from expressions. But when he gets to pictures of actors, Si-mons demurs. "So accustomed to dissemble," professional performers present faces the outward expression of which "give no idea of the in-ward workings of the mind." Thus outward appearance can be trusted as a sign of inward workings only if the sitter can be induced toward a "natural," not a histrionic or theatrical, expression. "No set rules can be given for the artistic arrangement of the sitter," he had written ear-lier in his 1858 manual, *Photography in a Nut Shell*, "and yet it is of the ut-most importance. . . . It is advisable to allow sitters to assume their natural positions which if awkward, may be improved upon, but not to such an extent as to lose the likeness."

The "passion series" may well have confirmed for Simons that speech in pictures could as easily be false as true, that states of mind or "passions," if they are to be "true" utterances, cannot be detached from the people who feel and express them in the exact moment of the picture. Because the camera will portray the inauthentic and the authentic with the same fidelity, the artist should strive for a "natural" (undissembled) expression of faces and bodies. At the same time, the series reveals how fictive are all representations of "expression," how formulaic even "natural" expression might be. How is one to know for certain what is "natural" and what merely performed, an imitation rather than an authentic expression?

From its beginnings the profession of portrait making in photography (which, in the United States, was almost exclusively confined to the daguerreotype from 1839 to the mid-1850s) worried over a central question, a specifically *photographic* question: how inwardness might be conveyed through a faithful (i.e., photographic) depiction of outwardness. How might the daguerreotype speak? Or, to put it more precisely, how might it be given to a viewer's imagination as capable of speech? A fiction of the "natural" came to dominate the profession, as putative assurance against inauthenticity and fraud. Recall Holgrave's famous words in Hawthorne's *The House of the Seven Gables*: "There is a wonderful insight in heaven's broad and simple sunshine. While we give it credit only for depicting the merest surface, it actually brings out the secret character with a truth no painter would ever venture upon." The performed "passions" of the Valentine group would have struck Simons, then, as a metacommentary on the inner logic of the entire daguerrean project of catching and fixing (or reproducing) likenesses on polished plates.

In 1912 the critic Sadikichi Hartmann revived the old question of how daguerrean images might "come to life":

The daguerreotype speaks a language of its own that touches the common chords of life. The daguerreotype possesses the pictorial magic and historic power to fascinate the many as well as expert minds, for it conjures up to contemporary view and truthfully portrays forms and faces long passed away, things that are dead and lost to living eyes because it was, as [Henry] James would put it, "the real right thing" in its own peculiar time.

What is dead and lost returns, resumes itself in the "living eyes" of the fascinated, those whose fascination excites their own eyes to new life. Hartmann describes a magical spell cast by the fascinating object, a conjuration, an enchantment, a seduction: the condition of readiness to hear and decipher the daguerreotype's "language of its own," restoring to life that "dead language, never spoken, and seldom written" whose loss Simons lamented.

A language exercised in silence. The speech Hartmann speaks of is, of course, imagined speech, words viewers conjure from within themselves to translate, as it were, unspoken messages. Fascination empowers us toward an act of empathetic imagining. Only by means of the word, the dead language resuscitated, might the image come to life. In the silent spaces of the image lies a story of its being, but how might we retell it? Simons aligns key elements of the process—absence, writing, likeness—in one of his lamentations about the lost art of the daguerreotype:

> If an absent friend whom I had not seen for a long time should write me, "What sort of a likeness shall I send you?" I would reply, "If possible, a daguerreotype." This, like all sun-pictures, is a perfect reflection of the face, and is, as it were, like standing behind a friend while he is looking into a faithful mirror.

Just as Whitman exhorted his reader, "You shall stand by my side and look in the mirror with me," Simons instructs his absent friend that looking at my daguerreotype will repeat my own self-apprehension in a mirror; I will be unto you as I am unto myself, a mirror image. By such faithfulness of reflection, Simons suggests, the daguerreotype itself might serve as a letter, a missive, a surrogate for writing. "As silent as a mirror is believed," in Hart Crane's gnomic trope, daguerreotypes translate intimacy across space and time—letters indeed from the dead.

And dead letters they most often seem, encountered most often on the auctioneer's block or among the stock of some dealer in antique photographs. Hartmann anticipated that these magical-seeming relics would command "exceptional prices at future auctions"—a prophecy fulfilled beyond all expectations. Daguerreotypes now have a currency in more than one sense: traded, exchanged, bought and sold, passed from hand to hand like chips in a revolving game of speculation and chance. The cash value into which they so readily translate belies their anterior value as untranslatable emblems of desire, belief, and hope. Whose memory is it that waits to be knocked down on the auction block? Uprooted, scattered, lost to their origins, they are dead letters, millions of them—indecipherable messages tasking our powers to imagine a world in which they made immediate and compelling sense.

Hartmann imagined coming upon a daguerreotype lying among other old things, a discarded and forgotten memory. "A daguerreotype—There it lies in its case among old papers, letters and curios." The story I want to tell begins with the equivalent of opening such a drawer as Hartmann evokes: a large ($^3/_4$ plate) square daguerreotype portrait of a man and woman seated on a wrought-iron bench, an unusual pose on a plate unusual in size and shape, with an embossed seal on the rear of the case identifying the maker as our M. P. Simons of Philadelphia, found among an ensemble of other objects: another, smaller daguerreotype of a mother and child, the image mounted in a gilded wooden frame; a shadow box frame with two painted miniatures on ivory of the persons shown in the large daguerreotype, along with a hair bracelet with an initialed clasp, and a watch piece of twisted satin rope, to which is attached a gold coin holder. Along with these objects, curios and images, the ensemble—first encountered in its latter-day emanation as a verbal description in an auction catalog in 1989— indeed includes old papers and letters that proffer bits of information about the pictured couple and child, about the ensemble itself and its history—a history of memory preserved and cherished—and also additional leads to archival sources of further information. In sum, a rich mine for the studious and provocations for the fascinated.

The ensemble of images, objects, and words suggests a story braided of several strands: a family, a place, a time, a romance. The place is the antebellum South, the town of Warrenton in Warren County, in the northern tier of North Carolina. The family is prominent, which is to say rich in slaves, land, and the resources of culture. The region is one, we learn from a National Register of Historic Places document, "of remarkable wealth and culture that produced many town and plantation houses of sophisticated design." Indeed, in the 1850s Warren County was known as the richest county in North Carolina, then one of the poorest states in the Union. By frequent travel to Philadelphia, Richmond, and Petersberg, Virginia, its main market town, and as a result of the many itinerants who visited the town and country—craftsmen, miniature-portrait painters, and daguerreotypists, as well as evangelists—Warrenton gentry enjoyed a remarkably cosmopolitan style of life. Furniture, other home furnishings, and books and newspapers, along with painted miniatures and daguerreotypes, were commonplace possessions among the planter class. They were thus able to think of themselves as sharing in a national upper-middle-class culture, which helps account for the particularly profound sense of dislocation brought on by the Civil War.

One focal point of the story is the plantation house called Elgin, described in the same document, a "nomination form" submitted in 1972 to the Register, as "a handsome temple-form dwelling, surrounded by well-tended boxwoods and framed by a variety of tall trees." Elgin was built in the late 1820s by the father of the young lady pictured in the daguerreotype. Peter Mitchel had come from Scotland in 1797, thrived as a merchant, and in 1824 married the daughter of a wealthy local planter, who "settled upon the couple a large farm near Warrenton where they had built a fine house in the latest fashion." As late as 1988 two Duncan Phyfe chairs from Elgin were still in possession of family descendants. At his death in 1846 Peter Mitchel owned more than two thousand acres at Elgin, at least that much elsewhere in the county, large tracts in Tennessee, and as much as fifty thousand dollars in "slave property." The plucky, land-hungry Scotsman, father of the young lady in the daguerreotype, had married into slavery, and henceforth his family enjoyed the fruits and services of the labor of black slaves.

An unusual abundance of family information accompanies the Simons daguerreotype, though not without certain lapses and blanks. Two of the eight children of the couple shown, the eldest son and eldest daughter (the infant in the small daguerreotype), will, late in their lives, in the 1920s, publish books that include memories of their childhood in the 1850s. In that fateful decade, the son, Peter Mitchel Wilson, wrote, "Warrenton was the nucleus of spreading plantations owned by old-time Carolinians of the prosperous, so-called 'aristocratic' class . . . typical of the best ante-bellum life of the state." Until, he adds, "the final curtain of civil war blotted out the scene." We have the makings of a story of something past, lost, blotted out, which helps explain both the persistence and the nostalgic glow of the memories of the scene before the "final curtain." The daughter, Lizzy Wilson Montgomery, quotes Southey in her book, *Sketches of Old Warrenton*: "Whatever strengthens our local attachment is favorable to individual and national character. Our home—our birthplaces, our native land— think for a while what the virtues are which arise out of the feelings connected with these words." Her book, she explains, answers a request from her son to put down "some reminiscences" of her birthplace (and his), a request "made out of warm love for, and genuine interest in, the old town and its people." The book is an act of piety to past and future generations. As late as 1984 a descendent writes about the painted miniatures that they "are to stay in *my* family" and describes them as "my most prized possessions from Miss Betsy," who was Lizzy's daughter. The cherished objects obviously put a face to memory, and a body; for family descendants they make the past visible and palpable, a treasure, a private hoard of ancestral bones.

The hoard of relics and the documents culled from archives can be read to tell a story broader and deeper than that of the daguerreotype itself, a family narrative rooted in a specific region of the universe of American enterprise from about 1820 to the Civil War, a story of the founder's "lust for land," as his grandson Peter M. Wilson put it, of wealth wrung from exceptionally fertile land by contented slaves (so the children recalled), of gorgeous plantation houses dressed as Greek temples, and of the community of masters and mistresses, the principal players, their parties, card games, racing, their pictures painted and taken, and their supporting cast of mammies, house servants, craftsmen, and field hands, of whom no pictures exist—though many of them are named in the children's memoirs. "My memory [is] warmed by recollections of the kindly care with which the colored servants surrounded my life and that of my brothers and sister," wrote Peter M.

Wilson many decades later. "One quaint illustration of this kindliness recurs in the picture of 'Mammy Rena' (Serena) putting sweet potatoes in the ashes and coals at night, before she tucked us into bed." "My personal feeling for the colored people who lived on our place was one of deep and sincere affection. I used to love to play with the Negro children and to eat with the darkies in their cabins."

Family history is thronged with memories of happy slaves faithfully serving their betters and faithfully looked after by their masters. Indeed the daybooks of Janet Wilson disclose one form of the proprietorial care that it fell to the lot of plantation mistress to execute; she lists names, ages, birthdates of the slaves, the provisions provided them, food, blankets, and clothing, with as much precision as she inventories other household goods and supplies. "The prevailing attitude in Warrenton toward the colored people was very kindly. There were, of course, instances of unfair treatment but they were not common. The sort of thing written of in *Uncle Tom's Cabin* was usually the result of absentee landlordism."

Whether it occurred to the children that kindness is not the same as equality is not recorded. Still, between the lines, cold realities can be glimpsed. Lizzy recalls by name some twenty-five "colored people" living on the family's "home lot" in town, including "Mammy Charlotte, my mother's nurse when an infant." "The burying ground for our colored people," she adds, "was the 'old place' two miles from town." "Good feeling exists between the races," she writes in *Sketches*, "as has always been the case; and it is a proverbial saying in all the adjoining towns and cities, that Warren County servants [*sic*] are the most intelligent and reliable of all the domestic help." The son recalls in *Southern Exposure*, however, without comment, that large revival meetings were never permitted in the town. "At nine o'clock curfew rang for all the colored people. . . . It was not considered wise to have too many of the emotional black race gathered in a crowd."

How does this story of experiences mentionable and unmentionable, these fragments of a narrative of plantation culture and its inbred silences, impinge on our reading of the central text in this hoard, the double-portrait daguerreotype made in the northern city of Philadelphia by a photographer known for his strong republican convictions?

Turning to the image, we see a young couple crowded snugly against each other on a rather cramped wrought-iron bench, knees almost touching, shoulders actually touching, her hands crossed demurely at the wrist, the left hand (the image is no doubt reversed, as is typical of early daguerrean portraits) falling limply over the right forearm in a properly ladylike manner, displaying a ring; his left arm out of sight behind her back (perhaps clutching the back of the bench to secure his rather awkward position), his right hand falling toward her extended fingers, coming to a rest high on his right thigh. Is it not, in a casual glance, an altogether touching scene with an air of intimacy: an adoring man gazing upon the expressionless face of his beloved? She, wide-eyed, unflinching, stares directly at or into the lens (that is, at and into us, into our eyes, daring us to look back with living eyes); he, his body twisted toward her as if his body doesn't quite fit the bench, his head turned almost to a full profile view, gazes at or toward her with what seems to be yearning and desire.

Or so it seems at a glance. Look more closely at his eyes, one barely visible in deep shadow. He is looking not at her but at a point beyond the frame of the picture, a bit forward of her. Thus his line of vision actually crosses hers, placing in the foreground of the image an imaginary triangle formed by the intersecting lines of vision and a line between the two heads (or noses). This apparitional triangle lies horizontally flat at eye level, repeated and reinforced by the forceful lines of his bent legs, and the implied direction of her legs, barely traced by the heavy cloth of her long enfolding dress. The foreshortening of the image, the tight placement of the figures so that they occupy more than three-quarters of the frame, the canting of the camera so that the bench sits at a slightly oblique angle to the picture plane, enough so that the woman must twist her head, just barely but visibly, in order to aim her eyes directly ahead, the more obvious twist of the man's body and the planting of his legs on the floor at the bottom edge of the frame, the force of which is expressed in the rumpling of his trouser legs and of his shirt front and cravat—all create a sense of dynamism not only physical but also emotional. Heads, eyes, shoulders, hands, and legs are all put to work as compositional elements in a design more complex and difficult than usual in such cases.

Is the picture a double portrait, or perhaps a genre scene? A man seated by a woman on a bench gazes longingly toward her with eyes and body, while she sits quiet and demure, a veritable icon of the proper young lady. But his eyes are not really on her; they look off into space in her direction and seem inward looking. Is he all physical and emotional expectation, and she all feminine disposition, preserving, in her blankness almost to the point of vacuity, a sentimental self-image of feminine reserve? The bodies touch, yet the space between the heads, the obliquely angled untouching of their eyes, do they suggest absent meanings, ambiguities, or simply, again, sentimental propriety? Is sexuality asserted only to be repressed? Has the photographer composed not merely a commemorative portrait but a scene from a unwritten narrative, perhaps a scene from a marriage?

A good guess is that the picture was made in the summer of 1847 on the journey the couple undertook to Niagara Falls immediately after their wedding on July 14 at Elgin. The groom, Thomas Epps Wilson (b. 1817, in Greensville County, Virginia), had taken a degree in medicine at the University of Pennsylvania in Philadelphia in the early 1840s, and a stopover in that city during the wedding journey is plausible. Evidence internal to the daguerreotype—the seal, the gilded paper mat, the oddly sized square plate—suggest that 1847 in Philadelphia is a likely date and place of its making. After a brief medical practice in Alabama, where he fell seriously ill with malaria, Wilson learned of a practice for sale in Warrenton, a "high and healthy" region, his daughter Lizzy wrote in an unpublished memoir, "one of the richest of the State, good lands, fine timber, and negro [*sic*] slaves numbering three to one of white population." He arrived there in 1846.

His own upbringing had been within a landed though hardly prosperous family that, according to daughter Lizzy, "had a very limited landed estate, but very little negro [*sic*] property." He remembers having to walk four miles to school when he was seven years old, but his industrious older brother, in charge of his younger siblings after the parents died, was able to send him to boarding school in Louisburg, North Carolina, then to the University of Pennsylvania for a degree in medicine. He began his practice on another relative's plantation in Alabama, where he came down with malaria, prompting his move to

Warrenton. Not exactly from the other side of the tracks, well-bred, still he seems to have retained a sense of the struggles of his early years. "He told his children," wrote Lizzy, "that he married our mother, a woman of fortune, and he resolved by his own industry in his profession to make each year as good an income as came from her property, which resolve he more than carried out." Her inherited property included a farm to which they eventually moved, and at least the twenty-five slaves allotted to him, in a legal document of 1849, "in right of his wife," worth $10,675: Phil Jones, for example, valued at $600, Lucy at $500, Charlotte at $400, and so on. The son records that their father had "never bought a slave and he never sold but one," and then so that a wife could rejoin her husband, a slave on a neighboring plantation who had been "removed" farther South in the owner's "search of the wealth of the cotton fields."

Whether Dr. Wilson had known Montgomery Simons during his student days in Philadelphia is impossible to say. What is known, and this information comes from Lizzy Wilson Montgomery, chief keeper of the family flame into the twentieth century, who had these facts from her father "during long rides in his buggy" when the family resettled in Virginia in 1870 when she was twenty and he fifty-three (he would die of a stroke six years later), is that when he was about twenty he had fallen tenderly in love with and married a classmate in Virginia, who then died after about a year. The family of his first wife showed him "unusual affectionate interest" throughout his life. It was his deceased wife's brother's plantation in Alabama to which he made his way with his new medical degree. While a student in Philadelphia he had a miniature of himself painted (perhaps by the prominent artist Chester Harding) for his first wife's sister, his "favorite sister-in-law," who, writes Lizzy, "gave me the miniature of my father that I still value so highly."

No mention appears in surviving family documents of the miniature of the mother, Janet Mitchel Wilson, a picture of an adolescent girl, probably made in Richmond where she attended a boarding school in the early 1840s, to be sent home as a sentimental memento, perhaps for her dear friend Mary Pope, daughter of the Dr. Pope from whom Thomas Wilson would purchase the medical practice in 1846.

Its style suggests the work of the much admired John Wood Dodge, who is known to have worked in the South in the 1840s. In fact, in the memories of their children the father seems strikingly more vivid than the mother. Their maternal grandmother, Elizabeth Mitchel, seems to have made more of an impression on the children than did their mother. Although the rule of primogeniture that Elizabeth Mitchel's husband obeyed strictly in his will gave her no share of ownership of Elgin, after his death Elizabeth took over management of the plantation, until her son, the bequeathed owner, came into his majority. Elgin is described as similar in scale and in diversity of its products to a small New England manufacturing town, which gives some measure of the widowed Mrs. Mitchel's managerial skills within the male-dominated plantation hierarchy. She was an ardent reader of novels (Scott especially), owned a copy of *Uncle Tom's Cabin*, scribbled poems of her own invention into notebooks. She kept up with current events, did not hide her proclivities for the Whig party and her opposition to secession, though she supported it sympathetically once it happened and willingly saw her sons off to war. Her grandson recalls her as a "feminist, without the self-consciousness of feminism."

Apparently without her mother's ardency, Janet Wilson is described as "a most devoted wife, mother, daughter, and sister," her domestic role apparently defining her in the eyes of her children. At local schools and then at Mrs. Meade's School in Richmond she learned well the arts and crafts of proper ladyhood for her future duties as wife, plantation mistress, and mother. The sentimental ideal of true motherhood to which she was reared can be gleaned from these verses her friend Mary Pope set down in a notebook: "As a fond mother viewed with glistening eye / Her infant offspring as they gather round, / Heard their complaints—attuned to every cry— / Watched each motion, comprehended each sound, / To one, perhaps, she gives a kind embrace, / And seats another gently on her knee, / While on her foot another claimed a place, / And yet another on her breast may be / . . . With fond regard for all her bosom glows."

The poem rejoices in "mother," of course, not "mammy," who by all accounts performed much of the primary mothering of white infants and young children on plantations such as those of Warren

County. As elsewhere in the country in the antebellum years, "mother" was the image upon which an entire culture of sentiment, the system of images and values fundamental to an emergent national middle-class culture, was founded. The adulation of motherhood was one sign of how fully Warrenton, despite its relative isolation from cosmopolitan centers in the North, participated in the national culture. The exclusion from its celebrations of any reference to slavery, to the mothering role of black slave women, adds an ironic and poignant note to its idealizations. In "An Address Delivered to the Students of the Warrenton Male Academy" in 1849, the Reverend William Hill Jordan encapsulated that ideal in typical figurative language:

> Who loves like a mother? Whose patience endures like the patience of a mother? Whose sympathy is so pure, whose smile of approbation so sweet, as that of a mother? . . . As the eagle spreads her wings and hovers over her new-born progeny, so does the mother bend with cherished hopes and sweet anticipation over the interesting little pupil by her side, as from the lips of maternal tenderness, he learns the first rudiments of knowledge. And as the little stammerer stumbles along, over the uneven surface of b-a—ba, and a-b—ab, his first tardy accents of beginning knowledge are sweeter to the ears of maternal love than all the silver tones of Plato's tongue.

The purpose of the many private boarding schools for wealthy young woman in the antebellum South, such as Mrs. Meade's School in Richmond, attended by Janet Mitchel, was to prepare their charges, usually between the ages of twelve and sixteen, for their coming roles as wives and mothers. The schools provided some useful learning, much refinement of manners, and of course, a haven during these vulnerable years for the cherishing and preservation of chastity, in preparation for a lifetime of marriage and pure motherhood. Peter Wilson recalls, in *Southern Exposure*, that his mother taught him "how to read and to make my letters," and Lizzy remembers her mother as a "delightful pianist" and "a fine home-maker, as well as a good housekeeper," to which the care and precision of her entries and inventories in her daily notebooks testify. Typical of plantation wives, she managed daily affairs as well as social obligations, while remaining subordinate to her husband in the plantation hierarchy. "Warrenton was famous for its housewives," wrote the son Peter, "who took pleasure and pride in the best cooking and the beautiful service of that cooking." Dr. and Mrs. Thomas Wilson were among the shining lights of their local gentry.

One wonders what sort of presence the old wedding daguerreotype may have had in the filial memories of the parents, what role it may have played in the children's imagining of their parents' voices, and of an original romantic moment between just-married husband and wife. Did they take the picture as a moment within a family narrative, a story of courtship and marriage? Imagine the impression on the young heiress of the tall, handsome, gentle Virginian who appeared in town in 1846, she barely eighteen years old, he eleven years her senior, still bereaved and perhaps still sallow from malaria. We can assume, in the absence of tangible remains, a conventional courtship of visits, parties, balls, rides in the country, letters, soft words of endearment. "The personality of my father was very attractive," writes Lizzy, "a handsome straight figure, very erect," with a walk distinctive to his family, "a very deliberate, unhurried walk." "There was a movement of his legs and feet that was striking and dignified," wrote one of his sons fifty years after his death. Lizzy quotes Hans Nunnery, "a well-known [*sic*] of Warrenton at that time," saying to him, "Doctor, I wish I owned as much of this world as your walk would seem you do." But Lizzy also recalls her father as extremely modest, polite, considerate, patient, generous, "always amiable and sweet tempered," and a fine conversationalist, "always at ease in manner, in any company knowing what he wished to say and saying it in a fine graceful manner." "He explained the lay of the land," recalls the son five decades after the father's death, "how the streams flowed, told me of the soils, why certain crops were suited to the land North and others South of the Railroad and a lot of lore that comes naturally into the knowledge of country people." The son's memory rings with remarkably durable filial piety. "He was a healer of wounds, and allayer of suffering, advisor to the sick and disturbed, a restraining hand to the over-anxious and nervous. . . . After half a century and only half of his children survive, his impress of character grows upon our maturity as or more than it did years ago. We see and hear him more distinctly." The son's figurative language suggests that the father had daguerreotyped (*impressed*) himself upon his children's memory as a living picture, distinctly seen and heard.

Of what, then, does the portrait of the couple on the bench speak? The chance intersection of a young Southern couple of the planter class with a young "staunch republican" Philadelphia artist, about the same age as Dr. Wilson, smitten with the possibilities of making living pictures as daguerreotypes, must be counted as one thread of the story. How much Simons knew of the lives of his sitters matters less than what his perceiving eye understood as an opportunity for a picture. The old Boston master of the daguerreotype Albert S. Southworth said in an address in 1870: "What is to be done is obliged to be done quickly. The whole character of the sitter is to be read at first sight; the whole likeness, as it shall appear when finished, is to be seen at first, in each and all its details, and in their unity and combinations." In our effort to bring the image to life, to speech, to hear its tale as richly and deeply as history has endowed it with richness, depth, and ambiguity, the artist's presence in the picture must also be felt and acknowledged. The sitters play their roles, given to them in part by the history we are able to recount, but also in part by the artist who staged the enactment of their drama. We can study the image, to paraphrase Roland Barthes, as a datum within a history we already know from other sources. And we can allow the image to fascinate us, reveal to us a trace or still-vibrant vestige of a moment of triangulated force: the woman, the man, the photographer.

The picture exists among other pictures, the smaller mother-and-child portrait, the two painted miniatures; it gives its own face and body to the sitters. And the ensemble can be taken as a small but telling model of kinds of visual representation practiced at a specific time in a specific culture. And surely, for students of Montgomery Simons, or of daguerreotype portraiture in the United States, the picture offers evidence of studio style and pictorial intention. But once we are caught in the emotional register of the image, confidence in what we can know erodes rather rapidly. In the end the full story of the lives caught in the

few seconds of the duration of the daguerreotype, the story of those
few seconds themselves, remains untranslatable. We are left to look at
the image, and to look again and again, feeling its *punctum*, in Roland
Barthes's evocative phrase, straining for a voice. Much as the contextual written voices enlighten us about social and familial identities, the
image itself finally denies reliable transparency to what we construct as
a history anterior to it. It is too rich as a picture in its own right, excessive, one might say haunting, in its interpretative possibilities. Because
of the art of the daguerreotypist, in producing an image so fully realized and specific to the point of ambiguity, an opaque curtain seems to
fall between the history gleaned from shards of memory and the
drama composed by the artist. We reach this point of final dubiety
only by listening for speech, by gathering external evidence, and most
important, by surrendering to the trope of the speaking picture. Only
by such efforts do we apprehend the absence which, in the end, makes
this image so compelling a visual and imaginative experience. Its ultimate silence becomes the picture's most eloquent testimony of coming
to life.

THREE

SEEING AND BELIEVING

Hawthorne's Reflections on the Daguerreotype in
The House of the Seven Gables

I

I don't much like pictures of that sort,—they are so hard and stern;
besides dodging away from the eye, and trying to escape altogether. They are conscious of looking very unamiable, I suppose,
and therefore hate to be seen. . . . I don't wish to see it any more."
Phoebe's unease occurs in Nathaniel Hawthorne's *The House of the Seven
Gables*, a narrative in which daguerreotypes figure consequentially both
in the plot and in the literary theory internalized as a major theme
within the fiction. For if the narrative launches itself in the preface as
an argument on behalf of "Romance" over "Novel," the figurative
rhetoric by which Hawthorne embodies that distinction, so crucial to
his undertaking, draws on the same daguerrean effects to which
Phoebe reacts. Sharing features of both "Novel" and "Romance," of
science and magic, of modernity and tradition, the daguerreotype
plays a strategic role in the narrative as an emblem of the ambiguity
that the tale will affirm as the superior mark of "Romance"—if not exactly "Romance" itself, at least a major narrative resource for defining
and apprehending what that term means.

A writer of novels, the "Author" explains in the preface, "is presumed to aim at a very minute fidelity, not merely to the possible, but
to the probable and ordinary course of man's experience." Too glaring

First published in *American Literary History* 9, no. 3 (1997): 460–81.

to miss, the analogy of novel writing to photography seems confirmed by the mimetic intentions of both. But Hawthorne's description of the latitude of the romancer—the allowable deviations from a strictly faithful mimesis—also evokes photography, particularly daguerreotypy: the romancer "may so manage his atmospherical medium as to bring out or mellow the lights and deepen and enrich the shadows of the picture." The literary distinction between two kinds of mimesis—one strictly adherent to an imitation of the probable and the ordinary, the other less constrained and freer to deploy atmospheric effects—corresponds to a distinction already well formulated in theories of photography at the time, between merely mechanical and self-consciously artistic uses of the new medium. While "minute fidelity" seems incontrovertibly to associate photography with "Novel," with its recurring imagery of light and mist and shadow, the preface subtly recruits the daguerreotype for a key role in the definition of "Romance" that the narrative will unfold.

Two sentences are especially important. "The point of view in which this Tale comes under the Romantic definition, lies in the attempt to connect a by-gone time with the very Present that is flitting away from us." The present flits away just as does the picture on the mirrorlike surface of a daguerreotype. But how are we to take "connect," especially in light of the rejection of "very minute fidelity"? Farther on, the "Author" warns against reading the tale as a too literal picture of an actual place and says that such a reading "exposes the Romance to an inflexible and exceedingly dangerous species of criticism, by bringing his [the author's] fancy-pictures almost into positive contact with the realities of the moment." How are we to understand the difference between dangerous "positive contact" and presumably benign "connect"? We are teased into imagining another mode of fidelity to "Present," to "realities of the moment"—that is, the mode of "Romance," which defines itself not by an absolute difference from "Novel" or by a rejection of mimesis but by the positing of another kind of mimesis, atmospheric, shadowed, faithful to that which flits away: a kind of mimesis that the narrative will apprehend with the help of its ambiguous and problematic daguerreotypes.

A present that flits away, fancy pictures that might be brought "almost" into "positive contact" with "realit[y]," portraits that dodge the eye and try to escape (to escape detection?)—Hawthorne's figures play nicely on what by 1851 had become a fairly common experience: that apparent trick of the mirrored metallic face of the daguerreotype image, seeming at once here and gone, a positive and a negative, substance and shadow. What one sees, shadow or image, or indeed one's own visage flashed back from the mirrored surface, depends on how one holds the palm-sized cased image, at what angle and in what light. The image materializes before one's eyes as if out of its own shadows. Because of the daguerreotype's peculiar construction, built up, as one recent expert explains, through accumulated surface granules rather than suspended in an emulsion (as in paper prints), what is required for the image to seem legible—or, as they said at the time, to "come to life"—is a specific triangulation of viewer, image, and light.

In the face of such contingency and instability of seeing, no wonder that some like Phoebe felt disconcerted by the experience. Phoebe's outcry and the suggestive language of the preface signal how deeply engaged this narrative is with daguerrean seeing, its ambiguities of affect and, I shall argue, ambivalences of purpose. How are we to understand, for example, the motives and purposes of the novel's ardent daguerreotypist, Holgrave? "I misuse Heaven's blessed sunshine by tracing out human features, through its agency," the young man confesses to Hepzibah. Surely we want to read "misuse" as coyly self-ironic, a nicely turned disclaimer of anything irregular in his craft. Is not his practice of daguerreotypy a sign of Holgrave's most appealing traits—his experimental bent, his adventuresomeness, his facility with modern tools? To be sure. But Phoebe personifies the sun's purest rays, and Holgrave comes close to misusing her; her feminine innocence we are surely meant to take as the novel's least controvertible value; in the end it is what saves Holgrave from himself. Our smile at "misuse" fades into a deeper, more shadowed concern when we learn of Holgrave's secret purpose of revenge against the Pyncheons in whose house he at present resides. Is he tenant or spy? In any case he resides in disguise, perhaps even from himself. Might not the craft he practices in the deep recesses of the old mansion as well as in his public rooms in the town be viewed as a purposefully atavistic regression to the witchcraft of his ancestors, the original Maules from whom Colonel Pyncheon, founder of the family, had stolen the land for his estate and house two hundred years earlier?

Etching his text with strokes of ambiguity and dubiety, Hawthorne draws widely on figural terms from the popular discourse of the daguerreotype circulating in the print culture of the 1840s and early 1850s. He draws on that gothicized discourse not for the sake of local allusions alone but as a vehicle of his deepest intentions in the romance, which are to probe the implications of the new order of things of which photography serves as the auspicious type. Alternative views of the daguerreotype portrait, of the autoptic process of apparently unmediated seeing and believing that the camera putatively represents, and of the physiognomic principles of portraits as such serve the tale's ulterior purposes. To be sure, a narrative more of picture than action, of tableaux than plot, of Gothic device than dialogic interaction, *The House of the Seven Gables* leaves its largest questions unsettled, its complexities and complications aborted by the quick fix of a hastily arranged fairy-tale ending in which Holgrave seems to abandon daguerreotypy (this is not clear), along with his resentment and radical politics (this is clear), for pastoral squiredom. It is as if, Walter Benn Michaels provocatively suggests, the daguerreotype of the dead Judge Pyncheon releases them all from both the burden of a weighty "Past" and the instabilities of a flitting "Present," frees them altogether from "Novel" to spend their days within the stone-protected realm of "Romance." Whatever authorial purposes account for the novel's odd ending, it reflects in part on daguerrean visibility, on photography's cultural work within a society rapidly undergoing unsettling change toward market-centered urban capitalism. No wonder Melville found in the narrative an "intense feeling of the visable truth," meaning by that, he wrote to Hawthorne, "the apprehension of the absolute condition of present things as they strike the eye."

II

Hawthorne focuses his inquiry into means and ends of the daguerreotype on the figure of his hero. At present Holgrave lives as an itinerant daguerreotypist, a fact that seems at first marginal to the main action of the narrative, which in summary resembles popular Gothic melo-dramas: a decaying old house, an ancient crime, a family curse, a thirst for revenge. The story centers on Judge Jaffrey Pyncheon's effort to ex-tract from his cousin Clifford, just released from a lengthy unjust im-prisonment, information about a missing family deed to lands in Maine. The judge had framed Clifford, giving false evidence that convicted his cousin of the murder of their wealthy uncle. Jaffrey's treachery and his greed make him seem an avatar of the original seventeenth-century Pyncheon, founder of the once magnificent, now decaying House of the Seven Gables. Two descendants whose decrepi-tude matches that of the ancient house occupy the dwelling: the penu-rious Hepzibah, whose rather helpless try at selling groceries in a wing of the house opens the action of the novel, and her sadly ruined brother Clifford. They are joined by their sprightly country cousin Phoebe and the ambiguous tenant, the young daguerreotypist with alarmingly radical views on the sinfulness of inherited property and other social conventions. It will emerge that the young man has coun-terfeited his identity, for he is none other than a descendant of the Matthew Maule from whom the original Pyncheon had wrested the parcel of land on which the house sits. That legalized theft followed Maule's conviction on charges of witchcraft, a false accusation that provoked Maule's wrathful curse from the gallows that the lying, over-reaching Pyncheon will drink blood. The stern old man's sudden death in a paroxysm the very day his house was completed (Maule's son Thomas was the chief carpenter) seemed to fulfill Maule's curse, the curse of the dispossessed and the resentful.

By legend the curse persists: virtually every generation has seen a Pyncheon who resembled the hard, unbending founder, even to the point of dying suddenly with a gurgling sound in his throat. The pres-ent judge is the latest avatar and the final one, for Holgrave's camera will show beyond cavil that his death was natural after all, the result of an inherited ailment. The curse lifted, Clifford exonerated, Phoebe and Holgrave married—the entire cast of characters, including the old re-tainer Uncle Venner, betake themselves to the judge's country estate, now restored to rightful heirs, the newly wed and redeemed descen-dants of both Maule and Pyncheon. With harmony between the antagonistic families (a distinctly class antagonism) finally achieved, the story closes happily as Hepzibah, out of the largesse of her newly recovered wealth and social station, dispenses silver coin to the town "urchin."

Like many readers, D. H. Lawrence puzzled over this curious tale of sinful fathers, vengeful sons, and compliant daughters in a bizarrely modern world: "The Dark Old Fathers. The Beloved Wishy-Washy Sons. The Photography Business. ? ? ?" As far as the plot goes, only the final evidentiary picture of the judge's death makes a difference, as a kind of messenger from the gods. But Hawthorne has his purposes, slyly insinuated in the daguerrean figures already quoted from the preface. The fixed picture that preserves what flits away had been a popular trope in the photographic trade for more than a decade: "Seize the shadow ere the substance fade." "Fancy-pictures" and "flitting" suggest that Hawthorne in some manner saw his own text as bearing a resemblance to the daguerrean image and its uncanny effects. One critic remarks that the narrative itself might be read as a "flickering" apparitional, here-again, gone-again daguerreotype portrait. The fact that Holgrave is also an author (his name can be read as self-written) carries the suggestion further of a metadiscourse on the art of narrative. Does Holgrave's daguerreotypy serve as a heuristic analogy to Hawthorne's writing of romance?

It is significant in this regard that Holgrave's daguerreotypes appear within a political universe, a world threatened by both past and future, by inherited corruption founded upon illegitimate class privilege, and by the discordant energies of modernity, the railroad, the telegraph, market society. Moreover, associated at once with sorcery through the Maule eye of Holgrave and with modern mechanical instruments of change, Holgrave's daguerreotypes combine elements of past and present, of tradition and change, of magical and rational systems of knowledge. The narrator situates the products of Holgrave's equivocal craft within a radiating web of implication.

It is noteworthy, then, that the first daguerreotype presented to a viewer in the narrative is a failed image, one that misses its intention: a dour picture of the judge that so displeases Phoebe that she turns away. The exchange occurs, not incidentally, in the Pyncheon garden near the bubbling waters of Maule's Well. The picture was "intended to be engraved," Holgrave explains, presumably for the judge's use in his campaign for governor. What seems to ruin the image is the incorrigible hardness of the judge's physiognomy:

> Now, the remarkable point is, that the original wears, to the world's eye—and, for aught I know, to his most intimate friends—an exceedingly pleasant countenance, indicative of benevolence, openness of heart, sunny good humor, and other praiseworthy qualities of that cast. The sun, as you see, tells quite another story. . . . Here we have the man, sly, subtle, hard, imperious, and, withal, cold as ice. Look at that eye! Would you like to be at its mercy? At that mouth! Could it ever smile? And yet, if you could only see the benign smile of the original! It is so much the more unfortunate, as he is a public character of some eminence, and the likeness was intended to be engraved.

Holgrave's explanation of the failure, often taken as an unequivocal endorsement on the author's part as well as his hero's, of the new medium, echoes the Enlightenment rationalist ideology embedded within popular commentary on photography. Yet it will prove to be every bit as equivocal as the young Holgrave-Maule himself: "There is a wonderful insight in heaven's broad and simple sunshine," he explains to Phoebe. "While we give it credit only for depicting the merest surface, it actually brings out the secret character with a truth that no painter would ever venture upon, even could he detect it." Knowing that the self-authored Holgrave himself travels under a false sign, that he too harbors a "secret character," is warning enough for us to hold these words at some distance. Is his mention of "secret character," like his present disguised tenancy in the house of his family's dispossession, a tactical move toward his own inherited interest in exposing the Pyncheons' illegitimacy and destroying them? Like the actual pictures he makes—three are mentioned: two portraits of the dubious Judge Pyncheon (one after his death), and another we never see directly, of Uncle Venner, the town's storyteller and down-home philosopher—Holgrave's words about his craft are freighted with implications eventually to be drawn forth.

Other readers have shared D. H. Lawrence's suspicion of something secretive and covert about the novel. "It is . . . full of all sorts of deep intentions . . . certain complicated purposes," remarked Henry James, adding that what Hawthorne evidently "designed to represent was not the struggle between an old society and a new . . . but simply . . . the shrinkage and extinction of a family." If not "struggle" between the old and new, then at least, as Frank Kermode nicely puts it, the narrative registers "a transition from one structure of society, and one system of belief and knowledge, to another." James notes cogently that the characters "are all figures rather than characters—they are all pictures rather than persons." In the "history of retribution for the sin of long ago," as the narrator describes his tale, Holgrave, who had taken up the daguerrean line "with the careless alacrity of an adventurer," plays a kind of avenging angel, not with a sword but a camera or, better, a certain kind of eye that adapts itself with alacrity (less careless than he admits) to the daguerrean mode of vision. Holgrave's "deep, thoughtful, all-observant eyes," the Maule "family eye," in which "there was now-and-then an expression, not sinister, but questionable," are there to witness the final act of what he conceives as a drama: "Providence . . . sends me only as a privileged and meet spectator." Author, actor, and privileged audience—his role is foretold in the shadowy, teasing way the past repeats itself in the world of the narrative. He is the Maule "descendant" whom Hepzibah imagines seeing her fall from lady to hucksteress as "the fulfillment of his worst wishes" (ironically so, for he is also "her only friend"). He represents the "posterity of Matthew Maule" who, through "a sort of mesmeric process," can make the "inner region" of the family looking glass come "all alive with the departed Pyncheons; not as they had shown themselves to the world, nor in their better and happier hours, but as doing over again some deed of sin, or in the crisis of life's bitterest sorrow," as he may indeed have made the judge look in the failed daguerreotype.

"They are all types, to the author's mind," writes James, "of something general, of something that is bound up with the history, at large, of families and individuals." Like each of the principal characters, Holgrave is both himself and not himself, a person and a type, a figure in his own right and a figure in an ancient, repetitive drama. Indeed, the inner life of the plot shapes itself around the need Holgrave feels most acutely to resolve the ambiguity of identity he shares with the Pyncheons: at once themselves and not themselves, copies of ancient originals "doing over again some deed of sin."

Thus within the drama of the romance Holgrave's often cited words about the sun's "wonderful insight" appear to the reader, if not to Phoebe as double-edged, covert, shadowed. Can he mean that the sun, sheer material light, does in fact possess an "insight"? Or that he, descendant of the wronged Maules and privy to the ancestral gift of witchcraft (their power to torment bestowed on them by the projected guilt of their oppressors), already knows the "secret" written on the "merest surface" of Judge Pyncheon's self-betraying face and knows craftily how to bring it out? Is the sun aligned with the "Black Arts" Hepzibah affectionately suspects him of? Associations of daguerreo-typy with alchemy abounded in the 1840s and 1850s, for obvious rea-sons. The pedagogy he offers to Phoebe in the garden next to Maule's Well is a lesson not so much on the superiority of photography to painting as on a larger matter related to the "complicated purposes" of the romance: the unreliability of appearances, of representations alto-gether. Can we believe what we see, the "merest surface" of things and people, crafted surfaces such as paintings, maps, even mirrors, and es-pecially the appearances put on by such public benefactors as the cap-italist, politician, and horticulturalist Jaffrey Pyncheon, whose public face is all smiles and benignity? Is there a trustworthy way of seeing through surfaces, interpreting them as signs of something not seen, a "secret character," an invisible writing?

Hawthorne deepens and complicates the issue by raising yet an-other question about that "character" beneath the judge's smiling exte-rior disclosed by the sun, a question about its origins. Is the judge's character his own, or is it merely a copy of his ancestor's, a replay, like his death, of an inherited infirmity? If he is indeed only a copy of an ancient original, then the "secret" part of his "character" signifies something different from simple hypocrisy or duplicity. The "truth" the sun "brings out" may be hidden from the judge himself. It lies in his history, a family history of illegitimate class privilege and abrogated power, and particularly of the use of established authority to lend an official seal to the original theft of Maule's land. It is in the Pyncheons' interest to keep that origin secret, to repress its threatening truth, and when repression becomes habitual, it produces a secretiveness that no longer understands what it hides or why. What the sun reveals through Holgrave's failed daguerreotype, then, is not the judge's ineptitude in maintaining an affable façade before the camera but his alienation from his own "character." What the sun reveals, in short, is not just something to be glimpsed beneath a façade, something merely visible, but something to be interpreted. A visibility incomplete in itself, the daguerrean image Holgrave offers to Phoebe's eyes is in search of an explanatory narrative.

III

Near the heart of the plot lies a document, "a folded sheet of parchment" hidden behind the ancestral portrait of the first Pyncheon. "Signed with the hieroglyphics of several Indian sagamores," this "ancient deed," which Jaffrey is desperate to lay his hands on, represents the legislative "grant" on which the original Pyncheon based his "claims" against the "right" of Matthew Maule to possess what, "with his own toil, he had hewn out of the primeval forest, to be his garden-ground and homestead." This mere piece of paper, these undecipherable scrawls in a language no one remembers, recall the "recondite documents" Bartleby labors to copy in Melville's "story of Wall Street," or the scraps of paper Ike McCaslin puzzles over in the commissary in Faulkner's "The Bear." Hawthorne represents as an American version of original sin an originating act of ruthless theft the knowledge of which calls into question all constituted authority. The missing deed, with its inscriptions of Indian "hieroglyphics," of course addresses the issue of real estate and "title," extending the horizon of conflict back to the first transactions between Europeans and native inhabitants. Might we not imagine that an appropriate decipherment of those hieroglyphics would deny the validity of European concepts of property and ownership altogether? The few references in the text to Indians hint that matters prior to and deeper than the class conflict between the two European families may be at issue in the tale. What the judge's "secret character" hides even from himself is the fact that his historical being arises from a crime, his ancestor's deed against "natural right" disguised as a legitimate "claim" in an undecipherable legislative "deed." "Deed"—the conflation of act and word places a lexical pun at the heart of the original sin: the deed (act) of displacing the Lockean "right" to ownership of the products of one's labor with "claims" based upon a cryptic deed (word) written by distant legislators or even more distant sagamores. "Secret character" behind "merest appearance" revives the pun on "deed," signifying at once character as accumulated acts (the judge's personal sin against Clifford) and character as a written inscription (the judge's figural reenactment of the first Pyncheon's crime).

Only by restoring this history, which requires a new way of thinking about the relation between self and past, can Holgrave render his daguerreotype of the judge legible as revelation of hidden truth. The light of the sun alone cannot suffice, contrary to the claims of Holgrave's compeers in the real world of commercial portrait photography. Working photographers proffered visibility as their commodity, the sun their warranty of reliable truth. In a moral climate in which citizens felt anxious about "character," eager to trust the façades projected in images of men holding public trust yet distrustful of their own eagerness, photographers offered their goods as a social good, a guide to virtue. For was not character readily discernible in the face? And did not the daguerreotype provide the republic with its most foolproof means of discerning character?*

---

*So thought the Philadelphia daguerreotypist Marcus Aurelius Root, who wrote in 1864 that in the power of the face to express inner character, and in the daguerreotype to capture that expression, "lies a valuable security for social order, insuring, as it does, that men shall ultimately be known for what they are." The famed Boston daguerreotypist Albert Sands Southworth, sometimes taken by critics as a prototype for Holgrave, offered an interesting variation on this theme, which veers toward the Hawthornian notion of "Romance." He argued that the power of penetration beneath surfaces belonged not to the mechanical medium but to the "genius" of the true artist. "Conscious of something besides the mere physical, in every object in nature," the true artist will feel "the soul of the subject itself." With these preternatural abilities in play, something emanates from the camera as forcefully as the lightborne impressions that enter it. "The whole character of the sitter is to [be] read at first sight." At the same time, "defects are to be separated from natural and possible perfections. . . . Nature is not at all to be represented as it is, but as it ought to be, and might possibly have been."

By allowing Holgrave a set of words that seem so in accord with this popular republican ideology of the image, Hawthorne slyly encourages the reader to lower his or her guard. The issue turns on the ambiguity within another key word: "character" as what is true about a person, "character" as an assumed role, such as the public face put on by the judge, or indeed that performed by the contemporary Maule in his "character" as Holgrave, daguerreotypist. In that drama Holgrave performs as both author and actor: "in this long drama of wrong and retribution, I represent the old wizard." This confession holds the crux of the matter: the conflict between character as a set of moral traits engraved within and visible without, and character as a performed role in a scripted drama. Changing occupations like so many roles, "putting off one exterior, and snatching up another, to be soon shifted for a third," without ever altering the "inner most man," Holgrave is the figure within whom tension between self and role most overtly plays itself out. At stake is whether he will remain a "type," in the sense of a foreordained copy, or become a free historical agent, a self in historical time, free to script his own roles.

Hawthorne formulates Holgrave's inner conflict as that between a commitment to historical time and one to eschatological time and represents the conflict as an issue of interpretation. How are we to understand the failed daguerreotype of Judge Pyncheon? Not one of those photographers Walter Benjamin calls "illiterate," who "cannot read his own pictures," Holgrave knows (it is, we might say, his secret knowledge) that the meaning of the daguerreotype cannot rest in the unsupported image alone but resides only within a particular system of meaning. The system activated by his words to Phoebe is a rather bland but nonetheless distinct version of Christian typology, in which secrets are foreknown by providence. In Hawthorne's half-serious, half-skeptical use of the typological method of interpretation, "secret character" refers to a residue of prophecy uttered in the past: Maule's curse. The face, then, is an inscription that can be known only by reference to something antecedent to itself. The serious side of Hawthorne's typological method says that the secret of faces lies in the fact that they are really copies of absent originals. The skeptical side says that the original is not so much an absent figure (the portrait of the ancestral Pyncheon to whom the judge bears an uncanny resemblance, or the lost deed) but a continuing process, an ongoing history. Judge Pyncheon is either a pure figural reflex of a determining original sin or a free historical agent responsible for his own badness, his own corruption.

Her shuddering initial reaction to the daguerreotype of the judge initiates Phoebe into typological explanation. "I know the face" she cries, "for its stern eye has been following me about, all day. It is my Puritan ancestor, who hangs yonder in the parlor." That misidentification is her first lesson; the uncanny resemblance brought out by the daguerreotype points her directly to the typological source of her uncle's "secret character": "It is certainly very like the old portrait." The process begun in the garden continues when Phoebe encounters the judge face-to-face; beneath his sunny exterior she recognizes the "hard, stern, relentless look" of "the original of the miniature [daguerreotype]." As she notes in a recurrence of the uncanny, the "original," the face before her, copies the features of the ancestor whose portrait in its antique, faded condition "brought out" the "indirect character of the man." The ancient portrait strikes her as a "prophecy" of the modern man, and in her "fancies" that in the living judge "the original Puritan" stood before her, she gives a start. Thus the process of interpretation inaugurated by Holgrave teaches Phoebe a lesson essential to the system of meaning that Hawthorne takes as his object of investigation, one in which material substance of today seems to cast shadows of yesterday.

The process of interpreting the first daguerreotype culminates in the final taking of a likeness, the death portrait that will prove, typologically speaking, that in effect the good judge had been dead all along, "fixed" as only the dead can be in an unalterable "character": "Death is so genuine a fact that it excludes falsehood, or betrays its emptiness." For the reading instigated by Holgrave in the garden begins the torturous process of converting the judge into a scapegoat, to be ritually slain by the camera. On the disclosure of his death everything else depends in this narrative of magical consummations. Both magical and political, Holgrave's reading of the judge's image, of the judge himself as an image, dissolves corrupt public authority by disclosing the corpse, the rotten "deed" decaying just behind the elegant façade. Holgrave's is that "sadly gifted eye" whose knowing look "melts into thin air" the "tall and stately edifice" the judge had constructed for the "public eye."

The narrative elaborates this architectural figure. The judge's self is like a marble palace constructed of "the big, heavy, solid unrealities" of wealth and power and "public honors," its windows "the most transparent of plate-glass," its dome open to the sky. The architectural figure recalls nothing so much as one of the era's novel creations, a mercantile shop posing as a neoclassical palace, while its stateliness recalls the original appearance of the House of the Seven Gables itself: "There is something so massive, stable, and almost irresistibly imposing, in the exterior presentment of established rank and great possessions, that their very existence seems to give them a right to exist; at least, so excellent a counterfeit of right, that few poor and humble men have moral force enough to question it, even in their secret minds." The political point of Holgrave's hermeneutics becomes clear: to penetrate "exterior presentment" in order to disclose the "counterfeit of right" it claims for itself.

Holgrave's lesson in the reading of the daguerreotype (both typological and historicist) sheds light, moreover, on the role of picturing as such within the texture of the book. The preponderance of looking, seeing, gazing, scrutinizing—for example, "To know Judge Pyncheon, was to see him at that moment"—declares the reading of images, reading in the sense of comprehending the look of things and persons, as a core issue in the narrative. Often the verb is made explicit: Clifford "reads" Phoebe, "as he would a sweet and simple story"; Holgrave too "fancied that he could look through Phoebe, and all around her, and could read her off like a page of a child's story-book." People stand to each other as texts, transparently legible or guardedly cryptic. There are texts within texts, not only figurative storybooks and the "legend" of Alice Pyncheon composed by Holgrave but also a host of pictures: "quaint figures" ornamenting the exterior of the house; "pictures of Indians and wild beasts grotesquely illuminat[ing]" the map of the legendary Pyncheon territories in Maine; "grotesque figures of man, bird, and beast" painted over the old tea set, "in a world of their own"; and the gingerbread figures of animals and "the renowned Jim Crow."

Some are ephemeral, vanishing as quickly as they are seen: the "continually shifting apparition of quaint figures, vanishing too suddenly to be definable," of Maule's Well and the "brilliant fantasies" that depict the world "in hues bright as imagination" on the "nothing" surface of Clifford's soap bubbles. And, of course, there are the most prominent pictures: the ancient portrait of the founding ancestor, the Malbone miniature of Clifford that Hepzibah cherishes, and the daguerreotypes of the judge. How does one read images of the world, the world deflected into image? The question of visuality as cognition lies athwart the entire narrative.

Indeed, the narrator introduces the larger question at the outset: "The aspect of the venerable mansion has always affected me like a human countenance, bearing the traces not merely of outward storm and sunshine, but expressive also of the long lapse of mortal life, and accompanying vicissitudes, that have passed within. Were these to be worthily recounted, they would form a narrative of no small interest and instruction, and possessing, moreover, a certain remarkable unity, which might almost seem the result of artistic arrangement."

Interpretation appears here at the outset not just as a correlation of outer trace and inward life but also as "narrative" with its own laws and codes of "arrangement." Here is the method of "Romance" promised in the preface, the method that presumes a relation between outer and inner as inherently ambiguous. Is the narrative true or only a plausible guess, governed equally by the desire for "unity" and by reference to actual fact or document? Indeed, as it proceeds, the narrative more and more adduces what it calls "tradition" against "written record," a polarizing of modes of telling that becomes part of a diagrammatic structure of oppositions: on one hand, public records, official, "cold, formal, and empty words"; on the other, "the private and domestic view," homely truths, gossip, rumor, chimney-corner tradition. Parallel to this contrast, substantially between writing and speech, is "the vast discrepancy between portraits intended for engraving, and the pencil-sketches that pass from hand to hand, behind the original's back." Holgrave's daguerreotype, recall, was indeed "intended for engraving," but the measure of its failure was its resemblance to a satiric pencil-sketch view of the judge. A corresponding opposition in the schema of personae has the judge, the archpublic figure, set in polar opposition to Uncle Venner, the book's gossip, who mediates between the sphere of women (he makes daily rounds in the town from kitchen to kitchen) and of men: the judge, who takes "his idea of himself from what purports to be his image, as reflected in the mirror of public opinion," and the uncle, the "man of patches" whose wardrobe consists of throwaways, "a miscellaneous old gentleman, partly himself, but, in good measure, somebody else."

How are we to understand Holgrave's art of daguerreotypy within this structure of oppositions? The daguerreotype occupies a paradoxical position. The narrative comes down on the side of tradition, gossip, and pencil sketches, linked through Uncle Venner and Phoebe to an older village culture, a republican culture founded on community and consensus. The old ways survive into and provide a perspective upon a present characterized by two localized but intense images of change: Hepzibah's fantasy of a "panorama, representing the great thoroughfare of a city," and the railroad car vista of Hepzibah and Clifford, during their mad flight from the threatening judge, of "the world racing past." The latter is more nightmarish and metaphysical, as Clifford discourses crazily in the rattling car on electricity as "an almost spiritual medium," on the blessings of the railroad, and on the insubstantiality of real estate. The scene is a severe gloss on the deceptively milder "fluctuating waves of our social life" by which the narrator had introduced Hepzibah's reopening of the shop. If that moment of transformation of a patrician into a plebeian hints at the upheavals of the Panic of 1837 and its aftermath, the effects of the railroad ride seem momentous: villages "swallowed by an earthquake"; meetinghouse spires "seemed set adrift from their foundations"; the "hills glided away." "Everything was unfixed from its age-long rest, and moving at whirlwind speed." Something even more calamitous awaits the time-stricken couple at "a solitary way-station": an abandoned church "in a dismal state of ruin and decay . . . a great rift through the main-body of the edifice"; a farmhouse black with age, "relics of a woodpile" near the door, gruesome icons of the new mechanical civilization that unfixes everything and bequeaths a wasted godless landscape.

Hepzibah's earlier fantasy in her shop depicts an equally new landscape of modernity but one obverse to the ruinous scene: prosperous mercantile capitalism confidently enjoying its high commercial stage. In place of the riven church, glittering shops; in place of the eye of God, a mirror: "Groceries, toyshops, dry-goods stores, with their immense panes of plate-glass, their gorgeous fixtures, their vast and complete assortments of merchandize, in which fortunes have been invested; and those noble mirrors at the farther end of each establishment, doubling all this wealth by a brightly burnished vista of unrealities! . . . this splendid bazaar, with a multitude of perfumed and glossy salesmen, smirking, smiling, bowing, and measuring out the goods!" The very figure of Broadway, the fantasy reenacts a world of goods and shoppers doubled by mirrors into unrealities (who can tell the copy from the original?), just as goods double or reduplicate themselves in the guise of their invisible agency, money. The mirror of unrealities leaps out as the apt emblem of commodity culture, the very agent of reproduction, transforming substance into image in a process that itself mirrors the apparent magic whereby money vanishes into goods and reappears as profit. The mystery of such market transactions arises, as Marx famously pointed out in his formulation of "commodity fetishism," through the effacement of all signs of labor by which goods might be recognized and known as the investment of toil. Condensed in Hepzibah's fantasy lies the historical secret of the judge—not only of his wealth garnered from the "crime" of appropriation in the capitalist market but also his "public character" raised by a trick of mirrors into an edifice resembling a commercial emporium disguised as a domed, neoclassical palace. The judge sees himself only in the mirror of his market self, takes the "unrealities" of doubled wealth as the truth of his being.

Can we doubt Hawthorne's purpose in these alternating views of modern change: a kaleidoscopic view of the old countryside, unfixed, ruined, deprived of God; a panoramic view of the new city as a marketplace with no perspective outside itself, only an internal mirror doubling its surfaces into "unrealities"? Widely separated in the narrative, the two views form a composite dialectical image less of a "struggle between an old society and a new" than of an already accomplished victory of new over old. If the new has no substance, in the old sense of solid reality, the old has no resources, except the resources of "Romance," which imagine the persistence of the older republic of rural virtue in the shadowed regions of the new society.

Recall the ending of the romance: the happy resolution, following the fortuitous demise of the judge, of the ancient quarrel between Maule and Pyncheon. Holgrave gives up his Maule eye, quits photography, retires with Phoebe and the others to a country estate, a house of stone—the "lapse of years . . . adding venerableness to its original beauty"—while the inhabitants "might have altered the interior" as they wish. Withdrawing behind protective walls, the group forms, in Holgrave's anticipatory image, a magic circle against the threat of a political economy that reproduces the world as image-commodities. The happy ending evokes another political economy, transmuted by "Romance" from archaic practice into imaginative value, a critical, even if defenseless and rearguard, perspective upon the new society.

Consider Phoebe, who represents the Pyncheon line melded into the folkways of the old New England countryside. She enters the narrative just as Hepzibah ventures into modernity by opening her shop, as if elicited magically as an antidote to the threatening mirrored panorama of the city market. Consider the village market Phoebe re-creates in her management of the Pyncheon shop. With her first customer, an old woman who "was probably the very last person in town, who still kept the time-honored spinning-wheel in constant revolution," she barters her goods for homemade yarn as the two voices "mingl[e] in one twisted thread of talk." With her "gift of practical arrangement," her "natural magic," she makes her own goods, such as yeast, beer, cakes, and breads, instinctively following Uncle Venner's old "golden maxims": "Give no credit! . . . Never take paper-money! Look well to your change! Ring the silver on the four-pound weight! Shove back all English half-pence and base copper-tokens, such as are very plenty about town! At your leisure hours, knit children's woollen socks and mittens! Brew your own yeast, and make your own ginger-beer!"

Can it be only a coincidence that Venner's mention of silver and copper links his "golden maxims" surreptitiously to Holgrave's daguerreotypes, images made on silver-plated copper and often "fixed with pure chloride of gold, so that it is impossible that the pictures can fade for ages"? No matter how oblique, the allusion clarifies brilliantly the paradoxical predicament of the daguerreotype within the text: its association on one side with all the unsettling elements of modernity and, on the other, with traditional modes of figurative cognition and social exchange. Associated with an eye that makes edifices melt away, with forces that unfix, the daguerreotype not only fixes the fleeting image but also fixes it as a "secret character," something solid and definite beneath the judge's insubstantial surface of smiling munificence. It partakes of the invasive technologies of modern life, the public "gaze" Hepzibah fears, the "eye-witnesses" who report to the judge on "the secrets of your interior," and represents the black or Maule side of Holgrave's own analytic eye. Yet it is also allied with the solid coin of Venner's maxims against the fluid paper wealth of the judge, his investments, speculations, membership on corporate boards. If the judge's edifice of appearances resembles money and what Marx called its all-confounding powers, the daguerreotype redeems paper (or the outmoded, debased copper) into the hard specie of silver and gold. If, as popular writers at the time claimed, "character . . . [is] a kind of capital," "like an accumulating fund, constantly increasing in value," then Holgrave's silver-plated image drives out false currency and its unrealities.

No wonder, then, that the narrative's third daguerreotype is of none other than Judge Pyncheon's foil, the good Uncle Venner himself. "As a mark of friendship and approbation, he readily consented to afford the young man his countenance in the way of his profession—not metaphorically, be it understood—but literally, by allowing a daguerreotype of his face, so familiar to the town,—to be exhibited at the entrance of Holgrave's studio." Here again Hawthorne evokes a common practice of the daguerrean trade, a display of wares to tempt the public into the rooms upstairs. The familiarity of the face would make good bait. But there is a symbolic aspect to the linkage between the young and the old man afforded by the exhibition, heightened all the more by the fact that we never see the actual image. Like the analogy between maxims of gold and silver and the materiality of the daguerreotype, its absence renders Venner's picture all the more potent as a kind of amulet. To grasp the implications of Venner's face as advertised trope for Holgrave's daguerrean practice, we need to look more closely at the old "patched philosopher"—and his relevance to the typological theory of character in play in the narrative.

According to the typological view, characters are not free to choose their destinies; Holgrave must behave as a wizard and Judge Pyncheon as a greedy hypocrite. But Hawthorne allows Holgrave a will to change; he endows him with an inviolable "innermost man." He has nothing to hide, only something hidden within himself he needs to ferret out and overcome. The process of coming to himself, a process enacted in the historical time of the narrative, requires that he exorcise the ghost haunting the house, a ghost in the form of that very typological system that prophesies Maule to be Maule and Pyncheon Pyncheon, and by which Holgrave-Maule must expose and exorcise the corrupt judge. Jaffrey must die that Holgrave be free. The need is ontological: as long as a representative of the old, tyrannical system of representation lives, the cyclic drama continues. And the camera proves just the right instrument of execution. First, it raises the old legend by revealing the judge's typological "character" beneath his surface appearance. Second, in the death portrait it turns around and disproves the legend by revealing the death to be of natural causes. In each case the camera's report is meaningful only by interpretation: in the first instance, the old typological account of why the judge is evil; in the second, a "scientific" account that accords with a view of the judge as a historical creature, with a view of history as process rather than cycle.

In the end Holgrave abandons the camera, or so we assume, as he enters his estate as a country squire. The modern instrument has served his purpose of a deconstructive politics, of exposure and exorcism. By itself, he has shown, the camera has no theory of character, no independent ideology; it serves the discursive needs of its practitioners and clients. It either provides the compliant mirror images the judge desires and lives by, or subverts those images, allowing inner corruption to show through surface displays of virtue. Is there an alternative to these two versions of character—one doomed to repeat the past, the other doomed to live always in the eye of others? An answer lies with "wise Uncle Venner," who presides over the fairy-tale ending, who is seen last as the curtain falls, and whose replica exhibited at the entrance to Holgrave's studio holds the key to the daguerreotype's equivocal place in this tale of many equivocations.

Venner condenses an alternative theory of society and character. As "immemorial personage," "patriarch," the "familiar" of the "circle" of families he visits daily, he stands (even too obviously) for continuity, the redemptive folk memory; he is the secular "clergyman," venerable and venerated, whose liturgy is gossip, story, and maxim. He welcomes Holgrave into the storytelling circle as a "familiar." And by exhibiting Venner's image at the entrance to his studio, Holgrave declares his allegiance to continuity, sympathy, communal sustenance, and a theory of character consistent with Venner's "miscellaneous" appearance, his wardrobe of ill-assorted hand-me-downs. "Partly himself, but, in good measure, somebody else," Venner is neither entirely self-made (like Holgrave in his adventuring phase) nor other-made (like the judge). He appears as both a copy and an original, whose patched exterior at once discloses and conceals his inner truth. One can imagine his daguerreotype portrait only as a perfectly equivocal construction; hanging by the door, the portrait declares Holgrave's studio to be, like "Romance" itself, the very place of equivocation, where "merest surfaces" lose their self-sufficiency and seek their meanings in communal narratives, such as Venner's sustaining stories.

To save himself from himself Holgrave must slay the scapegoat, surrogate of the bad father, and replace him with a good father, the venerable Venner. Venner saves the young man from the radical implications of his youthful politics, from the dangerous illusion that programmatic politics can effectively shape the tides of change. In the end, a historicist view of history proves too difficult to encompass, the railroad ride of Clifford and Hepzibah too menacing to be sustained. In Hawthorne's method of romance, as James recognized, this point cannot be made in narrative action; it can be supplied only as an authorial observation. Thus the narrator interpolates a remark regarding Holgrave's revolutionary hatred of the past: "His error lay, in supposing that this age, more than any past or future one, is destined to see the tattered garments of Antiquity exchanged for a new suit, instead of gradually renewing themselves by patchwork." Venner is a walking theory of social change as slow accretion rather than sudden irruption or the imposition of rationalist utopia. He leads the survivors to a recomposed middle landscape, in which the values of an economy based on barter and solid coin are transmuted into values of true exchange among familiars, well protected by solid stone walls. And significantly, some degree of social deference is restored: Hepzibah distributes her largesse, providing Uncle Venner himself a cabin on the edge of the property. Thus the anxiety of visibility is tempered by an imaginary restoration of rank.

The meaning of the ending may lie precisely in its unbelievability, its transformation of an already defeated culture into a permanent value: the republican ideal, associated with Andrew Jackson, of an exchange economy among producers and small shopkeepers in a market free of manipulation by banks. A lost vision of entrepreneurial, petit bourgeois social relations elevated into a historical impossibility, the dream of a restored "circle": only its impossibility, Hawthorne has us realize, endows the ending with the redemptive power of "Romance." Hawthorne proposes "Romance" as a power to preserve a lost idea of a republic of virtue, at the expense, we must note, of imagining a historical action that might resolve the modern version of the Maule-Pyncheon class conflict. The marriage of Maule and Pyncheon accomplishes what the daguerreotype by itself cannot: it wishes away the nemesis of the modern market, a monied class of investors, speculators, and manipulators.

Hawthorne's view of the daguerreotype seems in the end as equivocal as the political vision of the text as a whole. The popular ideology assumed (or desired) a transparent relation between face and character, between expression and truth. It endowed the mirror image with power to stir emulation, to provide models of visible virtue, to preserve the presence of the missing and the dead. "It is as if the subject of a daguerreotype is in some sense already dead," writes Walter Benn Michaels. In the godless labyrinth of the marketplace, the mirror might serve as a way back toward familiar paths but only within typological narratives in which physiognomy doubles as psychology. Without such narratives, Hawthorne understood, photography threatened to let loose additional ambiguities, confusions between copies and originals. By questioning popular assumptions about the medium, by casting a skeptical eye on the claims of a photographic power independent of self-reflective structures of meaning, Hawthorne represents photography as a new political mode of seeing with unforeseen consequences. Confronting the "visable truth" of his age, in Melville's words, "the absolute condition of present things as they strike the eye," Hawthorne recognizes in the modern engine of visibility a new version of the old challenge of seeing to believing.

FOUR

LINCOLN'S SMILE

Ambiguities of the Face in Photography

Ah! what tales might those pictures tell if their mute lips had the power of speech. —Walt Whitman, 1846

WHITMAN'S fancy that photographed faces have tales to tell seems to have gone the way of kindred tropes of authenticity, swept out of fashion by the radical skepticism of our fin de siècle. The old belief was that, in Georg Simmel's words, "in the features of the face the soul finds its clearest expression." Today we are more likely to hear denials that portraits are anything more than artifice. In 1942 Edward Weston remarked that the "primary purpose" of the portrait photographer is "to reveal the individual . . . the essential truth of the subject." To which Richard Avedon has replied, "You can't get at the thing itself, the real nature of the sitter, by stripping away the surface. The surface is all you've got." The gap between the two conceptions seems unbridgeable. Face as theater, "soul" as performance: such postmodernist notions seem a wholesale inversion of beliefs like Weston's in "the thing itself" and Whitman's that photographic portraits gave access to "real" if indeterminate individuals. The typical aim now is to intrigue rather than to reveal. All that the

First published in *Social Research* 67, no. 1 (Spring 2000): 1–22.

photoportrait can be said to register is its own occasionality. Openly staged and contrived expressions, as in Cindy Sherman's celebrated work, seem now trustworthier as vehicles of meaning. We distrust depths, interiors, hidden "truths." Meanings lie on surfaces, artifacts of an occasion rather than truths about persons. We speak of "persons," even, with some trepidation. It's "identity" that one looks for in photo-portraits, how it's "constructed," the assumed, the imposed, the impro-visatory gambits of which all identities consist. In place of persons with revealing faces we look for contingencies, cracks and fissures in façades that disclose the paint and wires. Name resolves into contingent ap-pearance, "soul" into a glint in the eye, a lucky event of angled light.

Where once photographers strived to eliminate blurs of accidental motion or unintended shadows, which gave away the artifice of the show, photographic portraitists today revel in such signs of random-ness. Sophisticated looking at photographs now wants the inscription within the image of signs of its making, marks of its being a photo-graph after all and not a timeless truth. We seek the mark that will un-make "picture" on behalf of "trace," signs of the camera subverting its own presumptive privilege. The photographed face is now looked upon as opaque and possibly devious, a collaborative construction among artist, sitter, and viewer. The codes for the reading of faces once taken for granted and so finely internalized they seemed "natural" are now often, as in Cindy Sherman's early *Film Stills*, thrown back into the viewer's face. What is a code but an act of coercion, an expectation that young women look like this and play this or that role? Can anyone any longer be said to own his or her face? Perhaps only those who know that faces are masks to be donned and discarded as one desires. Perhaps the only way to recover possession of one's face, the authority to use it as one will, is to disown it by masking it.

The old belief had been shaped into a pillar of support for the bur-geoning commerce in photoportraits in the 1850s, and Whitman took reassurance from it that the new sprawling urban crowds would not obliterate individuality. Earlier in the century Wordsworth wrote in the London section of *The Prelude*, "The face of everyone / That passes by me is a mystery!" For Whitman the mystery of the crowd gave way to the penetrative power of eyesight, dissolved in a glance, transformed by an exchange of looks. Whitman's earliest poems register the challenge of a new problem of recognition. "Sauntering the pavement, thus, or crossing the ceaseless ferry," he wrote in 1855, "faces, and faces, and faces":

> Features of my equals, would you trick me with your creas'ed and
>   cadaverous march?
> Well, you cannot trick me.
>
> I see your rounded never-erased flow;
> I see 'neath the rims of your haggard and mean disguises.

Does he mean that his cruising eyes have no trouble recognizing "equals," other men desiring men? Very likely. But in the event he endows perception of the face with utterly revelatory power. "Writing and talk do not prove me, / I carry the plenum of proof and every thing else in my face." Every person's face similarly shows proof of hidden individuality, a soul surging to express itself through its body. No wonder one of the places he enjoyed most to saunter was among the new galleries of lower Broadway, where photographed face upon face lined the walls, each promising a separate yet cognate tale. The gallery was the street, the ferry transformed, modeled into a place of encounter.

Has something important been lost in the recent abandonment of belief in the face as text? The view that photographed faces make transparent the inner workings of subjective consciousness is, of course, unsupportable, taken with complete literalness. Moreover, recorded faces and bodies, particularly of women, can without difficulty be exposed as projections of biased desire and fantasy, the "gaze," constructions of male-dominated studios and the culture they represent and reproduce. The idea that formal portraits frequently represent asymmetrical power relations in the guise of putatively transparent facial expression makes good sense. But there's more at stake in the abandonment of transparency as a culture-bound illusion. Reading further in Simmel's Kantian argument in his essay "The Aesthetic Significance of the Face," we learn that, in his view, the ability to perceive in living faces a visible manifestation of something otherwise invisible implicates the entire question of "significance" or the signification of material signs, and at the same time the question of the possibility of "society."

For Simmel, the face is the test case of significance in visibility. He takes the face as a field of mobility within unity, in which any single change, a curling lip, a frown, "immediately modifies its [the face's] entire character and expression." It represents "unity out of and above diversity"; no change in one part of the face fails to affect "every other part at the same time." The face is unique in this regard. "Within the perceptible world, there is no other structure like the human face, which merges such a great variety of shapes and surfaces into an absolute unity of meaning." Unity is key, for without it, the variously and diversely changeable face would be "something quite abstruse and aesthetically unbearable." We call this unity "soul," something "lying behind the features of the face and yet visible in them." Changes indicating inner emotion, moreover, "leave lasting traces," giving face and soul a perceptibly temporal character. And soul perceptible in and through the face, Simmel argues in his most telling point, is similar to and a model of "the spirit of a society," "the content of those interactions which go beyond the individual . . . which is more than their sum, yet still their product." Like society, soul in its facial visibility is a product of "interaction, the reference of one to another" of the separate, changeable features of the face in motion. We can say that by the fact that the face is the "geometric locus" at which the character of each feature is integrated with the character of every other, the face (understood in this light) helps make society or sociation possible. With the eye as its chief organ, both performing and representing perception, the face gives "intimation," by "mirroring the soul," that all problems of perception "which involve soul and appearance," or significance, might be solved. "Appearance would then become the veiling and unveiling of the soul."

Simmel's brief essay makes no mention of earlier systems of interpretation, already discredited by the time he wrote, known in the eighteenth and nineteenth centuries under the heading of "physiognomy." Not content with the commonsense perceptions by which we normally recognize grief or joy, pain or pleasure, anger or tranquillity from the look on a face, physiognomists wanted absolute certainty, wanted outer proof of either permanent character traits inscribed in the shape of skulls or the inner meaning of passing facial "expressions." They wanted the face as a sign charged with meaning, an index of "character" or a kind of semaphore signaling inner feelings with the reliable consistency of a code. The appeal of physiognomy to early photographers was that it seemed to raise common sense to practical principle. Doesn't everyday experience tell us that faces are texts, something given to be read, a surface molded by a depth, a screen through which the sympathetic eye could detect an invisible but palpable interior being? A rhetoric of surface/depth and penetrative seeing appeared at the beginning of portrait photography, and it persisted through the long nineteenth century as a cardinal touchstone of the medium. There's an inner essence, it manifests itself in facial "expression," something fleeting but capturable by the camera's powers of instantaneous reproduction. Technical "improvements" in the early decades of the medium aimed at increasingly immediate transparency, recruiting the positivism of science to enable "capture" of spiritual essences. It was in the practice of portraiture that photographers first came to think of themselves as "artists," trained in perception as well as technique, equipped with intuitive as well as mechanical means. To portray the face as more than a likeness (the camera alone can do this) but a revelation, what is "necessary and requisite," wrote the Boston daguerreotypist Albert Sands Southworth in 1870, is "genius" for close observation, "discipline of mind and vision," and especially an "acquaintance with mind in its connection with matter." The gift of the portraitist is like "another sense." The artist, unlike the mere "operator" of a camera, will feel "the soul of the subject itself." Indeed, writes Southworth, one of the masters of the old daguerrean portrait, "the whole character of the sitter is to be read at first sight." The rest is technique, the skill to manipulate sitter, light, and apparatus to achieve an image true to "character" and "soul."

Some physiognomies defied picturing. Whitman thought Abraham Lincoln's was one, a face like those of some old farmers or sea captains (Whitman made this note in 1864, a year before Lincoln's assassina-

Figure 2 Mathew Brady, portrait of Abraham Lincoln, January 8, 1864. (National Archives)

tion) which, "behind their homeliness, or even ugliness, held superior points so subtle, yet so palpable, making the real life of their faces almost impossible to depict as a wild perfume or fruit-taste, or a passionate tone of the living voice." Yet Lincoln was perhaps the most photographed American of his day. Typically solemn, a tentative smile or something like a smile often playing or arranging itself along the strong lines of his full lips, Lincoln's face seemed the epitome of an expressive exterior (Figure 2). But can one tell from the pictured face what the man was in and for himself? Hawthorne might have been looking at photographs when he described Lincoln as "about the homeliest man I ever saw, yet by no means repulsive or disagreeable,"

Figure 3 Alexander
Gardner, portrait of
Abraham Lincoln, between
February and mid-April
1865. (Meserve Collection)

his physiognomy "coarse" but "redeemed, illuminated, softened, and brightened by a kindly though serious look out of his eyes, and an expression of homely sagacity." He saw Lincoln's "aspect" as that of the "pattern American." Eventually the whole history of the nation and its most typical character traits came to seem inscribed and indexed by the face of Lincoln. How can we look at Lincoln's photographed face without seeing the debates with Douglas, Fort Sumter, the Emancipation Proclamation, Gettysburg, the Second Inaugural Address, John Wilkes Booth? Is it Lincoln's face we see, or versions (there are many) of the history of which he partook? The most famous photographed face in American history may be the most overdetermined, the easiest, and at the same time, the most difficult to read as the expression of a person. The images are saturated with history, likeness transformed into a surfeit of meaning. What do we make of what looks like a smile on Lincoln's last portrait, just weeks before his death—melancholy, relief, resignation, amusement, a private communication with himself during the sitting (Figure 3)? Our readings depend on larger stories we tell (or hear) about the man and his history.

Likeness alone, mere indiscriminate verisimilitude, presented the greatest hurdle for the early photoportraitists. Painted portraits flattered, yet the camera, as one commentator put it, was not given to "fancy-work." Obliged to record whatever appeared before it according to its own properties of focal length and sensitivity to light, the camera lens alone could not be trusted to "portray" as well as to delineate; it had to be disciplined, subordinated to the artist's will. In one of the leading handbooks of the time, the Philadelphia daguerreotypist and writer Marcus Aurelius Root explained that just as the "true artist" never represents a face "exactly as it is," the photographic artist "should not only be able to see at a glance the best view of each face and feature, but to rouse the intellectual faculties of his sitter" by whatever means available—conversation, Reynoldsian or Rembrandtian portraits on studio walls—in order "to sketch the moral as well as the physical lineaments."

The idea that a photographed face might reveal interior truth, might "tell" a tale, provided a commanding aesthetic fiction for bourgeois culture in the nineteenth century. Drawing on popular physiognomic beliefs, about midcentury an emergent discourse of photography endowed the medium with penetrative as well as descriptive powers. The face showed the person, traces of personal history, and what lay inside: dispositions, desires, inclinations. Photography encouraged scrutiny of faces for clues to meaning, signs of intentions; the medium seemed a second eyesight, capable of "fixing" ephemeral facial gestures for close and even closer examination. Did not physiognomies show all? If the face is itself a representation, an ensemble of signs signifying an invisible interior, then the photographed face, a representation of a representation, put you in the presence of the face's own referent, the interiority of the sitter. Understood as a picture with a tale to tell, the photographed face seemed a surety that persons were knowable in their visage, the image offering a surrogate for face-to-face sociality in an increasingly impersonal social order.

This was an outcome not immediately anticipated when "photography" can be said to have begun in 1839, with announcements within weeks of each other by Louis-Jacques-Mandé Daguerre in France and William Henry Fox Talbot in England of the results of quite different experiments and different methods of "fixing" an image. Daguerre doubted that the slow lenses, time-consuming preparation, and long exposures required made his process suitable for portraits. The French scientist N. P. Lerebours concurred, viewing the first efforts as "cadaverous-looking specimens." "The very idea of a portrait by the daguerreotype excited a repulsive feeling," he wrote. Compared to painted portraits (including miniatures), early camera portraits in both versions of the medium, the encased polished-metal plate under glass of the daguerreotype, the salted-paper print of the Talbotype, seemed fatally flawed by the sin of exactitude. "The Daguerreotype will never do for portrait painting," wrote the American Lewis Gaylord Clark, "its pictures are quite too natural." We are so accustomed to thinking of photography as a medium of portraiture that it comes as a surprise to learn that at the outset the camera was deemed ill suited to the rendering of faces. The camera and its process had to undergo acculturation, so to speak, to suit the needs of bourgeois portraiture. Technique had to be "improved" with faster lenses and contrived studio systems of natural lighting (skylights with northern exposure), and styles had to be learned to mitigate the harsh literalness that seemed natural to the camera.

We see this development best, in its formative moment, in the daguerreotype. A one-of-a-kind image produced directly on a metal plate without mediation of a negative, packaged in a molded and embellished thermoplastic (or leather) case adopted from the miniature painting on ivory, the daguerreotype had all the outward marks of a transitional mode. By the mid-1850s it would be replaced by more efficient processes, which issued in endlessly reproducible paper prints from glass-plate negatives. Once daguerrean practitioners and entrepreneurs set their sights on bending the new medium toward portraiture, the aim was a seamless, fluent image of continuous tones from edge to edge; a neutral field for the placement of a designed scene; a body depicted with a degree of verisimilitude unachievable in paint as an instantaneous event, in a pose performed in a space made over to resemble a sitting room—a face, then, furnished with recognizable prestige-endowing appurtenances. Fusing the authority of science and of art, the daguerreotype achieved a harmony of Enlightenment values in a distinctly modern amalgam. Filters for light, tints of color added to the image to model the face, carved wooden chairs, drapes, and pedestals in way of props: portrait studios soon emerged; by mid-century a trade in faces already flourished. Before long (the small *cartes de visite* gave the process a major boost) the photograph overwhelmed all other graphic modes of picturing faces. Looking at photographed faces, tokens of familiarity and celebrity, making the world seem present in its absence, emerged as a defining act of modernity. Photographed faces initiated the first mass experience of mechanically produced simulacra (with their implicit claim of being "manifestations" rather than "copies" of real subjects) intervening between mind and world, between consciousness and a "reality" still assumed to be the first-instance referent of the image. Faces staged as public events became available for intimate viewing.

It's in daguerrean portraits that photographic space first appears as theatrical space, a place gotten up to resemble another place, or, better, empty space furnished with an illusion of "place" in Wittgenstein's sense of the term: "a possibility: something might exist in it." Daguerrean adaptation of old conventions to a new mode instantiated, then, something provisional, a staged scene, as the locus of "face," the portrayal of physiognomy, an act of outward "expression" (even "self-expression") of inwardness. Provisional, abstract, elusive; a "there" that refers to nowhere, all signs removed that the scene was also a site of work: the fictive place where "portrait" occurs can be taken as an analogue to the bourgeois idea of the discrete, autonomous, self-governing individual. It's a two-sided self, public exterior/private interior, whose performance as "portrait" represents a free act of presenting oneself, as image, into social discourse. Might not the appearance in the 1870s of the extreme close-up, disembodied faces floating in indeterminate space, faces of celebrated men of distinction in art and science, Carlyle, Herschel, Tennyson by Julia Margaret Cameron, be taken as a culmination of the studio portrait of the isolated self-expressing "individual"?

In sum, the formal portrait, not native to the raw process of photography, had to be constructed out of available cultural and technical resources to earn its role as the world's dominant medium of pictured faces. It's hard to say just how important (if at all) systematic physiognomy was to this fateful development, to the actual work on the part of sitters and photographers in the making rather than the interpretation of portraits. More important than exact formulas for staging faces before the camera was the pervasive cultural supposition that a pictured face manifested innerness. Charles Bell's *Anatomy and Philosophy of Expression* (1844), which Darwin thought a more rigorous and useful work than the physiognomic theories of Le Brun and Johann Caspar Lavater, was often cited and paraphrased in photographic journals and handbooks. "Expression is to passion what language is to thought," Bell wrote, a formula quoted happily by Marcus Aurelius Root. Countless handbooks, such as Root's, proffered pedagogy for photographers and sitters alike in methods of "arousing the expression desired at the moment of portrayal": what to wear, where to sit, how to look. Another handbook offered this:

> The posture of the person sitting for the portrait should be easy and unconstrained: the feet and hands neither projecting too much, nor drawn too far back; the eyes should be directed a little sideways above the camera, and fixed upon some object there, but never upon the apparatus, since this would tend to impart to the face a dolorous, dissatisfied look.

Not too exact or exacting a formula, but the goal, clearly, was a picture with a predetermined look, a "portrait." Root advised: "The sitter, before a transcript of him is taken, should be put into a mood, which shall make his face diaphanous with the expression of his highest and best, i.e., his genuine, essential 'self.' " One went to the studio not just to obtain a likeness of oneself but also to have one's character traced by one's face.

What actually occurred in studios was very likely a more complex transaction than the one-sided scrutiny implied by the handbooks. Hegel included in his *Phenomenology of Mind* a rigorous refutation of the claim of physiognomy, in Alasdair MacIntyre's account of the argument, that "the face is an expression of human character," that "what a man is, appears in his face." The best portraitists, knowing from their practical experience that expressions had more often to be elicited and staged than simply "caught" as a natural event, would very likely have assented to Hegel's observation that how the face looks is an act rather than a sign; it is *of* and *for* itself, rather than a representation of something separate from it, such as "character" or emotion. MacIntyre writes, summarizing Hegel's refutation:

> But we do not treat the facial expression simply as a sign of something else, the outer sign of something inner, any more than we treat the movement of the hand in a human action as a sign of something else, the inner meaning of what is to be done. We treat the expression of the face and the movement of the hand as themselves actions, or parts or aspects of actions.

In Hegel's own words, the "externality" of the "inner" takes the form of "the deed, the act, in the sense of a reality separated and cut off from the individual." Facial expression, then, is one of the "outer expressions in which the individual no longer retains possession of himself per se, but lets the inner get right outside him, and surrenders it to something else." The surrendered look on the face in the fixed portrait refers in the first instance, Hegel would insist, to the act performed by the face in the portrait-making situation rather than to an ahistorical inner essence. What the neo-Kantian Simmel reads as "soul" expressing itself in and through the face, Hegel would have us understand as an event, the action of the face in a particular situation.

Hegel wrote before photography, but his critique of physiognomy has an uncanny pertinence to the making of photoportraits. The aim of pedagogies such as Root's was to get the sitters to act in certain ways, to perform what the photographers led them to believe is their best self, the self they wish to reveal in public. Working photographers would have understood that expressions are not emanations but performances. Adapting the model of the portrait studio developed in the fine arts, photographers fashioned their studios as surrogate theaters, places not wholly of make-believe, but something close. The aim was not to perform a scripted role but to perform oneself. Painters like Joshua Reynolds in England typically engaged their sitters in collaborative efforts to sum up personal history, to portray through costume, posture, and setting an idea of what is typical and most noteworthy about themselves. Sitters brought their accumulated experience and their already achieved public identities with them to this effort. The photoportrait undercuts the studio premise of a typical representation. An instantaneous event, the photograph presents a "now" and delivers it as a continuous present. It gives us, in Roland Barthes's definition, a "having been," something past, transpired and expired in a flash. Beginning and ending coexist (virtually) in a single image, and staged performances appear as precisely that: staged performances.

Studio and camera, this line of argument suggests, coexist in uneasy, contradictory relations. This might well have been the lesson of the project of Montgomery Simons in 1853, as designed to illustrate a system of physiognomic interpretation (see above, pp. 30–31). Commissioned by Mann Satterwaite Valentine II, a young man of wealth with enthusiasm for art and philosophy, Simons made some thirty daguerreotypes intended to depict not persons as such but expressions of mental and emotional states. What does it look like to feel rage, inspiration, scorn, desire? What is the look of having a thought, of being at attention or in admiration? Valentine put the metaphysical question driving his curiosity in a note attached to his list of passions for "Daguerreotype picturing": "What excites these passions?" Were the daguerreotypes part of an effort to seek causes? Was it supposed that the pictures themselves, pictures of passions rather than persons, would provide answers?

A few days before the sitting Valentine noted in his diary: "[William James] Hubbard [an artist friend] has been engaged the past week or ten days in some strong work for my pursuits in metaphysics, physiognomy. Desiring to possess myself of a key to the passions, he has fallen upon a beautiful system of illustrating them." The system was derived from Charles Le Brun's famous lecture of 1668, "*Conférence sur l'expression générale et particulière,*" illustrated editions of which were readily available in English. A clue to the ambition of Valentine's project is a sheaf of loose sheets, otherwise blank but bearing at the bottom quotations from Le Brun's description of particular passions: "Admiration. In this passion the eyebrow rises, the eye opens a little more than ordinary . . . the mouth half opens . . . ," and similarly for scorn, anger, compassion, remorse, and so on, each passion described as a modification of eyes, eyebrows, mouth, forehead, nostrils. The already captioned blank sheets seem to await Hubbard's drawings. Instead, we have the cased daguerreotypes, uncaptioned, unspecified, merely fascinating pictures of two young men performing what they believe to be the look of what for ages have been called "the passions."

A group of extraordinary images survives this metaphysical exercise. Valentine and his friend Hubbard performed some thirty passions, apparently in a single sitting on January 2, 1853. Intended as metaportraits, the results, while stunningly dramatic, can only be described as antiportraits (Figure 4). They obliterate the person on behalf of a performed "passion." In this they unwittingly cast a certain light of dubiety on the mechanistic assumptions of the Le Brun system, a particularly photographic light.

From Descartes's *Les Passions de l'âme* Le Brun drew the idea that emotions originated in the motions of an incorporeal "soul," which, through an intricate system of physical attachments from pineal gland to blood system to nervous system to muscles, registered its affections directly on the face: thus, in what E. H. Gombrich called a "dial theory," a mechanistic account of the presumed mind-body split, face indexes soul and mind. With his detailed description of each of the passions taken almost verbatim from Descartes, Le Brun proposed in effect a simplistic semiotics intended to give painters, especially of historical subjects, models for depicting faces in states of high emotion. As Norman Bryson argues, Le Brun's motive was to inscribe textuality upon the painterly image, to bring contingent motions of the face within a discursive frame of reference, to impose a coded system and thereby render material appearance meaningful. Significance lies in textuality, the name of the emotion and the verbal description, rather than in observation. Le Brun provided both line sketches and drawings, which have to be seen as visual approximations of ideal types, models, rather than exact depictions. It's as if each of his figured heads asks to

Figure 4 Montgomery P. Simons, "Passion Series," 1853. Just what passion this image is meant to display Simons does not say. (Valentine Museum, Richmond, Virginia)

be understood as a part in an allegory about the expression of human emotion.

What the photographer thought of this game is unrecorded. But Valentine found the results not fully satisfactory for his metaphysical investigation. In a note he describes "faults" in the picturing (see p. 31). It's the abstract verbal or discursive model against which Valentine measures success, a standard unsustainable in photography, an instrument wholly of observation. The fault lay in the performance, not in the depiction of the performance. What the pictures show is not "the passions" but two young men putting on faces before a camera, contorting features, theatricalizing body parts. Like any good daguerrean artist, Simons shared with Whitman the belief in the photograph, as he wrote years later about "looking over my Photographic album," as a "tell-tale"; one can usually tell something about the sitter, he observed, except when it's an actor, who may very well be feigning an emotion. The "passion series" may well have confirmed for him that the apparent tales told by pictures are as likely to be false as true, that states of mind or "passions," if they are "true" utterances, cannot be detached from the people who feel and express them in the exact moment of the picture. Because the camera portrays the false as truly as it does the true, the portraitist should strive for a "natural" (undissembled) expression of faces and bodies. At the same time, the "passion series" reveals how fictive are all picturings of "expression," how formulaic even "natural" expression might be. How is one to tell what is "natural" and what is staged, a performance rather than an "expression"?

Thus the logic of photographic studio portraiture contains an unconscious aporia, an underlying doubt and contradiction about the ontic status of its productions, which, we can say, has been recovered and articulated by recent postmodernist artists. At stake is a question of biography (and autobiography), the telling of a tale as if it were a life story. The nineteenth-century theory of the photographed face, absorbing and revising inherited theories of the representation of persons in painting, quickly won a place as an emblem of a lie. It is still assumed, though denied by a higher sophistication, that photoportraits have a part to play in the telling of lives. Is it wise to take this implicit claim with a grain of salt? Whitman wrote out his great confidence in the communicative power of the face: "You shall stand by my side and look in the mirror with me." Photoportraits ask the same of us. Must we abandon our attachment to images and self-images as messages as if from a mirror? Do we need another pedagogy?

Interestingly, the enjoyment of snapshots, a popular ritual of life in modern societies, has sustained the possibility of the speaking mirror image, the picture-with-a-story-to-tell, which you are prepared to believe, at least for the moment. It's a different kind of story from the revelation of interiority assumed in nineteenth-century photography. Snapshots passed around among family and friends usually go with conversation; they inspire stories, how the picture was made, what it shows, what you make of the relations among the figures in the image. Typically they come in batches, perhaps in sequences. They trigger memories, excite speculation and thoughts about past and future. They take their place within familiar narratives of family or friendship, adding, subtracting, or revising details, changing or confirming judgments. Snapshots are understood intuitively as stories rather than abstract truths, as depictions of events even if it's just a certain look on the face. That look belongs to whatever story one can imagine would explain it; it may refer inward to the way we all know this person to be in the presence of a camera, but mainly it points outward, to the interactive situation assumed by the image. We understand about faces in snapshots what we do not regularly assume about faces in formal portraits of the old school, that they are engaged in some form of what the sociologist Erving Goffman calls "face-work." Goffman writes that in interactive situations "the face clearly is something that is not lodged in or on his [the interactant's] body, but rather something that is diffusely located in the flow of events in the encounter." What we call the "look" on the face refers to a situation either depicted in the image or invisible to but nonetheless constitutive of its expressive content. In the ritualistic functions and pleasures of snapshots we can construct an alternative both to the old idea of revelation and the new idea of unknowability, the alternative of storytelling. It's a conversational, a dialogical alternative; it sees the image not as a translatable proposition about its depicted figures but as an occasion for unlimited hypotheses, questions seeking answers in the knowledge that they are not likely to be found and may have to be invented.

Suppose you see a picture of a smiling face. Suppose you take it as a kind smile, or perhaps a malicious one. "Don't I often imagine it," asks Wittgenstein, "with a spatial and temporal context which is one either of kindness or malice? Thus I might supply the picture with the fancy that the smiler was smiling down on a child at play, or again on the suffering of an enemy." Like Lincoln's fragile smile, ambiguities of the photographed face find resolution, and then only of a provisional sort, in the narratives we imagine by way of explanation.

FIVE

PHOTOGRAPHS AS SYMBOLIC HISTORY

I

NOT long after the birth of photography in 1839 Oliver Wendell Holmes cast a curious eye toward the millions of images already gathering on tabletops and in drawers across America, the countless albums and prints and cards, and wondered what was to come of such an "enormous collection." Writing in *The Atlantic Monthly* in 1859, the noted doctor and philosopher confessed himself enraptured by the new medium, smitten by its uncanny "appearance of reality that cheats the senses with its seeming truth." Photographs were magical illusions. But even more than that, he explained, they were matchless pieces of information, descriptions of things, scenes, and persons infinitely more vivid than words. As if photographs were the very skin or surface of things stripped and preserved, they seemed miniature worlds: not copies, but the things themselves. Eventually, he foresaw, photography would reproduce the entire world, reducing all solid objects to thin film images. Indeed, the time was fast approaching when everything under the sun would be available "for inspection" as images.

That time has long since arrived, and now, almost one hundred and fifty years after the invention of photography, we wonder how the

First published as the introduction to *The American Image: Photographs from the National Archives, 1860–1960* (New York: Pantheon, 1979), pp. ix–xxxii.

world ever managed its business without it. Photographs have become so thoroughly ingrained in our way of life that we rarely give them a second thought. They seem part of the air we breathe, as natural as language. And very much like language, they frame our world. They show us how things look, how we ourselves look, and often, in advertisements and pictures of celebrities, how we may want to look. Photographs are compelling things, and more than we may want to admit, they fashion and guide our most basic sense of reality.

Writing on the threshold of its career, Holmes anticipated the camera's immense power to shape our world, and this led him to make a remarkable proposal. All those fabulous pictures, he explained, "will have to be classified and arranged in vast libraries, as books are now." Fascinated particularly by the stereograph, which created a three-dimensional effect when viewed in a special holder, he envisioned a library of stereo cards. But his words ring true, and prophetic, for photography as a whole. "We do now distinctly propose," he wrote, "the creation of a comprehensive and systematic stereograph library, where all men can find the special forms they particularly desire to see as artists, or as scholars, or as mechanics, or in any other capacity."

At least another generation passed before libraries began systematically to collect and classify photographs. But Holmes's proposal, and his enthusiasm, seem notably appropriate as an introduction to this book of photographs culled from one of the world's most important and unique collections. Like the collection Holmes envisioned, the pictures in the holdings of the National Archives touch upon almost everything under the sun, literally from nuts (and fruits) to bolts. But what makes the collection truly extraordinary is its unique ties to American life, to the history of its everyday affairs as much as to the history of its major events and personalities. Here we can see American history made vivid and concrete—vivid, concrete, and dramatic in the special ways of photography. The pictures are examples of one of the nation's major resources for the study of its life, past and present. For photography *is* a resource, as Holmes understood, without precedent and without peer: a special kind of knowledge available to all interested parties. The pictures presented here are documents of history, but they are also experiences in their own right; they offer us a privileged opportunity to witness the past as if it were momentarily present. The book is a history lesson of sorts. It is also—and this is very much part of the lesson—an opportunity to think about the special resources and properties of photographs, and of what gives them the power that moved Oliver Wendell Holmes, and a multitude of other commentators, to proclaim a new era in human knowledge.

II

Pictorial histories are certainly not a new phenomenon. For many years, since the invention of efficient halftone reproduction of photographic images in newspapers and books in the 1890s, editors and writers have combed picture archives for striking and colorful images, either to illustrate history texts, or, as in Frederick Lewis Allen's *American Procession* (1933), to construct a panorama of American life. Recently interest has grown in studying photographs not simply as illustrations of history but also as revealing documents and expressions, as the source of insight as well as information not so readily available in other media. True, Mathew Brady's famous picture of General Sherman (Figure 5) "illustrates" his appearance, his uniform, his military decoration—and the black crepe sash tied in a bow above his elbow as the official sign of mourning for the death of President Lincoln. But the picture discloses even more about the grizzle-bearded warrior, stiff and straight in his chair against a plain background. Everyone can recognize the picture as a "portrait," not a candid snapshot, and so we take for granted that Sherman is knowingly *posing*, that he prepared himself for a picture he realizes will represent him, his visage and his image, to the world. True, he has not taken any great pains to brush his hair or straighten his tie; neither he nor Brady wanted especially to show a man too scrupulous about his neatness. Instead, Sherman makes his point about himself by his military posture, by the arms folded with certainty and self-assurance across his chest. His eyes peer off toward the distance: does he mean to show what he looks like on a battlefield, gauging enemy fortifications, or is he in fact in a blank stare? In any case, he is not looking directly into the lens, preferring

Figure 5 General William Tecumseh Sherman, wearing on his left arm the mourning sash required of all military men during the six-week mourning period for Abraham Lincoln, 1865. (Brady Collection, Records of the Office of the Chief Signal Officer [111-B-1769], National Archives)

Figure 6 Franklin D. Roosevelt and Winston Churchill at Marrakech, French Morocco, on January 24, 1943, following the Casablanca conference. Photographer unknown. (General Records of the Department of the Navy, 1798–1947 [80-G-35190], National Archives)

perhaps to be *looked at* without giving the viewer a feeling that the general is exchanging a glance with his public.

If we look closely at the photograph, as we would at a painting, we see that we can actually *read* the picture, that it reveals more than it merely illustrates. We can reconstruct some small drama, or sequence of happenings before the taking of the picture, that itself tells us more than meets the eye about Sherman, and also something about Brady's willingness to allow the camera to record such a direct, undisguised encounter. In venturing such reconstructions out of photographs, moreover, we begin to reach critical points of difference between camera-made images and those painted or drawn by hand. A painting, for example, tempts and invites us to reconstruct not a happening that the painting imitates but some vision and intent of the painter's, something in his mind's eye, even though he may be copying a scene from real life. We involve ourselves differently with photographs. True, we look for personal vision and intention, but also signs of real life. These signs are not always obvious, nor are they simple to see and to read. Compare the portrait of Sherman with that of President Roosevelt and Winston Churchill at Marrakech after the Casablanca conference in 1943 (Figure 6). The differences are striking and point not only to different cameras and lenses (the photographer here was obviously able to get closer, in vision if not in body, with a longer lens), but to an entirely different relationship between the camera and its subject, and the picture and its viewer. The Brady portrait expresses an era when photographic portraits were almost entirely formal in pose and decorous in style. It is not likely that Brady would photograph a public figure unawares, without his cooperation. The candid picture of the two wartime leaders—a fascinating study in contrasts—presupposes that both the subjects and the viewers of the picture accept the legitimacy and indeed the accuracy of candid, informal pictures of public figures. The picture conveys a kind of intimacy with person and scene simply not true of Brady's portraits: like a movie close-up, the picture gives us the illusion of being invisibly present as emotion unfolds. We feel that such images are somehow more "real" because more "immediate" than the studied composures of face and body in Brady's pictures.

Such differences among pictures made at different moments in history are instructive, for they reveal how powerfully photography is influenced by prevailing assumptions about pictures of all kinds, and about such subjects as the proper appearance of a public figure. Of course the rapid development of photography as the predominant visual medium of communication itself influenced these assumptions, giving to the image a power over ideas of "truth" and "reality" never possessed by any other medium. But truth and reality are relative terms. Compare, for example, typical photographs made during the Civil War with those made in the two twentieth-century world wars. What did the photographer intend in the picture of the *Chickamauga* (Figure 7)? Merely to show an army transport being loaded somewhere along the Tennessee River? Or does the positioning of the camera at a site above the scene, distant enough for us to have a whole view of all the sundry activities, give us, the viewers, a particular role to play? The elevated perspective makes the scene a vista. An "overall, distant view

Figure 7 The *Chickamauga*, 1864. A lightly armed Army transport, it carried supplies along the Tennessee River. Photographer unknown. (Records of the War Department, General and Special Staffs [165-C-607], National Archives)

of things dominates" in the Brady Civil War pictures, as Joel Snyder accurately points out, a view that corresponds to the theory implicit in most photographic practice at the time: that the camera was like the eye of eternity. Every event had its place in a comprehensible scheme of things. The loading of the *Chickamauga* was worthy of depiction because it fit a larger unfolding story. Positioned on that elevation, the viewer is like a detached though interested audience of a drama. The eye-level perspective of the group portrait "Section of Keystone Battery" serves a similar function. The group is placed in middle distance, as if on a stage before the viewer, and the men position themselves in a manner part formal, part casual, as if before an audience. As the "Keystone Battery" they are performing a role, albeit a small one, in a destiny. The contrast with typical twentieth-century war scenes could hardly be more stark. Here, as Snyder points out, the photographer seems to be "in the center of the action." The soldiers—the Twenty-third Infantry gun crew in World War I, "U.S. Marines pinned down

Figure 8 "U.S. Marines pinned down on Peleliu," September 22, 1944. Photographer unknown. (General Records of the Department of the Navy, 1798–1947 [80-G-435697], National Archives)

on Peleliu" in World War II (Figure 8)—are oblivious to the camera, just as, for the viewer, they are rather blurred images of figures and movement, not distinct individuals. Action—and its spontaneous and authentic representation (often entailing blurs and slanted angles)— seems the essence of these pictures, not destiny. Changes in the photographic image of war follow changes in the very conception of war, of the individual's role within it, and the role of the home-front viewer.

A photographic history lesson, then, must first awaken in the viewer a sensitivity to the *language* of photography—or the several languages, for a variety of styles, of methods, of functions abound in the history of the medium. And a rich assortment of kinds of pictures along with a fascinating range of subjects confront the viewer and invite his or her close attention in this selection from the National Archives. Of course photographs give pleasure as well as history lessons, and among these photographs we find many that are simply beautiful to look at, to contemplate and muse over. But the particular point of this group of pictures is to open a path from the present to the past, to bring the past into our present lives with the vividness, immediacy, and gripping concreteness that photographs make possible.

The photographs collected by the National Archives are especially appropriate as a source for such a lesson in reading history. By and large, photographs appear in the Archives only if they have already served some purpose linked to "history"—that is, if they have been part of the work of a government agency. There are exceptions, of course—the Brady Collection is the most notable—but on the whole the Archives photographs represent documents accumulated in the course of government work. Pictures are not collected for their aesthetic importance or because they represent significant moments in the history of photography. They are collected simply because they once played a useful function. The mission of the National Archives (founded in 1934) is to provide a place for records no longer in active use—to keep, preserve, and make available "the experience of the Government and people of the United States as it is embodied in records of the Federal Government and related materials." A somewhat fuller statement in the *Guide to the National Archives of the United States* (1974) explains that the material it holds "was originally created or received by legislative, judicial, or executive agencies of the Government in pursuance of their legal obligations or in the transaction of their official business. This material was maintained by these agencies as an official record of their activities or because of the value of the information it contained."

The Archives gives the impression of a virtually bottomless repository of historical memory. It keeps and displays documents sacred to the nation's memory, such as the Declaration of Independence and the Constitution, and also items that might strike the casual browser as the most trivial and incidental of records of government operations. Everything is organized according to "record group," each containing the papers of a particular agency or bureau—papers that have outlived their original purpose and are now transformed, as it were, into "history." Of course such records are simply inert facts or objects until they are brought to life again by some new use, a new purpose. "What is past is prologue" is the motto of the National Archives, and the *Guide* is like the map of a forgotten terrain, a systematic key to that portion of the past that lies within the domain of government work—or that part of the past created by the activities of government. The latest *Guide* lists 409 "record groups," the number hinting at the size and range of government domain. And what one is likely to find in that domain, what records and what details of American history, is often quite surprising.

As for photographs, they are often among the most pleasant and disarming of surprises. It is actually an advantage, for a variety of reasons, that photographs belong to the Archives by virtue of their historical rather than aesthetic value. This is not to say that many of the photographs are not interesting simply for their visual pleasure. The landscape photographs by Timothy O'Sullivan, Jack Hillers, and Carleton Watkins are among the acclaimed masterpieces of the art of photography, and the collection includes distinguished pictures by many other figures accepted as artists in the medium of photography (Mathew Brady, George Barnard, William Henry Jackson, Lewis Hine, Edward Steichen, Dorothea Lange, Russell Lee, and Ansel Adams among others). But the opportunity to see famous and lovely pictures in the context of other pictures—less interesting in form or visual excitement—heightens the surprise we feel in discovering that a beautiful picture may also have a specific, valuable, historical meaning embedded within its value as an aesthetic experience. All photographs—the great, the merely interesting, the commonplace—have a place in the Archives only as they fall within a "record group" (including the miscellaneous group called "Gift Collection"), only as they relate *in some fashion* to a government activity. Usually they are filed under a specific subject matter within a "record group"; rarely are they filed by the name of the photographer, a practice widely at variance with that of "art" collections. The surprises that await the researcher often lie in finding pictures that seem only tangentially connected to any imaginable function of a particular agency—or, often enough, not connected at all in any apparent way. Sometimes verbal documentation can be found explaining why a particular picture was deposited within a particular "record group," but such information cannot always be counted on.

In what sense is this situation, anomalous among archives of art works, an "advantage"? Partly because it leads to an extraordinary feeling of adventure, which staff members of the Audiovisual Archives Division and other researchers often feel. And partly because it compels the researcher and viewer to confront pictures directly, head-on, from the point of view of their meaning and value as historical documents. If they are also strong pictures from a strictly visual point of view, so much the better; their value as documents is then enhanced. A stronger picture will invite a closer inspection, a more detailed analysis, a deeper involvement on the part of the viewer. Most likely he or she will feel compelled to think about the information in the picture along with the *form* by which the picture informs—to think, that is, about the connections between aesthetics and history.

Such connections are, of course, often the subject of fierce controversy among scholars and critics in the field of art. Some art historians insist upon a separation of the form of a work of art from its content, from the story or scene or person it represents. From this point of view the circumstances under which a painting was created, its relation to the biography of the artist, the influence of the historical moment, are incidental concerns, important only as they illuminate the picture and enhance our appreciation of it as an artwork. In most photographs the content or subject matter is so prominent—it is, of course, what we initially look at and see—that a separation of form and content often seems unnecessary, or a barren exercise. The connection between a photograph and its subject seems so immediate, so certain, so inevitable, that form and content appear as one. Perhaps for this reason, and also because of the high degree of mechanical or automatic procedure in the making of a photograph, art histories have tended, until recently, to ignore photographs, to exclude them from the variety of visual expressions that qualify as art worth looking at and thinking about as significant experiences. Very often photographs have been relegated by art historians (whose own books, by the way, rely heavily on photographic reproductions of paintings or images of sculpture and architecture), and also by general historians, to the status of illustrations, or visual examples of a certain subject matter.

By filing photographs under "record groups" rather than by photographer or by subject, the National Archives collection makes it equally difficult to take the photograph either as simply an illustration of a subject or as purely an aesthetic object. Of course anybody can take either point of view, or any other, toward any picture. But the particular *form* of the Archives collection does invite an experience of pictures without preconceptions. If one looks, for example, among the 75,089 photographs listed within the records of the Bureau of Reclamation to find pictures that effectively describe or recount aspects of American life, what is one likely to find? The results are surprising, and revealing. Bureau activities included power and irrigation projects throughout the West, and projects concerned with "roads, bridges, rivers, floods, drought conditions" in the West and South. Researchers found a group of pictures made in the Far West and Southwest between 1905 and 1908 by W. J. Lubken, presumably a staff photographer for the Bureau, and several others by other hands. The explicit subjects in most cases do indeed seem related to Bureau activities: two men operating an "Ingersoll drill" in a "diversion channel" project (Figure 9), a newly completed dam, a reservoir, a group of trappers and hunters, a fisherman, a government automobile. The most overt illustrative level—probably the chief reason each picture was taken—is only the beginning, however, of the experience of these wonderfully

Figure 9 "Class E9 Ingersoll drill at work in diversion channel," Minidoka Project, Idaho and Wyoming, July 30, 1905. Photographer unknown.
(Records of the Bureau of Reclamation [91`15-JO-187], National Archives)

Figure 10 W. J. Lubken, "Native fisherman of the Colorado River, fishing in the Imperial Canal," August 16, 1907. (Records of the Bureau of Reclamation [115-JI-323], National Archives)

evocative pictures. They evoke a host of additional perceptions, recognitions, provocations of curiosity, incitements to thought. The "native fisherman of the Colorado River, fishing in the Imperial Canal" (Figure 10) shows a man in a wet loincloth and shirt standing barefooted on the rocky bank of a stream from which he may have just emerged with his equipment—a net hung between two rough-hewn poles. He looks directly at the camera, in a position of pause and attention we recognize as a "pose." It seems obvious he would not take such a position unless a photographer had wandered along and asked him to hold still. The question is, What is the photographer doing? Why did he want or need a picture of a man and a method of fishing that virtually everyone likely to see the picture would call "primitive"? Was the Imperial Canal designed with the needs of such fishermen in mind, in which case does the picture say that the purpose of the construction is being fulfilled? Or can we take the rubble on the banks of the stream to suggest that the construction of the canal is still in progress, that the fisherman is not so much fishing in a government-made canal but in what he might consider native waters, and thus that the picture is meant to mean something like "transition," "an image of old ways passing out of existence"? Perhaps deep in the records of the Bureau there rests a written document that answers such questions, or proves them irrelevant and foolish. Without such documentation we are intrigued, perhaps baffled, but certainly engaged by the picture and its possible implications.

Take all of the Bureau of Reclamation pictures as a separate group, just for the moment, and the image of the "native fisherman" takes on even more suggestions as a *contrast* to the government work of changing and controlling the shape of the land. A contrast is pointed and urged upon us simply by the form of the fisherman picture and that of the Ingersoll drill, which, as a power-driven tool, takes entirely different kinds of muscular exertion and control than does the fisherman's net, and imposes a different relation between itself and its human manipulator, a difference in physical tension and finally in the basic relation (which includes emotions) between man and his tools. The drill picture has provocations in its own right: mainly a picture of a man at work, it is probably a picture of a man posing *as if* he were at work. In operation the drill would certainly be in motion and it and the worker would leave only a blur on the photographic film. The glance of the seated figure toward the camera is a key that both men are aware of the presence of a camera. Moreover, it appears that another camera is stationed in the picture—though out of range of clear focus—in the left-center middle ground (standing on a tripod): an extremely incidental detail, but one that suggests a larger theme, that the presence of a photographer often disrupts and modifies a scene, making it over into a *photographed* scene. The photographer's intervention results in a scene that is not quite "true," not quite "reality" as it is lived, with all its complexity and unpredictableness, yet bears some close relation to that reality, close enough for us to acknowledge the picture as a fairly reliable image of what once existed. Still, the question arises and persists: How much of the picture belongs to the photographer's arrangement, how much to any sitter's collaboration, and how much simply to the scene as it was in fact?

One final example from this group. "Raising and lowering gates at newly completed diversion dam at head of main Truckee canal on Truckee river at the opening of the Truckee-Carson project" (Figure 11) is, like its caption, a picture with more in it than the previous two. The others can be usefully described as "portraits"—a term taken from painting and indicating one of the large areas in which photography has followed the lead of older media of representation—in that they concentrate on single figures (two in the case of the drill picture) who, while relatively informal in their postures, do take notice of the photographer and pose for him. This picture is obviously entirely different. It is a view from a distance of both a structure and an event (or many small events) that sprawls across it: the opening of the dam gates together with the activity of watching the event (and even, along the lower left-hand corner, photographing it). The photographer is not looking at single individuals, who seem oblivious of him. He is at a distance, on a rise—like the Civil War photographer who took the picture of the *Chickamauga*—taking in the scene as if he were detached from it, a mere observer. Thus the picture seems merely to illustrate an event within a scene.

But in fact the picture shows more than the event itself, more even than the dam's structure, which is also part of the documentary interest of the picture. The structure and the activities occurring on and

Figure 11 W. J. Lubken, "Raising and lowering gates at newly completed diversion dam at head of main Truckee canal on Truckee river at the opening of the Truckee-Carson project," Newlands Project, western Nevada, June 17, 1905. (Records of the Bureau of Reclamation [115-JQ-178], National Archives)

around it occupy not much more than the lower half of the picture. The rest is given over to space, a spreading flat plain that reaches to the base of a range of mountains that in turn rises in curves and slopes, virtually billowing to the top of the picture frame. We realize that this upper section of the picture is there because the photographer meant it to be, and moreover, that he has placed his camera in such a way that the lines in the actual terrain can be seen from such an angle, in such a perspective, that our eye is guided toward the elevation in the distance. We realize, in short, that the picture has been *composed* rather carefully and artfully, that the happenings around the dam have been placed within a landscape, and that the landscape in turn gives us yet another perspective upon the main event. Perhaps the intention was to enhance the event by showing it in a setting of grandeur. Moreover, the setting itself is curiously and intriguingly reflected in the structure of the dam, its curves and slopes, its pillars and arches repeating shapes that we see in the mountains. We might begin to see the entire picture in strictly formal terms, a disposition of lines and shapes, an interesting geometric design emerging from the literal details of the scene. But the picture remains literal, as its cumbersome caption reminds us, and returning to its subject matter after thinking about its abstract form, we can then recognize ways that the form contributes to the subject, clarifies not only what it is—an opening ceremony of a construction project within the wide spaces of the Far West—but also its meanings. The relation of diagonals to curves, for example, might be taken as the *form* of the relation of the mechanical to the natural, between the work of human technology (dam and railroad streaking along the straight horizontal path at the base of the mountains, and also cameras) and the work of natural time (the patterns of erosion in the distant hills). The human forms seem partly to imitate the natural forms, only leveling them out, straightening their bumps and irregularities into machine-made lines. And meanwhile the people themselves, in their variety of postures (see the marvelous lines of characters stationed at the gates above the pillars on the left), occupy a middle range of regularity and irregularity, nature and civilization, between the two poles of the absolutely natural and the absolutely mechanical.

The picture, then, holds a provoking subject matter in a tense relation to a compositional design, and we are left wondering if W. J. Lubken, on assignment to make a record of a ceremony, had all this in mind when he placed his camera where he did—or if it matters whether he saw and intended everything we see. For the picture documents certain implicit ideas of both a disruption between man and nature, and a subtle continuity with nature in the forms of man's buildings, as much as it documents a specific event. And those implicit ideas are as authentic and valid data of history as the literal dam itself.

III

Not without cause, people are more prone to "believe" a photograph than they are a painting or a drawing. This trust, of course, is often naïve; the camera *can* lie as often and as cleverly as any other tool wielded by people intent on telling lies. And even in the best of cases, where the photographer is as honest as one can wish, his or her picture will inevitably show only what the particular lens on the camera is capable of showing, in the way of depth, clarity, and spatial relations. The very frame of the photograph is itself something of a distortion or imposition; had we been present at the scene, standing where the camera stood, we all know that we would have seen more than what the frame allows us to see. Cropping of a scene cuts off the viewer from other details that may well be relevant to an understanding of the picture. This is, to be sure, obvious and commonplace. But these inherent limitations in the truth-telling capacities of photography point to one of its essential characteristics and one of its major differences from paintings and drawings: the picture could not have been made had not a camera been present at the scene of its making. Photographs cannot be made from memory. A photographer does not retire to a studio to render a scene he has witnessed; he makes the rendering at the same time that he witnesses the scene. Of course many artists also paint or draw before a living scene, either a person or an object or a view. But the camera makes its exposure and its record on film instantaneously. The photographer has considerable leeway in the darkroom to alter tones and to crop even further; he may also retouch or manipulate the image in other ways. But when he does so he is altering a picture that already exists: the picture formed in the chemical changes on emulsified film in the fraction of a second measured by the click of the shutter. Any straight, single-negative photograph tells us that at the very least a camera was *there*, where something happened.

Simply as a property of the technique of the medium, a photograph lends a special kind of presence to what it depicts, quite decidedly different from the presence one feels in objects, persons, or places in a painting. Every unaltered photograph is a record of time past. We may look at the picture as timeless, but a closer look will usually betray the sign of a specific happening present to the lens at a specific time. O'Sullivan's monumental picture of the ruins at Canyon de Chelle (Figure 12) is an excellent example. Look closely at the original print—this is obscured in halftone reproductions—and you will notice several inconspicuous human figures, members of the photographer's party, in

Figure 12 Timothy H. O'Sullivan, "Ancient Ruins in Canyon de Chelle, N.M." (New Mexico Territory, later Arizona). Lt. George M. Wheeler Expedition of 1873, in a niche 50 feet above the present canyon bed. (Records of the Office of the Chief of Engineers [77-WA-11], National Archives)

various postures among the ruins; one figure, low in the left-hand corner, holds the scaling ropes by which the two men looking toward the camera mounted the highest ruins. What is the photograph a picture of? The four figures, the ropes, the signs of an exploration party? All these small items need to be included in any answer. They give to the picture the presence proper to a photographic record of a definite moment in time and space. Of course painters often attempt and achieve a similar kind of specificity of time and place. But what is present to the viewer of a canvas is not so much the action of light recording itself as it falls on film, but the rendering of a vision in the eyes and mind of an artist, whose hands and fingers are skilled enough to make the vision clear and palpable for others. The painting refers back to the artist as its origin; the photograph points both to the camera and to the scene in its field of vision.

Then is the photographer himself of no real importance? It runs deeply against the grain of our convictions to say so. Yet in one very limited sense it is true. Anyone can make a photograph. And any photograph, as dull or as unfocused, or as conventional as it may be, will have its points of interest. That interest, as an astute Englishwoman, Lady Elizabeth Eastlake, put it as early as 1857, in the *London Quarterly Review*, is "historic":

> Every form which is traced by light is the impress of one moment, or one hour, or one age in the great passage of time. Though the faces of our children may not be modelled and rounded with that truth and beauty which art attains, yet minor things—the very shoes of the one, the inseparable toy of the other—are given with a strength of identity which art does not even seek. Though the view of a city be deficient in those niceties of reflected lights and harmonious gradations which belong to the facts of which Art takes account, yet the facts of the age and of the hour are there, for we count the lines in that keen perspective of telegraphic wire, and read the characters on that playbill or manifesto, destined to be torn down on the morrow.

Because of its special mode of endowing its image with presence, as if by automatic action, the photograph is a unique historical record, one that allows us to read, to count, even to measure what once existed.

From this point of view, simply of what can be measured, what facts and details identified and counted, the group of pictures presented here have unmistakable historical value. Here we can see in vivid detail, almost as if we had been present, scenes from the familiar passages of American history in the hundred years between 1860 and 1960: the battlefields of three wars, the faces of many famous Americans, the Western landscape as it appeared to government survey and exploration expeditions in the 1870s, frontier settlements, Native Americans both in their own settlements and in photographers' studios in their full get-ups, men, women, and children in factories, people at picnics or in living rooms, and so on. War, exploration and settlement, rise of the city, mechanization, immigration, racial conflict: these and other of the major themes by which historians have tracked the history of these years can all find some visual evidence—perhaps visual equivalents—in these pictures. And even in this limited light, as sheer documents of the look of things, these pictures also add something to our historical knowledge. The past is always immeasurably more complex than any written narrative can suggest. Because of the particular way photographs are made—by the action of light—they record small details of the sort usually ignored (if only for efficiency's sake) by historians: precisely what kind of clothing—hats, shirts, suspenders—were worn by "Negro laborers" as they are shown in the Brady picture, and what kinds of facial expressions they are likely to put on when asked to pose as a group before a photographer; what General Martin T. McMahon and his staff thought of themselves and their image as warriors, as heroes, as best we can tell from their postures and their appearances in the group portrait made just after the Civil War; or what we can read of the complicated situation of Native Americans in the 1870s from the differences in how they present themselves to the camera between O'Sullivan's "Navaho Group" at their own dwelling (Figure 13), and Will Soule's "Navajo Silversmith" (Figure 14), taken in the same years; or what life was like for "convalescent officers" in World War I ("Mrs. W. E. Corey playing cards with the wounded officers on the porch"), and for wounded soldiers ("The American Advance in the Argonne"); or what difference radio made in the way a family gathered in the living room down on the farm ("Sometimes the whole family gathered around the receiving set" [Figure 15]), and then the difference of television, in the age of media images. Note the photographs on the wall, and how the TV image holds all members of the family equally, in "A family watches a debate between John F. Kennedy and Richard Nixon" (Figure 16).

To be sure, there is much more to reading a photograph than recognizing its details and connecting what they show with a larger frame or scheme—in this case, our common knowledge of American history—and we will have to confront that "more." But it is worthwhile to continue in this vein a bit further, for this group of pictures taken as a whole (rather than as single expressive images) does make a significant addition to historical knowledge simply on the level of what is represented. The pictures document a changing society and they do so,

Figure 13 Timothy H. O'Sullivan, "Navaho Group." Canyon de Chelle, Arizona, 1873. (Records of the Smithsonian Institution [1106-WB-305], National Archives)

Figure 14 Will Soule, "Navajo Silversmith." About 1870. (Records of the Bureau of Indian Affairs [75-BAE-242b-6)], National Archives)

Figure 15 "Sometimes the whole family gathered around the receiving set. This Hood River County, Oregon, farm family is listening to the radio." July 20, 1925; photographer unknown. (Records of the Federal Extension Service [33-SC-48949], National Archives)

Figure 16 A family watches a debate between John F. Kennedy and Richard Nixon during the 1960 presidential election, September 26, 1960. (Don Phelan/UPI. Copyright © United Press International #NXP 1249267. Records of the United States Information Agency [306-PS-60-16872], National Archives)

much more than is the case in most history textbooks from the point of view of people who experienced change: not only the children working in a coal mine, crammed into a tight space for a photograph by Lewis Hine, but the families tuned in to radio and television. There is still a conviction, though it may be changing, that history is made by leaders and governments, by larger-than-life heroes and villains—and that plain people only live in their wake. The thematic emphasis in these pictures is upon plain people, and especially upon people engaged in work. Work, physical labor, is a powerfully recurring motif here. The sequence of pictures opens with views of monumental and symbolic buildings in construction, and this theme of construction runs throughout, counterpointed by scenes of ruin and devastation in warfare. Think of the variety of kinds of work displayed here; we see explorers, sailors, hunters, prospectors, farmers, miners, soldiers, teamsters, cowboys, convict laborers; we see women in factories and on farms, and children in mines and mills as well as schools. Simply as visual fact, this particular photographic history underlines the presence of working people in our history. It also underlines the fact, until recently blocked from the consciousness of many white Americans, that ours is a multiracial population, that blacks and Indians and Asians share an American identity just as they share work and play.

Taken as a single ensemble of views of American people and places, a stitched-together panorama, the pictures can tease us into a kind of interpretation we might give to a work of literature. We might, as our imaginations play over the sequence, pick out certain motifs, watch them develop, reappear, fuse with other motifs and images, and coalesce in our minds into a new insight. Take the various images of natural terrain, of what, as an idea, we call "nature." They range from the swamp and ruminating cows in the foreground of a scene that rises toward the Capitol dome, to the solemn Cathedral Spires of Yosemite (Figure 17) and the cavernous gulches and strata of erosion in the Grand Canyon—all three rendered by the photographer as "landscapes" following painterly compositions in organizing their views. An enduring idea that flourished especially among painters and poets and clergymen in the nineteenth century, and persists still, is that America has a special affinity with "nature," that the country is in a sense

"God's country." Surely many viewers will look upon the Western landscape photographs in this light. The scale of the pictured landscape among the canyons and rock formations and giant trees of the West is awesome; human figures are dwarfed yet often seem in peaceful harmony with the natural setting. For viewers so disposed these par-

Figure 17 John K. Hillers, "Yosemite National Park, California: Cathedral Spires in Yosemite Valley." (Records of the Geological Survey, 1871–1879 [57-PS-28], National Archives)

ticular pictures might well support a religious or an aesthetic view of nature, in which the terrain of rocks and sky and vegetation and water is an inspiration, perhaps a solace. Another point of view might see the open spaces of the plains, the Rockies and beyond, as many Americans did in the nineteenth century, as beckoning the new society forward, toward a "manifest destiny," an American empire in the West. It seems likely that many of the photographers themselves entertained one or all of these cultural outlooks.

But whatever fancy these pictures evoke in us, seen within this particular sequence of images, they dramatize the overriding *fact* of a particular natural terrain within which American history occurs: "nature," that is as geography, issuing its own imperatives and having its own say in shaping human actions. The mountains, rivers, canyons, prairies, deserts, are not only capable of serving as symbols (religious, aesthetic, or philosophical), but they are also real places in a human historical enterprise. This may in fact be a buried point in one of the most stunning and moving of the pictures in the group, O'Sullivan's famous photograph of his wagon "darkroom" in the Carson Desert, Nevada (Figure 18). The power of the picture lies in its apparent simplicity: the dark forms of the wagon and team of mules against the light sand dunes behind, bordered at either edge by darker forms etched against a bright noon sky, indicated by the position of the shadows under the mules and wagon. O'Sullivan often depicted stark edges of rock formation and receding planes of sloping hills against the sky. In general his pictures seem the least conventionally composed of the Western photographs, the most attuned to the drama of line, shape, texture, and light that the camera itself can detect or elicit and record. Here he seems to want to show no more than the presence of his wagon within such an empty, inhuman, and with the desert heat we can assume, threatening setting. But showing that, and the footsteps that seem to lead from the wagon toward the camera position, he achieves something more, a symbolic statement that reflects upon the entire enterprise of exploring and surveying the Western lands and making photographs of their wild, unexpected natural forms. For the wagon and the footsteps are signs of his own presence in this scene, a presence that disrupts the perfect *natural* harmony of the scene, that in effect ruptures the idea that the photographer's subject is a pure, unspoiled, and unsullied nature. The picture is rich with suggestion: are these the sands of time that will before long efface the tracks of man, just as the imposing rocks and mountains in other pictures might be taken as silent sentinels, reminders that the land itself has a natural history that far exceeds America's? But one suggestion that wins support by its echo in other pictures is that the wagon represents not only "man," but a particular kind of work—the work most prominent in the entire group of pictures—that of the photographer himself. In its simplicities of contrast the picture seems to factualize "nature," to remove it from mystery and place it within the range of experiences capable of being photographed, an act, the picture seems to say, that subtly modifies the natural, transforms it for human consumption. The wagon not only measures the scale of the hill of sand, but it also makes that hill available to our comprehension. We no longer have a "landscape" with its associations of devotion, reverence, sublime emotion. Instead, we have the land in one of its most barren forms, and a photographer: and in

Figure 18 Timothy H. O'Sullivan's photograph of his wagon "darkroom" in the Carson Desert, Nevada. About 1868. (Records of the Office of the Chief of Engineers [77-KS-P-46], National Archives)

the transaction between them, an image that might serve as a symbol of the complex relations between man and land, society and geography, that runs throughout American history.

IV

O'Sullivan's wagon darkroom picture takes us swiftly from a discussion of the literal content of the photographs to their symbolic suggestions. In reading pictures as symbols—and we do this with paintings as well as photographs—we try to get inside the mind of the artist, to ferret out his intentions, or to point out ways his picture may say even more than he realized or intended. But symbolic interpretation is an enterprise full of risks, not least of which is the temptation to be reckless, to venture guesses without evidence. Like all pictures, photographs invite interpretations, but the interpreter needs some controls upon his own imagination, some limits and a boundary between sense and nonsense. Where are they to be found, and where placed?

The problem of interpreting photographs is like opening a can of worms. It is hard to get a solid hold on it. Of all the modes of visual expression the photograph is perhaps the least understood, the least commonly agreed upon. There is little help to be found in the kinds of strictly formal analyses appropriate to paintings, though some awareness of the effect of lines and relations of shapes and tones is essential. Formal analysis, moreover, tends to confine the photograph to a narrow range of meanings. It cannot do justice to the special relationship that exists in the photograph between its form and its content, a relationship based on the photographic presence already discussed. And it adds little to the question that interested Oliver Wendell Holmes: What is special, what is different, about photographs as *knowledge* of the world? Can we *know* through a photograph what cannot be known through any other means?

It may well be that the question is unanswerable, or that a simple answer is negative—that is, that photographs are really not unique either as pictures or knowledge. But writers on photography have suggested some positive answers, and one in particular seems at least useful enough to warrant a brief discussion. That is, to see photographs not so much as formal pictures but as events, actions, performances, communications. The principle is to recognize that the meaning of a photograph—what the interpreter is after—is rarely a given within the picture but is developed in the *function* of the picture, in its particular social use by particular people. Photographs have a multitude of uses, some private, some public, and we can take each use as its context or, to borrow a term from the sociologist Erving Goffman, as "frame." A baby picture in the frame of private consumption by mother, father, grandparents is a different picture from the very same image examined by a doctor for evidence of skin eruptions or malstructure, or by a photohistorian as an example of a popular genre. Change the frame, and the meaning also changes, though the image remains the same. Of course the same can be said of all pictures, but in fact paintings are usually already framed, literally, and set aside from commonplace experience as "art," properly viewed on a wall. Photographs have simply developed a far wider range of social functions and are that much more difficult to pin down to a single definition.

One common feature of these pictures is that we have by and large lost the original frames. The "record group" location of the National Archives photographs, as we have seen, is only haphazardly helpful in reconstructing that frame and thus in recovering an original meaning. Internal evidence sometimes helps, especially in studio portraits, where the picture is often itself a clear record of a collaboration and an intention. But internal evidence alone is not fully reliable. Was the picture published, and if so, where? Assuming that most of the National Archives photographs were produced as public communications, not as tokens of private transactions within families or among friends, the missing frame is likely to represent some communication within a definite social scene. Captions usually identify subject matter and photographer, but not the scene in which the photograph was meant to play a role. Clearly, much more verbal documentation is wanted if we wish to reconstruct all the original purposes, contexts, and frames of these pictures. Such a reconstruction would take a monumental task of research, and its results would add invaluable new knowledge about the history of American life, its many small patterns of interaction, its changing modes of exchange and communication among people. For photography is a form of behavior—or many forms, each bearing important information about the daily lives of Americans, about those expectations and implicit values that make up the everyday life of any society. This is to say that the historical and documentary value of these photographs does not lie wholly in their visual subject matter—in what they are as recorded perceptions—but also in the buried and hidden social uses they originally performed. Each picture, then, represents more than itself: each is a symbol of meanings, of frameworks within which the picture performed its original work, that in turn lead as if by infinite regress into the patterns, values, and beliefs of American culture at any given moment of its history.

To explicate the "meaning" of each picture in this archaeological sense is, to be sure, a hopeless task. We need far more detailed information about how photographers worked, about their relations of obligation and commercial arrangement with clients, their ways of presenting pictures to particular audiences, particular publics. We need to know much more than we do about how people behaved toward such public pictures (leaving aside the even more intricate matter of the private use of photographs within families), whether they preserved them, hung them (and where), inscribed them in memory, or whatever. The photographs we see here are surely an enormous enrichment of our historical knowledge, let alone our visual pleasure, but they also remind us how impoverished we are in many regions of knowledge, especially in the history of common, everyday life. And that reminder can lead us back to the pictures themselves, perhaps with an added hunger for more information, more detail, more clarity of purpose and meaning.

Recognizing how much more we need to know in order to know perfectly the meaning of the pictures, we can then begin to ask leading questions, to construct frames of our own for the use and appreciation of these images. Our questions may be aesthetic, or art historical, or political, or broadly historical and cultural. We can take O'Sullivan's "wagon darkroom" as a marvelous design in form (which it is), a sign of the individual talent of this extraordinary photographer, and a sign too of a phase in the history of photography (the use of wet-plate equipment for open-air work). It is all of this, and all such questions are legitimate. It is also, as we have seen, a thoughtful statement about man and nature, the West, and also about photography; on this level of idea its interest is very much historical and cultural. It comments upon a particular moment in a changing way of life. When we "frame" it culturally, with questions drawn from our own interests in the history of American life, it discloses new possibilities of meaning, without neglecting or disturbing questions of aesthetics and photographic history.

But a counterquestion might arise: Were not Timothy O'Sullivan, W. J. Lubken of the Bureau of Reclamation, and the dozens of others whose pictures appear here really just *working* photographers, craftsmen of the camera, doing the best job they could on particular assignments? Of course. Very few, if any, thought of themselves as "artists," producing pictures for display in art exhibitions. Their work was to record a specific scene or event. Primarily their work is straightforward, honest, accurate. They show what their client—often the government—wanted to see and have shown to a public. The purposes of government photography were varied and precise. They included, as the archivist Joe D. Thomas explains, efforts "to supplement the written record of exploration with visual information." And education: "to increase the public's knowledge of their national resources, as in photographs taken by the National Park Service and the Forest Service." Identification is another purpose, of military personnel and military materials, of farm products and the results of agricultural experiment. Documentation of the construction of government buildings is yet another separate category. The viewer will easily recognize pictures that obviously served each of these general functions. Yes, the photographers were first and foremost craftsmen of documentation. But it is because they did their jobs so well, with so little attention to extrinsic and secondary matters of formal aesthetics, that their pictures survive their first purpose and can now serve additional purposes within our own frame of reference. It is because they were so good as photographers that their work is so good now as historical pictures.

The explanation of this residual power and usefulness goes back to one of the fundamental properties of photography, a property that so impressed Oliver Wendell Holmes, Lady Eastlake, and others: its capacity to represent what was *there*. Or, to put it differently, its inability *not* to show what appears to the lens. A photograph is a record of a past event. It also makes that past moment seem present, here and now: it makes the past present to us, and makes us, as it were, present to the past. It is a complex psychological relationship, as anyone who keeps family photographs in albums or shoe cartons realizes. A painting, of course, is in some measure *always* here and now; its "past" is the imagination of the painter, not real light rays that once passed through a lens onto a plate or film. A painting may be a *rendering* of a past moment—like John Trumbull's famous conception of the signing of the Declaration of Independence. But it cannot be a direct, physical *impression* of the actual light bouncing off the surfaces of that event. An honest, straight photograph cannot but put us in touch with history in a manner unique to itself.

Photographs give immediate access to a past. Thus they make vivid and near at hand what written history is about. At the same time, as we have seen, the immediacy is always qualified in some way, in some manner often hidden from us. We can usually tell at a glance what a photograph is about. But the image does not always tell us everything we want to know about it. Viewers of photographs are in a position akin to Helen Keller's in her pictured meeting with President Eisenhower (Figure 19), grasping by touch what she cannot hear. We need to read by interpretation, not by sight alone. And photographs differ yet again from painted or hand-drawn images in that intelligent reading usually begins by looking *through* the picture before looking *at* it. That is, we normally bring to a photograph the skills we have learned in our own everyday lives to recognize gestures, appearances, the signs whereby people and objects signal their functions and intentions to us in real life. Photographs may help us realize, in fact, how much we rely in real life upon acts of *picturing*, of presenting ourselves to others in prepared ways, ways appropriate to certain situations. Every person posing in these photographs is in effect the maker and manipulator of a picture, which the camera then records as a picture *of* a picture. This relationship is quite plain in photographs of theatrical performance like "Elsie Ferguson in 'The Spirit That Wins,' " or the still from the Liberty Loan film "Stake Uncle Sam to Play Your Hand," or in the astonishing picture of the "164th Depot Brigade, Camp Funston,

Figure 19 President Eisenhower with Helen Keller and Polly Thompson, November 3, 1953, by Abbie Rowe. (Records of the National Park Service [79-AR-2196-A], National Archives)

Kansas" (Figure 20), at once a mass portrait, and a picture made *of* a picture already made by the formation of the brigade into the figure of a banner holding a single star. But some degree of theatricality, of performance, appears in most pictures of people. Such self-authored images as that of the "forest service ranger" showing off his bear skins and guns, and the three men calling attention to their skills and their luck in capturing the amazing "Short-nosed sturgeon" contain obvious keys to the performance: the trophy defines the character. And the camera defines the stage—or it provides the opportunity for the performance, just as the photographic process defines its first object or purpose: the production of a physical object that will give the performance a certain permanence, making it available for future reference. The performed roles are pretty clear in these pictures, as in the studio portraits of "unidentified Indians from Southeastern Idaho Reservations." But where the presence of the camera does not elicit a complete studiolike decorum—William Henry Jackson's "a group of all the

Figure 20 "164th Depot Brigade, Camp Funston, Kansas," 1918 or 1919. (Records of the War Department, General and Special Staffs [165-WW-78G-2], National Archives)

members of the survey made while camping in Red Buttes," for instance—roles are not so clear. In the Jackson example, some figures seem aware of the camera and adjust their positions accordingly; others seem oblivious and appear as if "caught" in an action that would have occurred even if the camera were not present. Scenes of people at work in factories, in the Mint, in fields, are of this sort, and it is impossible there to make out any specific response. Still, it is evident that one way or another, by posing or framing (cropping) or actually rearranging, the camera itself makes a difference; it too, as an apparatus as well as a photographer's intention, is part of the picture. For this reason, the past we are given access to is not a "pure" objective truth, but a truth already processed and reprocessed by human intention and mechanical limitation.

V

We see, then, that photographs are complicated, difficult objects: complicated by their social functions, made difficult by a relation to the world that is both clear and obscure, simultaneously transparent and opaque. Like miniature replicas, they give us worlds to ponder and amaze ourselves with. They trap our attention and often lead us to bafflement, to mystery. "Son of Clabe Hicks, miner" (Figure 21), in the picture by Russell Lee, may well be a good, sweet, innocent child. The picture is part of a series documenting conditions in West Virginia coal-mining regions. Framed as he is in the curtained doorway, the kitchen table behind him (is the meal set, or has it ended?)—framed too by the flowered wallpaper, the domestic photograph of dog and litter above the door, the wonderfully protective slogans tacked on either side ("You Can't Do Wrong and Get By"; "God Bless Our Soldier Boy So Brave and True")—the boy's strangely inexpressive face and his gun (is it a toy? is it loaded?) make a picture of menacing ambiguity. It is a picture *made* of materials that were there, and the making of it condenses those materials into a powerful statement that involves us on several levels, driving us toward questions about Bradshaw, McDowell County, West Virginia, on August 27, 1946—and further, into the corners and shadows of the culture represented by such slogans, such wallpaper, such objects as guns (toy or real) found in the hands of children.

What are we to make, in a remarkable instance of mysteriousness, of a lost frame, of the picture captioned "Meridian Hill Park. View showing texture of concrete in lower wall. Maid with small children in view" (Figure 22)? The caption neglects the tree, or what the wall is doing there, what system of walls it may be part of, and why the texture is

Figure 21 Russell Lee, "Son of Clabe Hicks, miner." (Bradshaw, McDowell Co., West Virginia, August 27, 1946. Records of the Solid Fuels Administration for War [245-MS-2010 L], National Archives)

worth photographing. The photographer is listed as "unknown," but surely the way he or she treated this assignment gives as clear and potent a presence as one can hope for. There are other ways to photograph textures of concrete. But the photographer also saw something else—what appears to be a small drama in process, a visual drama in whites and blacks—as well as textures of cloth and of skin—of truly unknown import. Is the picture an accident? Here is an example of an apparent violation of a frame: the assignment of picturing textures for the Office of Public Buildings and Public Parks of the National Capital. But the photographer must have had another meaning in mind, if only "human interest." We appreciate the audacity as much as we puzzle over the intention.

Figure 22 "Meridian Hill Park. View showing texture of concrete on lower wall. Maid with small children in view." Washington, D.C., about 1910; photographer unknown. (Records of the Office of Public Buildings and Public Parks of the National Capital [42-SPB-18], National Archives)

Like such ambiguous pictures, history itself is also a provocation. Its corridors are also blocked by walls without apparent reason or meaning, its written records also pointing toward unexplained actions. The obscurity into which many photographs plunge their contemporary viewers is very much like the obscurity that challenges the historian to get at the bottom of things. One question gives way to another, and the route toward a reliable truth, about photographs as much as history, lies often through a labyrinth of false leads. What other pictures might have been taken of the same subject at the same time, from a slightly different point of view? What really existed beyond the edge of the picture's border? Every photograph takes its image from a living setting; it is always made at the expense of another image that might have been made by another camera with another eye behind it and another purpose in mind. Reading photographs is an active, gymnastic process, as

Walt Whitman said about reading poems. It does not require a special skill, only a special attention and an active curiosity. Unexpected pleasures are one reward. Another is the sense one can achieve of participating in the continual public process of making sense of history, of interpreting the past from the perspective of the present. Hardly simple illustrations, photographs can be framed by judicious questions and made into symbols of lived experience: symbols that illuminate just as they provoke further questions. The National Archives collection is a national public resource of immeasurable value. It provides an opportunity to realize one of the ideals of democracy, to make every person a historian.

PART TWO

SIX

WHITMAN'S LESSON
OF THE CITY

T HE chief street of a great city," wrote Whitman in an article
titled "Broadway" in 1856, "is a curious epitome of the life of
the city; and when that street, like Broadway, is a thoroughfare, a mart, and a promenade all together, its representative character
is yet more striking." In his poems Whitman's city shares these representative features of Broadway, the conjunction of thoroughfare,
promenade, and marketplace: a place of passage, movement of people,
goods, and useful knowledge, and a place of display and spectacle, of
things in the guise of goods in shop windows and of persons in the
guise of exchangeable social identities. His city, "an endless procession," is at once material place and mode of perception.

What we seek is that nexus, the rapport between procession as
Broadway life and procession as a way of taking life in, processing and
representing it. How does the city's materiality, its hidden or obscurely
visible political economy and its economy of social relations, figure itself in the tapestry of perception Whitman weaves as he sets out to
model the city as poetry? Passage from street to poem, itself an endless
and intricate procession, is the issue at hand.

Broadway persists in Whitman's memory as the archetypal place of

First published in *Breaking Bounds: Whitman and American Cultural Studies*, edited by Betsy Erkkila and
Jay Grossman (New York: Oxford University Press, 1996), pp. 163–73.

urban instruction, its "representative character" implying but also withholding a pedagogy. In a late poem (1888) he addresses the great city's "chief street" as "portal" and "arena," salutes it as "Thou visor'd, vast, unspeakable show and lesson!" What is the visor'd lesson, and why unspeakable? Epitomized by its greatest thoroughfare, Whitman's city brings people together in countless varied and fluid transactions, unutterable in their variety and veiled in their changeableness. People pass blindly and mingle unknowingly with others who are their immanent "you." The street instructs the poet to interrupt the flow without dispersing it, to seize "whoever you are" as the necessary occasion for "my poem," for my coming to be myself.

> Whoever you are, now I place my hand upon you, that you be my
>   poem,
> I whisper with my lips close to your ear,
> I have loved many women and men, but I love none better than
>   you.
>
> O I have been dilatory and dumb,
> I should have made my way straight to you long ago,
> I should have blabb'd nothing but you, I should have chanted
>   nothing but you.

The audacity of "that you be my poem" confirms the extremity of need: only You gives voice to I, only the fusion of I and You that is the poem brings me to myself, and you to yourself. Whitman's city is the imaginative space where such things happen—not a place he represents but a process he enacts. The lesson of Broadway, its instruction in the mutuality and interdependence of I and You, constitutes Whitman's poesis: not a speakable lesson but a continuing process, the originating event of his discourse.

A process undertaken and undergone, moreover, as William James understood, not for the sake of sensation alone, the quivering touch or ecstatic vision, but for the sake of a state in which self and other fuse into a new sensation of being, quivered into new identities. Whitman cruises the city in search of significant others—as James will put it,

"the significance of alien lives"—and finds his "You" in every encounter. "You have waited, you always wait, you dumb, beautiful ministers. . . . Great or small, you furnish your parts toward the soul." The
poet interpolates the other, whether person or thing, as "soul," the You
that realizes the I. Soul names the ground on which enactments of new
identity occur. James called this way of being in the city "rapture," and
in a popular lecture of the late 1890s, "On a Certain Blindness in Human Beings," he recruits Whitman's rapt attention to the city as exemplum of a vision he too wishes to promulgate.

According to James, Whitman "felt the human crowd as rapturously as Wordsworth felt the mountains." James portrays Whitman as
"rapt with satisfied attention . . . to the mere spectacle of the world's
presence" and presents this open-eyed receptivity to "mere spectacle"
as an antidote to that "blindness," as he puts it, "with which we all are
afflicted in regard to the feelings of creatures and people different from
ourselves." We cannot see beyond the horizon of the "limited functions
and duties" of our practical lives, our "single, specialized vocation,"
and in that private darkness we nourish our own "vital secrets," blind
to "the significance of alien lives" and thus to the fullest significance of
our own. Calling this a certain blindness in human beings, James seems
to assert its universality as an existential, transhistorical human condition. Without diminishing the general character of the condition—and
James speaks of a person's unknowing relation with his or her dog to
underscore that dimension—he also localizes a present version of this
blindness with pointed allusions to a common predicament shared by
his audience. And he alerts us to seek similar evidence of a historical
social condition and predicament in Whitman's rapture and raptness.

James gave his lecture on "a certain blindness" principally at
women's colleges, but it embraces a larger range of middle-class citi-
zenry, the "we of the highly educated classes (so called)," that is, specialized professionals or students looking forward to academic or
professional or corporate careers. Perhaps he chose this theme to perform before young women aspiring to professionalism because he
deemed women, for whom professional and academic careers were still
novel and scarce, more sympathetic than college men to the insight
that the highly educated have drifted "far, far away from Nature."

We are trained to seek the choice, the rare, the exquisite exclusively, and to overlook the common. We are stuffed with abstract conceptions, and glib with verbalities and verbosities; and in the culture of these higher functions the peculiar sources of joy connected with our simpler functions often dry up, and we grow stone blind and insensible to life's more elementary and general goods and joys.

Whitman doubtless helped James write such lines, emboldened him to prescribe that we "descend to a more profound and primitive level," that we learn from "the savages and children of nature, to whom we deem ourselves so much superior."

This agitation toward a more vigorous, natural, emotional, and risk-filled life signals a distinct motif of the middle-class 1890s, a yearning for revitalization, a protest against a metropolitan malaise of conformity and repression among white-collar workers, the new managerial-professional class of incorporated urban America that James addressed. "Deadness" toward the world of others is "the price we inevitably have to pay for being practical creatures," which is to say, incorporated creatures. James tells his young women listeners that it is all right, it is healthy, it is tonic, to go sensuous, savage, and irrational. "The holidays of life are its most vitally significant portions, because they are, or at least should be, covered with just this kind of magically irresponsible spell."

Holiday of course grates, seeming to trivialize alien lives by offering touristic excursions to their significance. Diction like "magically irresponsible spell" must have embarrassed James himself, for when he published the lecture in a volume in 1899, he noted in the preface that "it is more than the mere piece of sentimentalism which it may seem to some readers." Those who have read his philosophic essays, he wrote, will recognize the essay's seriousness as an expression of "the pluralistic or individualistic philosophy." By pluralistic universe he means that "truth" being "too great for any one actual mind," we need to learn to see through many lenses, multiple perspectives. "The facts and worths of life need many cognizers to take them in. There is no point of view absolutely public and universal. Private and uncommunicable perceptions always remain over, and the worst of it is that those who look for them from the outside never know *where.*"

This authorial gloss on the underlying philosophical argument of the essay also glosses the role of Walt Whitman as James's rapturous city poet. Without saying so, James portrays a Whitman who intuits pragmatism, the view that truth is plural and partial, subjective, fragmented, scattered. James alerts us to the presence of "many cognizers" in Whitman's domain, to the significance of scale of perspective, shifts of point of view, positions of the moving eye. As an instance of Whitman's rapt attention toward the crowd and its otherness, James inserts in his lecture a passage from an 1868 letter to Pete Doyle that James found in what he called "the delicious volume" published as *Calamus* in 1897. It is Whitman of the omnivorous and voracious eye describing a ride atop a Broadway omnibus.

"You know it is a never ending amusement and study and recreation for me to ride a couple of hours on a pleasant afternoon on a Broadway stage in this way. You see everything as you pass, a sort of living, endless panorama—shops and splendid buildings and great windows . . . crowds of women richly dressed continually passing . . . a perfect stream of people . . . and then in the streets the thick crowd of carriages, stages, carts, hotel and private coaches . . . and so many tall, ornamental, noble buildings many of them of white marble, and the gayety and motion on every side: you will not wonder how much attraction all this is on a fine day, to a great loafer like me, who enjoys so much seeing the busy world move by him, and exhibiting itself for his amusement, while he takes it easy and just looks on and observes."

It's not so much what or how Whitman sees here that so captivates James, not the city's great promenade and marketplace taken in as a panoramic spectacle, but the flow of the passage, the speaker's taking it easy, his guiltless loafing while life passes by, "this mysterious sensorial life, with its irrationality," as James says later in the lecture.

As urban loafer, flaneur of Broadway coaches and Brooklyn ferries, the Whitman James stages for us plays a crucial demonic role in the argument. Of all the literary authorities James raises in support of his argument (Wordsworth, Emerson, Stevenson, Tolstoy), Whitman looks most the part of disreputable tramp, "a worthless, unproductive being." By his very otherness he demonstrates James's point that you don't have to go to such extremes of errant behavior, that vacations from the office might suffice to see the world in a new, nonhabitual light. The letter to Doyle and the Brooklyn ferry poem show the antithetical conception of productivity and worth that James argues alone makes ordinary everyday conceptions tolerable. Feeling "the human crowd as rapturously as Wordsworth felt the mountains, felt it as an overpoweringly significant presence," Whitman says in effect that "simply to absorb one's mind" in the crowd "should be business sufficient and worthy to fill the days of a serious man." For James's Whitman the mere seeing of things means serious business, yielding profits of a different order from those recognized by the practical, productive, specialized world: "To be rapt with satisfied attention, like Whitman, to the mere spectacle of the world's presence, is one way, and the most fundamental way, of confessing one's sense of its unfathomable significance and importance."

This term, "rapt," calls for closer attention. Whitman himself understood the arrogant impropriety of his stance, the insult to the ideology of private ownership in what he found sufficed, his satisfaction in saying "I see, dance, laugh, sing." In the passage that follows in section 3 of "Song of Myself," Whitman acknowledges the voice of the bourgeois superego by asking, in regard to the hugging bedfellow who withdraws at the peep of day leaving behind swelling baskets covered with white towels:

> Shall I postpone my acceptation and realization and scream at my
>   eyes,
> That they turn from gazing after and down the road,
> And forthwith cipher and show me to a cent,
> Exactly the value of one and exactly the value of two, and which
>   is ahead?

The eyes gaze after, naturally rapt; the antithetical condition is to cipher and count, to apply the calculus of ownership to an incalculable act of love.

Rapt attention, then, stands opposite conventional forms of possession, ownership, property. Mulling over the mystery of private property
in the years just before 1855, Whitman noted that "the money value of
real and personal estate in New York city is somewhere between five
hundred millions and a thousand millions of dollars." What does this
mean, he asked? "It is all nothing of account—The whole of it is not
of so much account as a pitcher of water, or a basket of fresh eggs,—
The only way we attach it to our feelings is by identifying it with the
human spirit,—through love, through pride, through our craving for
beauty and happiness." He might have said through our rapture. In
another notebook entry in the same years he wrote: "What is it to own
any thing? It is to incorporate it into yourself, as the primal god swallowed the five immortal offspring of Rhea, and accumulated to his life
and knowledge and strength all that would have grown in them." In
"There Was a Child Went Forth," one of the originally untitled 1855
poems, going forth means swallowing the world: "And the first object
he look'd upon, that object he became." To be rapt in attention toward
someone or something, in Whitman's presumed gloss on James's figure,
is to become that person or thing, to incorporate it as nourishment,
knowledge, strength.

Yet, to be rapt also says to be seized, carried off, taken from one
place to another, transposed, perhaps by force or by emotion, a state of
transport, ravishment: James's terms project an excess beyond the figure of exultant poet for whom the city stands in for Wordsworth's "nature," source of ultimate refreshment, verification, and meaning. Rapt
and rapturous, with hidden kinship to rape, convey an inchoate sense
on James's part of a violence immanent in Whitman's version of the
city, in his crowds, in his apparent surrender as passive panoramist to
their inducements and promises. Indeed, if we think of "City of
Ships" and especially the haunting "Give Me the Splendid Silent Sun,"
Whitman's Civil War city is filled with the clamor and agitations of
war, but signs of siege appear even earlier, a discordant note at the
deeper frequencies of his urban vision.

Consider the first appearance of a distinctively urban place in
"Song of Myself," the initially untitled opening poem of the 1855 edition. It occurs in what would later become section 8 and presents not
an entirely heartening picture: a kaleidoscopic display of colliding im-

ages, visual and aural, fragmented narrative shards composing a tableau of untold stories, "living and buried speech" echoing from "impassive stones." A hallucinatory air hovers over this Broadway passage, which seems more typical of Baudelaire or T. S. Eliot than the Whitman of William James:

> The blab of the pave, tires of carts, sluff of boot-soles, talk of the
>   promenaders,
> The heavy omnibus, the driver with his interrogating thumb, the
>   clank of the shod horses on the granite floor,
> The snow-sleighs, clinking, shouted jokes, pelts of snow-balls,
> The hurrahs for popular favorites, the fury of rous'd mobs,
> The flap of the curtain'd litter, a sick man inside borne to the
>   hospital,
> The meeting of enemies, the sudden oath, the blows and fall,
> The excited crowd, the policeman with his star quickly working his
>   passage to the centre of the crowd,
> The impassive stones that receive and return so many echoes,
> What groans of over-fed or half-starv'd who fall sunstruck or in
>   fits,
> What exclamations of women taken suddenly who hurry home
>   and give birth to babes,
> What living and buried speech is always vibrating here, what howls
>   restrain'd by decorum,
> Arrests of criminals, slights, adulterous offers made, acceptances,
>   rejections with convex lips,
> I mind them or the show or resonance of them—I come and I
>   depart.

The scene verges on an implosion into private rage and pain, into passionate disorder. In its fragmented inventorial form the passage resembles a newspaper page, a reenactment of such a page with juxtaposed accounts of riots, street fights, sudden illness, criminals apprehended. What does the poet make of this spectacle in which rich and poor, overfed and half-starved, fall together in sunstroke or fit? How does the poet relate to the policeman with his star, the figure of coercive authority who pushes his way to the center of the crowd, indeed at the exact center of the passage itself? What does "I come and I depart" in the closing line (in 1855, "I come again and again") reveal about the poet's place in the scene, the speaker's way of being in such a city place?

The concluding line retrospectively discloses the presence of the poet in a curiously paradoxical posture of minding (in both senses of watching and caring about) and not minding the scene, gripped yet independent of it: an oddly tentative closure swinging between coming and going, staying and leaving, turning toward and turning away. What can we make of this alternating motion in Whitman's relation to the crowd? James might say that the poet's rapture demands the freedom from practical commitments, from family and job, which coming and going imply. To enjoy the pleasure of merely watching life go by, to stay open to what James calls the "vital secrets" of other people's lives, you had better not make a profession of it.

This pragmatic explanation has merit, for it reminds us that Whitman's posture is that of a person with a definite calling, a vocation of his own to avoid vocations that entrap one within fixed identities. But we seek a formal explanation as well, an account of the form or typical forms of Whitman's representation of his poet in the city: a formal account, moreover, through which we might better understand Whitman's response to the pressures and opportunities of the historical moment.

Perhaps the coming-and-going or ebb-and-flow pattern provides an enabling condition for Whitman to confront the crowd in the first place, to confront it "face to face" as a condition of his own being, as the "dumb, beautiful ministers" who minister to harmony with the world at the close of "Crossing Brooklyn Ferry." Section 42 of "Song of Myself" restates the earlier dynamic relation of poet to crowd in somewhat more opaque but paradoxically illuminating terms:

A call in the midst of the crowd,
My own voice, orotund sweeping and final.

A voice heard from without yet recognized as originating from within—"my own voice" as "a call" heard from within "the crowd."

Whitman's speaker makes the ecstatic claim of the mystic, that he stands at once inside and outside himself, within the crowd that comprises the city, part of it yet detached enough to hear his own voice. The poet minds his own voice calling at once to the crowd and to himself, calling himself through or by means of the crowd: an act of self-interpolation, himself as the "performer" in the following lines:

> Come my children,
> Come my boys and girls, my women, household and intimates,
> Now the performer launches his nerve, he has pass'd his prelude
>   on the reeds within.

And a few lines later, in an ecstatic fit:

> My head slues round on my neck,
> Music rolls, but not from the organ,
> Folks are around me, but they are no household of mine.

The poet comes to himself through the intermediary of the crowd; the call emerges from and expresses the oneness of being close and being distant. Coming and going define a mode of acceptance, Whitman's way of placing himself in the crowd yet holding (or withholding) himself free and aloof from it, far enough away to witness it, to discern its patterns, to re-create it as an element of his own being, what he calls "soul," as in the final lines of "Crossing Brooklyn Ferry":

> You furnish your parts toward eternity,
> Great or small, you furnish your parts toward the soul.

"Crossing Brooklyn Ferry" recapitulates the ebb-and-flow pattern in the representation of crowd and the self's relation to the crowd. The capacious, vehicular structure of that poem invites the epithet processional, a form of movement, in this case stately, majestic, with great formal feeling, though in the case of the kaleidoscopic panorama in section 8, agitated, uncertain, edgy. In "There Was a Child Went Forth," "Broadway Pageant," "City of Ships," and "Give Me the

Splendid Silent Sun," whatever the emotional tonality of the procession its effect is to produce an idea of a totality, an assembly of parts constituting an immanent even if not yet present whole. Processional form signals a hope of unity at the site of difference and conflict: it is Whitman's crowd control, we might say, his way of subduing and containing recalcitrant particulars within his dream of an American oneness—his answer (in the sense of equivalence) to the cop's star or club at the center of the crowd.

We can better approach the problem of dissonance in Whitman's city, then, by looking at his compositions. When Whitman writes to Doyle, "You see everything as you pass, a sort of living, endless panorama," he is being serious about the worth and value not just of seeing but of this particular mode of urban perception, a moving mode of dynamic panorama, the mode of procession. It constructs itself as a recounted movement through city space, a passage that attempts to comprehend a whole in its parts, to create an impression of a totality out of disparate, disjunctive parts.

A mode of this sort had arisen in the popular press of the new industrial metropolises of Europe and the United States in the 1830s and 1840s, and Whitman took as if naturally to the emerging conventions of moving panorama as early as his 1840s newspaper accounts of life in the burgeoning city. As a visual and kinetic form the panorama procession occupied theatrical space within the city; as a written form in the penny press and periodicals it developed out of the "ramble" familiar to London readers in the late eighteenth century, drew upon the "city mysteries" genre of Eugène Sue and Lippard and Poe, and in Whitman's city poems takes a new turn as a nuanced method of structuring and comprehending urban experience. "Crossing Brooklyn Ferry" is Whitman's most exquisitely realized work in the processional mode, but we find it in much of his journalism and incidental prose and in other poems of passage through city space.

James doesn't comment on the formal composition of Whitman's rapturous utterances, except to remark dimly and perhaps archly that "his verses are but ejaculations—things mostly without subject or verb, a succession of interjections on an immense scale." But had he examined the structure within which these interjections performed their work, he might have found in Whitman's processional order evidence of something he evokes earlier in the lecture. Speaking of that moment of swiftly changing consciousness, as when "the common practical man becomes a lover" and "the hard externality give[s] way," illuminating us by "a gleam of insight into the ejective world," James wrote that "the whole scheme of our customary values gets confounded, . . . our self is riven and its narrow interests fly to pieces, then a new centre and a new perspective must be found."

New center and new perspective offer a clue to the radically urban mental configuration embodied in Whitman's processional form. It allows the speaker of his poems access to ever-changing perspectives from a flexible point of view because it understands the constancy and thus inevitable incompleteness of its need, a permanent, agitating need, for the other, for You. A common pattern in the poems is the idle saunter unexpectedly ruptured, and then a zoomlike shift from wide-field panoramic perspective to close-up scrutiny:

By the city dead-house by the gate,
As idly sauntering wending my way from the clangor,
I curious pause, for lo, an outcast form, a poor dead prostitute
    brought,
Her corpse they deposit unclaim'd, it lies on the damp brick
    pavement,
The divine woman, her body, I see the body, I look on it alone,
That house once full of passion and beauty, all else I notice not.

The shift in perspective away from the clangor of the main thoroughfares to the "outcast form" produces the poem's most dramatic perspectival shift, from within the clangor that knows the prostitute as outcast, to the poet's own outcast act of looking alone on the dead body, the wondrous but ruined house of the corpse, a look in which the surrounding city of substance and power—"the rows of dwellings . . . Or white-domed capitol with majestic figure surmounted, or all the old high-spired cathedrals"—loses its priority and its reality: "That little house alone more than them all—poor, desperate house!"

A similar pattern of a turn in space and a constriction of perspective, a narrowing and sharpening of focus, occurs in "Sparkles from the Wheel":

> Where the city's ceaseless crowd moves on the livelong day,
> Withdrawn I join a group of children watching, I pause aside with
>   them.

And as in the dead-house poem, this turn is followed by an obsessive close-up and an attendant shift in the long view of the enclosing city space: in this case, the city vastness rising up as if newly perceived from the perspective of the small group of children, poet, and knife grinder, "an unminded point set in a vast surrounding." Moreover, the sparkles from the wheel suggest a new perception, of city substance collapsing into mere sensation: "Myself effusing and fluid, a phantom curiously floating, now here absorb'd and arrested." The effusion and the arrest suggest a pattern of distintegration of substance into sensation, of matter into light, which elsewhere—"There Was a Child Went Forth," for example—accompanies doubts about the reality of appearance:

> The doubts of day-time and the doubts of night-time, the curious
>   whether and how,
> Whether that which appears so is so, or is it all flashes and specks?
> Men and women crowding fast in the streets, if they are not
>   flashes and specks what are they?
> The streets themselves and the façades of houses, and goods in the
>   windows,
> Vehicles, teams, the heavy-plank'd wharves, the huge crossing at
>   the ferries,
> The village on the highland seen from afar at sunset, the river
>   between,
> Shadows, aureola and mist, the light falling on roofs and gables of
>   white or brown two miles off,
> The schooner near by sleepily dropping down the tide, the little
>   boat slack-tow'd astern,
> The hurrying tumbling waves, quick-broken crests, slapping.

The strata of color'd clouds, the long bar of maroon-tint away
solitary by itself, the spread of purity it lies motionless in.
The horizon's edge, the flying sea-crow, the fragrance of salt
marsh and shore mud,
These became part of that child who went forth every day, and
who now goes, and will always go forth every day.

An astonishing and immeasurably beautiful enactment of dematerialization, here in Whitman's processional mode lies the condition for fusion of I and You, for integration into a new identity and achievement of the soul.

The energy of Whitman's processional lines in such a passage, and throughout the majestic "Crossing Brooklyn Ferry," invokes in us a sense of the fragility of the triumph of such lines. They are won against forces of distintegration that Whitman may have understood less gothically than Poe and Melville but with an equal sense of their menace to the integrity of selfhood. But Whitman, like James, also sensed a promise within the decentering forces of the market and of modernity in general, the promise of new registers of selfhood achieved in relation to the "significance of alien lives." He invented his urban processional as a way of moving through the city, through its encountered others, directly to the soul, Whitman's great trope for communal love, labor, and spirit, the only means of attaching the city's incalculable collective wealth, "the money value of [its] real and personal estate," to human experience. Is this not the office of those "dumb, beautiful ministers" in "Crossing Brooklyn Ferry," those persons and things encountered in the crossing no longer alien, who always wait until "we receive you with free sense at last, and are insatiate henceforward"?

This receiving of the world with free sense is exactly the function of Whitman's processionals. Procession dissolves the world into sensation in order to accomplish this reintegration. It is a lesson in a mode of being, a way of remaining within the float even while disentangling oneself from it. No wonder James saw within it, saw even farther than he may have realized, a remedy for a certain blindness. Seeing processionally is Whitman's most radically urban way of seeking the soul, a way of freeing people from the hold of money and ownership to seek possession of themselves, in Karl Mannheim's terminology, through the ecstasy (ex-stasis) that comes with recognition of oneself in others. Whitman's lesson of the city, his vision of ecstatic community, lies in the turn in consciousness that the unspeakable life of the street provokes.

SEVEN

READING
THE GILDED AGE CITY

READERS seeking the city in nineteenth-century American literature often find themselves in the curious predicament Jean-Paul Sartre experienced during a visit to New York in 1946. "I was looking for New York," he wrote about himself on a midtown street corner, "and couldn't find it." Similarly many readers of what have been considered classic American texts of the nineteenth century, a century of steady and massive urbanization, have remarked on the apparent absence or invisibility of an urban landscape, of such familiar literary versions of city phenomena as Dickens's London, Balzac's Paris, Dostoyevsky's St. Petersburg. Of course Whitman's Manhattan stands out as an exception, the "crowds of men and women attired in the usual costumes" of his great ode "Crossing Brooklyn Ferry" absorbed by the poet as a natural part of his own selfhood:

I too walk'd the streets of Manhattan island, and bathed in the
    waters around it,
I too felt the curious abrupt questionings stir within me,
In the day among crowds of people they sometimes came upon
    me.

But in American fiction it is not until the early twentieth century, until the appearance in 1900 of Theodore Dreiser's *Sister Carrie*, that the city makes its first unequivocal appearance as a place in its own right, as deeply felt and richly detailed as Thoreau's piece of nature at Walden, as Melville's whaler cruising the watery portion of the globe, as Mark Twain's great river. Dreiser's achievement has seemed to represent a decisive change, a sharp break in what has struck some observers as a distinctly anti-urban bias in American writing—a bias described by some scholars as a reflection of a deeply seated preference in American culture for a pastoral way of life: a preference, in the collective imagination, at least, for small homogenous communities, for frontiers and farms and small towns, for closeness to nature, for traditional values and simple, uncomplicated relations.

Before Dreiser, according to this view of American writing and culture, writers either avoided city themes or dealt with them with a divided heart and mind. For example, when in the Gilded Age the presence of the big city could no longer be denied as a dynamic force in American life, William Dean Howells abandoned the romantic courtship themes of his early novels of manners and, in *A Modern Instance* (1882), *The Rise of Silas Lapham* (1885), and *A Hazard of New Fortunes* (1890), turned his attention to city matters. Yet compared to Dreiser his efforts even in these bold and courageous books have seemed to readers halfhearted, constrained by a barely concealed distaste for and fear of the modern city, colored by nostalgia for simpler rural places, more harmonious times. And Stephen Crane's city tales, his vivid sketches of life in the slums, seem to be surreptitious, half-guilty excursions into forbidden regions. Not until Dreiser, according to the conventional literary history, does the city appear in American fiction as a landscape every bit as natural to human existence as any other terrain: a place neither good nor bad, neither blessed nor wicked, but unmistakably there, a given of contemporary human experience.

This standard version of the city in classic North American writing is, I believe, mistaken and misleading, and it gives a distorted interpretation of urbanism in the United States. Adopting as its own point of view the very outlook it claims to diagnose, it interprets literary versions of the city as predominantly negative, alien, disruptive. It mistakes notions of good or bad, positive or negative, as objective reflections of historical fact rather than as cultural responses, tropes, or literary figures conditioned by the subjective realm of value and desire. Cultural history concerns itself with collective pictures, modes of representation, ideological narratives that seem indistinguishable from social fact. And such refracted pictures and cultural stories themselves perform a role in the larger social and political histories of society. Negative pictures and moralistic condemnations of city life belong as much to the history of the city as more solid-seeming texts on demographic patterns, mass transportation, political governance, and changes in land use. The cultural picture can provide a particularly sensitive index or trace of historical meanings of urban experience, complementary to the findings of social science.

Seeking the city in the fiction of the Gilded Age, what can we learn from Sartre's predicament of looking and not finding? Sartre explained his peculiar situation in New York as a matter of subjectivity. He had come with a European idea of a city in his mind, the experience of a place in which "streets run into other streets" and, "more than mere arteries," are "a social milieu" where you might stop, "meet people, drink, eat, and linger." New York presented a different fact, a different physiognomy. The "numerical anonymity" of its streets and avenues made him feel that he was "simply anybody, anywhere": "No valid reason justifies my presence in this place rather than any other, since this one is so like another. You never lose your way, and you are always lost."

Sartre opposes the intimate familiarity of European cities with the anonymity and disorientation a stranger feels in New York. And it is precisely this sense of the city as a strange terrain, a place that baffles and mystifies the visitor, that one finds predominating in American writing before the Civil War: in Charles Brockden Brown's *Arthur Mervyn*, in Edgar Allan Poe's "The Man of the Crowd," in Nathaniel Hawthorne's "My Kinsman, Major Molineux" and certain scenes in *The Blithedale Romance*, and perhaps most powerfully in Herman Melville's "Bartleby the Scrivener: A Story of Wall Street" and *Pierre, or The Ambiguities*. The remark "You never lose your way, and you are always lost" seems apt indeed in describing the predicament of characters, often visitors from elsewhere, typically from the countryside, in these and many other works of the early and mid-nineteenth century. In an extreme but characteristic moment of entry into the city, for example, Melville's Pierre encounters an ominous sense of obscurity. The lamps along the "great thoroughfare" leading into the city seemed "not so much intended to dispel the general gloom, as to show some dim path leading through it, into some gloom still deeper beyond." The city seems constructed of depths beneath depths, of "dismal side-glooms," of "dark beetling secrecies of mortar and stone." At the same time the still innocent Pierre encounters a "garish night-life," is accosted by a "scarlet-cheeked" woman of the night whose figure is "horribly lit by the green and yellow rays" of a storefront. To the stranger newly arrived the city presents a fearsome look of labyrinthine depths, deceptive and unnatural appearances that hint of crime and sin.

A familiar story. But why, we might ask, have American writers, even "realists" and "naturalists" in subsequent generations who wrote in a less charged and feverish rhetoric, chosen frequently to write about the city from the point of view of the stranger, the visitor from outside, from elsewhere? One answer lies in the power of literary convention. American city writing at first tended to follow the lineaments of a genre known as the "mystery," best represented by the French writer Eugène Sue's *Mysteries of Paris*. The city "mystery" employed Gothic devices and motifs to portray a dense, lurid, forbidding terrain. Then realism, advocated by Howells as a way of representing "commonplace" experience, sought to dispel mystery and to render the city, or any subject, transparent and comprehensible. As defined by Howells, realism proposed an opposing literary mode, wishing to shed the "light of common day" upon the obscure corners and thoroughfares of the gothicized city. Gilded Age realism shared with contemporary reform movements the motive to purge the city of corruption, immorality, crime, and general disorder, to portray the city differently, as a community in which moral reason could find a place. While reform movements sought to demystify the urban world by replacing corrupt political bosses with an elite of well-bred, disinterested leaders, realism sought to portray a world in which this process would seem necessary and possible. Both literary realism and political reform wanted to change the conventions and the prevailing picture: to replace mystery with clarity, obscurity with light, corruption with moral purpose.

To be sure, the transactions between conventions of "mystery" and of "realism" are less simple than a stark contrast suggests. Both literary and pictorial conventions had complicated and ambiguous elements; their relationship was interactive, dialectical, and heterogeneous. Also, there were important differences in the audiences for realism and mystery; realism in America assumed middle-class readers, urban homesteaders, property owners, families in a domestic scene, while mystery in popular fiction, sensationalist journals of crime and exposé, and daily newspapers tended to find readers among the working class and immigrants, groups less attached to a vision of social order founded on respect for property, more familiar with poverty, crime, sexuality, and violence in everyday life. Yet neither is a pure mode; when we look closely at the fictional cities of realists such as Howells, Crane, and Henry James, we find mixed modes, elements of Gothic romance interwoven in the fabric of representations that present themselves as pictures of the "real." At key moments in realist texts we find authors resorting to "mystery" as a necessarey adjunct of "realism."

I'd like to suggest an approach to the fictive city of the Gilded Age by sketching several key persisting features in the convention of "mystery." The first can be called the trope of illegibility, the encounter with a sign that cannot be read or understood. This figure of a blocked understanding of the visual texts of the city appeared with great force in Romantic writing of the early nineteenth century and survived as a powerful legacy into the age of realism. In Poe's great tale of the 1840s, "The Man of the Crowd," the sign is the inexplicable behavior of an old man who wanders obsessively through crowded city streets, day and night, in compulsive flight or pursuit. The story begins:

> It was well said of a certain German book that *"es lässt sich nicht lesen"*—it does not permit itself to be read. There are some secrets which do not permit themselves to be told. Men die nightly in their beds, wringing the hands of ghostly confessors, and looking them piteously in the eyes—die with despair of heart and convulsion of throat, on account of the hideousness of mysteries which will not suffer themselves to be revealed.

Thus speaks the narrator, a figure who in turn pursues the old man with a compulsion similar to that of the pursued. And in his pursuit the narrator himself becomes another "man of the crowd," another enigma among enigmas, another illegible sign of the city. Strangers to each other in their circular chase, they enact the elusiveness of the city's own reality: it does not permit itself to be read.

The city makes all its inhabitants—as well as its visitors, if they are at all self-aware—into strangers; to be conscious in the city is to be conscious of one's own estrangement. "I wander all night in my vision . . . ," writes Whitman in "The Sleepers" (1855), "Wandering and confused, lost to myself, ill-assorted, contradictory." It's not a condition of American writers: recall Wordsworth wandering among the "spectacles" of London in Book VII of *The Prelude*, seeing the city as a book of arcane inscriptions:

> . . . the string of dazzling wares,
> Shop after shop, with symbols, blazoned names,
> And all the tradesman's honours overhead:
> Here, fronts of houses, like a title-page,
> With letters huge from top to toe.

Everywhere among "those labyrinths" of streets London presents signs and symbols that "ape / The absolute presence of reality"—shams and imitations, "lies to the ear, and lies to every sense." With its "staring pictures and huge scrolls, / Dumb proclamations," Bartholomew Fair presents itself to the poet's estranged and questing eye as "blank confusion! true epitome / Of what the might City is herself."

The convention of the illegible city took shape in the literary imagination in Europe and America at a time of vast, unsettling growth in the size, shape, and visible texture of cities. The literary convention can be understood as a response to social change—not only to increases in size and density and heterogeneity of population, but also to deep, less visible changes in patterns of ownership, of distribution and control of power. In America the process of urbanization started later and proceeded more rapidly than in Europe, with perhaps more radical effects in the constant upheaval or urban landscapes unmitigated by the survival of ancient and medieval urban sections. Estrangement and mystery of the sort Sartre expressed seemed more intense, more thoroughgoing and decisive in the United States than in the Old World. Moreover, the virtually unchallenged Protestant outlook in nineteenth-century America had its effect by stamping the city as evil: the city as Sodom and Gomorrah. John Bunyan's powerful book, profoundly influential in eighteenth- and nineteenth-century Protestant households, *The Pilgrim's Progress* (1678), depicts the road to salvation as running from the City of Destruction to the City of Zion, that Celestial City which "stood upon a mighty hill." Along the way the Pilgrim passes through and escapes the clutches of such infamous places as the Town of Carnal Policy, the Town of Vanity with its notorious fair where, Bunyan relates, can be found "all such Merchandize sold as Houses, Lands, Trades, Places, Honours, Perferments, Titles, Countryes, Kingdoms, Lusts, Pleasures and Delights of all sorts." Such images of nefarious urban dealings echoed throughout American culture before the Civil War, an inescapable legacy of popular imagery of the city, especially as the smoke, dirt, and pressing crowds of the new industrial cities seemed to give life and credibility to Bunyan's damning vision of urban damnation. The worldy city stood in contrast in Bunyan's eyes to the Celestial City of God, a white city upon a hill. His vision reverberated with the inaugurating words of American Protestantism— John Winthrop's oft-repeated commandment: "Wee must consider that wee shall be as a Citty upon a Hill, the eies of all people are upon us."

The persisting power of the convention of "mystery," the city as the site of evil, of estrangement and alienation, of crime and corruption, gains force from its contrast with the image of a pure, white city shining in the distance. The Puritan message was that, should the colonists fail to produce in their worldly city a simulacrum of God's Celestial City, then it would be their unhappy fate to inhabit one of the godless cities of destruction and vanity, of "Thefts, Murders, Adulteries, False-swearers, and that of a blood red color," in Bunyan's vivid admonitory phrases: a message brought home to the Gilded Age by scores of evangelical voices raised in alarm and outrage at the state of urban affairs. For example, Josiah Strong in his best-selling tract of 1886, *Our America*: "Here luxuries are gathered—everything that dazzles the eye, or tempts the appetite. . . . Dives and Lazarus are brought face to face . . . here is heaped the social dynamite; here roughs, gamblers, thieves, robbers, lawless and desperate men of all sorts, congregate; men who are ready on any pretext to raise riots."

In the evangelical version of "mystery," the Gilded Age city is portaryed as mammon, as "storm center," as "most serious menace" to "our America." A spokesman for the Home Mission movement, Josiah Strong attacked the city with the zeal of a revivalist missionary. But similar images drawn from secular versions of the city mystery informed even less zealous enterprises of reform. Frederick Law Olmsted, the landscape artist and designer of Central Park, a leading voice for rational order and planning, wrote in 1870: "Every day of their lives they [city people] have seen thousands of their fellow-men, have met them face to face, have brushed against them, and yet had no experience of anything in common with them." The city estranged even those in closest contact with each other, it mystified human relations. "We want a ground," Olmsted continued in explanation of the value of city parks, "to which people may easily go after their day's work is done, and where they may stroll for an hour, seeing, hearing, and feeling nothing of the bustle and jar of the streets. . . . We want the greatest possible contrast with the restraining and confining conditions of the town, which compel us to walk circumspectly, watchfully, jealously, which compel us to look closely upon others without sympathy." Against the city mystery, the illegible city, Olmsted proposed to recreate a pastoral landscape within the precincts of the city: "a simple, broad, open space of greensward" with "depth of wood and enough about it . . . to completely shut out the city"—nothing less than an act of redemption, the mystifying street displaced by a restored community of virtue, a symbolic city upon a hill: people will assemble, he wrote, "with an evident glee in the prospect of coming together, all classes largely represented, with a common purpose, not at all intellectual, competitive with none, each individual adding by his mere presence to the pleasure of all others, all helping to the greater happiness of each."

The reformer clearly intended here to reorganize the city's spaces in order to plant within them a physical, moral, and psychological contrast to the competitive alienating life of the street. A literary analogue to this deliberate establishment of a pedagogical contrast within the city—encouraging people to view their daily lives from the pastoral and communal point of view of the park—appears in Edward Bellamy's famous utopian fiction *Looking Backward* (1888). Bellamy's hero awakes one day in the year 2000 to find himself in a new society based on a rationalized system of production and distribution; poverty has been eliminated, as well as inequality, profit, selfishness—and the familiar urban contrasts of rich and poor, slums and mansions, filth and cleanliness. Under Nationalism, Bellamy's name for the socialism he advocated, the city has been thoroughly demystified and placed under a rational and hygienic regime. At the close of the narrative the hero dreams he has returned to nineteenth-century Boston, wandering its streets with greater consciousness of mystery, of estrangement, than ever before:

> I had passed through Washington Street thousands of times before and viewed the ways of those who sold merchandise, but my curiosity concerning them was as if I had never gone by their way before. I took wandering note of the show windows of the stores, filled with goods arranged with a wealth of pains and artistic device to attract the eye. I saw the throngs of ladies looking in, and the proprietors eagerly watching the effect of the bait. I went within and noted the hawk-eyed floor-walker watching for business, overlooking the clerks, keeping them up to their task of inducing the customers to buy, buy, buy, for money if they had it, for credit if they had it not, to buy what they wanted not, more than they wanted, what they could not afford. At times I momentarily lost the clue and was confused by the sight. Why this effort to induce people to buy? . . . I had been in this quarter of the city a hundred times before . . . but here . . . I now first perceived the true significance of what I witnessed.

The former Gilded Age Bostonian has since been elsewhere, he has walked the streets of the Celestial City, and now his estrangement measures a difference in values, the degree to which the scales have fallen from his eyes.

Like the reformer, the Gilded Age realist focused often on divisions

in urban space, especially on the barriers and separations that com-
partmentalized activities, functions, and people. Indeed, spatial barriers, the fragmentation of the urban terrain, became an obsessive image
in literary culture, low and high. In popular writing, titles such as "People We Pass," "The Nether Side of New York," "How the Other Half
Lives" catered to the public's interest. In the most important city novel
before Dreiser, *The Hazard of New Fortunes*, Howells gives a vivid account of just this sense of spatial estrangement from the point of view
of his hero, Basil March, who has an unappeasable curiosity to peer
across social barriers. In the New York Elevated Railroad, an early
form of mechanized transport in the Gilded Age city, March finds
what seems a perfect vehicle for exactly his kind of high-minded
voyeurism:

> . . . the fleeting intimacy you formed with people in second and
> third floor interiors, while all the usual street life went on under-
> neath, had a domestic intensity mixed with a perfect repose that
> was the last effect of good society with all its security and exclu-
> siveness. He said it was better than the theatre, of which it re-
> minded him, to see those people through their windows: a
> family party of work-folk late at tea, some of the men in their
> shirt-sleeves; a woman sewing by a lamp; a mother laying her
> child in its cradle; a man with his head fallen on his hands upon
> a table; a girl and her lover leaning over the window-sill to-
> gether. What suggestion! what drama! what infinite interest!

Thus Basil March and his wife, newly arrived in Manhattan from
Boston, enjoying their conjugal chats after a ride on the El "of the superb spectacle." They seem to have overcome or repressed the estrangement that the convention of city mystery would impose, to have
overcome it by making another convention, that of the "spectacle," the
idea of city life as "theatre," the spectators enjoying both their security
and their exclusiveness in their passenger seats on the elevated train.
    Howells's tone is gently ironic here, for it is precisely this sense of
comfort in the notion of a picturesque theatricalized spectacle, viewed
at a distance, that his hero will find shattered as a result of the unfold-

ing events of the narrative: the conflict between the German Socialist radical Landau and the newly made millionaire Dryfoos; the streetcar strike and its violence; the death of the millionaire's son, a Christian Socialist who attempts to intervene in the strike. The underlying issue of this novel, which centers on the founding of a new popular literary journal backed by the ignorant, narrow-minded millionaire, concerns the possibilities of reconciliation among the conflicting and contending forces in the new city. " 'If you can make the comfortable people understand how the uncomfortable people live,' " says the young Dryfoos, " 'it will be a very good thing, Mr. March. Sometimes it seems to me that the only trouble is that we don't know one another well enough; and that the first thing to do is this.' " Which is to say that March's journal and Dryfoos's reform share the identical end of dispelling that mystery which the novel contemplates: the mystery of otherness, of class and ethnic separation, and of new mechanical forces represented by that same elevated train that seems to provide a means, in the spectacle it discloses, for overcoming social distance by no more effort than the paying of a fare and the taking of a seat.

The pressures upon the heart of Howells's literary version of the historical city can best be grasped in the mixed emotions and thoughts aroused by the El.

> "Look at that thing! Ain't it beautiful?"
> They leaned over the track and looked up at the next station, where the train, just starting, throbbed out the flame-shot steam into the white moonlight.
> "The most beautiful thing in New York—the one always and certainly beautiful thing here," said March; and his wife sighed, "Yes, yes." She clung to him, and remained rapt by the sight till the train drew near, and then pulled him back in a panic.

In that panic, a moment that passes quickly, lies a feeling of irreducible and unresolved threat. Like the city as a whole, the El is at once picturesque spectacle and chaotic energy.

In another extended revery on the El, March perceives the potentially destructive feature of the new mechanized forces reshaping the

city, only to back away from the implications of his perception. He remarks upon "the insolence with which the railway had drawn its erasing line" across the fronts of buildings, how it dishonors and flouts a
Corinthian theater and interferes with "vistas of shabby cross streets,"
affecting the vision of passengers and pedestrians "always in wanton
disregard of the life that dwelt, and bought and sold, and rejoiced or
sorrowed, and clattered or crawled, around, below, above." As a new
principle of rectilinear order, as a force against mystery, the elevated
train has introduced its own mystifications, creating a "frantic panorama." The passage concludes with an image that seems to link this
thing of human will and energy with forces of nature. Perhaps the El
represents mere accident, a planless energy like that of nature itself in
the "fierce struggle for survival," in which destruction of the weaker by
the stronger seems the only order. Indeed, "the whole at moments
seemed to him lawless, godless; the absence of intelligent, comprehensive purpose in the huge disorder." Perhaps, in short, mystery remains,
heightened and deepened by the very forces of rationality, of science
and technology. This difficult, troubling thought affects March with no
more than "a vague discomfort" and a "half recognition," however.

In this passage, as in the novel as a whole, Gilded Age realism finds
itself at a limit. The El represents something Basil can understand only
by resorting to images of mystery. The imagery proves inadequate as
an explanation of new historical realities yet is a perfect sign of the
bafflement produced by them. Howells seems to edge toward a new literary mode, the mode of Dreiser, of acceptance of the urban world as
man's nature, ruled by forces over which society has gained no measur-
able control. Dreiser will dispel mystery by naturalizing the city. Howells draws back; the conventions of mystery, a touch of the Gothic in
the image of a sublime beauty exciting panic, remain a resource for
characterizing the impressions of the city upon consciousness.

In *The American Scene*, the book written about his visit to the United
States in 1905 after an absence of twenty-five years, Henry James remarked of the forces unleashed and taking shape in the new commercial tall buildings of lower Manhattan—buildings akin to Howells's El
in their sublimity and mystification—that New York was not likely "to
produce both the maximum of 'business' spectacle and the maxi-

mum of ironic reflection of it." The city awaits an American Zola, he suggested—whose name, of course, would be Dreiser. Meanwhile, as if thinking of his old friend Howells and his valiant effort to comprehend the new in the terms of the old, James noted: "The reflecting surfaces, of the ironic, of the epic order, suspended in the New York atmosphere, have yet to show symptoms of shining out, and the monstrous phenomena themselves, meanwhile, strike me as having, with their immense momentum, got the start, got ahead of, in proper parlance, any possibility of poetic, of dramatic capture."

James's words seem juridical and final. By the close of the century the actual social and economic mysteries and mystifications of the historical city seemed to have surpassed their literary versions. A certain idealism, a wish for a world ruled by high moral values and love of beauty, lay close to the heart of literary realism, sharing with painting, sculpture, and architecture in the Gilded Age a hope that art could make something orderly and redemptive out of what seemed the imminent chaos of America's burgeoning commercial and industrial cities. Could the new urban forces be brought under control by acts of imagination? The realists and idealists hoped so. In 1893 they erected on the shore of Lake Michigan in Chicago a simulacrum of their dreams, a plaster of paris White City purged of evangelical rhetoric and presented as a perfect emblem of classical rationality and beauty. The following year, after the great Columbian Exposition at Chicago closed, the White City went up in flames, while the strike and boycott called by workers against the Pullman company, and the resulting arrival of federal troops to keep the trains moving, filled the city with violence and destruction of property and led its citizens to fear outright class conflict. Contradictions between dream and reality, between the dream of "realism" and a reality of persisting and deepening mystery, were abounding in the American world.

Henry Adams gave expression to just this moment of danger and frustration with the collapse of conventional understandings in a passage, dated 1905, in the final chapter of *The Education of Henry Adams*:

The outline of the city became frantic in its effort to explain something that defied meaning. Power seemed to have outgrown its servitude and to have asserted its freedom. The cylinder had exploded, and thrown great masses of stone and steam against the sky. The city had the air and movement of hysteria, and the citizens were crying in every accent of anger and alarm, that the new forces must at any cost be brought under control.

Adams, like Howells trembling before the sight of the El, reaches for images of mystery to convey his sense of peril: the desire for order and control struggling vainly against the reality of the city as sheer chaotic power. The explosion of forms in Henry Adams's eyes provided a fitting conclusion; the rupture he perceived held premonitions not only of the demise of realism but also of the rise of new artistic experiments in making urban mystery legible.

EIGHT

HORATIO ALGER'S
RAGGED DICK

When Dick was dressed in his new attire, with his face and hands clean, and his hair brushed, it was difficult to *imagine* that he was the same boy.

He now looked quite handsome, and might readily have been taken for a young gentleman, except that his hands were red and grimy.

"Look at yourself," said Frank, leading him before the mirror.

"By gracious!" said Dick, staring back in astonishment, "that isn't me, is it?"

"Don't you know yourself?" asked Frank, smiling.

"It reminds me of Cinderella," said Dick.

—*Ragged Dick*

L IKE the new suit of clothes for his astonished hero, the appearance of *Ragged Dick* in book form in 1868—a shorter version had run serially the previous year in a periodical for schoolchildren—inaugurated a "new life" for its author, Horatio Alger Jr. Two years earlier Alger's luck had hit rock-bottom, his identity as a gentleman called into question. Born in 1832 the son of a cultivated and earnest Unitarian minister in Marlborough, a small town

First published as an introduction to *Ragged Dick: Or, Street Life in New York with the Boot Blacks* by Horatio Alger, Jr. (New York: Signet Classics, 1990), pp. v–xx.

near Boston, Alger had dreamed of living by his pen. He entered Harvard College in 1848, contributed to student literary journals, won prizes, was chosen class odist, and graduated in 1852 eighth in his class. Writing, editing, and teaching occupied him for a few years, and he enjoyed some success placing moral essays and sentimental tales and poems in the liberal Unitarian press and in such esteemed journals as the *North American Review* and *Harper's Monthly*. But earnings were slight, and to supplement his income he turned to divinity—a disastrous move, as it happened, for in 1866 he was accused of (and did not deny) performing "unnatural" acts with several boys in his congregation in Brewster, Massachusetts.

Alger fled to New York, narrowly escaping prosecution by pledging, through the good offices of his father, never again to seek or accept a ministry. Alone in the big city he pulled himself together, it seems, by composing *Ragged Dick*—a story of the metamorphosis of an undeservedly outcast boy into a "quite handsome . . . young gentleman." The book launched him in a new direction, not toward lavish success—*Ragged Dick* would be his only best seller—but toward at least a regular, reliable career as a writer. He had found a marketable identity. Henceforth this mild-tempered, bookish, pink-skinned, and very petit (his mature height was five feet two inches) son of the same New England tradition that produced Ralph Waldo Emerson and Harriet Beecher Stowe would win fame and fortune (both more modest than commonly believed) as a writer of "stories for boys."

The material facts of Alger's writing career cannot be stressed enough. The name Horatio Alger has come down to us as *the* synonym for capitalist ideology. We still think of him as an "apostle of the self-made man," a true believer in "pluck and luck," "rags to riches," "bound to rise," and so on. But as critics and historians now recognize, this simplisitic view of Alger is based on a misconception of his motives, message, and literary methods. Moreover, the stereotype deflects attention from the primary fact of his career: before anything else he was a professional *writer*, a producer for a market, a competitor with other private entrepreneurs for the rewards of literary commerce. Not so much the ideology but the *actuality* of a literary producer's self-interest lay behind his decision to write the works by which his name became one of America's most potent, yet little understood, household words.

Those rewards—prestige bestowed by reviewers as much as cash earned by publishers' advances and royalties—were undergoing vast change during Alger's career in the last three decades of the nineteenth century (he died in 1899). Like other industries, American publishing emerged from the war years a big business; serious fortunes were to be made in the line of books and magazines. Technology provided one impetus—steam-driven presses for mass production of print commodities; railroad lines reaching untapped markets. Like other manufacturers, publishers learned the secrets of "marketing," tailoring products to specific consumers. The literary market became segmented and stratified not only by categories of gender, age, vocation, levels of education, and region, but also by cultural status—calibrated distinctions of prestige conferred by reviewers, critics, ministers, teachers. Any writer who counted on writing for a living, Henry James and Mark Twain no less than Horatio Alger, understood the fine points of the system, especially the nexus between rewards of reputation and of cash.

Just as he was decidedly not the single-minded ideologue for acquisitive capitalism he has been made out to be—a careful reading of *Ragged Dick* makes that clear—Alger was no fool about the business of writing. His choice of a vocation as author of "stories for boys" was just that: a choice dictated by market conditions he had already, by 1868, spent almost two decades testing. "When I began to write for publication," he explained in an article titled "Writing Stories for Boys" for *The Writer: A Monthly Magazine for Literary Workers* in 1896,

> it was far from my expectation that I should devote my life to writing stories for boys. I was ambitious, rather, to write for adults, and for a few years I contributed to such periodicals as *Harper's Magazine*, *Harper's Weekly*, *Putnam's Magazine*, and a variety of literary weeklies. I achieved a fair success, but I could see that I had so many competitors that it would take a long time to acquire a reputation. One day I selected a plot for a two-column sketch for *Harper's*. It was during the war. Thinking the matter

over, it occurred to me that it would be a good plot for a juvenile book. I sat down at once and wrote to A. K. Loring, of Boston, at that time a publisher in only a small way, detailing the plot and asking if he would encourage me to write a juvenile book. He answered: "Go ahead, and if I don't publish it, some other publisher will." In three months I put in his hands the manuscript of "Frank's Campaign." This story was well received, but it was not till I removed to New York and wrote "Ragged Dick" that I scored a decided success. . . . I soon found reason to believe that I was much more likely to achieve success as a writer for boys than as a writer for adults. I therefore confined myself to juvenile writing.

Stalled by only "fair success" in the high-prestige circle of *Harper's* and *Putnam's*—fourteen dollars was all he got for an essay in *North American Review*—Alger tried another product for another set of customers.

Of course this is not the whole story behind his "confining" himself (he well understood what this meant as far as literary reputation goes) to juveniles—a commitment, in his case, as much to actual youngsters (he would surround himself with companions among the young "street-Arabs" of New York and supported some of them) as to a genre and a style of writing. The choice of popular authorship was not, to be sure, merely cynical calculation but showed a practical prudence similar to that of Ragged Dick: "for in the street-life of the metropolis a boy needs to be on the alert, and have all his wits about him, or he will find himself wholly distanced by his more enterprising competitors for popular favor." Exactly Alger's own predicament as a writer courting "favor" of readers. "A writer for boys should have an abundant sympathy for them," he wrote in 1896. "He should be able to enter into their plans, hopes, and aspirations"—in short, *identify* with his desired readers, put himself in their place. "It seems to me that no writer should undertake to write for boys who does not feel that he has been called to that particular work," Alger wrote in *The Writer*.

In *Ragged Dick* Horatio Alger discovered not only a formula for literary success within a limited literary market but also a personal gift, a calling for just such stories, and a role in which he might continue to love boys without overt passional indiscretion. He learned to consult the "boy" in himself, to transmute and recast himself—his genteel culture, his liberal patrician sympathy for underdogs, his shaky economic status as an author, and not least, his dangerous erotic attraction to boys—into his juvenile fiction.

It is impossible to know whether Alger actually lived a double life, closeted as a secret homosexual. But there are hints that the male companionship he describes as a refuge from the streets—the cozy domestic arrangements between Dick and Fosdick, for example—may also have been an erotic relationship, or at least physically close enough so that the few instances of boys touching each other tenderly, or older men laying a light hand on the shoulder of boys, might arouse erotic wishes in readers prepared to entertain such fantasies. Nothing prurient appears in *Ragged Dick*, but the vision of happiness in Dick's safe harbor with Fosdick, and the allure of the good-looking youngsters for kindly older men—images that project Alger's critique of the same aggressive individualism he is supposed to have celebrated—may also imply a positive view of homoeroticism as an alternative way of life, a way of living by sympathy rather than by aggression. In any case, in *Ragged Dick* we see Alger plotting domestic romance, complete with a surrogate marriage of two homeless boys, as the setting for his formulaic metamorphosis of an outcast street boy into a self-respecting citizen.

Historians have given more attention to the formula than to the personal elements in Alger's fiction. In shaping the pattern that would serve as template for the rest of his career, Alger drew on a number of popular sources—didactic children's books, popular since the 1830s (the Rollo books of Jacob Abbott, for example), with their homilies about frugality and piety; stories, common in the 1850s, of poor city youths, newsboys and bootblacks, rising to fame and fortune. These sentimental romances with overlapping plots included a goodly amount of adventure and detection thrown in. Alger did not invent his formula but boiled down the conventions to make a more refined brew, with a style accessible both to young and to adult readers; clever dialogue and vivid descriptions; characters representing a range of moral positions; a physical setting itself part of the action. Alger also incorporated the conventions of city guidebooks, including their advice about confidence games, cheats, and crooks. *Ragged Dick* takes place in actual New York spaces, in definite streets and buildings, streetcars and ferryboats.

Like any genre writing, the Alger formula is a kind of machine; each story reproduces all the others. Like other mass-market writers, Alger conceived his books in series or cycles, with the same characters recurring in successive stories, sometimes under different names and guises. In effect Alger told the same story in his hundred-odd novels. Part of what is meant by "hack" is just this practice of rearranging fixed component parts. But repeatability is also a feature of folktales, legends, and myths. Stories of gods and larger-than-life persons like Paul Bunyan have an anecdotal quality similar to the sequence of encounters, adventures, confrontations, and coincidences that comprise the narratives of Ragged Dick and Tattered Tom and their kin among Alger's legion of boy heroes.

"Alger is to America what Homer was to the Greeks," wrote the novelist Nathanael West. West means that the core story of "poor boys who make good" comes from the heart of America; Alger gave it classic form. It matters little whether his stories can be believed; like Homer's, they people the imagination with figures immune from skepticism and disbelief. In *A Cool Million* (1934) West brilliantly parodied the formula in a way that honors its power even as it devastates its tragic naïveté. For West the mythic aspect of the Alger story lies in its sublime indifference to obstacles, to all the dense obstructions to desire that the daily newspaper or naturalist novels like Dreiser's report. But repetitive form counts as much as this content. The power to arouse and sustain disbelief is equally a function of the recurring forms of Alger's fictions.

Doubtless a large part of Alger's effect does lie in his repetitiveness, his faithfully recharging the same battery. But Alger's first boy's novel, *Ragged Dick*, retains the freshness of a beginning, the start of something. And this work better than others puts misconceptions to rest. Rather than great wealth and high social position, Ragged Dick and his friends desire much simpler things—a steady job, a decent place to sleep, a suit of clothing, respect from others. The wish for self-improvement is satisfied by modest jobs as clerks and office boys, by the opportunity to wash one's face every day, save one's earnings, plan for the future. The didactic lessons taught by the Alger narrator have less to do with the sharp-dealing and tooth-and-claw practices of the Jim Fiskes and Daniel Drews in the actual business world of the late 1860s than with simple self-respect. For Alger bourgeois life means security, comfort, cultivation, companionship, responsibility—the reverse of cut-throat competitiveness. He wants his boys to read and write, to look neat and speak well, to show kindness to younger children and old people. He also wants them to take pleasure in watching the interest on their savings accounts grow little by little—but this is always a means to the end of self-respect.

There is a lesson for adult readers as well. The 1868 edition of *Ragged Dick* carried the revealing subtitle: *or, Street Life in New York with the Bootblacks*. In his preface Alger addressed the social theme implicit in the full title:

> The author hopes that, while volumes in this series may prove interesting as stories, they may also have the effect of enlisting the sympathies of his readers in behalf of the unfortunate children whose life is described, and of leading them to co-operate with the praiseworthy effort now making [*sic*] by the Children's Aid Society and other organizations to ameliorate their condition.

These children, he wrote in the preface to the final book in the Ragged Dick series, *Rufus and Rose* (1870), are the "material out of which good citizens may be made, if the right influences are brought to bear upon them. In every case, therefore, the author has led his hero, step by step, from vagabondage to a position of respectability."

More important than individual success, then, is communal redemption, the making of "good citizens." Alger's stories, particularly the Ragged Dick ones, openly mention and support such charitable institutions as the Children's Aid Society and the Newsboys' Lodging House, which provided not just shelter and food but also moral instruction to homeless and working street children. As Charles Loring Brace,

who founded the Children's Aid Society in 1853, put it in the introduction to his *The Dangerous Classes of New York and Twenty Years' Work Among
Them* (1872), the aim was to "draw them [homeless children] under the
influence of the moral and fortunate classes, that they shall grow up as
useful producers and members of society," to redeem "the abandoned
and destitute youth of our large towns" as a prevention against crime,
anarchy, and possible uprisings by "the proletaires." Brace described
his book as consisting of "little stories of the lot of the poor in cities"
and offered the hope that "incidents related of their trials and tempta-
tions, may bring the two ends of society nearer together in human
sympathy." As his own prefaces make clear, Alger entertained a similar
hope for his stories, that they might do good by closing social gaps between rich and poor, adult and child.

One way of accomplishing this was to make his ragged boys attractive, good-looking, and instinctively well behaved. Dick may have certain faults—he smokes, gambles, speaks ungrammatically—but he is
not one of the dangerous kind, is really one of us: "He was above doing anything mean or dishonorable. He would not steal, or cheat, or
impose upon younger boys, but was frank and straight-forward, manly
and self-reliant. His nature was a noble one, and had saved him from
all mean faults." Making his hero so eminently redeemable, Alger redeems his reader as well, by offering an occasion for an act of sympathy across class boundaries hardening so visibily and dangerously on
New York streets in the post–Civil War era. Moreover, just as Dick
looks up to genteel models like Frank Whitney and his father, so there
is something to be learned from Dick. The action of the book can be
seen as an interlocking series of exchanges. While Dick learns about
gentility, Frank learns how to cross busy streets, what sights to see, how
to avoid the traps set for the unwary by New York's cheats and
swindlers. Both gain in the exchange, and the adult reader learns a lesson in expanded social sympathy.

"I ain't knocked round the city streets all my life for nothin.'" Dick
has a distinct tone of voice—worldly, rough edged, colorful, often bit-
ingly sarcastic—a voice that, like his red and grimy hands, betrays his
street identity even in his "new attire." "That's the misfortun' of being
rich. Astor and me don't sleep much for fear of burglars breakin' in

and robbin' us of our valooable traesures.' " He sees through the disguises of street life, can meet threats with a nimble sidestep that throws Mickey off balance, or can play dumb in order to trap Travis. Fast talking, quick to meet a jibe with a better one, he himself is part of the continuous drama of street life, its star performer. And his steady flow of wit has one major constant typified by the glaring discrepancy between himself in his rags and Astor in his mansion. Dick is a satirist, whose deadpan account of "Demon of the Danube," the "great play at the Old Bowery now," compares well with one of Mark Twain's deflations of sentimental and blood-and-thunder romance in the voice of Huck Finn.

But Dick is destined to lose these verbal powers, to surrender them at the altar of respectability whence he is conducted by Alger's plot. Ragged, he charms; in smart clothes (especially in the later books), he can be a prig. To justify so appealing a street boy Alger makes him not only savvy but "noble." For Alger has an ideological as well as an erotic muse to serve, and Dick is finally a vehicle for a social vision.

> He was a thorough democrat, using the word not politically, but
> in its proper sense, and was disposed to fraternize with all whom
> he styled "good fellows," without regard to their position. It may
> seem a little unnecessary to some of my readers to make this ex-
> planation; but they must remember that pride and "big feeling"
> are confined to no age or class, but may be found in boys as well
> as men, and in boot-blacks as well as those of a higher rank.

Alger presents Dick to the adult reader, presumed to be of a superior social class, as an object of respect as much as affection. For respecting Dick can bring out the democrat in us, teach us a lesson in fairness, in fraternalism. Alger cannot be accused of patronizing his working-class hero, and that is admirable. But Dick cannot remain as he is. To justify himself as worthy of the respect of readers, he must undergo the self-imposed ritual of "improvement." What we see in the mirror through his eyes, in his "new attire," is our own "respectable" image—ourselves idealized in the guise of a reformed Dick. Dick's fate in Alger's plot is to change, to metamorphose, as much for the reader as for himself.

For unlike writers of the city "mysteries," Alger is little interested in actual poverty except as the ground on which metamorphosis occurs. Not poverty but its opposite is the mystery Alger confronts: the interior places of the bourgeois city, the downtown counting rooms and Fifth Avenue drawing rooms to which his outcasts aspire. While his deepest ambition for his boys is not wealth as such but the security of a good name and a steady income, nevertheless Alger constructs his world on the foundation of money, the hard cash that can transform desire into goods, bootblacks into clerks, Ragged Dick into Richard Hunter, Esquire (we ought not miss the hint of irony in Dick's voice as he adds the title to his name). Like other genteel patricians Alger disdained finance capitalism and makes Dick "too sensible not to know that there was something more than money needed to win a respectable position in the world." His benevolent adults are not industrialists or financiers, but come from the older and already passing merchant class. They are educated, gentle, sympathetic to youngsters, and manly. The explicit argument of *Ragged Dick* is that a streetwise bootblack might well have in him, like a chrysalis, the makings of just such a figure, for in most important regards (excepting education and incentive) Dick already possesses the requisite character traits.

The first step toward realizing the potential is self-respect. The lesson comes from genteel bourgeois spokesmen such as Mr. Whitney, who himself had started as a printer's apprentice, worked on a farm, and won his fortune by inventing a machine. He tells Dick, " 'All labor is respectable, my lad, and you have no cause to be ashamed of any honest business.' " He also advises him to develop " 'a taste for reading and study' "—not just as an economic utility but an end in itself: " 'My studious habits paid me in money, as well as in another way.' " Until something better comes along, he urges Dick, " 'Earn your living in the way you are accustomed to, avoid extravagance, and save up a little money if you can.' " " 'It's an honest business,' " another model adult tells Dick—"a sensible man and a worthy citizen" who happens to be a policeman. " 'Stick to it till you get something better.' "

The lesson for bootlacks and other poor kids might be translated as follows: "keep the peace, follow the law, curb your instincts, replace anger with tranquility, despair and resentment with the hope of 'something better.' " While Alger clearly disapproves of unbridled individualism, the virtues he advocates are hardly unconventional or antibourgeois: honesty, thrift, obedience. His world remains under the eye of the Protestant ethic, with the emphasis falling on benevolence and friendship more than on competition, striving, and aggression. Self-denial remains the great underlying principle—denial of immediate pleasures like the Old Bowery theater, cigars, an oyster stew, an occasional game of chance—for the sake of future goods. Because he has reformed his spendthrift habits and banked a few dollars, Dick can help his friend Tom Wilkins pay the rent—a "generous and disinterested action." The narrator draws the lesson: "In more ways than one Dick was beginning to reap the advantage of his self-denial and judicious economy."

Judicious economy is key in Alger's imagined world. It represents his effort to secularize the mystery of money, to bring it under the rational control of human will. Savings "earn" interest (a mystery in itself that even knowledge of arithmetic cannot explain), which then becomes discretionary income Dick can spend on doing good, thereby exchanging potential capital for the more valuable (exchangeable) good of self-approval—a step toward attainment of the highest good: respectability. Thus Alger transfigures capitalist investment from an economic into a moral act: Dick exchanges the unearned increment of his savings (interest) into a gift that then earns him an intangible but real increment of moral value, in turn marketable as "respectability." There may be something more than money needed to win a respectable position in the world, but that something resembles nothing so much as money itself.

Even if Dick's motives derive from elsewhere—his innate belief in Christian charity and fellowship, not to say his erotic attachment to his fellows—the logic of his behavior follows from capitalism, which helps to account for the most transparent device of Alger's plots: the role of luck. In one sense the Alger luck is no more than a heavy (and heavy-handed) dose of those coincidences by which narratives as such make their way through the world's dangers and pitfalls. Plots depend on coincidence—the unexpected but convenient discovery of an old letter, an accidental meeting that turns out to be fateful. Coincidence is the secular storyteller's magic, the surrogate of providence. If we cannot call it God's will, we call it luck. Alger has his own brand of luck—nothing supernatural or extraterrestrial but as normal in his world as the interest that unaccountably accumulates in Dick's savings account. Luck and money run together in Alger's world, two ways of explaining another mystery: the presence of social divisions, classes of poor and rich, propertied and propertyless. How did the world get this way? " 'Remember that your future position depends mainly upon yourself, and that it will be high or low as you choose to make it.' " Mr. Whitney's voice of bourgeois confidence bolsters Dick's resolve to "improve" himself, and it is Alger's task to make the homily seem reasonable. "*Mainly* upon yourself" offers an escape hatch, however, for the unspoken fact of Alger's world is that "yourself" alone is not enough to depend upon—that "future position" depends entirely on unlooked-for help from benefactors (older men) who appear on the scene, like the merchant James Rockwell on the ferry with his clumsy little boy, by sheer chance. Unable to explain social divisions by personal virtue alone, Alger explains them away by the device of luck.

Luck serves in Alger's stories as the sign of everything inexplicable in Dick's world: the coexistence of Mott Street and Fifth Avenue, of homes and prisons, of churches and banks; why some boys make it and others do not. And at the heart of the story sits the graven mystery of money: how it reproduces itself, remakes identities, transforms Ragged Dick into Richard Hunter. Of course it runs against Alger's genteel grain that money might rule without challenge. "But Dick had gained something more valuable than money," he writes about the boy's exemplary study habits. Money is not everything, but it *is* something. Luck allows Alger to insinuate a force superior even to money—though it amounts to the same inexplicable thing.

Luck can be seen finally as a defense mechanism within the unconscious of Alger's fiction, defense against the sundry threats of the city—the unwashed Irish bully Mickey Maguire (even he will be redeemed in a later novel) and the cowardly thief Jim Travis—and the less palpable threat of money begetting money and becoming an all-consuming end in itself. Alger's skill lies in making this wish fulfillment seem credible or desirable (which amounts to the same thing) for the duration of the tale. The real magic and charm of *Ragged Dick* lie in the way the narrative makes money and desire coincide. There is something fabulous and otherworldly about such consistency. In Horatio Alger's world, once mistaken by countless readers young and old for America itself, all good wishes come true.

NINE

THE FORM OF FREEDOM IN *ADVENTURES OF HUCKLEBERRY FINN*

ERTAIN literary works accumulate an aura that possesses the reader before he ventures into reading itself; it gives him a readiness to respond and a set of expectations to guide his response. Who has come to *Adventures of Huckleberry Finn* free of associations, even of some intimacy with characters and episodes? An aura can be considered a mediation that situates the book and guides the reader toward an available interpretation. Books like *Huckleberry Finn* can be powerfully predetermined experiences; the reader encounters them, especially at certain stages of their career, from deep within the culture shared by reader, author, and work. How any book achieves an aura is a problem for the historian of culture: a book's career implicates the history of its readers.

Huckleberry Finn became a cultural object of special intensity during a period after World War II when many Americans seized upon literary experiences as alternatives to an increasingly confining present. Mark Twain's idyll seemed to project an answerable image—an image of wise innocence in conflict with corruption, of natural man achieving independence of a depraved society. It seemed to project an image, in short, of freedom. But not freedom in the abstract; the values of the book were seen by readers as the precise negation of all the forces felt

First published in *The Southern Review* 6 (Autumn 1970): 954–71.

as oppressive in the 1950s. Common to the several major interpretations of the book was one absolute theme, that the book's most prominent meanings were, as Henry Nash Smith wrote, "against stupid conformity and for the autonomy of the individual." Autonomy vs. conformity: the terms condense a memorable passage of recent American history. The conception of freedom and individualism that pervades the criticism reveals as much of the subliminal concerns of the critics as it does the themes of the book and should be understood in light of the political and social anxieties of the postwar period.

But does *Huckleberry Finn* deserve its celebration as a testimony to freedom? What exact place does freedom have among the book's themes? To say that a theme does not exist apart from its verbal matrix may seem commonplace. But criticism has often addressed itself to extractable elements in this novel such as imagery, symbol, and episode rather than to the total and continuous verbal performance. Granted, the book's susceptibility to a variety of readings—its ability to come apart into separate scenes and passages that affect us independent of the continuous narrative—is a mark of strength. But a firm grip upon the complete and total text is necessary to understand the form freedom takes in the book.

We want first to locate the problem implied by "autonomy" and "conformity," the problem of freedom, within the text, and if possible, to identify the thematic problem with a formal problem. In the broadest sense, the theme of freedom begins to engage us at the outset: Huck feels cramped and confined in his new condition as ward of Widow Douglas and closet neophyte of Miss Watson. The early episodes with Tom Sawyer add a complicating paradox: to enjoy the freedom of being "bad"—joining Tom's gang—Huck must submit himself to his adopted household and appear "respectable." With Pap's arrival the paradox is reversed; now he can enjoy his former freedom to lounge and choose his time, but the expense is a confinement even more threatening, a virtual imprisonment. The only release is escape, flight, and effacement of the identity through which both town and Pap oppress him; he can resume autonomy only by assuming "death" for his name.

In brief and general terms, such is the inner logic of the theme of freedom as we arrive at the Jackson Island episode. With Jim's appearance as a runaway slave a new and decisive development begins. We now have two runaways, and their conjunction generates the rest of the narrative, deepens the theme, and forces nuances to the surface. Jim's situation is both simpler and more urgent than Huck's. His freedom is no more or less than escape from bondage, escape to free territory. He expects there to assume what is denied him in slave society, his identity as an adult man, husband, and father. The fact that the reader is made to share this expectation with Jim, that the novel does not allow us to anticipate a reversal of hope if Jim reaches free territory, is important; as readers we are freed of normal historical ambiguities in order to accept as a powerful given the possibility of fulfilled freedom for Jim. Thus by confining the action to the area of slave society, Mark Twain compels us (at the expense of historical accuracy, perhaps) to imagine the boundary between "slave" and "free" as real and unequivocal, and to accept that boundary as the definition of Jim's plight: on one side, enslaved; on the other, free.

Jim presents himself, then, unencumbered by the paradoxes of Huck's problem: to be free, to possess himself, to reveal a firm identity—these will be equal consequences of the single act of crossing the border. The effect of such a simplifying and unambiguous presence in the book is, first, to bring into relief the more subtle forms of denial of freedom, forms that cannot be overcome by simple geographical relocation, and second, to force Huck, once the boy commits himself to the slave, into a personal contradiction. Jim can say, as soon as he escapes from Miss Watson, "I owns myself," while Huck is still "owned" by the official values supervised by his "conscience." Once Jim's freedom becomes Huck's problem, the boy finds himself at odds with what Mark Twain called his "deformed conscience." Huck's "sound heart" may respond to Jim's desire to recover his humanity at the border, but his conscience wants to repress that response.

In light of this conflict, implicit in Huck's words at the end of Chapter 11, "They're after us!" what would constitute freedom for Huck? Clearly, getting Jim to the free states would not be enough. He would need to free himself of moral deformity before he too can say "I owns myself." Just as clearly neither issue is resolved in the novel. And the book's indecision is reflected in criticism. The controversies regarding the "Evasion" at the Phelps farm need not be reviewed here, but it is useful to point out that the question of the ending eventually becomes a question of *form*, of judgment about the book's unity of tone and intention. Those who wish for Jim's release through a heroic act by Huck tend to feel the ending flawed, and those who wish for Huck's escape from all consciences, including a "good" abolitionist conscience, tend to accept the ending. In either case the burden of both meaning and form has fallen on the question of unity, of the wholeness of the narrative as a patterned action.

The question of unity is, however, only one of the formal problems of the book. If form is understood as the shape given to the reader's consciousness, as the unique engagement the text makes available, criticism might profit by an account of that engagement, of the reader's participation in the book's flow of words. And from this point of view the first fact we encounter is that the book is the speech of a single voice. At the outset we learn that Huck is teller as well as actor, that we are listeners as well as witnesses of action.

Reading begins by acceding to the demands of the voice. "You don't know about me," Huck begins, and his accents identify him immediately as a recognizable type, a Western or frontier speaker whose vernacular diction and syntax stand for a typology that includes dress and posture along with characteristic verbal strategies. Huck asks to be heard, as if he faced a live audience from a stage. The first-edition frontispiece has him posing with a smile for the reader, in rags and tatters, the familiar long-barreled rifle in hand; the bow and flourish in the concluding illustration confirms the quasi-theatrical stance. Huck appears before us, at least in part, within the conventions of an oral tradition. But if Huck is by convention a storyteller, Mark Twain is at the same time a novelist, a maker of a book that asks to be read as "literature" even if its mode is in some ways preliterary.

The book is born for us under the aegis of a dual tradition, a dual vision of art. The dualities are not always in accord with each other, and some tensions between an oral and a written, especially a "high" or sophisticated tradition, account for technical problems, problems that, I mean to show, bear on the theme of freedom. The book is marked by an uneasy accommodation between seriously differing modes of literary art. Before I detail some of these, it is worth commenting that the pressure to fuse a vernacular verbal style and its methods of narrative with an accepted form of "literature"—a book-length fiction—characterized all of Mark Twain's mature work. As Justin Kaplan has made clear, Clemens's career contained many unresolved tensions and ambivalences, and none had more consequence for his work than his simultaneous though uneven commitment to two kinds of audience. On the one hand he saw himself as popular spokesman for a vast, nonliterary readership. "My audience is dumb," he wrote, "it has no voice in print." He claimed "the Belly and the Members" as his people, not the "thin top crust of humanity," and insisted, not without defensiveness, that it was unfair to judge his work by "the cultivated-class standard." At the same time that standard appealed to him, and even if his paranoia before it represented social as well as literary anxieties, he did bow toward the established conception of "literature" held by readers of *The Atlantic Monthly*. "*It* is the only audience that I sit down before in complete serenity," he confessed. Writing books that resemble novels is one capitulation to that audience, while marketing his books through the subscription system kept him in touch with his large "dumb" audience.

Even as an "author," however, Mark Twain clung to his root notion of literary art as a performance by a speaking character, usually a non-literary figure with a calculatedly vernacular voice. Such a figure—Simon Wheeler in "Jumping Frog" is a good instance—characteristically deflates expectations and values associated with the "cultivated-class standard." But he does so on behalf of a standard of "common sense," of common and humble humanity. Rather than pose one class standard against another, the vernacular tradition in American humor offers a universal standard, open to all, skeptical of hierarchies, self-evident in its truths. Through a fusion of vernacular values with "literature," Mark Twain strived to achieve exactly such a universal, classless appeal. "I can't stand George Eliot, & Hawthorne & those people," he wrote to Howells in 1885; their "labored & tedious analyses of feeling & motives" were suspiciously aristocratic. Instead he preferred Howells's own *Indian Summer*. "It is a beautiful story, & makes a body laugh all the time, & cry inside." This describes just the kind of response he wished from his own readers: direct and uncomplicated and moving.

What better means did he have toward this end than to create vernacular characters unencumbered by analysis or excessive introspection, whose universality was obvious to every reader? Matching his manner of creation to his self-conception as a popular writer, Clemens seemed always more comfortable inventing such characters than filling out complete books or imagining narrative actions. He might even be better considered a maker of figures, like Huck and Tom and Jim, and "Mark Twain," who populate a general fictional realm unconfined by specific verbal contexts, than a maker of particular books. The tendency of his characters to live in the mind apart from their texts is a revealing feature of Clemens's talent.

But our aim is to hold the characters fast within their verbal settings. Transforming an oral art to a written one presented Mark Twain with difficulties apparent in almost all his long narratives. Consider the matter of filling out a book that wants to be the "adventures" of a vernacular voice. One difficulty is simply how to bring such a book to a close. The ending of *Huckleberry Finn* does, to be sure, bring the action to a point of general resolution: Jim is freed, masks are stripped away, misunderstandings are cleared up, some sort of order is restored. But the loose plot that calls for resolution has been kept out of sight during much of the narrative, and we cannot avoid feeling that the plain duration of the book has depended more upon the arbitrary postponement of any event (such as the recapture of Jim) that might end things too soon than upon an inner logic of plot. The only conclusive ending is the drop of the curtain, the final words, "The End. Yours Truly, Huck Finn," and silence. The performance of Huck's voice does not so much complete itself as exhaust itself.

To begin with, then, the problem of the ending is a technical problem of *an* ending. The source of the problem is the attempt to accommodate the opening convention of a vernacular storyteller, whose story simply unwinds, to the imperatives of a book-length written narrative. But the ending is a relatively minor matter. Of more consequence are the pressures upon the narrative voice through the entire course of its performance. An enormous burden is placed upon Huck, who must not only tell the story but enact it as the leading player. My discussion focuses on this double role, assessing Huck's role in articulating the narrative in order to assess his role as a character within the narrative. What freedom means in the book, and what form freedom takes, cannot be understood without such an assessment.

What part of Huck's life in the book derives from the inner necessities of his "character," and what part derives from the outer necessities of his role as speaking voice? Huck has precisely the split identity this question implies. The consequent tensions within the narrative have been obscured in criticism by the great attention given to "identity" as a theme. The pervasive deployment of disguises, verbal and sartorial, through which Huck extricates himself from tight spots alerts the reader to the significance of hidden and revealed identities. When Huck is taken for Tom Sawyer in Chapter 32, he accepts the name with relief (it saves him the trouble of having to invent yet another name), "for it was like being born again, I was so glad to find out who I was." The line follows one of Huck's meditations on death, and some critics have been moved to discover a pattern of death and rebirth throughout, a pattern in which Huck's true name finds protection in the "death" of assumed identities. The motif is familiar in oral literature (see the excised "Raftsmen" passage), and the fact that Huck is legally dead through most of the book adds suggestive weight. At least as long as Pap lives, and as long as Huck is associated with Jim's escape, it seems impossible for the boy to own up to his true identity. The motif of disguise thus seems to harbor a dilemma directly related to the question of freedom: is it possible for Huck to both show and be his true self? To show himself as a runaway who has faked his own death and is aiding an escaped slave would invite disaster. This is a given of the narrative: to be himself Huck must hide himself.

What are the sources of this commanding paradox? Social reality, for one: Miss Watson, Pap, slavery, general avariciousness, all constitute an environment of treachery. Some critics argue too that the need to hide derives from deep psychic needs, from the extreme vulnerability expressed in Huck's character, especially his recurrent feelings of guilt. In this view, colored by psychoanalytic rhetoric, Huck's disguises represent a shrewd reality principle that acts to protect the very shaky equilibrium of his inner life, the life of a "lost" boy who prefers the pleasure of a precivilized and precharacterological state of nature. This is a compelling and widely held view of Huck. "You feel mighty free and easy and comfortable on a raft." Pleasurable drift and unruffled harmony seem the conditions Huck demands for "free and easy" selfhood.

The issue is subtle and difficult. Do Huck's traits derive in fact from an inner life at odds with social necessity, or from, I want to add, imperatives of his role as narrator? Obviously we need not make an either/or choice. But the second alternative has been so little present in criticism it is worth considering at some length. The crux of the matter is whether Huck presents a consistent character, whether a sentient inner life is always present. Some critics have suggested not. Richard Poirier finds that after his reversal of attitude toward Jim in Chapter 15 (the "trash" episode) and the defeat of his "white" conscience in Chapter 16, Huck gradually disappears as an active agent in the narrative. Unable to continue the developing consciousness implicit in these scenes, Poirier argues, Mark Twain became absorbed in sheer "social panorama," to which Huck is a more or less passive witness. Henry Nash Smith makes a similar point. After losing Cairo in the fog, and losing the raft in Chapter 16, Mark Twain set aside the manuscript, and when he resumed several years later, he "now launched into a satiric description of the society of the prewar South." Huck becomes Mark Twain's satiric mask, which prevents him, Smith argues, from developing in his own right.

These are promising hints regarding Huck's status as a fictional character. Of course any criticism that charges Mark Twain with failing to continue a developing consciousness assumes such a development is a hallmark of fictional character. It might be countered that such a standard is inappropriate to this book, as Clemens himself may have suggested in his attack on the "cultivated-class standard," or that Huck's so-called disappearance in the middle section is actually another disguise, profoundly enforced by an increasingly hostile setting. His retreat, then, after the Grangerford episode, might be consistent with what had already developed as his character.

Even to begin to discuss this issue we need to understand what we mean by a "fictional character." Our expectations derive from the novelistic tradition, in which character and action have a coextensive identity. Henry James insisted in "The Art of Fiction" (consider the differences implied between this and the title of Mark Twain's comparable essay, "How to Tell a Story") upon the inseparability of character and action by describing the novel as "a living thing, all one and continuous, like any other organism." "What is character," he wrote, "but the determination of incident? What is incident but the illustration of character?" The reciprocity of character and action implies, moreover, a process, a twofold development in which character fulfills itself just as it reveals itself to the reader. By development we expect a filling out, a discovery of possibilities and limitations. We also expect a certain degree of self-reflectiveness in character to register what is happening internally.

We need not remind ourselves that *Huckleberry Finn* is not a Jamesian novel. But it is important to know what sort of novel it is, to know what to expect of Huck as a character. What happens to Huck in the course of the narrative? Is he a changed being at the end from what he was at the beginning? In the opening scene Huck chafes at the "dismal regular and decent" routine of Widow Douglas, says he can't stand it "no longer," and "lights out" to his old rags and hogshead and "was free and satisfied." He returns only to qualify for Tom's gang. At the end of the book he again "lights out," this time for "howling adventures amongst the Injuns, over in the Territory." Has anything changed? The final words rejecting civilization, this time Aunt Sally's, do seem to register a difference: "I been there before." These are precious words for the reader; they confirm what he has discovered about civilization. But do they mean the same thing to Huck?

The difference we want to feel between the two rejections of civilization that frame the book parallels the indisputable difference between the two instances when Huck decides to go to hell rather than obey moral conscience. In Chapter 1, Miss Watson tries to frighten the child into sitting up straight by preaching about the bad place and what is in store for boys who don't behave. Huck retorts that he wishes he were there; if Miss Watson is heading for heaven, he would rather not try for it. In Chapter 31, in Huck's famous struggle with his conscience, this comedy of inverted values recurs, but with much expanded significance. In the first instance the preference for hell is expressed in a raffish, offhanded manner; it is a joke, not a serious commitment. In Chapter 31, in a much analyzed passage, we witness a genuine choice, preceded by an inward struggle. The language, first of self-condemnation ("here was the plain hand of Providence slapping me in the face"), then of self-reproach ("and he was so grateful, and said I was the best friend old Jim ever had in the world, and the *only* one he's got now"), externalizes the opposite perspectives of sound heart and deformed conscience. The feat of language itself convinces us that Huck has now earned a meaningful damnation on behalf of his friendship with Jim. This episode has a structure of modulated feeling entirely missing in the first case. Moreover the much deeper implications for Huck's freedom in the second instance are affected by the location of the moment in the narrative, after the exposure of greed, corruption, hypocrisy, and violence in the river society. If the Grangerfords and all the others name heaven as their goal, then hell is by far a better aspiration. Huck's decisive words, "All right, then, I'll *go* to hell," are a release for the reader, for he too has been in "a close place." The line affirms Huck's fundamental rightness.

The deepened implications of "I'll go to hell" and "I been there before," implications that have led critics to impute to Huck a self-generated liberation from moral deformity, arise from the context of narrative action. But does Huck actually catch the same implications? Does he know and understand exactly what he is saying? Of course we might argue that the implications are finally comic precisely because Huck does not understand them. But if this is the case, can we also say that he is a conscious character? If we cannot believe that Huck shows himself just at the moment when we most approve of his words, then we necessarily claim we are superior to him. We fix him in an ironic relation to his own words: he says more than he knows. But then again, does he not by nature *feel* rather than think? If we say so, if we excuse him from an intellectual act we perform, then are we not exploiting our sense of superiority and condescending toward him? Of course Huck is clearly mindful of the seriousness of his impasse, that he is deciding "forever, betwixt two things." Even earlier in the narrative, however, Huck had settled moral dilemmas by choosing what to him is the easiest, most comfortable course; we approve his choices and smile at his handy rationalizations (some of which he learns from Pap). A similar pattern finally emerges in Chapter 31; after his "awful thoughts, and awful words" about hell, he "shoved the whole thing out of my head; and said I would take up wickedness again, which was in my line, being brung up to it." A beautiful line—but beautiful because of its perfect ironic tone. Is Huck aware of the irony? Has he learned what we have learned as witnesses, overhearers, of his conflict? Can we be sure, here or at the end of the book, that we are not extrapolating from our own lessons in expecting Huck to share our recognitions?

In at least one episode Huck does achieve an unequivocal self-awareness, and the scene is the measure of Huck's behavior elsewhere in the book. I refer to the colloquy with Jim that concludes Chapter 15, after Huck had played his joke on Jim during the fog. The scene is unusual in the book, in part because of its realized tension between Huck and Jim, in part because of the completely unfettered, "free" and honest speech by Jim ("What do dey stan' for? I's gwyne to tell you. . . . Dat truck dah is *trash*; en trash is what people is dat puts dirt on de head er dey fren's en makes 'em ashamed"). Huck is forced by the speech to reckon with Jim as a person who has developed specific human expectations regarding Huck. By reckoning with such expectations Huck must reckon with, must confront, himself as a social being whose acts make a difference. He experiences himself through the sense compelled by Jim's speech of how another person experiences him. Huck once more wins our approval, but more important, he wins a self-conception that issues into an action—his apology "to a nigger."

The implications of a deepening human relation between Huck and Jim fail to materialize in the book; they have no other dramatic conflicts of this sort. But perhaps one confrontation is sufficient; perhaps the implications are buried in order to return in Huck's comparably "free" speech in Chapter 31, which recalls the circumstances of his friendship with Jim on the raft. It is curious, however, in light of the growing consciousness of these moments of mutual perception and self-perception, that the book, filled as it is with so many characters, is so barren of human relationships. The superficial quality of how people deal with each other (and themselves) is, of course, a deliberate element in Mark Twain's portrait of river society. It is also true that in Huck's experience people usually represent problems rather than possibilities, objects rather than subjects. His disguises are manipulative; he usually plays the role of the victimized orphan boy in order to exact enough sympathy to permit an escape. His many encounters leave him relatively untouched by memory (with a few notable exceptions); threads of meaning do not appear between episodes. Pap, Miss Watson, Tom, cannot be said to exist for Huck as subjectivities in their own right: if Tom were here he would do this or that, Miss Watson is a nuisance, Pap is a threat.

The scarcity of complicating relations, of *dramatic* encounters, does in fact qualify the reader's relation to Huck. To repeat what I propose is the critical issue at stake, we want to learn if these features of the narrative follow from Huck's "character," the demanding needs of his inner being, or if they in some way reflect the double role he plays, as a narrator who tells a story and a character who has a story. We need to look more closely at Huck's technical and dramatic roles.

The absence of serious complications helps account for the book's universal appeal. Compared to the "analytic" works Mark Twain condemned, *Huckleberry Finn* seems "easy" reading. Mark Twain could rely upon a readership already trained to recognize and "read" a comic vernacular speaker, to place him within its verbal universe; Huck appears within the guise of local color conventions (dialect, regional dress, essential "goodness" of heart). As a storyteller he intervenes very little between the events and the reader; he rarely projects a mind that calls attention to itself apart from the immediate experiences it records. Verbally, Huck displays a prepositional exactness in defining himself in space but more or less imprecision in regard to time; his language is keyed more to geography than to the clock—as befits a mind with little active memory. The intervals between episodes, which themselves have fairly concrete temporal structures, are filled usually with drift: "So we would put in the day, lazying around, listening to the stillness." The mythic force of many separate passages in the book arises from the absence of an obtruding sense of historical time. In the drift, one thing follows another without more relation than sequence: "Two or three days and nights went by"; "Soon as it was night"; "One morning."

But if sequential time matters little in the narrative structure, "timing," the arch device of the oral storyteller, does. In "How to Tell a Story" Mark Twain speaks of the importance of a studied nonchalance, and appearance of rambling purposelessness, and of the strategic pause. The storyteller holds his listener in a relation that has a strict temporal order of its own. Within that order, generated by the verbal posture of casualness, the placement or the withholding of details is of first importance. Thus the comic story tends to appear within longer narratives as a set piece, such as Huck's account of the Grangerford household, or his colloquy with Jim about "Sollermun." Within these pieces, Huck's role follows what Clemens called "the first virtue of a comedian"—to "do humorous things with grave decorum and without seeming to know they are funny." Grave decorum and seeming humorlessness well describe Huck's appearance. But is he so guileful as to dissemble his appearance for the reader? Who is the controlling comedian of the book, Huck or Mark Twain? Is humorlessness, the deadpan, Huck's trick on us, or Mark Twain's? Is grave decorum a feature of Huck's own character, or of Mark Twain's deployed mask?

We need to consider deadpan, not only as a mode operative in specific passages but also as the dominant mode of the entire narrative, even when it does not lead to a punch line or reversal. The mode is based on a form of trickery, of saying less than one means. As such it can be taken as a form of insincerity, benign though it may be. "I never seen anybody but lied, one time or another," says Huck in the fifth sentence of the book. The comment disarms in several ways. It evokes a village world where the highest premium is placed upon "telling the truth." To admit that the official value of truth telling is often violated by everyone, including Miss Watson and Widow Douglas, requires either the courage of an iconoclast, which Huck is not, or a personal station outside the official values. As a vernacular character, Huck is free to speak this way; his manner is not aggressive or muckraking, but grave, decorous, and deadpan. (Contrast, for example, the tone of Colonel Sherburn's speech.) At the same time, the offhanded, flat manner of the admission hides the fact that the statement is of more than passing importance in the book. Lying, indeed, is a major and complex theme. The reader will eventually recognize instance after instance of lies passing as truths, deceptions sanctioned by the social order. Moreover, liars often believe their own lies, are unable to distinguish truth from appearance. On a level of considerable abstraction, the book offers as a basic deception the notion that Jim is "worth" eight hundred dollars, or that money can be traded for human value. Tom seems to think so when he pays Jim forty dollars "for being prisoner for us so patient"; Jim's being "pleased most to death" is one of the jarring notes in the Phelps conclusion. Another variation of the theme belongs to the Duke and the King, perhaps the supreme liars of the book. Cynicism liberates them to purvey appearance as truth without qualms. For this reason they are among the abstractly "free" characters; without thoughts of heaven, without conscience, they menace not only the social order but the fragile harmony of the raft. They represent an ultimate freedom in which the "other" is entirely an object, a freedom Huck ostensibly has overcome in himself after his elaborate lie to Jim after the fog in Chapter 15.

Deadpan exists in a complex relation to lies. It too is a falsehood, a manipulated appearance. But it is a lie in the service of truth or "reality," an honest lie whose effect as humor is based on our ultimate recognition of its falseness. As James Cox writes of the tall tale—a variant of deadpan—it "is true in that it is the only lie in a world of lies which reveals itself to be a lie." Commonly the procedure is to dramatize in the comic voice an apparently unrecognized discrepancy between what is perceived (the awful gimcrackery of the Grangerford sitting room) and what is felt (Huck's sentimental approval). The reader is allowed to accept the feelings as provisionally his own, only to be thwarted by the details that normally arouse a contrary response; he is released from the false feelings by recognizing their cause to be ludicrously inadequate. The reader is initially taken in by Huck's manner so that he or she may, so to speak, be saved from Huck's foolish approval.

But does Huck really approve? If so, he is indeed a fool, and we laugh at him as well as the complacent Grangerfords. In the convention of deadpan the teller is only apparently a fool. We permit him to practice deception on us because in the end some absurdity will be exposed to the light of universal common sense; we will gain an advantage over the world. The teller's manner is a mask that steadily, deliberately misleads us, until at the critical moment the mask falls. Behind the mask we might expect to find the real Huck, sharing our laughter, perhaps laughing at us for being momentarily taken in. The revealed comedian becomes at least our equal. But is this model at work here? Again we face Huck's paradoxical situation, as teller and as character. If we say that Huck's manner is a deliberate guise on his part, what happens to his gravity, his solemnity, his innocence, which we have normally taken as traits of character? Apart from depriving, or freeing, him of these elements of personality, such a reading would seriously upset the delicate balance between reader and narrative voice established at the outset. The voice presents itself as genuinely literal minded; it presents itself as inferior in its own mind to the civilization of Widow Douglas and Tom Sawyer. We quickly make the judgment Huck seems unable to make for himself, that literal mindedness is notably superior to the respectable lies of the town. The obvious superiority of Huck's frankness frees the reader from the deceptions of a world where respectability is the qualification for membership in a gang of robbers. To assign duplicity to Huck (by claiming he knows more than he is saying) would disturb this effect. To serve as our liberator Huck must remain ignorant and solemn. He must remain so in order to serve as Mark Twain's comic mask. In short, Mark Twain may have removed himself from the frame of the book, as the guileful, controlling voice, but the control remains in force, internalized and sublimated. The outside speaker who in earlier versions of vernacular presentation appeared, as in the Sut Lovingood stories, as a colloquist, now hides in the mask, a secret character in the book.

Deadpan predominates, and with it, Mark Twain's use of Huck's surface manner to reach the reader on a level of common values. But Huck's speech periodically escapes studied solemnity to become either lyrical, as in the sunrise passage that opens Chapter 19, or dramatic, as when he faces up to himself after Jim's "trash" speech. Such moments usually occur after actions that begin within the comic mode. Deadpan in part neutralizes the world, holds it at bay, seems to remove the threat of harm. But genuine harm frequently springs up to threaten the comic mode itself. One of many instances occurs in Chapter 18; the deadpan technique exposes Buck's explanation of the feud as absurd (the scene parallels the exposure of Tom's absurdities in trying to enforce an oath upon his fellow robbers in Chapter 2). Before long the slaughter begins and we hear, "Kill them, kill them!" The sunrise passage and the idyllic account of the raft follow in Chapter 19. Huck's lyric-dramatic voice seems to require a violation of his surface deadpan manner for release. The book alternates between a voice given over to deadpan trickery and narrative, and undisguised, direct feeling. The second voice generates needs for dramatic realization the author does not accommodate. Mark Twain's own needs, perhaps for some revenge against Southern river society, seemed to require a Huck Finn who is ignorant, half deformed, and permanently humorless. To put the case strongly, we might say that Huck's character is stunted by his creator's need for him to serve as a technical device. The same devices of irony that liberate the reader by instructing him or her about civilization and human nature also repress Huck by using him; they prevent his coming into his own.

Huck's freedom, I want finally to argue, requires that he achieve a conscious moral identity. Huck cannot be free unless Mark Twain permits him a credible and articulate inner being, with dramatic opportunities to realize his self. Of course this is to make perhaps impossible and therefore inappropriate demands upon this novel. But I think Mark Twain came close enough to such a realization for us to judge the book by its own best moments. Consider the raft, often taken as the symbol of freedom. The ethic of the raft is stated eloquently: "You feel mighty free and easy and comfortable on a raft." Yes; but this mood is possible because Huck had earlier humbled himself before Jim and decided to give up the pleasure of playing tricks. The raft has a tacit code, what we might call its own conscience. When the Duke and King arrive, that code bends to accommodate the rascals, for, as Huck tells himself as justification for not letting on to Jim that the men are frauds, "what you want, above all things, on a raft, is for everybody to be satisfied, and feel right and kind towards the others. . . . It's the best way; then you don't have no quarrels, and don't get into no trouble." "Free and easy" of the first passage has become "satisfied" and "no quarrels . . . no trouble." The difference is subtle but crucial. The raft is no longer free. Dissembling has returned. Huck decides in the name of "peace in the family" not to share with Jim his insights into the intruders: "it warn't no use to tell Jim." No one but the wary reader recognizes that trickery and deception have returned for the sake of the comedy Mark Twain can wring from Jim's ignorant wisdom about kings. True, Jim plays a pastoral role in his discussions about royalty with Huck, but his stature is reduced. Long before the Phelps episode he is required to submit to being tied up and left alone in the wigwam, or to donning "King Lear's outfit" to play a "Sick Arab." No one protests, and "Jim was satisfied."

The raft cannot defend itself against imposture. In the end imposture itself seems the only resort for Huck and Jim. From this point of view the elaborate theatricals at the Phelps farm seem an appropriate conclusion: how else might the two fugitives be returned to a possible world without real harm, without damaging the comic expectations of the novel? But what then can we say about freedom? Are we to judge the vulnerability of the raft, the necessity of a concluding "Evasion" (necessary to have any conclusion at all), to mean that by *its nature* the difficult freedom of owning oneself is impossible? Are we too hard with this book to blame it for failing to sustain the self-consciousness and process of self-discovery implicit in several scenes? Or more to the point, is that failure part of Mark Twain's design, or a result of technical limitations? Does the book project a fully realized vision, or is the vision blocked by the author's inability to sustain a novelistic development? These questions characterize the critic's dilemma in assessing the book.

Of course a vision and the verbal means of its realization and execution are virtually inseparable. Mark Twain saw the world the best he was able to, given his special verbal resources. My argument has meant to say that the formal problems that proceed from the initial conception of a book-length narrative in a mainly deadpan vernacular voice themselves enforce a certain vision. Mark Twain's work as a whole suggests that he seriously doubted the possibilities of personal freedom within a social setting. He seems to have taken freedom as true only when absolute and abstract, outside time. The imagery of drift in this novel is invested with such longing perhaps because it represents a condition already lost and insubstantial the moment it is imagined. The other side of the image reveals the fully invulnerable trickster, whose cynicism releases him from the control of any conscience. The dream voyages and mysterious strangers that obsessed Mark Twain's later years are anticipated in *Huckleberry Finn.*

The book is finally more persuasive as a document of enslavement, of the variety of imprisonments within verbal styles and fictions than as a testimony to freedom. Of course its negativity implies an ideal. I would like to identify that ideal with the "free" speech of Huck and Jim at the moments of engagement. I have tried to explain why such speech breaks out so rarely, why moral identity was so difficult to attain given the technical resources of the book. But we should recognize that the limits placed upon Huck's character are also forceful imperatives from the society within which Mark Twain portrays him. Moral character requires that social roles be credible to young people about to assume them. The society rendered in *Huckleberry Finn* deprives all roles of credibility when viewed from a literal-minded vernacular perspective. Rationalization and improvisation have convincing survival value, and virtuosity of disguise earns our admiration. Pap, after all, did bequeath a fatherly heritage by teaching Huck how to cheat and get away with no more than a bruised conscience. Perhaps the book's Americanness is most profoundly revealed in this heritage of eluding fixed definitions, in the corrosive decreation of established roles. Jim's presence reminds us, however, of the cost history has exacted from a society that drives its children to negativity. The cost is charged most heavily against Huck; he pays with his chance to grow up.

TEN

EXPERIMENTS IN
ANOTHER COUNTRY

Stephen Crane's City Sketches

IN the nineteenth century the big city appeared often in the guise
of mystery. To be sure cities always have baffled the stranger with
their labyrinths of streets and lanes, moving crowds, noisy markets,
obscure carvings on gates: each a unique entity of family and clan and
inner places closed to the outsider. Concealment in some measure is inherent in cities. But with new developments in the nineteenth century,
particularly in large centers like Paris, London, and New York, mystery
deepened beyond initial appearances and developed into a pervasive
response. It was deeper too than the middle-class curiosity about the
demimonde to which Eugène Sue catered, although the veiled lives of
outcasts and criminals contributed a large share to the sense of urban
mystery. The pervasive image now shows the city as a perilous and
problematic experience for its own citizens as well as strangers, its
whole reality hidden within denser crowds, closed off much the way
older vistas are now blocked by taller, inexplicable buildings. We find
the image on all levels—in guidebooks and newspapers, in popular
gothicized "mysteries," in serious poetry and fiction: the city as a
swarming mass of signals, dense, obscure, undecipherable.

Of course, what was happening in and to nineteenth-century cities
was in most ways not mysterious but calculable as the result of new

First published in *The Southern Review* 10 (April 1974): 265–85.

forces of production and distribution pulling in a working class from the countryside, creating on one hand intensely crowded living quarters close to places of work, and on the other new places for display of goods and for shopping. Divisions of space and of styles of life, between production and consumption, were the most visible marks of a new social order imposing itself on older sites. The process was plain and disclosed itself in the growing divisions between rich and poor that beset mid- and late-nineteenth-century urban society. The literary trope of mystery might itself serve as a form of mystification, as Karl Marx showed with exuberant irony in his lengthy analysis of Sue's *Mysteries of Paris* in *The Holy Family*: a device for confirming the social order while seeming to expose its hidden facts. But within the pervasive idea of mystery there does lie an irreducible condition that was fundamental to much urban literature. The physical city had become divided in so many small, insinuating ways that it defied comprehensibility. Its reality had become elusive, always seeming to flee into the shadows of another street. The motto of Edgar Allan Poe's haunting tale of pursuit, "The Man of the Crowd," sums up the essence of the deeper mystery: *Es lässt sich nicht lesen*. The city and its obsessive characters are like a book that does not permit itself to be read. The story of the compulsive wanderer among crowds, and the pursuit of the wanderer to penetrate his mystery, enacts the dilemma of comprehending the incomprehensible in a pristine form. Jean-Paul Sartre formulates this paradox that lies at the heart of the city mystery:

> A *city* is a material and social organization which derives its reality from the ubiquity of its absence. It is present in each of its streets *insofar as* it is always elsewhere, and the myth of the capital with its *mysteries* demonstrates well that the opaqueness of direct human relations comes from this fact, that they are always conditioned by all others. *The Mysteries of Paris* stem from the absolute interdependence of spots connected by their radical compartmentalization.

Experienced as an absence, as radically incomplete in any of its moments, the city thus invites pursuit, requires investigation, invasion of other spaces. The image of an impenetrability that provokes quest settled into urban culture, shared in different ways by poets, journalists, and social reformers in Europe and America.

Friedrich Engels describes himself as "a traveler" in London roaming "for hours," submitting himself to the "imposing" impressions of river, docks, houses. "All this is so magnificent," he writes, "that one is lost in admiration." Then leaving the "main streets" and turning into the slums, into an "elsewhere" that enlarges and complicates the picture of London's social reality, the traveler has it "dawn upon him that the inhabitants of modern London have had to sacrifice so much that is best in human nature in order to create those wonders of civilization with which their city teems." The city's physiognomy begins to reveal itself only as the investigator changes his perspective, shifts from one space to another. The problem of point of view, of the appropriate physical stance from which to gauge the social meanings of scenes witnessed, is at the core of investigation, the reformer Charles Booth realized:

> East London lay hidden from view behind a curtain upon which were painted terrible pictures:—Starving children, suffering women, overworked men; horrors of drunkenness and vice; monsters and demons of inhumanity; giants of disease and despair. Do these pictures truly represent what lay behind, or did they bear to the facts a relation similar to that which the pictures outside a booth at some country fair bear to the performance or show within?

"This curtain," writes Booth about his masterly *Life and Labor of the London Poor*, "we have tried to lift."

The street in particular appeared as the locus of curtained, displaced experience. The idea of mystery came to be particularized as the notion of space fragmented, regularized, specialized. The consciousness of differentiated space use can be traced in guidebooks for "strangers" and street directories, themselves perfect expressions of the radical incompleteness of any street experience. Often dressed with literary devices and Gothic coloration drawn from the *mysteries*, these verbal maps convey the city as interlocking spaces occupied by functions increasingly unintelligible to each other, in short, as space mystified. Men brought up "in the streets," wrote Frederick Law Olmsted in 1871, develop a particular kind of hardening of the surface of their private spaces. He conceived of the city park precisely as an overcoming of the oppressive mystification of the street. Olmsted's parks were designed as antitheses to the city, which appeared now as closed and enclosing, as a denial of experience.

By the end of the century spatial barriers appeared threatening and intolerable, and in the rhetoric of reformers the idea of *mystery* itself was the veil that hid the sight of the lower orders and their quarters from the "public," the readers of newspapers and the payers of taxes for whom the slums were par excellence an "elsewhere" shrouded in awe and fear. What Stephen Crane called "the eternal mystery of social conditions" begged for solution. Such popular titles in the 1890s as "People We Pass," "The Nether Side of New York," "How the Other Half Lives," confirmed the by then conventional trope of a fragmented urban landscape; the *mystery* or problem is located entirely in the alarming incommunicability among what Robert Park early in the twentieth century described as the "moral regions," the patterns of segregation that make the city "a mosaic of little worlds which touch but do not interpenetrate."

In 1894 Crane published a number of city stories and sketches in the daily press in New York. He thought well enough of these experimental pieces to consider collecting them as "Midnight Sketches." Considering their origins as newspaper sketches, these mainly short, deft impressions of New York street life seem more like apprentice work than finished inventions. One of the reasons for their interest is, however, exactly the fact of their having been produced for the press as newspaper performances. If the stories show the young writer, still in his early twenties, experimenting with language to develop an appropriate style, the newspaper itself must be taken into account as a given of the experimental situation. Crane derived the form itself, the "sketch," from the newspaper, and at a deeper level the form provided a challenge, a barrier to be overcome.

The big city daily, especially as it developed in the 1890s, has its raison d'être chiefly in the mystification of urban space, a mystification it claims to dispel as "news" yet simultaneously abets as "sensationalism." The newspaper addresses itself abstractly to a "public" that is the collective identity each isolated urban consciousness is invited to join, a neutral space held in common as the negation of hidden private space. The motive of the metropolitan press, Robert Park writes, is "to reproduce as far as possible, in the city, the conditions of life in the village." In villages "everyone knew everyone else, everyone called everyone by his first name." The tactic of searching out "human interest," of making the commonplace seem picturesque or dramatic, is an attempt to fill the distances inherent in mystified space with formulaic emotion fostering the illusion of distance transcended. In their daily recurrence newspapers express concretely the estrangement of an urban consciousness no longer capable of free intimacy with its own material life. In their form the wish for the commonplace or the demystification of social distance coexists with the wish not to dispel mystery, to retain as surrogate experience the aura of awe, allurement, fear that surrounds street experience.

Crane was not an ordinary reporter on assignment; he wrote as a "literary" observer, a personal reporter of city scenes. His sketches were not "news," nor were they entirely fiction, though he was capable of "making up" an account of a fire that never occurred and placing it in the *New York Press* as a signed report. The sketches present themselves as personal reports from and on *experience*, frankly colored by a personal style. The convention of such stylized reporting already existed in New York journalism as an expression of the newspapers' need to transform random street experience into *someone's* experience. The convention provided Crane with an opportunity to cultivate an authentic style as a vehicle of personal vision. The danger was that pressure to distinguish his vision, to make his signature recognizable, would lead to stylization.

Choosing themes familiar to newspaper, magazine, and novel readers, Crane developed a distinctive manner, a kind of notation that rendered physical scenes in highlighted color and sound. "When Everyone Is Panic-stricken," his fire report hoax, opens:

We were walking on one of the shadowy side streets west of Sixth Avenue. The midnight silence and darkness was upon it save where at the point of intersection with the great avenue there was a broad span of yellow light. From there came the steady monotonous jingle of streetcar bells and the weary clatter of hooves on the cobbles. While the houses in this street turned black and mystically silent with the night the avenue continued its eternal movement and life, a great vein that never slept nor paused. The gorgeous orange-hued lamps of the saloon flared plainly and the figures of some loungers could be seen as they stood on the corner. Passing to and fro the tiny black figures of people made an ornamental border on this fabric of yellow light.

The effect is painterly, precise, impressionistic. Crane's eye for detail, his ability to take in a scene and convey its sense, its contours, in a few telling strokes, suggest important correspondence between his visual intentions and that of impressionist painters and photographers. The notation here, and typically in the city sketches, seizes a passing moment and formalizes it as a picture drawn from a precise physical perspective—from the shadowy side street toward the great avenue and its gorgeous yellow light. Within the formalization the scene contains motion, the potential for change, for the appearance of the sudden and the unexpected. The potency is held in the carefully constructed spatial relation between the black, silent houses in "this street" and the unsleeping, flaring life of the avenue. The relation has, moreover, the potential of an ironic contrast, one that does in fact emerge as the "grim midnight reflection upon existence" of the narrator and his companion (identified only as "the stranger"), "in the heavy shadows and in the great stillness" of the street, are disputed by a sudden "muffled cry of a woman" from one of the "dark impassive houses" and the "sound of the splinter and crash of broken glass, falling to the pavement." The pictorial patterns of the opening paragraph give way to the frenzy and excitement of a midnight fire. Like the shadowy street itself the stranger suddenly flares into life, clutches the narrator's arm, drags him to the blazing house, himself a mirror of its vehemence. Through his responses Crane registers the effective transformation of the scene from shadow to blaze, from grimness to frenzy: "The stranger's hand tightened convulsively on my arm, his enthusiasm was like the ardor of one who looks upon the pageantry of battles. 'Ah, look at 'em! look at 'em! ain't that great?' " The spatial relations and contrasts of the opening picture contain, in short, visual elements corresponding to the little drama that this fake news story performs.

A similar dramatization of visual detail and spatial relations to deepen and complicate conventional newspaper action appears in many of the sketches. Their interest lies in the fact that Crane used the occasion—the "personal" or "feature" reporter in search of copy—to develop techniques for rendering events on city streets as unique and complex experiences. Defining his literary problem from within such conventions posed certain difficulties; literalism, sensationalism, sentimentality were the ogres of the newspaper story Crane had to slay in his own work. From within the conventions Crane was able to discover a ground for genuine creation. That ground lay chiefly within the spatial structure of the common city story. Crane grasped the element of *mystery* within that structure and made it the basis of his point of view.

The most prominent and sensational of the spatial images in this period was that of the "other half," represented by the maze of streets and alleys and courtyards in lower Manhattan. In his famous exposures of living conditions in the slums, Jacob Riis, reporter for the *New York Sun*, excavated place names like Mulberry Bend, Bottle Alley, and Bandit's Roost. These names joined the "Bowery" as signals of forbidding and exotic territory. Illustrating his stories and books with photographs that explored to the "darkest corner," Riis established a pattern of spatial penetration that provided his readers with vicarious expeditions into mysterious quarters. His technique was that of a guided tour; his aim, to convert the reader from passive ignorance to active awareness and caring. In the sensations of his disclosures lurks some residue of the city *mystery*.

Leaving the Elevated Railroad where it dives under the Brooklyn Bridge at Franklin Square, scarce a dozen steps will take you where we wish to go . . . with its rush and roar echoing yet in our ears we have turned the corner from prosperity to poverty. We stand upon the domain of the tenement . . . enough of them everywhere. Suppose we look into one? No.—Cherry Street. Be a little careful, please! the hall is dark and you might stumble over the children pitching pennies there. Not that it would hurt them; kicks and cuffs are their daily diet. They have little else. Here where the hall turns and dives into utter darkness is a step and another, another, a flight of stairs. You can feel your way, if you cannot see it. Close? Yes! What would you have? All the fresh air that ever enters these stairs comes from the hall door that is forever slamming and from the windows of dark bed-rooms that in turn we see from the stairs the sole supply of the elements God meant to be free, but that man deals out with such niggardly hand.

And so on. The strategy is to place the reader in a moral relation of outrage, indignation, or pity. But it remains a touristic device; the reader is not permitted to cross into the inner world of the slums—into its own point of view—and see the outer world from that perspective. The moral stance that defines the "other half" as "problem" assures distance.

The portrayal of "low life" in much of the popular writing of the period employed analogous devices to preserve distance—devices of picturesque perspective or sentimental plot that protected the reader from the danger of a true exchange of point of view with the "other half." The danger appears as such in an interesting passage in the essay "New York Streets" by William Dean Howells. In his walks through the "wretched quarters," he writes, he permits himself to become "hard-ened, for the moment, to the deeply underlying fact of human discom-fort" by indulging himself in the "picturesqueness" of the scene: "The sidewalks swarm with children and the air rings with clamor as they fly back and forth at play; on the thresholds the mothers sit nursing their babes and the old women gossip together," etc. He remarks then, shrewdly, that "in a picture it would be most pleasingly effective, for then you could be in it and yet have the distance on it which it needs." To be *in it*, however, is "to inhale the stenches of the neglected street and to catch that yet fouler and dreadfuler poverty-smell which breed from the open doorways. It is to see the children quarreling in their games and beating each other in the face and rolling each other in the gutter like the little savage outlaws they are." This reality, if you are a walker in the city, "makes you hasten your pace down to the river" and escape. The passage confesses at once to the denials of the picturesque view and the offensiveness of an unmediated view.

How then was "low life" to be viewed? For Howells, for Riis, and for many concerned writers, a moral posture supplied the necessary screen of protection from an exchange of subjectivities. But the possibility of such an exchange—indeed its necessity if the logic of the convention were to complete itself—is implicit in the spatial pattern. It is precisely this possibility that Crane recognized in his city sketches—a possibility that provides the formal structure of two of the most ambitious of the city stories, the companion pieces "Experiment in Misery" and "Experiment in Luxury," and that illuminates his stylistic intentions throughout the sketches. Already in *Maggie: A Girl of the Streets* (1893) and *George's Mother* (presumably composed in 1894, in the same period of the city sketches), Crane had discarded the moral posture of the tourist and had tried to convey physical landscapes equivalent to his perception of the subjective lives of his characters. His materials for *Maggie* seem to have been derived almost entirely from written accounts of the lives of slum people by investigators like Riis and the evangelist T. Dewitt Talmage. The story is, in effect, a retelling of a familiar plot: Maggie (the name itself was virtually generic), pure blossom of the slums, driven by indifference, selfishness, sexual exploitation, first to streetwalking and then to suicide in the East River. For Crane the plot was an occasion to tell a familiar tale with vividness, with exactness of observation, and most of all, with sufficient irony to make it apparent that the characters themselves viewed their world melodramatically, through lenses blurred with the same false emotions they inspired—as "low life"—in the many popular tellers of their tale. Crane aims at accuracy, not compassion. The story is a complicated piece of parody written with a serious regard for the task of rendering a false tale truly. Crane's version of "low life," in *George's Mother* as well as *Maggie*, aims to represent the subjectivities of his characters. Each of the characters in these two novellas lives inwardly in a withdrawn psychic space, possessed by the shadowy feelings and escapist yearnings of the city's popular culture. Each is self-deceived, estranged from all others, occupying an imaginative world of his or her own.

Crane's recognition of the "mosaic of little worlds" and its demands upon representation is manifest in one of the best-known of the street sketches, "The Men in the Storm." The sketch is of a crowd of homeless men observed on the street during a blizzard as they wait with growing impatience and dangerous discontent for the "doors of charity" to open. Images of the homeless and jobless waiting for charity on the street were common in the writing and graphics of the period. Crane's piece differs from the standard treatment in several crucial ways. It is not a social study; it neither excites compassion for the men nor induces social guilt in the reader for their plight. It is a rendering of a scene, a depiction of a space, as objective as Alfred Stieglitz's street photographs with a handheld camera in the same year. Crane's concern is with the phenomenon before him, and his writing is almost surgical in its sureness of stroke. He writes to achieve an accurate statement of the feeling of the scene, and his details are physical correlatives of the men's feelings of pitiless cold, biting wind, and snow that "cut like knives and needles." The men are driven by the storm "like sheep in a winter's gale." Viewed from without, they are also seen as possessing a collective subjectivity. For example, in their fierce condition they still can swear "not like dark assassins, but in a sort of American fashion grimly and desperately it is true but yet with a wondrous under-effect definable and mystic as if there were some kind of humor in this catastrophe, in this situation in a night of snow-laden winds."

A picture of a desperate scene—of men subjected to cold wind, snow, and hunger, alternately clinging to each other for warmth and fighting with each other for shelter—the sketch is also a highly pointed study in the problematics of point of view. Drawn from a detached floating perspective, the sketch contains several limited points of view, each located spatially and each characterized by a feeling linked to its space. The opening paragraphs present a picture of late afternoon busy streets as the blizzard begins to swirl upon pedestrians and drivers of vehicles and horses. The mood is grim at first: people are huddled, drivers are furious, horses slip and strain; "overhead the trains rumbled and roared and the dark structure of the elevated railroad stretching over the avenue dripped little streams and drops of water upon the mud and snow beneath it." But the next paragraph introduces a more hopeful note. The perspective shifts momentarily to an interior, "to one who looked from a window"; the clatter of the streets, softened by snow, "becomes important music, a melody of life made necessary to the ear by the dreariness of the pitiless beat and sweep of the storm." The warmth of the interior in which such musings are likely pervades the paragraph; the shop windows, "aglow with light," are "infinitely cheerful," and now "the pace of the people and the vehicles" has a "meaning": "Scores of pedestrians and drivers wretched with cold faces, necks and feet, speeding for scores of unknown doors and entrances, scattering to an infinite variety of shelters, to places which the imagination made warm with the colors of home." The objective scene has been constructed to reveal a subjective mood—the storm is pitiless but the imagination warms itself with images of doors, entrances, home: "There was an absolute expression of hot dinners in the pace of the people." Crane then introduces a conjectural point of view inspired by the scene: "If one dared to speculate upon the destination of those who came trooping, he lost himself in a maze of social calculations. He might fling a handful of sand and attempt to follow the flight of each particular grain." But the entire troop has in common the thought of hot dinners: "It is a matter of tradition; it is from the tales of childhood. It comes forth with every storm." Social calculation might be pleasant, diversionary, but trivial. All classes are reduced to those who speed home in the blizzard warmed with the thoughts of food, and those who do not. At this point Crane performs the sketch's most decisive modulation of perspective: "However, in a certain part of the dark West-side street, there was a collection of men to whom these things were as if they were not." The stark negative halts all calculation.

The narrator has subtly worked upon the reader's point of view, freeing it from the hold of customary feeling so that it might receive freely a newly discovered "moral region," the territory of "half darkness" in which occurs another kind of existence. In the description that follows Crane twice again introduces a shift in perspective in order to confirm better the spatial independence of his own. At one point, across the street from the huddled men, the figure of a stout, well-dressed man appears "in the brilliantly lighted space" of the shop window. He observes the crowd, stroking his whiskers: "It seemed that the sight operated inversely, and enabled him to more clearly regard his own environment, delightful relatively." The man's complacency is echoed at the end of the sketch as the narrator notes a change in expression in the features of the men as they near the receiving door of charity: "As they thus stood upon the threshold of their hopes they looked suddenly content and complacent, the fire had passed from their eyes and the snarl had vanished from their lips. The very force of the crowd in the rear which had previously vexed them was regarded from another point of view, for it now made it inevitable that they should go through the little doors into the place that was cheery and warm with light."

By projecting in the contrasted points of view a dialectic of felt values, Crane forces the reader to free his or her own point of view from any limiting perspective. Crane thus transforms the conventional event of turning corners and crossing thresholds into a demanding event: a change of perspective that as its prerequisite recapitulates a number of limited perspectives. Crane's "Men in the Storm" differs, for example, from a characteristic "literary" treatment of the same theme such as Howells's "The Midnight Platoon" by its achievement of a point of view superior to, yet won through a negation of, perspectives limited by social, moral, or aesthetic standards. Howells's piece concerns a breadline as it is perceived from a carriage by a man who comes to recognize himself as comfortable and privileged. The figure in the story approaches the scene as a "connoisseur of such matters," enjoying the anticipation of "the pleasure of seeing"; he wants to "glut his sensibility in a leisurely study of the scene." The breadline is to him "this representative thing," and he perceives in the crowd of hungry men "a fantastic association of their double files and those of the galley-slaves whom Don Quixote released." His mind wanders in conjecture:

> How early did these files begin to form themselves for the midnight dole of bread? As early as ten, as nine o'clock? If so, did the fact argue habitual destitution, or merely habitual leisure? Did the slaves in the coffle make acquaintance, or remain strangers to one another, though they were closely neighbored night after night by their misery? Perhaps they joked away the

weary hours of waiting; they must have their jokes. Which of
them were old-comers, and which novices? Did they ever quarrel over questions of precedence? Had they some comity, some
etiquette, which a man forced to leave his place could appeal to,
and so get it back? Could one say to his next-hand man, "Will
you please keep my place?" and would this man say to an inter-
loper, "Excuse me, this place is engaged"? How was it with
them, when the coffle worked slowly or swiftly past the door
where the bread and coffee were given out, and word passed to
the rear that the supply was exhausted? This must sometimes
happen, and what did they do then?

Aware that the men look back at him with equal curiosity, he suddenly
recognizes his own "representativity." To them, he realizes, he stands
for Society, the Better Classes, and the literary picturesque notions dissolve as he feels himself face-to-face with the social issue. Howells here
confronts the social distance, portrays it as filled with middle-class rationalization, and ends with a "problem": What are "we" to do about
these men and their suffering?

For Crane, that question is as if it were not. He writes from a curiously asocial perspective—or, at least, a perspective disengaged from
that of the typical middle-class viewer; he approximates (though he
does not yet achieve) the perspective of the men. That is, what Howells
sees as a thoroughly social matter of how the classes view each other,
Crane sees as a technical problem: how to represent the scene before
him. He is not concerned with converting the reader to social sympathy (perhaps distrustful or weary of the condescension of such a
stance), but with converting the sheer data into *experience*. He writes
as a phenomenologist of the scene, intent on characterizing the consciousness of the place (which includes its separate points of view) by a
rendering of felt detail. Each of Crane's images resonates with significance as a component of the episode's inner structure of feeling; the
exactness of the correlation of detail to feeling leads, in fact, to the frequent mistake of describing Crane as a Symbolist. His *realism*, however,
in the phenomenological sense, points to the significance, indeed the
radicalism, of these sketches. For Crane transforms a street scene, a

passing sensation for which a cognitive mold is already prepared in his reader's eye, into a unique experience.

If, following Walter Benjamin, we require that works be "situated in the living social context," then the immediate context is that established by the author with his reader; it is in that relationship that the possibility of each becoming "real" and particular for the other exists. In this case, the relationship is mediated by the sketch's appearance in a newspaper, and at a deeper level, by its formal expression of the newspaper motive: a "human interest" observation on a street. But typically the newspaper does not permit its own formal qualities to have so intense and exact a realization. Newspapers respond, as I have pointed out, to the increasing mystification, the deepening estrangement of urban space from interpenetration, from exchange of subjectivities. But their response is to deepen the crisis while seeming to allay it. In their typographical form, their typical verbal usage, they serve, Benjamin writes, "to isolate what happens from the realm in which it could affect the experience of the reader." By isolating information from experience, moreover, they deaden the capacity of memory; the lack of connection among the data of the newspaper page reduces all items to the status of "today's events." The newspaper, Benjamin writes, "is the showplace of the unrestrained degradation of the word." In *War Is Kind* Crane wrote:

> A newspaper is a collection of half-injustices
> Which, bawled by boys from mile to mile,
> Spreads its curious opinion
> To a million merciful and sneering men,
> While families cuddle the joys of the fireside
> When spurred by tale of dire lone agony.
> A newspaper is a court
> Where every one is kindly and unfairly tried
> By a squalor of honest men.
> A newspaper is a market
> Where wisdom sells its freedom
> And melons are crowned by the crowd.
> A newspaper is a game

Where his error scores the player victory
While another's skill wins death.
A newspaper is a symbol;
It is fetless life's chronicle,
A collection of loud tales
Concentrating eternal stupidities
That in remote ages lived unhaltered,
Roaming through a fenceless world.

The poem expresses nicely Crane's recognition of the constricting function of the newspaper as a "market" in which are sold "loud tales" to a world that appears fenced in. He has no illusions about the newspaper and the degradation of literature it represents.

Yet, as Benjamin argues, within the logic of the newspaper lies a possible condition for the salvation of the word—in the new relationships it fosters between writer and world, between writer and reader. Crane accepted the condition of newspaper production and produced within it work that, with the complicity of his careful reader, converts the data of street life into memorable experience. He thus transvalues, or as Benjamin would put it, "alienates" the apparatus of production and forces his reader to become an accomplice, that is, to become himself or herself an experimenter in mystified space. The best example among the sketches, an example that reveals Crane's motives almost diagrammatically, is the often misunderstood "Experiment in Misery." In this and in its companion piece, "Experiment in Luxury," published a week apart in the *New York Press*, Crane presents a figure, a "youth," who enters opposite social realms—in the first a seedy lodging house, in the second the mansion of a millionaire. The report in both cases is of the quality of life, of the awareness that inhabits each interior. The method in each "Experiment" is to convey the inner feeling by having the youth "try on" the way of life. The spaces are thus presumably demystified by the youth's assuming the point of view implicit in the physical structures and the actions of their interiors. For example, as he lounges with his rich friend, smoking pipes, the youth feels a sense of liberty unknown on the streets. "It was an amazing comfortable room. It expressed to the visitor that he could do supremely as he chose, for it said plainly that in it the author did supremely as he chose." Before long "he began to feel that he was a better man than many—entitled to a great pride." In each case the narrative point of view projects the youth's consciousness; he is made into a register of the world as it is felt in the particular setting. In this way Crane transmutes social fact into experience.

The stories are not identical in their strategies, however. Both begin with a frame in which the youth is encouraged by an older friend, in a conversation on a street, to undertake the experiment. As companion pieces they together confront the great division that was the popular mode through which "society" was perceived in the culture of the period: luxury and misery, rich and poor, high and low, privileged and underprivileged. Intentionally, then, they comprise a social statement. In the "luxury" piece, unlike the other, Crane consciously works from a social proposition: his "experiment" is an attempt to discover if indeed the inner life of the very rich justifies the "epigram" "stuffed . . . down the throat" of the complaining poor by "theologians" that "riches did not bring happiness." The motive of the "misery" story is less overtly ideological: it is to learn of the "tramp" "how he feels." The narrative technique of the "luxury" story differs from the other in that the youth carries on his "experiment" along with a simultaneous inner dialogue based on observation and self-reflection. He learns that the rich do, after all, live pretty well, if insipidly. He could "not see that they had great license to be pale and haggard." The story assumes a point of view in order to shatter a social myth. Being rich makes a difference.

Discursive self-reflection plays no role in the companion sketch. In fact, to intensify attention on the experience itself, and to indicate that the social drama of displacing one's normal perspective already is internalized in the action, Crane discarded the opening and closing frames when he republished the story in a collection of 1898. In his revision he also added to the opening paragraphs a number of physical details that reinforce and particularize the sense of misery. Streetcars, which in the first version "rumbled softly, as if going on carpet stretched in the aisle made by the pillars of the elevated road," become a "silent procession . . . moving with formidable power, calm and irresistible, dangerous and gloomy, breaking silence only by the loud fierce cry of the gong." The elevated train station, now supported by "leg-like pillars," resembles "some monstrous kind of crab squatting over the street." These revisions and others suggest an intention more fully realized: the creation of physical equivalents to the inner experience of misery.

The first version makes clear that the youth's "experiment" is a conscious disguise in order to search out "experience." "Two men stood regarding a tramp," it opens; the youth "wonders" how he "feels" and is advised by his older friend that such speculations are "idle" (a finely ironic word, as is "regarding") unless he is "in" the tramp's condition. The youth agrees to "try" it: "Perhaps I could discover his point of view or something near it." The frame opens with an awareness, then, of what the older man calls "distance," and establishes "experiment" as a method of overcoming it. So far the situation recalls the wish of Howells's witness of the breadline to penetrate distance, as it does the situation in many similar down-and-out pieces in the period. For example, in *Moody's Lodging House and Other Tenement Sketches* (1895), also a collection of newspaper sketches, Alvan Francis Sanborn writes: "the best way to get at the cheap lodging-house life is to live it,—to get inside the lodging house and stay inside. For this, un-less one possesses a mien extraordinarily eloquent of roguery or misery, or both, a disguise is helpful." Crane's youth borrows a disguise from the "studio of an artist friend" (this suggestive detail is dropped in the revised version) and begins his experiment: as Crane puts it with a note of irony, the youth "went forth." The irony is directed at the hint of naïve chivalric adventuresomeness in the youth and prepares for the authentic conversion of his subjective life to follow.

In what follows the youth proceeds downtown in the rain; he is "plastered with yells of 'bum' and 'hobo' " by small boys, he is wet and cold, and "he felt that there no longer could be pleasure in life." In City Hall Park he feels the contrast between himself and the homeward-bound "well-dressed Brooklyn people" and he proceeds farther "down Park Row" where "in the sudden descent in the style of the dress of the crowd he felt relief, and as if he were at last in his own country" (this last significant detail was added in the revision). The youth begins to inhabit this other country, first by occupying himself with "the pageantry of the street," then "caught by the delectable sign," allowing himself to be "swallowed" by a "voracious" looking saloon door advertising "free hot soup." His descent deepens. The next step is to find someone with "a knowledge of cheap lodging houses," and he finds his man in a seedy character "in strange garments" with a strange guilty look about his eyes, a look that earns him the youth's epithet of "assassin." The youth confesses himself also a "stranger" and follows the lead of his companion to a "joint" of "dark and secret places" from which assail him "strange and unspeakable odors." The interior is "black, opaque," and during the night the youth lies sleepless as the dormitory takes on the grim appearance of a fiendish morgue. Near him lies a man asleep with partly open eyes, his arm hanging over the cot, his fingers "full length upon the wet cement floor of the room." The spirit of the place seems contained in this image. "To the youth it seemed that he and the corpselike being were exchanging a prolonged stare and that the other threatened with his eyes." The "strange effect of the graveyard" is broken suddenly by "long wails" that "dwindle to final melancholy moans" expressing "a red and grim tragedy of the unfathomable possibilities of the man's dreams." The youth feels now that he has penetrated to the deepest recesses of the tramp's condition.

But at this point Crane performs an important act of distancing the narrative from the point of view of the youth. Fulfilling the earlier hints of his naïveté, Crane now has the youth interpret the shrieks of the "vision pierced man" as "protest," as "an impersonal eloquence, with a strength not from him, giving voice to the wail of a whole section, a class, a people." An ideological romance settles in his mind, "weaving into the young man's brain and mingling with his views of these vast and sombre shadows," and he "lay carving biographies for these men from his meager experience." With morning and sunlight comes the "rout of the mystic shadows," however, and the youth sees that "daylight had made the room comparatively common-place and uninteresting." The men joke and banter as they dress, and some reveal in their nakedness that they were "men of brawn" until they put on their "ungainly garments." The normalization of feeling in this morning scene is crucial. When the youth reaches the street he "experienced no sudden relief from unholy atmospheres. He had forgotten all about them, and had been breathing naturally and with no sensation of discomfort or distress." The respiratory detail confirms the point; he is now indeed in his own country, where he might feel after breakfast that "B'Gawd, we've been livin' like kings." In the expansive moment his companion "brought forth long tales" about himself that reveal him as a confirmed hobo, always cadging and running from work. Together they make their way to City Hall Park, the youth now one of "two wanderers" who "sat down in a little circle of benches sanctified by traditions of their class." In the normalcy of his behavior he shows that his experience of misery, since the night before, has become less meager.

The story closes as the youth on the bench becomes aware of a new substance in his perceptions. Well-dressed people on the street give him "no gaze" and he feels "the infinite distance" from "all that he valued. Social position, comfort, the pleasures of living, were unconquerable kingdoms." His world and theirs were now separate countries. The separateness is discovered as a difference in perspective, in how the world is seen, felt, and accepted. Now, the tall buildings in the background of the park are "of pitiless hues and sternly high." They stand "to him" as emblems "of a nation forcing its regal head into the clouds, throwing no downward glances." "The roar of the city" is now "to him" a "confusion of strange tongues." Estrangement has become his own experience, no longer a "thought" about the original object of his perception, the tramp. The youth, and through him the reader, has attained an experimental point of view expressed in an act of the eyes in the concluding sentences: "He confessed himself an outcast, and his eyes from under the lowered rim of his hat began to glance guiltily, wearing the criminal expression that comes with certain convictions." The conviction itself, of being excluded by the overarching buildings, accounts for the new perspective.

The two "experiments" conclude that the rich are banal but live well and that the homeless poor are victims whose inner acquiescence is a form of cowardice. More important than such "meanings" are the strategies compressed in the word "experiment." In these strategies lie the specifically urban character of Crane's writings, a character that is his calculated invention out of the materials of the newspaper culture. Crane's "experiments" implicate Zola's but go beyond them. In the misery sketch "experiment" denotes the subject as well as the method; the sketch is "about" the youth's experiment, an anatomizing of the components of the naturalist's enterprise of investigating human life in its social habitat. But Crane is concerned with the investigator, with the exercise of the logic of investigation upon his subjectivity. The experiment transforms the youth, and it is through that transformation that the life of the city's strangers becomes manifest. The youth is transformed only provisionally, however; he is not converted, not reclassified as a tramp. His experiment is literally a trying-out, a donning of a costume in order to report on its fit and feel. In order to live provisionally as a stranger in another country he must have estranged himself even more deeply to begin with, that is, he must already have disengaged himself from all possible identities, from social identity as such. Crane recognized that the inner form of the newspaper culture was itself "experiment" and to fulfill its logic of disengagement was a prerequisite for recovering "experience" from the flux of the street. Crane's city sketches are experimental writing in the sense, finally, that they confront the transformation of literary relations (the writer's relation to his subject and to his reader) implicit in the big city's mystification of social and psychic space; they invent stylistic procedures for re-creating the word as experience.

Crane's direction was a descent to the street and to the constricted visions that lay there as broken images. Out of these he forged a unifying image of his own, a vision of a city peopled by nameless, desolate creatures, strangers to each other and to their own worlds. "The inhabitant of the great urban centers," writes Paul Valéry, "reverts to a state of savagery—that is, of isolation. The feeling of being dependent on others, which used to be kept alive by need, is gradually blunted in the smooth functioning of the social mechanism. Any improvement of this mechanism eliminates certain modes of behavior and emotions." Crane's vision is of a world already confirmed in its isolation, a world shocking in the absence of those "certain modes of behavior and emotion" that make subjective experience possible. The exchange of subjectivity performed by the youth rarely occurs among the characters of his city fiction; instead, violence always threatens as the promise of heightened sensation in defiance of the blunting mechanisms: a wail, a scream, a fire, a clutched arm. Crane's city people seem always ignitable, verging toward the discharge of feeling in riot. His own narrative point of view remains cool and aloof, however; his spatial penetrations end at the edge of sympathetic identification. Unlike Theodore Dreiser, he was little interested in character, little interested in exploring the versions of reality his style transcends. The expense of his expert technicianship was the larger novelistic vision Dreiser achieved. Dreiser also descended to the popular, to the banal, but the points of view of his characters were not provisional guises; he took them as self-sufficient acts of desire. Dreiser's city is a theme as well as a place: a magnet that attracts. Less than a place, Crane's city lies in the structured passages of his point of view; it is situated in his technique, in its processes of disengagement and recovery. His sketches are experiments in reading the "elsewhere" of the street.

ELEVEN

CIVIC IDEALISM IN STONE

Louis Sullivan's Auditorium Building

ONE of the earliest efforts by a major city in the United States to erect a monumental edifice serving several cultural functions, the Chicago Auditorium Building (1890) encloses within its massive walls a concert hall, a luxury hotel, and a commercial office tower. The challenge facing the builders, the young architect Louis Sullivan and his older partner, Dankmar Adler, was to conceive a form capable of harmonizing these distinct spaces and functions and a set of techniques to assure the stability of a building so heavy (the heaviest in the world at the time) and internally complex. And the challenge to the cultural historian today is to find in that form, in the building's composite purposes and spaces, a rationale, a governing idea, a meaning for its contemporary era, Chicago and the nation in the 1890s, and for today, more than a hundred years later. At the heart of the structure lay the auditorium itself, a space for the performance and experience of musical and dramatic art, of opera in particular. Culture in the form of orchestrated performance of "high art" gave the building its stated purpose, and the building in turn gave to "culture" a tangible, material form, an appearance in stone, wood, and mosaic. The Auditorium Building made culture tangible and visible; it gave to art,

Based on a lecture at Roosevelt University, Chicago, in November 1990, on the centennial of the Auditorium Building.

Figure 23 Auditorium Building from Michigan Avenue. (Photocopy of photograph #9853, Library of Congress, Prints & Photographs Division, Historical American Buildings Survey)

Figure 24 Auditorium Building interior, toward stage and electric lights. (Photocopy of photograph #9876, Library of Congress, Prints & Photographs Division, Historical American Buildings Survey)

to the several arts to which the structure dedicates itself, a distinctly urban look, an outdoor place on a city street for the indoor experience of aesthetic pleasure. We can take the building, then, as sign and instrument of an idea of culture, an investment of mind, emotion, and capital in an enterprise of civic art.

Louis Sullivan held that buildings represent the mind of one man, the architect. "Every building you see," he wrote, "is the image of a man whom you do not see." But in truth the man represented by any building is a composite figure: not the heroic artist alone, as Sullivan came increasingly to envision himself, but as he also occasionally observed, a figure representing a collective intention. "An architect alone cannot make a building," Sullivan often observed; the client also plays a role. Indeed the architect's function is nothing more than to realize "the client's thought." Or as his partner Dankmar Adler wrote in 1892 about the Auditorium Building itself: "The form in which we find this building is . . . the resultant of many conflicting causes and influences."

The Auditorium Building offers a seductive visual experience inside

Figure 25 Interior: theater detail. (Library of Congress, Prints & Photographs Division, Historical American Buildings Survey)

and out. The largest and tallest masonry building of its time, one of the last of the great masonry buildings in America before the steel frame came to dominate construction, the building shapes the experience of its visitors by an imposing array of columns, arches, staircases, ornamented walls, a lavish variety of woods and stones and mosaics, a stunning display of materials transformed into architectural space. The richness of display leads the visitor, through several circuitous routes, to a sensuous appreciation of a total design: the relation between exterior walls and interior spaces, the great arched doorways sweeping us inside where we meet elevators and a grand staircase. The dialectic of inside and outside, of up and down, of lateral and diagonal movements, discloses the building's basic divisions, its tripartite form as a single container of a theater, a hotel, and an office block. Sense experience leads us toward the building's controlling idea, its being a container of three simultaneous moments: art, travel, and commerce. In its modulated relations among these distinct realms lies its modernity. It points ahead toward a prominent phenomenon of our postmodern era, the multifunctional public structure such as the mall, the newest airports, colossal entertainment and sports centers.

In seeking the inner idea of the building the historian cannot overlook the extraordinary mind of Louis Sullivan. But at the outset we need to bear in mind that Adler and Sullivan's design reflected to the letter the wishes of their clients, the Chicago Auditorium Association and its three hundred or so stockholders. It was their vision in the first instance that the builders articulated, their desire, as Adler explained, for an opera house finer than New York's Metropolitan and, unlike that building, "self-sustaining," not "a perpetual financial burden to its owners." It was this encompassing commercial interest that, as Adler put it, "rendered necessary the external subordination of the Auditorium itself to the business building and hotel, which, together with it, form the Auditorium Building." The clients, at once real-estate speculators and philanthropists, conceived of the Auditorium Building as an instrument of profit as well as culture; the form of the building was shaped by the market in commercial space, and this without disguise or embarrassment. During the three years of construction, from 1886 to 1889, new considerations, mainly to enhance the building's profitability, required that the architects modify their plans—"not once," exclaimed Adler, "but a score of times; in fact, for each successive widening of the financial horizon of the enterprise."

As cultural historians we want to ask how Sullivan's design sat within that horizon not merely of financial constraint and client expectation but of their (and his) view of the place or role of "culture" in Chicago. One answer lies in the record of Sullivan's revisions in design. His first drawings proposed an ornate façade complete with oriel windows, turrets, dormers, pinnacles, and a tower capped with an elaborate pyramid. The final design, the exterior as we know it, eliminated these beaux arts elements for a much simpler rhythmic pattern of piers and arches emphasizing the building's great horizontal strength. The usual explanation for the change is that after finishing his original drawing, Sullivan found in the just-completed (1886) Marshall Field Warehouse, designed by the master of Romanesque public structures, H. H. Richardson, a powerful and irresistible inspiration and model. Yet Adler's discussion of the exterior design of the Auditorium Building complicates this explanation, and because Sullivan himself seems not to have commented on the matter, we must accept Adler's account as representing the view of both partners.

Adler admits that "every square foot of street exposure serves commercial purposes, and serves them well. . . . Still," he adds, and we cannot avoid detecting a defensive note, "one sees that the Auditorium is not an ordinary business building, but that its exterior is the embodiment of something nobler and higher than the desire to erect an inclosure for a rent-trap." The something nobler and higher, the common ground on which client and architects met, was that this building should represent as well as house a cultural institution. Though Adler insists that the final design aspires to nobility of statement, the façade's "severe simplicity of treatment" was a compromise with the original "nobler and higher" design. Adler attributes the final "simple and straightforward" design to "the financial policy of the earlier days of the enterprise." The building assumed its simplified form as a result of economics, then. Moreover, he adds, the directors of the Auditorium Association were themselves taken with Richardson's warehouse, and he implies that they saw in the aesthetic economy of the exterior of

that building a solution to the financial economy of their own investment. True, Adler concedes, the "highly decorative effects" of Sullivan's initial designs were an "indulgence." But he holds that the
coincidence of the clients' stringent financial policy and their attraction to the apparent straightforwardness of the Richardson building together "deprived the exterior of the [auditorium] building of those
graces of plastic surface decoration so characteristic of its internal
treatment."

To Adler the exterior of the building seemed in the end too commercial, not "noble and high" enough for a cultural center, a view
shared by the influential New York architectural critic Montgomery
Schuyler. Schuyler loved the interior, what he called "the essential
parts" of the building, the auditorium itself, its great stage, and the several lobbies. But the façade he condemned as untruthful and inexpressive of the building's "structural facts." The building contained a
"latent contradiction," he thought, and while he referred specifically to
the handling of the pillars in relation to the balcony in the Michigan
Avenue entrance, the term "latent contradiction" resonates with his
overall estimate of the structure. Schuyler perceives and Adler confirms that the architects faced an insuperable problem in attempting to
reconcile inherently contradictory elements. The building's exterior
design was "complicated with requirements irrelevant to its main purpose." The requirement to "envelop" the theater "in a shell of many-
storied commercial architecture . . . forbade them [the architects] even
to try for a monumental expression of their great hall," resulting in an
exterior that "appears and must be judged only as a 'business-block.' "
Schuyler does not blame either the clients or the architects and does
not scorn the clients for tampering with the architecture; to the
contrary, elsewhere he praises the influence of Chicago businessmen,
considering them the "most public-spirited" such group "of any commercial city in the world." He simply states a truth: that the Auditorium Building's attempt to integrate commerce and culture in a single
structure entailed contradiction from the start.

Most remarkable about Adler's own criticism is the light it sheds on
the choice of the Richardson warehouse as prototype for the final
auditorium façade. He makes it seem that the clients pushed it on the

architects as a model, perhaps to capitalize on the high prestige of that Romanesque masterpiece, perhaps because it seemed more appropriate to the priority they gave the commercial shell of the theater, or perhaps simply because they liked its aura of power and authority (Marshall Field himself was among the top subscribers to the Auditorium Association). In any case, Adler suggests that the Richardson model may not have been what the architects themselves would have chosen, that it seemed too commercial, lacking in "those graces of plastic surface decoration" of the auditorium's highly ornamented interior.

It is worth looking closely at the effect of the Richardson warehouse on the evolution of Sullivan's auditorium precisely because architectural historians invariably breathe a sigh of relief that Sullivan altered his earliest design. The historian Carl Condit writes: "Fortunately for architecture everywhere, Sullivan abandoned his propensity for elaborate exterior ornament and concentrated on the architectonic effect of mass, texture, and the proportioning and scaling of large and simple elements." That the Richardson building helped him achieve these architectonic effects can hardly be doubted. But influence is not simple. Did Sullivan and his clients understand the Richardson building in just this way, as a precursor of modernism? A closer look at Sullivan's well-known praise of the Richardson warehouse answers some of these questions and helps us refocus the issue of artistic influence and cultural meaning.

"Four-square and brown, it stands," Sullivan's famous paean to the Richardson building begins, "a monument to trade, to the organized commercial spirit, to the power and progress of the age, to the strength and resource of individuality and force of character." What thrilled him about the building was its strength and force, its mastery. Over and over Sullivan describes the building as *masculine*: "Here is a man for you to look at. A man that walks on two legs instead of four, has active muscles, heart, lungs and other viscera; a man that lives and breathes, that has red blood; a real man, a manly man; a virile force . . . an entire man." The building "sings the song of procreant power" and "bespeaks . . . the manliness of man."

Can we miss the erotic energy here, the sheer physical magnetism

Sullivan felt in Richardson's hymn to manhood? The language suggests that Sullivan felt a release in standing before the warehouse, discovered there a license for his own radical urges toward a sensuous, indeed an erotic architecture. At the same time, can we overlook Sullivan's association of manliness and trade, masculinity and the "organized commercial spirit"—in short, the idea held passionately, aggressively, and not a little defensively throughout American bourgeois culture at the time that business was the affair of men, that the market demanded manly strength, force, mastery, that competition tested one's virility? The same culture held that women symbolized (and were symbolized by) home, church, school, concert hall, places of nurturing, refinement, and spirituality. To be sure, beliefs in separate spheres and gender-specific behavior, indeed all the cultural notions of difference between male and female, masculine and feminine, were undergoing important change at the time and would soon burst into the open with the "new woman" and the flapper of the 1920s. But for now the rigid distinctions held fast as a matter of creed. And if business signified masculinity (and vice versa), and culture and art signified femininity, then Sullivan's problem in designing the Auditorium Building might be restated as a problem of reconciling not only separate activities and values but also separate gender spheres in a single design. How to join male and female together, how to integrate and harmonize precisely what the dominant culture imagined as separate and distinct, if not antagonistic to each other?

Did Sullivan and Adler think of their design problem in these terms? Whether or not, such distinctions belonged to the large semantic features of the auditorium project, the conjunction of parts representing the masculine sphere of business, the feminine sphere of culture, and the heterosexual sphere of leisure and pleasure signified by the hotel and theater. But Sullivan's frequent allusions to male and female in his writings, and his explicit comments on the "enchantment" of his ornamentation and color schemes for the theater proper, his emphasis upon the theme of music in the murals for the auditorium walls, reveal not just an intense awareness of these terms but also an equally intense and determined effort to realign them, to change their relationship, to overcome the cultural divisions between them by redefining them not as terms of gender and separate spheres but of human faculties present in all people.

It seems plausible that Sullivan wished to transpose the conventional male-female dichotomy and turn it into a critique of America's commercial civilization, its rigid rationality and its denial of nature. "You have not thought deeply enough to know that the heart in you is the woman in man," he wrote in an exhortation to American men in his essay "What Is Architecture: A Study in the American People Today" (1906). "You have derided your femininity, where you have suspected it; whereas, you should have known its power, cherished and utilized it, for it is the well-spring of Intuition and Imagination." Intuition, imagination, and thought, along with the masculine faculty that doubts, inquires, concentrates, and "makes very firm and sure," constitute for Sullivan a constellation of wholeness. In this essay Sullivan proposes to separate feminine and masculine traits from the male and female genders, to see these traits as belonging to humankind as a whole. Male-female terms become androgynous, freed from actual sexual identity and thus made available as terms of criticism, standards of judgment. To fuse the allegedly female trait of poetry with the allegedly male trait of building is to achieve a mutuality of human faculties and desires—an androgyny of architectural form. This, he seems to have fervently believed, is what his interior theater design achieved.

In standard architectural history Sullivan's cancellation of his earliest designs for the auditorium exterior is said to represent the liberating influence of the Richardson "monument to trade." But the inner story was more complex. Adler's remarks suggest that both partners would have preferred a more decorative, "feminine" exterior as expressive of the unleashed imagination and intuition of the interior, with its exotic play of color and light and form. A strictly Richardsonian exterior (which the final design only approximates in any case) would misconstrue not just the interior but the major function of the entire block as a place of leisure, art, entertainment, performance, and aesthetic delight—a place of spectacle instead of speculation. Ought a civic center look like a warehouse, even the finest in the world? We can speculate that while Sullivan and Adler hoped to invent a form to integrate trade and art, money and culture, male and female, the clients demanded a structure that in outer appearance would allude directly to Richardson's "monument of trade" and thus make a civic statement about what in their minds was the properly subordinate relation of culture to commerce, of feminine to masculine.

It should be clear, then, that many unsettled contradictions, psychodynamic as well as political and cultural, lay within the interrupted dialectic of outside and inside: the external spectacle of commerce raised monumentally before the face of the city, the interior spectacle of art blazing in electric lights and subtle orchestration of color—all supported by the preeminently masculine skills of construction, the deep-buried piles of the foundation and the internal trusses and beams supporting the massive building, the complex network of pipes, conduits, air ducts, electrical wires, telephone circuits, and elevator shafts that made this the most mechanized building of its time, and this entire revolutionary infrastructure hidden in the recesses of the building and its stolid masonry walls.

It is no wonder that Schuyler felt in the building a "latent contradiction," a vision of art darkened by the shadows both of money and of technology threatening to take control over architecture. To be sure, one might detect ambiguous overtones in Sullivan's spectacular interior, his overflowing poetry and the grandiosity of desire it enacts. He composed the theater to teach lessons, first about the nature and experience of theater in a new, boisterous, violent, class-ridden, and money-crazed American city, and more generally about art itself, about its place in American democracy and its function in achieving the kind of religious democracy Walt Whitman envisioned. Sullivan took Whitman's lessons to heart, particularly the poet's call in "Democratic Vistas" for a democratic culture based on native experience and on "nature." Sullivan's theater embodies such a Whitmanesque idea; its ornaments represent art evolving from the simplest natural forms, grains and seeds. With its superb acoustics and clear sight lines from all positions, the theater presents itself as a place of clarity, of unhampered access to the experience of art. By its Wagnerian orchestration of nature and art, space and time (the murals represent the passing seasons of nature and human life), color and light, the theater becomes and enacts a performance in its own right. It provides not only a stage but also a pedagogy, a lesson in aesthetic if not social democracy.

If the experiential democracy of the auditorium seemed at odds with the hierarchies and signs of moneyed power of the exterior façade, likewise Sullivan's androgynous and classless theory of democracy—at least what was implicit in the interior design—clashed with other interpretations of the meaning of "culture" in the Chicago of the 1890s. There was, first, the Chicago version of a national trend: the philanthropic sponsorship by the wealthy of new cultural institutions: libraries, concert halls, opera houses, art museums, universities, housed often in buildings imitating neoclassical and Renaissance marble palaces. With their air of distance, unchallengeable authority, and decorum, such monuments arose against a background of extraordinary unrest, with angry strikes, violence, new immigration, corruption in city governments, and an unstable boom-and-bust economy. Militant labor unions arose, which led to a national campaign for an eight-hour workday, culminating in the Haymarket Riot in Chicago in 1886; bombs were thrown, police killed, hysteria everywhere about foreign "anarchists" on the loose. In an atmosphere already charged with fear, the Haymarket Riot raised the specter of class warfare and symbolized the dangerously divided state of the nation.

It was partly in response to this frightful vision of social collapse ignited by class violence that art museums, opera houses, libraries, and universities began to appear in cities across the country. Housed in palatial edifices that lent a new look of elegance to city boulevards and plazas, cultural institutions adopted monumental styles appropriate to the loftiness of the idealism they represented. In Chicago new establishments such as the Chicago Symphony Orchestra, the Newberry Library, and the University of Chicago all got under way in 1889, the same year the Auditorium Building opened. These new institutions of high culture provided opportunities for new professional groups, curators, musicians, academic specialists, and of course architects. Genteel political and social reformers supported them because they might encourage a general improvement in the tone of civic life. There was a hope that high art would bestow a beneficent influence and be a source of unassailable civic values.

Civic idealism surged into prominence within the private clubs of the Chicago elite. Perhaps the wealthiest and most powerful of these was the Commercial Club, founded in 1877, limited in membership to sixty men prominent in business and dedicated to "the prosperity and growth of the city of Chicago." The club included civic reform among its concerns, and in 1880 put the following question to a forum: "Should not the commercial prosperity of great cities be attended by the cultivation of art, literature, science, and comprehensive charities, and the establishment of art museums, public libraries, industrial schools and free hospitals?" Within a decade arose an infrastructure of philanthropically endowed institutions. Significantly, in the same years Chicago underwent another kind of change: between 1887 and 1894 a mass transportation system including cable lines, electric surface cars, and elevated trains hastened the process of suburbanization and residential segregation by social class, rapidly erasing neighborhoods of mixed uses and populations, isolating social classes from each other except in the workplace, and sealing the fate of the Loop as a strictly commercial area.

It was before this same Commercial Club on May 29, 1886, that the promoter Ferdinand W. Peck put forth a proposal for a permanent civic center for performing arts at the downtown corner of Michigan and Congress. The date is telling: about three weeks after the bloodshed at Haymarket on May 4. The Commercial Club had responded to that event with an alarm typical of the Chicago elite; fearing the worst, its members donated land for a federal fort outside the city, and many of its members served on a private vigilante committee. The city was ablaze with antiforeign feelings, writes one historian: "People were thrown into jail without warrants, and freedom of speech and assembly seemed in danger of extinction." In this atmosphere of fear and desire for vengeance the club endorsed Peck's proposal, with handsome subscriptions from Marshall Field, Martin Ryerson, Charles Schwab, George Pullman, and scores of others, who in turn secured Peck's assurance of their right to vet the plans to assure that the building not only be "an ornament to the city" but that it properly represent the "good taste of its citizens."

Peck, wrote Sullivan many years later, "declared himself a citizen, with a firm belief in democracy—whatever he meant by that; seemingly he meant the 'peepul.' At any rate, he wished to give birth to a great hall within which the multitude might gather for all sorts of purposes including grand opera; and there were to be a few boxes for the haut monde." He was, Sullivan adds, "an emotionally exalted advocate of that which he, a rich man, believed in his soul to be democracy." Sullivan's sarcasm registers his distance from the clients' views of culture and democracy, from their desire to have an "ornament to the city" reflecting the "good taste" of the owners. Yet he faithfully followed their wishes and provided a design that met with their approval. How are we to understand Sullivan's commitment to that design as a fulfillment of Whitman's democracy?

Among its "latent contradictions" the Auditorium Building projects two versions of civic idealism. Sullivan's rhetoric, his words as well as his poetic ornamentation, point in one direction, while the building's compromised exterior along with the words of Peck and others point in another. In his address at the opening-night ceremonies, for example, Peck did not find it necessary even to mention the names of the architects, since the building so faithfully expressed the clients' wishes. The speech by the governor of Illinois, John Riley Tanner, delivered the key terms of celebration:

> The enterprise which conceived and the liberality which patronized [this] vast and truly philanthropic undertaking stand as proof that the demand of Chicago's civilization has not been lost in the dust of the warehouses nor trampelled beneath the mire of the slaughter pen. This Auditorium proves that culture and art are here keeping pace with the material developments nor surpassed by any in the world.

A chorus performed a cantata with words by the poet Harriet Monroe: "Hail to thee, fair Chicago! On thy brow / America, thy mother, lays a crown."

Thus sanctioned and sanctified, the auditorium quickly became the home of high culture in Chicago. A group of artists and writers and intellectuals, dubbing themselves with fine irony the Little Room, met regularly for tea and talk on Fridays after the matinee concert by the Chicago Symphony under the direction of the formidable Theodore Thomas. Thomas, an evangel of genteel civility and decorum, insisted on absolutely silent, respectful, well-behaved audiences. His creed held that "a symphony orchestra shows the culture of a community." "To form a refined musical taste among the people" was his goal, except, that is, children and "wage-workers," who, he wrote, fell short of the necessary intelligence. He thought the auditorium was a living embodiment of the ideal of cultivated refinement, of civility and decorum, as requisite for legitimate aesthetic experience.

Did Thomas address the multitudes imagined by Peck? It is likely that Peck, too, imagined the building as a place where multitudes might be instilled with properly obedient attitudes toward refined music. Is this what Sullivan had in mind? Is it what his murals, his ornaments, his lights and colors imply? Is refined sensibility a correct reading of his design: culture as noblesse oblige, as uplift, as decorum and civility?

In fact the auditorium can be seen as embodying a quite different notion of art, performance, and culture. The swirl of Sullivan's terracottas, the glow of his lighting and subtle harmonizing of his colors, the trumpetlike effect of his arches replicating the flow of sound from the stage into the seating area crafted by Adler into a perfect arena for listening and seeing, the stage itself, its deep plush curtain, its movable sets, its hidden contraptions of illusion, its hydraulic apparatus for simulating on stage, in Adler's words, "steps, terraces, rocks, hills, caves, pits," all "by mere movement of a few levers"—does not all this proclaim pleasure first and foremost, the pleasures of spectacle, illusion, performance? Adler and Sullivan wanted audiences to know through their bodies the sensuous experience of listening, watching, bending toward performances of visual, aural, and kinetic art. They designed a space not for abstract culture but for living art, and within the interior spaces, at least, they gave that idea monumental expressive treatment. The end of their design was delight, pleasure, and enhancement of being. Sullivan understood by democracy the enlargement of self through the senses, the fusion of thought and imagination, of masculine and feminine powers.

The very intensity of Sullivan's poetry heightens the tension between the theater proper and its enclosing commercial shell, structural analogues to social contradictions within Chicago itself. Inside and out the Auditorium Building could hardly avoid providing a site where contradictions manifested themselves. The opening scene of Frank Norris's novel *The Pit* (1903) discloses some of these. The heroine, Laura Dearborn, sits "spell-bound" at an opera in the auditorium: "It was wonderful, such music as that; wonderful, such voice; wonderful, such orchestration; wonderful, such exaltation inspired by mere beauty of sound. . . . How easy it was to be good and noble when music such as this had become part of one's life." But "a discordant element" interrupts this transformative reverie. Laura becomes aware of a whispered conversation somewhere nearby, a "hoarse, masculine whisper" about the price of wheat. "Why could not men leave their business outside," she asks herself; "why must the jar of commerce spoil all the harmony of this moment?" Then, when she and her party leave the opera, they encounter "an apparently inextricable confusion . . . policemen with drawn clubs laboured and objurgated. . . . furious quarrels broke out between hansom drivers and the police officers, steaming horses with jingling bits . . . plunged and pranced, carriage doors banged, and the roll of wheels upon the pavement was as the reverberation of artillery caissons." Beauty inside, warfare outside. And as her carriage makes its way through the Loop, Laura exclaims at another discordant sight. "The office buildings on both sides of the street were lighted from basement to roof. Through the windows she could get glimpses of clerks and book-keepers in shirt-sleeves bending over desks. Every office was open, and every one of them full of feverish activity." Laura feels suddenly stupefied, overcome by the contrasts. "Here it was, then, that other drama, that other tragedy, working on there furiously, fiercely through the night, while she and others had sat there in that atmosphere of flowers and perfume, listening to music. Suddenly it loomed portentious in the eye of her mind." For Norris the Auditorium Building triggers a portentious moral equation that sets art and business at opposite poles, unequal antagonists in a warlike struggle for the soul of the nation.

Citing this opening chapter of *The Pit* in his important book *American Apocalypse: The Great Fire and the Myth of Chicago*, Ross Miller observes wryly that in spite of "Sullivan's naive hopes, the art represented by the Auditorium's theater did not encourage class and social harmony." To the contrary, the building may well have exacerbated such hopes, especially by its association of culture with wealth, and by providing an arena for the display of the latter by bejewelled women. Hoarse masculine whispers about carloads of grain were not welcome in the feminine precincts Adler and Sullivan designed for the pure experience of art. Yet undoubtedly with the wives of their clients in mind, the architects did take into consideration another function, another role, for women, not as muses of intuition, imagination, and sympathy but as decorative figures of conspicuous display. The theater was a place in which to hear and to see, and also to be seen, to show forth who and what one was, especially in the boxes arranged in two tiers on each side of the theater. "When these boxes are filled with richly-dressed women," writes Adler, "the mass effect of the rich colors and stuffs is exceedingly fine, and blends quite harmoniously with the forms of the architectural details and the colors of the decorations." Adler and Sullivan saw that attending the theater was in itself a theatrical event, a dramatic occasion for self-display.

Women may have performed the main parts in the spectacle enacted there, and emblems of class difference and class power may have been the hidden nerve of display, but there was another, more specifically modern element in the theater's design for easy conspicuousness. The architects realized that the audience itself comprised a drama of its own, a drama of looking and wishing, of private imaginings. Adler understood that a new feature of the culture of modern urban nightlife was precisely the spectacle of mass display, a power in its own right even apart from the parading of class identity. Thus the room was at its best, Adler wrote, "when used as a hall for mass concerts."

> The chorus seems thus to blend with the audience, and the house is so open that one can see at a glance almost the entire audience and the whole chorus. The sight of thousands of men and women in festive array is always pleasing, and when every one of these has ample space for sitting in comfort, has fresh air and can see and be seen and hear every modulation of sound in its full effect the result is inspiring.

In asserting a new aesthetic of democracy founded in the body, the theater speaks to another expression of commercial society, the rise of a consumerist sensibility that seeks satisfaction in display for its own sake.

The original Auditorium Building balanced contradictory elements: aspects of genteel high culture housed within a commercial shell; both aligned with a new popular culture of nightlife, display, fanatasy; and in another dimension, Sullivan's cryptic inscriptions of a holistic democracy, the radical androgynous implication of the theater. The subsequent history of decline and deterioration and the building's narrow escapes from demolition sadly mocks the claim to unifying power and authority in the prophetic image of art Sullivan embodied in his design. But the preservation of the building gives the vision another chance, a second life. The transfigured spaces and functions of the urban university that now occupies the building alter the original message, just as they change the balance of social forces originally represented there. There changes revive questions addressed by Adler and Sullivan regarding the place of culture, of art and performance, of consciousness and sensibility, of mind and desire within a city and a society still ruled by business, commercial transactions, and inequality. The building's ambiguous and contradictory messages contribute a usable if enigmatic lesson in the city's and the nation's efforts to understand the past for the sake of an improved future.

PART THREE

TWELVE

MUMFORD IN THE 1920S

The Historian as Artist

I

"WE were the scouts and prospectors in a new enterprise," Lewis Mumford remarked in 1973 about his work in the 1920s: "the bringing to the surface of America's buried cultural past." He spoke of a collective enterprise, naming especially Van Wyck Brooks, Paul Rosenfeld, Waldo Frank, and Constance Rourke as fellow scouts in a "re-discovery of America." Mumford's own several books of that decade have seemed the most lasting, the most practically useful, of the "usable past" project. In *Sticks and Stones* (1924), *The Golden Day* (1926), *Herman Melville* (1929), and *The Brown Decades* (1931), we have perhaps the most significant beginnings of that vast revaluation of literature, architecture, and painting in America that decisively reconstructed the popular image of a native cultural heritage. Much that we now take for granted—the stature of Melville and Whitman, the importance of Richardson, Sullivan, and Wright to a native American art—was fresh discovery and original judgment in Mumford's books. *The Golden Day* preceded F. O. Matthiessen's *American Renaissance* by more than a decade in calling attention to an extraordinary creative flowering before the Civil War. Simply as excavations the books lay foundation stones for much subsequent work. And as interpretations, with their guiding theme of a continuing struggle between

First published in *Salmagundi* 49 (Summer 1980): 29–42.

cultural originality and independence against a "colonial mentality," between a communal and organic view of nature and society and an individualist, exploitative, and mechanistic view, they have left a major imprint on American studies as a whole.

But there is more to be said about these works. We miss something essential if we take "usable past" to mean only discovery, the digging out of buried ore. Mumford's books of the 1920s are also inventions, deliberate compositions, similar in spirit and ambition to works such as William Carlos Williams's *In the American Grain* (1925) and Hart Crane's *The Bridge* (1930). This is not to say that Mumford's studies are also works of art, either in the sense of being wholly aesthetic in their ends or of being immune to judgments of accuracy and validity of historical interpretation. But it is to say that they are not uncomplicated discourses in a conventional mode of historical narrative. What they attempt as discoveries cannot be separated from what they attempt as literary inventions. The motive, in fact, toward a "usable past" discloses itself as much in the form as in the content, as much in the invention as the excavation. For in the form, or let us say in the very concern with form, with presentation, lies the implication that "history" itself demands a creative response, that the past can become present only through a kind of personal encounter. This, of course, is the extreme aesthetic view of Williams and Crane, for whom "past" is constantly in the process of realization through fresh encounters, and history nothing if not realizable as personal experience. Mumford's books remain historical narrative, not poetry, but they attempt a fusion of discourses, a bringing forward of the past not just as fact previously neglected but as real experience continuous with the reader's present.

We have a subtle hint of this personal dimension, and of the terms in which it expresses itself, in Mumford's remark of 1973: "We were the scouts and prospectors in a new enterprise." Perhaps unintentional but nonetheless unavoidable is the hint of irony in this configuration of images: scout and prospector, new and enterprise, bring to mind the figures of the pioneer, the entrepreneur, the miner: figures Mumford and others had viewed as negative forces in America, representing inward repression for the sake of a merely physical exploitation and despoilment of the external, and a naïve, willful belief in the "new start," the

perpetual frontier. The irony, intended or not, points up the contrast between a pioneering that denies history and the value of continuity, and
one that searches purposefully for a continuous past. It points up a motive: not only to reclaim what had been "buried" by neglect, but in so
doing to demonstrate a kind of pioneering and prospecting of resources
that will place the historical corruption of these acts into perspective.
Mumford's scouts would redeem missed opportunities, would restore a
humane impulse to the activity of being American. Moreover, as Mumford continues to reflect upon the 1920s in his note of 1973, he and his
colleagues undertook not simply a "re-discovery of America," but a
"discovery of their own American heritage." If the aim was to restore
something lost in the culture at large, it was also to regain something
missing in personal life: an active heritage and a subjective meaning to
"American." In 1918 the Dutch historian Johan Huizinga had noted
that Emerson and Whitman had shared a common "consciousness of
their duty to speak as the voice of America to America." The comment
is apt for Mumford and his group as well; they too assumed a task of
speaking for what was buried, distorted, misappropriated: for what
Waldo Frank in 1919 called "Our America." Thus the subjective element, the identification of the tasks of scouting and prospecting with
the activity of being American, would define the cultural mission. The
personal and the historical would flow as one current.

In this confluence of the personal and the historical lay the source
of those "high energies and ever renewed hopes" Mumford recalled as
bright moments within the otherwise "sordid and even lethal characteristics of the twenties." The contrast is critical, for it emphasizes the
perception of the young scouts that their current ran against the tidal
patterns of the larger culture. The "usable past" prospectors took their
bearings from their sense of antagonism to dominant trends. The personal element exerted itself in opposition; indeed it provided the significant form of opposition. This cannot be stressed enough. The
assertion of self in the mode of a new historical awareness represented
a rebellion, a radical innovation in thinking about and identifying with
the past. Mumford understood this radical experimental element in his
labors of the 1920s perhaps better than most of his colleagues. He
seems always to have felt, at least, a need to view his own work in the

perspective of history, of a clear definition of the moment. In an essay of 1931, "Prelude to the Present," Mumford spoke at close hand of the 1920s as a decade of "spiritual eclipse" compared to the high hopes for cultural change in the years 1910–20, a darkness relieved only by the stirring of creativity among artists. The earlier period had witnessed the coming together of cultural rebellion and political reform: "a belief in a cultural America not identified with Colonial spinsterhood, with the antiquarian possessions of the museum, nor overallured by the sordid promiscuous jangle of Broadway or the Loop," and a "social conscience that made all the beginners in the decade turn automatically to Europe and to contemporary socialism as a source of value." The fruitful joining of culture and politics found its epitome, Mumford wrote, in the work of Randolph Bourne, who "declared war on colonialism" in the arts, who embraced education, architecture, and city planning in his range of criticism, and who "confronted the Power-state, when he found all his hopes and solicitudes about to be shattered in the diabolical mob-mindedness of war."

But with World War I, "darkness fell," and in the 1920s the two motives fell apart. Reformers, Mumford suggests, turned their backs on both cultural change and the more radical social vision they had entertained earlier: "they did not scheme generously enough . . . they carried into the promised land the customs appropriate to their older bondage." What remained of hopes in the 1920s, as he remarked in his note of 1973, were hopes "no longer for a great wave of utopian social improvement, but for achievements in art and literature that would enrich our days." Of course it is clear from a glance at his bibliography of periodical writings and reviews, especially his essays on architecture, city planning, regionalism, and "the machine," that Mumford himself continued to entertain and advocate hopes for social change as well as aesthetic enrichment. And his "usable past" books, while focusing on artists, are also works of social criticism. But it is in harmony with the artistic creativity of the decade that he (along with Brooks and Constance Rourke) focused on the buried heritage of art in his excavations, his new excursions into the past. Moreover, he hints that the new cultural historians felt more than a passing affinity with avant-garde artists. Evoking the mood of experimentation in the work of Hemingway, Eliot, Conrad Aiken, the sculptor Gaston Lachaise, and the photographers Paul Strand and Edward Weston, Mumford writes: "A display of intense individuality, a nourishment of idiosyncracies, was what precisely characterized the period, as this writer or that cast his line in waters that had never before been fished in." So the artists were, to the conventions they defied, rebellious and individual. Conventional academic scholars "had, in their pride over our natural endowments and our political innovations, overlooked the contributions that our ancestors had actually made to a new culture in literature, painting, architecture, and the machine crafts." If they celebrated writers it was only "the mediocrities," the imitative poets and authors who prided themselves on their European modes and styles. Condescension toward Mark Twain and Whitman, and dismissal of Melville, marked the standard versions of American history. To reclaim this wasteland that stood in place of a thriving tradition, the young scholars, Mumford implies, needed to work in the spirit of artists.

In 1918 Van Wyck Brooks had raised a resounding call to arms in "On Creating a Usable Past": "The present is a void, and the American writer floats in that void because the past that survives in the common mind of the present is a past without living value." The need as Brooks and Mumford saw it was to revalue, indeed to revise the past in order to reinsert the artist as a formative figure. Revisionary scholarship would perform a public cultural service by correcting the picture, and the performance of such a service is how historians now credit the "usable past" group. But their major goal was far more sweeping. It aimed to produce scholarship that would itself function as a kind of art: a manifestation (not simply a recounting) of the same creative spirit, the same buried and voiceless Americanness that was the subject of their researches. By their acts of imaginative scholarship the new scouts would not merely correct the picture but place themselves within it. As scholarship verged toward art, rediscovery assumed the form of self-discovery.

"Usable past," then, fused impulses toward self-expression with impulses toward a broad social criticism, a criticism founded upon values represented by art. This cannot be stressed enough, if we are to understand and make claims ourselves upon the work of Mumford and his colleagues as our own genuinely usable past. In the perspective provided by Mumford himself, that work in the 1920s took as its own immediate heritage the earlier rebellion, what Henry May has described as the break by progressive intellectuals with their "genteel tradition" elders. The initial rupture induced critics to view culture and politics in a single perspective. This early synthesis clarified itself best, as Mumford elsewhere indicates, in the journal *Seven Arts* (1917–18) and in the increasingly probing work of Bourne. The war caused a break in ranks, a split between social-political thinking and aesthetic experiment. The project to create a new cultural history out of new researches and new valuations aligned itself chiefly with experiment: by its placement of original and dissident artists at the center of the newly conceived American tradition, and just as important (and integral with its new orderings of the past), by its own manifestation of an experimental aesthetic spirit in the making of its own works, its new texts of scholarship.

To this brief and scanty overview must be added the notion, everywhere implied by Mumford in his comments on the decade, that while the new scouts were in search of *their own* heritage, they also sought to retain or to revive the synthesis of culture and politics of the earlier period. We find this effort toward what might be called a social aesthetics—a grounding of social criticism upon an aesthetic premise—in the criticism of popular culture by Waldo Frank (as well as in his larger syntheses such as the metaphysical *Re-Discovery of America*, 1939), in the essays on contemporary artists by Paul Rosenfeld, and in Mumford's own studies of American art and culture. In the scouting and prospecting of the decade, in short, quite apart from its specific achievements, we have an epitome of the attempted integration of culture and social life, of art and politics, that marked the beginnings of a radical intellectual tradition in modern America.

II

I suggest that we must look to the form of Mumford's books in the 1920s (to confine the matter to that decade) as much as to their sub-

stance—to their form as partaking of their substance and their meaning—in order to grasp their significance. By the 1940s and 1950s the
"usable past" project found its way (for reasons themselves revealing of
major shifts in American life) into the academy, especially into what is
known as the American studies "movement." It found its way into an
academic scholarly discourse, and perhaps for this reason, in confronting their own origins in the "amateur" scholarship of the 1920s,
American cultural historians have failed to notice the importance of
form, of style, of aesthetic presentation. The discourse of Mumford is
not simply that of an "amateur," a nonprofessional, a "generalist" (in
one of his favorite terms of self-description) rather than a specialist. It
is a discourse of a writer who conceives of history so deeply in an aesthetic mode that the category itself may seem tautological. This is to
say that his books perform their task of historical revision and reconstruction in the ambience of an idea of the centrality of art to culture,
an idea antithetical to the ruling cultural values of the age. The task of
the books is to revise historical memory by centering it upon the work
of artists, and thereby to revise the culture itself by fostering an aesthetic point of view toward the past as a mode of consciousness desirable in itself. And they perform their double task, of revising the past
and revivifying the present, by taking their own form as an occasion for
imaginative inventing.

The quality I refer to lies so securely entwined with the substance of
the books that we can hardly unstitch it without disturbing the entire
fabric. We can, however, indicate several outward signs of an inward
commitment to an aesthetics of history. Of course *Sticks and Stones*,
The Golden Day, and *The Brown Decades* all proceed faithful to a linear
chronological structure: an important sign of the acceptance of history
as development and unfolding, as accumulation of achievements and
energies in a single process that must be apprehended as a whole.
Mumford's aesthetic view of history is not to be understood as a sub-
jectification in any extreme sense. History is real in its externality and
firmness. But it is also internal and plastic, shapable by perception,
which in turn acts upon its own needs. It is, indeed, the wholeness of
history that demands an aesthetic viewpoint, and a need for form and
order that provoke imaginative revision. Chronology here serves as the

external form of apprehension. But within the chronological structure the historian, or we might say the narrative voice, frees itself from confinement to the "past" it contemplates. It speaks the voice of its own present—Mumford typically evokes "our generation"—and views the past as the present's "story," the occasion for self-contemplation.

The narrative voice is both storyteller and commentator. It is unmistakably present as a distinct voice, as *someone's* voice, an "I" that commits itself to judgment and valuation. The speech is dramatic in the double sense, first, of simply being speech, addressed to a listener also assumed to be present, attentive to a discourse, not simply a seeker of cataloged facts, and additionally, in the sense of its witnessing the past within a mode of conflict, of oppositions, of polarities. The speaker *dramatizes* just as he himself enacts a dramatic event, an address to an audience. The following passage from *Sticks and Stones* is characteristic:

> I have emphasized what was strong and fine in Richardson's work in order to show how free it was from the minor faults of romanticism; and yet it reckoned without its host, and Richardson, alas! left scarcely a trace upon the period that followed. Romanticism was welcomed when it built churches; tolerated when it built libraries; petted when it built fine houses; but it could not go much farther. Richardson was a mason, and masonry was being driven out by steel; he was an original artist, and original art was being thrust into the background by connoisseurship and collection; he was a builder, and architecture was committing itself more and more to the paper plan; he insisted upon building four-square, and building was doomed more and more to *façaderie*. The very strength of Richardson's buildings was a fatal weakness in the growing centers of commerce and industry.

The finely articulated balances and antinomies of the passage carry the dramatic form of conflict: the opposition between an older idea of craft in building and a new practice of rationalized and mechanized construction. In the sequence of oppositions—masonry/steel, original art/connoisseurship, builder/paper plan—larger issues arise, even deeper conflicts between originality and superficiality, between substance and façade, between commerce and art. The passage recounts the fate of Richardson's work, how in the eyes of its "host"—the new capitalist order after the Civil War—its very strengths appear as fatal weaknesses. But the passage resonates beyond its instances, discloses an entire historical moment. The disclosure follows, moreover, from the narrator's command of a shifting perspective: his raising the image of the host, tracing the instances of conflict, and concluding with the articulated irony of strength seeming weakness.

Of course we are speaking of style, of rhetoric, of devices of persuasion. But the critical element flows from a source below style, from the motive or bent of mind that determines in the first place that there should be a "style" in a written discourse, a manner as well as a flow of words and designations. Style represents the writer's presence, in this case as narrator: his caring to be present. The Richardson passage is one of many that can be chosen almost at random, in which it is clear that style represents the writer's intervention as the witness of the recounted event (or general situation), his taking it on, so to speak, as his own experience, an event in his own (or the present's) consciousness of the past: his remaking the past, in short, into *his* (or the present's) past.

There are, I think, two major impulses evident in Mumford's design of his narratives. One is the impulse toward unity, toward discernible pattern; the other is toward experience, toward a vividness and precision of detail that brings what is recounted forward as concrete experience as well as significant example. The two are not at odds, but a tension holds them together. The desire for unity shows in the obedience to chronology, and in the structure common to each book of concluding the linear narrative with an "Envoi" or summary that caps the story with a kind of moral, a dramatic aside, as it were, in which the storyteller reflects upon the tale and its wisdom. It also shows in the deployment of images and metaphors. The titles alone signify a metaphorical imagination governing the construction of the books, a thinking in images that itself rubs against the grain of conventional academic history and associates itself with the evocative power of poetic language. Taking the three books as a kind of trilogy, we can observe a deepening, an intensification of the metaphoric, that reaches a height in *Brown Decades*, where the title image runs through the work, releasing a complex and serviceable metaphor of color.

The structural possibilities of a controlling metaphor appear in the central chapter of *The Golden Day*, itself called "The Golden Day." Here Mumford stages the central event of the book—indeed of the authentic American culture he wishes to recapture in all three books—as the phases of a day, the passage of light in the course of a day. If certain figures such as "pioneer" serve as types in the drama of conflict that is Mumford's primary mode of narrative, this chapter chronicles the lives and works of Emerson, Thoreau, Whitman, Hawthorne, and Melville under the subheadings "The Morning Star," "The Dawn," "High Noon," "Twilight," and "Night." The image designates a metaphoric role for these concrete historical figures, a role tending toward typification, toward figuration, yet stopping short of complete translation of the literal into the symbolic. They remain themselves, with a hint of cosmic power befitting makers of culture. They function in the aura of a specific tonality of light, and at the same time represent that tonality as a moment of cultural history, a phase of the process whereby "then" becomes "now." Thus the light image illuminates them, and they in turn shed that light back upon the culture, in the eyes of the narrator, as a characterizing ray. Mumford makes the function of the image explicit in a passage in *Brown Decades*: "One might almost divide cultures according to their habit of viewing the world in the hard sunlight of midday or in the murky vistas and undecipherable horizons of night."

Unity achieved through metaphor (and through the formal mode of address of an envoi) declares itself, however inconspicuously, as a unity of perception and construction: an act that substantiates the presence (as well as the presentness) of an active narrator. The two impulses nourish each other, for the need to see the past whole appears in these works as a function of the need to *experience* the past in its livingness, to overcome not only the "officialness" of an arid, conventional history, but any purely instrumental or pragmatic view of history as mere record or lesson. Structural unity and metaphor both flow, in Mumford's case, from an organicist model in which wholeness, interconnectedness, integrity of parts among themselves, and process provide the key terms for both history and the writing of history.

The model, the needs out of which it arises, and the kinds of experiencing of the past as present it allows show best in *Brown Decades*. It is, in important ways, the most personal of the three books; that is, personal in the sense of its speaking most immediately out of and toward a generational need. "The commonest axiom of history," the narrative begins, "is that every generation revolts against its fathers and makes friends with its grandfathers." The book exfoliates from the "axiom," keeping the parental image central. This is a book by a grandchild who has "become conscious of a life not unlike our own" stirring "beneath the foreign trappings of the seventies and eighties." A sensed similarity "is the first claim to our sympathy."

> Like our grandfathers, we face the aftermath of a war which has undermined Western Civilization as completely as the Civil War undermined the more hopeful institutions of our country. The dilemmas, the hopes, the mistakes of the earlier period are so near to our own that it would be a wonder if we did not see its achievements clearly, too. But we need a fresh name for this period, if we are to see it freshly.

The grandchild perceives the grandfather in his own image; pursuing the similitude he pursues his own visage, his own being. *Brown Decades* has more the character of a mirroring, a quest in search of a past that will disclose the present, than either of the other books. Issues of an organic relation to the past, and also of literary structuring in the rendering of the past as narrative, lie closer to the surface here, more conscious, more programmatic. Thus the dependency of seeing upon naming—or shall we say of knowing upon metaphor—can be stated as a bold proposition.

Mumford no doubt expected his title to recall Thomas Beer's *The Mauve Decade* (1926), a spirited and somewhat novelistic account of the 1890s. Mumford refers to Beer's "uncanny eye for neglected materials and sources." Mauve, a faded or diluted purple, conveys a note of decline and decadence; it evokes an air rather than suggesting a

metaphoric interpretation. Mumford takes the interpretative implications of color much farther. Brown serves as more than a label; it
evokes a view of experience.

> There are occasional years when after spring has leafed and
> blossomed, a long series of storms and rains destroys one's sense
> of the summer. Suddenly one raises one's eyes to the trees and
> discovers that autumn has arrived: the leaves are sere, the gold-
> enrod stands brown and threadbare in the fields, the branches of
> the maples are stripped, and only the red berries of the black
> alder, or the dull persistent greens of the buttonwoods and
> poplars, remind one of the summer that never came.

Such an introduction to the meaning of brown is more than literary
embellishment. The natural imagery joins the generational allusion in
the opening sentences of the book as a way of grounding the writing of
this history within a wider, more concrete experience. The paragraph
that follows expands the seasonal image into a mode of historical experience, a metaphor not of explanation but of apprehension.

> There was such a violent stormy summer, and such a sudden
> push of autumn, in the period of American history that began
> with the Civil War. The long winter of the seventeenth century,
> a sturdy battle with the elements, had given way to the slow
> spring of the eighteenth: it was then that the ground was
> ploughed and the country made ready for a new political system
> and a new relationship to the institutions and customs of the
> past. Then, in the few warm weeks that elapsed between 1830
> and 1860, there had come a quick leafing and efflorescence. In
> the literary works of Emerson, Whitman, Thoreau, Melville,
> Hawthorne, new modes of thought and a fresh sense of the hu-
> man adventure became apparent. If there were few early fruits,
> the flowers were delectable and their promise abundant.

As in the temporal sequencing in "The Golden Day," the seasonal
metaphor here stresses process, cyclic change, organic growth, and de-

cay. The image provides an order, a unity, that lies elsewhere than in the sequential causation represented in conventional historical writing.

To be sure, the organic metaphor might seem also a principle of explanation, a version of the Spenglerian system of cyclic determination. But Mumford cautiously avoids any hint of a causal accounting from natural process. Instead the natural imagery offers a mode of experience: a naming for the sake of a fresher seeing. The metaphoric act seems more important than the specific metaphor itself. For in that act the past becomes "usable" as personal experience; metaphor creates an organic link of its own, and its ultimate aim is not merely to represent the past, but to bring the present to a fuller, surer sense of itself.

III

How are we to understand Mumford's efforts to compose history as art in the 1920s? The ambition arose, as I have suggested, out of dissent: dissent shaped by the need for a creative role in the present. Mumford makes the ambition explicit in the conclusion to *The Golden Day*. Here he speaks of example and implies that the need for art arises from, and provides the most significant form for, a criticism of the present state of culture.

> We cannot return to the America of the Golden Day, nor keep it fixed in the postures it once naturally assumed; and we should be far from the spirit of Emerson or Whitman if we attempted to do this. But the principal writers of that time are essential links between our own lives and that earlier, that basic, America. In their work, we can see in pristine state the essential characteristics that still lie under the surface: and from their example, we can more readily find our own foundations, and make our own particular point of departure. In their imaginations, a new world began to form out of the distracting chaos: wealth was in its place, and science was in its place, and the deeper life of man

began again to emerge, no longer stunted or frustrated by the instrumentalities it had conceived and set to work. For us who share their vision, a revival of the moribund, or a relapse into the pragmatic acquiescence is equally impossible; and we begin again to dream Thoreau's dream—of what it means to live a whole human life.

Art represents the "whole human life" that serves as an alternative vision to the present. Not simply *in* the art of the past, but in the active cultivation of an aesthetic outlook altogether lies Mumford's hope, as expressed here, for "essential links" to "that basic America."

Mumford's histories premise and evoke an aesthetic self, and in this they perform their own work as both art and cultural criticism. Art names a capacity open to all people, the capacity to shape experience by desire and thus to free oneself from negative limits. "Man is not merely a poor creature, wryly adjusting himself to external circumstance: he is also a creator, an artist, making circumstances conform to the aims and necessities he himself freely imposes." Art, Mumford continues, joins desire to social actuality: "without this union, desires become idiotic, and actualities even a little more so." Art is the activity from which springs culture itself: "Confronted by the raw materials of existence, a culture works them over into new patterns, in which the woof of reality is crossed by the warp of desire." The aesthetic, then, belongs at the center of social existence; in Mumford's eyes, only an aesthetic encounter redeems experience for human use. Thus artists, craftsmen, builders, makers of all kinds, emerge as the valued figures against the pioneers, explorers, hunters, and miners, whose energies address themselves only to instrumental goals, whose satisfactions are always deferred on behalf of a future that always recedes, and whose inner repressions cripple and disable.

We must recognize that the aesthetic priority Mumford shared with his fellow scouts bore no resemblance to an aestheticism of dilettantes and connoisseurs. It was instead a deliberately antagonistic concept, a vehicle of a criticism that deserves to be called social and political. We can better gauge the density of critical implication by uncovering its grain of opposition, its antagonism to its own "host" in the 1920s. Mumford's aesthetic of history shaped itself primarily in antagonism to the new formations in culture Huizinga described in the phrase "transitive culture," formations embodied in behaviorist psychology and a general mechanization of thought. Huizinga refers to a "psychological terrorism" that bans "summarily" all terms that belong to the realm of "spirit" rather than matter: terms like "meaning" and "consciousness." The reduction of all human phenomena to "behavior," Huizinga observed in his visit to the United States in 1926, is a form of submission to mechanism. To speak of human actions as "functions" is to prepare for an integration, an "adjustment" of man to environment of profound consequence for culture: "This obliteration of the boundaries between the individual and the environment, this interchange of object and subject, if I see things correctly, opens up the possibility of a reconciliation with a mechanized, leveled-down society, in which productive energy is transferred from the living arm and fixed in the dead tool." The "This, Here, and Soon" spirit of a "transitive culture" also denies reality to any dimension of experience not immediately understood as behavior, function, or physical need. Any transcendent impulse of desire, such as represented by art, is considered evasive, illusory. Moreover, in the pragmatists as well as the behaviorists Huizinga identified an "antimetaphysical attitude of mind" that "automatically includes an antihistorical one." History serves only "the utility of a warning," and exact description of past events substitutes for experienced continuity.

Devaluation of the past was a more serious barrier to culture, in the mind of Mumford and his colleagues, than mere distortion or misrepresentation. It was of one piece with devaluation of mind, of desire, of freedom outside the constraints of a corporate system. The aesthetic self posited by Mumford at the center of the engagement with the past is a figure, then, of resistance. The achievement of his American "usable past" studies appears foremost in his creation of such a figure, in his invention of narrative forms and a voice to give it expression. To read Mumford in this light is to realize a challenge to critical history, not only to turn its eye to the forms that convey the content that has absorbed most of our attention, but also to consider our own forms, our own narratives, the kind of figures we project at the center of our own studies. This is not to say that Mumford's kind of history must, or even can, serve our own needs. But that reading his history as art may bring us to a keener sense of the cultural predicament within which we perform our own work.

THIRTEEN

BROOKLYN BRIDGE AS
A CULTURAL TEXT

MONG the celebrants of Brooklyn Bridge in May 1883, one voice struck what might have seemed an oddly discordant note. It is a voice little heard in these days of rededication and reverence for the old bridge and its builders, and when heard, not always comprehended and appreciated. I refer to Montgomery Schuyler, the most important critic of architecture of his day, and to his article in *Harper's Weekly*, "Brooklyn Bridge as a Monument." Like everyone else on that festive occasion, Schuyler hailed the bridge as "one of the mechanical wonders of the world, one of the greatest and most characteristic of the monuments of the nineteenth century." Unlike the speakers at the opening ceremonies, however, Schuyler did not proceed to draw lofty conclusions about "progress" or the coming age of peace and reconciliation. To the contrary, when he cast his eye ahead, it was toward a very different future indeed: a postapocalypse scene, when New York lay in ruins, "a foresaken city." Suppose, he asked, only the massive stone towers of the new bridge survived, outlasting "every structure of which they command a view." Imagine the metal roadway and cables—"the web of woven steel that now hangs between the stark masses of the towers"—already "rusted into nothingness." The towers

First published in *Annals of the New York Academy of Sciences* 424 (1984): 213–23, on the occasion of the hundredth anniversary of the Brooklyn Bridge.

alone may now provide the only clue to what we once were, to what we are. And if so, if "our future archeologist, looking from one of these towers upon the solitude of mastless river and a dispeopled land . . . [has] no other means of reconstructing our civilization than that which is furnished him by the tower on which he stands," what might he make of us?

The question was, of course, meant to jolt the reader, and still effects a certain disconcertment. Schuyler asks: When viewed in such a distancing way, what does Brooklyn Bridge disclose about "our civilization"? Take the bridge as an ethnological fact of an otherwise unrecorded people (ourselves). What knowledge of a way of life lies inscribed in its structure, its materials, its form? Attempt to read it as if it were a hieroglyphic text. What messages can we detect in its wordless inscriptions? By what key might we decipher its purposes and functions, its original meanings? Schuyler's essay inaugurates such questions about the bridge as a cultural text, and his remains the most detailed and attentive study simply of its physical structure, shorn of all association or anecdote. The essay is also a polemical argument, an excursion in cultural criticism, and is, itself, a major text in the history of discussion and representation generated by this extraordinary object, the Great East River Bridge.

Schuyler concluded that with all its power as a "mechanical wonder," the bridge was a flawed work of architecture. The power of his essay lies less in this conclusion, however, than in Schuyler's method, which can be called a critical exegesis of the bridge as a form, a material structure. The method demands that we "recontextualize" the bridge in our imaginations in order to see it more clearly as a form. And we can better see the form of Schuyler's own argument, and more sympathetically assess his conclusions, if we replace his essay in its original setting of May 1883, in the context of the official opening ceremonies, where questions about the meaning of the bridge for "our civilization" were posed again and again, and where answers flowed with remarkable ease. By contrast complex, difficult, and in many ways decidedly unofficial, Schuyler's view of the bridge differed sharply. Thus, at the very outset of its career, the bridge occasioned quite distinct, even radically diverging views, and this fact—of differing and antagonistic interpretations of the bridge's import—constitutes a most telling feature of its role in American cultural history. Indeed, conflict over its significance has enhanced the resonance of Brooklyn Bridge as a charged image, a cultural text of unfinished meaning.

I want, then, to consider Schuyler's essay and the opening ceremonies in light of each other, to note differences of approach, of outlook, and thus perhaps to recover an original moment of tension in the career of the bridge as America's grandest symbol. We should understand at the outset, however, that the word "symbol" has at least two operative meanings relevant to this discussion. Normally when we speak of the bridge as a symbol, we mean that in someone's mind it "stands for" something—an idea, a state of being, another place or thing—besides its *bridgeness*, its function as a highway over a river. Then there is another, more technical sense by which "symbol" designates the normal, typical way a sense of reality gets constructed in the mind. Thus, language itself consists of symbols, and a culture can be defined as a structure of symbols, a "symbolic constitution of the world," as Marshall Sahlins has put it. In this sense of the word, even as a highway, Brooklyn Bridge is already a symbol, for the function of bridging makes sense only within a larger symbolic order. If the symbolic order of American culture at any given moment so powerfully governs how its members perceive reality, then Brooklyn Bridge is never a mere fact, it is always mediated by a symbolic meaning. When we use "symbol" in the first sense, then, we refer to what can be called a second order of meaning, something beyond the everyday object. The utterance of self-consciously named symbolic meanings occurs chiefly on certain distinct occasions: the ritual of an "opening" or a "rededication," the writing of a poem, or the painting of a picture. That this particular bridge evokes the need for such meanings beyond its everyday significance constitutes its claim as a complex cultural text.

Schuyler's view of the bridge embodies the notion that meanings are not fixed, not inherent in objects, but are products of interactions and the effects of a process: in the case of Schuyler's own interpretation, meaning derives from a close questioning of the form of the bridge in light of the function of its parts. What is disclosed at the outset to Schuyler's imagined archaeological eye is the bridge's status as "a work of bare utility." "It so happens," he writes, "that the work which is likely to be our most durable monument, and to convey some knowledge of us to the remote posterity, is a work of bare utility; not a shrine, not a fortress, not a palace, but a bridge." Not merely a bridge, moreover, but a bridge devoted to nothing more than the "bare utility" of crossing a river. From this fact—the striking prominence of a structure stripped of any reference to functions other than the utilitarian— follows another, equally characteristic, and even more expressive of the character of an age devoted to "bare utility": "its disregard for art." Taken as a form, the bridge rests "satisfied with the practical solution of the great problem of its builders, without a sign of the skill which would have explained and emphasized the process of construction at every step, and everywhere, in whole and in part, made the structure tell of the work it was doing." Proof of this failure of self-explanation meets the eye, Schuyler writes, in the flatness of the tops of the towers, their squared-off appearance. That flatness, he writes, "conceals instead of expressing the structure." Any one of the towers "without its cables would tell the spectator nothing," nothing of its purposes, of its "uses." "With its flat top and its level coping, indicating that the whole was meant to be evenly loaded, it would seem to be the base of a missing superstructure rather than what it is."

Disregard of art, then, is tantamount to a failure of expressiveness and explanation, of the capacity of the structure to "tell" its own story, the story "of the work it was doing." In earlier periods, Schuyler notes, "this aesthetic purpose would have seemed to the builder of such a monument as much a matter of course, as necessary a part of his work, as the practical purpose which animated the designer of the Brooklyn Bridge." With us, he concludes, "the utilitarian treatment of our monument is as striking and as characteristic a mark of the period as its utilitarian purpose. It is a noble work of engineering; it is not a work of architecture."

Some of us may want to insist, in rebuttal, that Roebling did in fact care for art, that the Gothic towers bespeak that caring, and that they have surely passed the test of time as honorably handsome and affecting images. The point remains arguable, and in the end, not very cogent or interesting. Much more to the point is the fact that Schuyler launches his critique of the masonry from two temporal sides: from the rear, so to speak, in the contrast between the medieval synthesis of art and engineering and the modern subordination of the former to the latter, and from the front, in the contrast between the very engineering of the bridge and its flawed "art." While "the anatomy of the towers and of the anchorages is not brought out in their modelling," in the central span of the bridge, in its cables and networks of stays, we have "anatomy alone, a skeletonized structure in which, as in a scientific diagram, we see—even the layman sees—the interplay of forces represented by an abstraction of lines." This is, he writes, "gossamer architecture," which speaks "its story more clearly and more forcibly" than traditional architecture. Schuyler's rapture is unmistakable: "This aerial bow . . . is perfect as an organism of nature. . . . There was no question in the mind of its designer of 'good taste' or of appearance. . . . His work is beautiful, as the work of a shipbuilder is unfailingly beautiful in the forms and outlines in which he is only studying 'what the water likes,' without a thought of beauty. . . . The designer of the Brooklyn Bridge had made a beautiful structure out of an exquisite refinement of utility, in a work in which the lines of force constitute the structure."

In Schuyler's reflections upon the bridge, then, the medieval wholeness of vision finds a modern counterpart in the work of the engineer when he confines his works to engineering alone. It is betrayed when the designer of bridges entertains thoughts of beauty and attempts monumental architecture. "To see the difference between a mechanical and a monumental conception of a great structure," Schuyler writes of the bridge, "compare these towers with the front of Amiens, or of Strasburg, or of Notre Dame of Paris." The comparison, Schuyler claims, serves all the more to highlight the intrinsic aesthetic power of the superstructure, its self-revealing anatomy of lines and curves. In his interrogation, then, Schuyler fuses the two perspectives—those of the Gothic builder and the modern engineer—into a single, coherent critique of the age: not of its architectural taste merely, but of a deeper failure to achieve a unified vision, an expressive form. Brooklyn Bridge serves as the occasion of this critique and also as the lens that brings it into focus. In Schuyler's view, the bridge stands in the end as quintessentially modern and American, its very flaws, its beguiling ambiguity, qualifying it as our most characteristic monument: a heuristic symbol for the culture as a whole.

Schuyler reads the bridge, it should be clear, not merely as a structure in space but as a cultural text, an object freighted with meanings that inform its smallest details. In this regard it is noteworthy that nowhere in the essay does he mention the designer of the bridge by name—Roebling is always the "designer" or "builder"—and the entire drama of construction is conspicuously absent from his account. Analytic rather than narrative, Schuyler asks only that the bridge itself, the material object of his exegesis, declare its own story. Schuyler extracts from the bridge its own confession, so to speak, as a characteristic structure of the times, one whose very flaws and internal contradictions are eloquent. In how the bridge is made to speak to its interrogator resides its cultural meanings: its monumentalizing of "bare utility," its utilitarian or mechanical treatment of its own monumentality. This contradiction qualifies the bridge to speak of its culture: in Schuyler's eyes, a culture riven by the "estrangement between architecture and building,—between the poetry and the prose, so to speak, of the art of building, which can never be disjoined without injury to both." The bridge thus represents its world ironically, an ambiguous embodiment of the culture's own self-estrangement. And it is all the more stunning, all the more provocative in its representation, because it contains within itself its own critique, its own sign of resolution, in the "gossamer architecture," the "exquisite refinement of utility," of the great central span. Here the bridge manifests, in Schuyler's critical eye, the promise of a culture capable of expounding itself in the form of a pure anatomy.

Contrast with the view of the bridge prevailing at the opening ceremonies could hardly be more stark. The event itself provided a structure of symbolic association: the bridge "presented" by the trustees of the "New York and Brooklyn Bridge" to the two cities, in the presence of the highest republican authority, the president of the nation, the governor of the state, and sundry lesser officials. Acceptance speeches on behalf of their respective cities were made by the mayors of New York and Brooklyn, and after a cornet solo by a Mr. J. Levy, two featured addresses by prominent representatives of the twin realms of the secular and the sacred: the Honorable Abram S. Hewitt, industrialist, philanthropist, and politician (then serving a term in Congress under the Democratic banner), and the Reverend Richard S. Storrs of Brooklyn. Rich in extravagant figures of speech and dazzling tropes, the rhetoric of the day held no surprises; it was a reprise of a familiar mode of public language, what Leo Marx has called a "technological sublime." For at least a half century in the United States it had been heard on like occasions—the opening of canals, railroads, bridges, and other public works. As to be expected, the keynote was "progress," man's domination of nature, and the tone was heartily optimistic. The bridge is a "trophy of triumph," we learn, "over an obstacle of Nature"; a fulfillment of man's "never-ending struggle . . . to subdue the forces of nature to his control and use." It is "the epitome of human knowledge," "the very heir of the ages." A "wonder of science," it was no less "a triumph of faith." Moreover, while "the glory of it belongs to the race," "yet it is distinctly an American triumph. American genius designed it, American skill built it, and American workshops made it."

To be sure, the occasion itself—the ceremonial embrace of the bridge into public consciousness as well as public space—called forth such language. The opening ceremonies received the bridge into a prevailing view of things, found a place for it in the mind, authorized it, so to speak, as possessing a public meaning beyond that of a mere traffic artery, a highway above a river. Indeed the orators of the day took the opportunity precisely to articulate those assumptions, to underscore that presiding worldview, of which the bridge seemed so compelling, so undeniable, so transparent and inevitable an emblem. Unmistakably an ideological event, the opening ceremonies represented a "ritual of assent," affirming the essential soundness of the body politic, the unity of American society, and the hegemony of a worldview compounded of faith in individual effort, in science, in peaceful relations between labor and capital, and in progress. Within the ritual, the Great Bridge served as text for the sermon, an image for typological interpretation. And appropriately it is the Reverend Storrs who finds in the bridge the very "type of all that immeasurable communicating system which is more completed every year to interlink cities, to confederate States, to make one country of our distributed imperial domain, and to weave its history into a vast, harmonious contexture." It is the "express palpable emblem" of such unity, of peace and harmony. And by linking together two cities that comprise a "magnificent gateway" to the nation, the bridge plays its symbolic part (as the figure of unity) "toward that ultimate perfect Human Society for which the seer could find no image so meet or so majestic as that of a City, coming down from above, its stones laid with fair colors, its foundations with sapphires, its windows of agates, its gates of carbuncles, and all its borders of pleasant stones, with the sovereign promise resplendent above it,—'And great shall be the Peace of thy children!' "

Thus the opening ceremonies baptized Brooklyn Bridge into its role as a ready-made symbol: text, type, sign and agent of "progress," of the American way, and in Storrs's final extravaganza, a pathway to John Bunyan's Heavenly City, which, "coming down from above" (by way of the bridge, presumably), might yet fulfill the old Protestant hope of founding in America a "city upon a hill." The bridge seemed on that day to plant itself as a veritable sermon in stone and steel. "Courage, enterprise, skill, faith, endurance," proclaimed one speaker, "—these are the qualities which have made the Great Bridge, and these are the qualities which will make our city great and our people great."

To judge by the exalted rhetoric, the worldview enunciated and affirmed at the opening of the bridge—an official worldview, we must remember, proper for utterance in the presence of the highest authority, the president of the nation—stood intact, free of such structural flaws and fissures of consciousness as those perceived by Schuyler. Yet the future tense in the just-quoted sentence should give us a pause, for it points to a somewhat less conspicuous feature of the rhetoric: that it often embodied a wish, a prayerful hope, that the bridge indeed *be* the emblem of unity, the symbol of peace and reconciliation, it was claimed to be, and that it serve truly to hold the world in place. When taken in the context of the open conflicts of the Gilded Age, and of the 1880s in particular—an age and a decade of staggering public corruption (affecting even the early years of construction of the bridge), of acrimonious political struggles between party machines and reformers, of chronic economic hard times, of increasingly bitter and violent strikes—the embrace of the bridge as an official emblem of an official culture makes clearer sense as an ideological event. The most explicit political interpretation and use of the image of the bridge occurred in the speech by Abram Hewitt, and appropriately so, considering Hewitt's role in New York City politics and culture.

Hewitt truly represented in his own life the values and worldview he articulated in his speech. He was a self-made industrialist who married into the solid burgher family and business of Peter Cooper; he stood as the city's most prominent patrician politician, a leading figure in the overthrow of Boss Tweed several years earlier, a Democrat unbeholden to the machine, a statesman above the fray who was willing to campaign for elected office. In his mind no issue surpassed in importance the worsening conflicts between labor and capital, and three years after the opening of Brooklyn Bridge, in 1886, he would run a fierce and angry campaign for mayor, barely edging out the radical Henry George, who, supported by the city's labor and immigrant voters, seemed to Hewitt an ominous threat to social order and stability. Order, stability, and intelligence: these were precisely the values Hewitt found so moving in the bridge, and which he extrapolated from the structure for application to the political world. The bridge represented a wanted alternative to the corruption and disharmonies of the age. It represented "organized intelligence," being in appearance a "motionless mass of masonry and metal" but in reality "instinct with motion." Hewitt saw in the bridge's design a political allegory: "It is an aggregation of unstable elements, changing with every change in the temperature and every movement of the heavenly bodies. The problem [is], out of these unstable elements, to produce absolute stability." Drawing the explicit lesson, he said: "If our political system were guided by organized intelligence, it would not seek to repress the free play of human interests and emotions, of human hopes and fears, but would make provision for their development and exercise, in accordance with the higher law of liberty and morality." By higher law his audience would have understood Hewitt to mean "free trade," a minimum of government regulation, and a natural harmony between labor and capital based on mutual recognition of rights and interests. Properly

heeded, the bridge might serve as symbolic pathway to social regeneration, to a secular version of Storrs's city "coming down from above":
"If, then, we deal successfully with the evils which threaten our political
life, who can venture to predict the limits of our future wealth and
glory—wealth that shall enrich all, glory that shall be no selfish heritage, but the blessing of mankind? Beyond all legends of oriental
treasure, beyond all dreams of the golden age, will be the splendor, and
majesty, and happiness of the free people dwelling upon this fair domain, when fulfilling the promise of the ages and the hopes of humanity they shall have learned to make equitable distribution among
themselves of the fruits of their common labor."

A trophy of triumph and a token of unity: Brooklyn Bridge
emerged from the ritual of the opening ceremonies as a public symbol
charged with meanings nothing short of utopian. How this came to be
so, how it happened that the bridge should release such visions of ulti-
macy as Hewitt's and Storrs's—and indeed as Hart Crane's a half century later, though his case differs profoundly—is yet another story. But
we might encapsulate the cultural drama of 1883 as follows: The
bridge was completed at a moment of crisis in American life, a moment of perceived threat to the system of meanings or ideology by
which many Americans took their bearings and imagined their relations to their real world—the ideology associated in the most influential minds not with a single class, but with America itself, and
embodied in such key terms as "individualism," "success," "stability,"
and "order." At such a moment the bridge seemed to promise that the
old ideology would remain intact, would prevail. Its own history, since
its beginnings in 1869, seemed a history of obstacles overcome, man-
made as well as natural, obstacles easily allegorized as tropes of similar
obstacles (corruption in high places, labor violence, growing heterogeneity of the population) facing the dominant American belief system. Of course no one actually believed the bridge would accomplish
anything besides making it possible to cross from one side of the river
to the other in seven minutes or less, but the occasion of the opening
ceremonies encouraged the speakers to imagine the bridge as the very
utopia of the governing ideology, that is, as the imaginary place, buttressed by its actuality as a bridge, a real pathway for crossing over, and

a very palpable achievement of modern tools, materials, and coordinated labor, where the ideology might represent itself as free of conflict, of threat, of contradiction. Here, in Brooklyn Bridge, at this moment, on May 24, 1883, the American way seemed manifest, liberating, and as true as nature.

The opening ceremonies, then, produced a Brooklyn Bridge as myth, as ideology, an idea of the bridge much in evidence when it was rededicated a century later.* If Hewitt's bridge is utopia, however, Schuyler's certainly is not. We do better to view Schuyler's bridge as an implicit cultural criticism, for in the bridge the critic discerned an unconscious enactment of clashing utopias, incompatible myths: the myth of tradition in the bad masonry; the utopia of utility, of modernity, in the perfect steel. The official bridge, then and now, is a transparent, self-evident emblem of a whole and stable society: a transcendent version of the real. Schuyler's bridge, on the contrary, represents its world obliquely, ambiguously, ironically, as a world divided against itself. This difference in readings entails, I am stressing, a difference in ontological status of the bridge itself, a difference in its status as an image of its respective versions of the world. Differences in reading, in symbolizing of the bridge, in short, arise from differences in outlook, in ideological need and perception.

And such differences as I have tried to reconstruct between Schuyler's view and that of the official orators have persisted in the remarkable history of representations of the bridge. Indeed, to speak of the bridge as having a significant history at all, beyond the narrative of construction and its anecdotes of courage, is to speak of that texture of representation by which the bridge has become, for those who wish to engage themselves with it in such terms, a prime cultural document.

---

*For example, the chairman of the board of Chase Manhattan Bank, writing in the preface to *The Great East River Bridge 1883–1983* (1983), a catalog of an exhibition at the Brooklyn Museum: "But the Brooklyn Bridge is also a symbol of the American spirit. The spirit which moved the project was the same that opened the West and built a great Industrial Revolution. This spirit was based on a firm belief in American technology, industry, and democracy. . . . The hundred years since the Bridge's opening have seen an extraordinary growth in our country. As the original engineers could build a bridge to last one hundred years—to carry traffic of a kind and amount unthinkable in 1883—so can we, with the same kind of perseverance and dedication, prepare for a sound and prosperous nation one hundred years into the future."

Of course the most significant chapter—that which permanently embedded the bridge within the dialectic of modern culture and the culture of modernism—was written in the 1920s by the extraordinary attention that artists and writers focused upon the structure: these include Georgia O'Keeffe, John Marin, Waldo Frank, Lewis Mumford, Henry Miller, and most significantly, Joseph Stella, Walker Evans, and Hart Crane. The cardinal document is, of course, Hart Crane's epic romance *The Bridge* (1930), a poem that crystallizes the tradition of antagonistic representation, of ideological difference, by attempting to imagine the bridge as fulfilling that utopia of unity freed of any social specificity claimed by the speeches at the opening ceremonies. The coincidence of Crane's wish and that of the 1883 orators is astonishing: the wish for a promise of unity, harmony, and repair of a broken world. Crane's utopia is, however, that of the exiled romantic artist in quest of a home, a tradition, a visionary ideal. We can speak of Crane's Brooklyn Bridge as representing a "usable past," thus indicating its debt to one of the major cultural projects of his generation. And as "usable past," the bridge of Crane's poem represents an energy, a form of coherence and transcendence utterly opposed to the forms of the cities, with their anarchy and deceits, that it joins.

> I think of cinemas, panoramic sleights
> With multitudes bent toward some flashing scene
> Never disclosed, but hastened to again,
> Foretold to other eyes on the same screen;
>
> And Thee, across the harbor, silver-paced
> As though the sun took step of thee, yet left
> Some motion ever unspent in thy stride—
> Implicitly thy freedom staying thee!

As in Marianne Moore's brief lyric "Granite and Steel" (1966), Crane's bridge is (in Moore's words) "implacable enemy of the mind's deformity, / of man's uncompunctious greed, / his crass love of crass priority." That such a bridge, in virtually absolute antagonism to the cities it links and the culture it serves, should have emerged in the

1920s as a cardinal emblem of the notion of the "usable past" says something of the urgency of need shared by artists and intellectuals in that decade of swift and decisive change. Now, the antagonism that Schuyler saw embodied within the bridge itself has become the leading fact of its relations to its cities: a reproach, in its perfect "curveship," to the deformities of a culture of office buildings, movie theaters, billboards, a culture with a terrible capacity to efface the past, to make Rip Van Winkles of us all. In his final walk "home" across the bridge in the concluding poem of his sequence, "Atlantis," Crane transforms the crossing over, the physical passage on the promenade, into a recovery of memory, of reconnection with all time and space. It is surely one of the most remarkable regenerative experiences in our literature. Whether the walk takes us to "Cathay," the elusive utopia of the history the poem recounts, remains an unanswered question. But the walk itself, its kinetic and visual repossession of the bridge, makes the bridge over into rhythm, into music, into an internal experience of the very harmony missing in the city's streets and in its tunnels.

> Through the bound cable strands, the arching path
> Upward, veering with light, the flight of strings,—
> Taut miles of shuttling moonlight syncopate
> The whispered rush, telepathy of wires.
> Up the index of night, granite and steel—
> Transparent meshes—fleckless the gleaming staves—
> Sibylline voices flicker, waveringly stream
> As though a god were issue of the strings.

Thus the "curveship" becomes a living thing. The walk across the bridge recapitulates, in "one arc synoptic," the history of which the poet had felt so utterly and desolately bereft. Here he attains his usable past.

There are, then, many Brooklyn Bridges, not all harmonious with each other. Difference, contradiction, antagonism have marked the bridge's continuing role as a symbolic presence. To speak of that role as continuing is, of course, to allude directly to our present occasion— not exactly, one would hope, a ritual of assent, but an occasion for scholarly and critical reflection upon an astonishing career of a magnificent bridge that is also a compelling cultural text. That we continue to reproduce this text, to consume the bridge not only as a medium of traffic but also a medium of meaning, may betoken our society's most revealing trait: a persistence of need for renewed images of utopia, for justifying myths, perhaps for a "city upon a hill" made permanently free of the deformities of "man's uncompunctious greed." We may wonder whether, bristling as it does with multitudinous and contrary implication, Brooklyn Bridge may yet address its future archaeologists with messages still unwritten.

FOURTEEN

PHOTOGRAPHY/ CINEMATOGRAPHY

T HE ideal film," remarked Vachel Lindsay in his incomparable tract of prophecy and fantasy, *The Art of the Moving Picture* (1915), "has no words printed on it at all, but is one unbroken sheet of photography." The image is jolting: an unbroken sheet of *photography*? Lindsay's association of cinema with the photograph, as free of text or captions, brings us back to the essential nature of the movies: cinema consists of a linear sequence of *still* photographic images, each differing in slight degree from the next and together creating the illusion of motion. Movement out of stillness is the paradoxical fact of the medium. Moreover the illusion of motion succeeds because the individual photographic image becomes invisible. The viewer cannot single out a particular still—a paradoxical and a well-concealed fact. This is an ironic casualty, so to speak, of that illusion of reality, that immediacy of representation, which is the camera's singular bequest to the art of the moving picture.

The relation of photography to cinematography in the emergence and shaping of cinema has not been carefully examined, and the exhibition of these early films from the so-called primitive era affords a special view. Cinema arose from the conjunction of two products of

First published in *Before Hollywood: Turn-of-the-Century American Film* (New York: American Federation of Arts, 1987), pp. 73–79.

technology: a device that presented a series of images so rapidly that there was an illusion of continuous motion, based on the phenomenon of "afterimage"; and an apparatus for projecting such continuous pictures. So far, photography proper plays no essential role. The projected images might well be hand drawn on a translucent ground. However, while there is no inherent reason for the image to be photographic, cinema without photography is almost unimaginable. By trying to imagine it, we can better appreciate the role played by photography in the emergence of the cinema.

The question of photography's role in motion picture history concerns cinema as an artifact made under particular circumstances. It is a question of form and of aesthetic analysis. As always, however, form remains inseparable from content, and aesthetics is inextricably entangled with history. Photography is not merely the camera apparatus. It is also the entire system of picture-making practices: the subjects chosen; the photographer's aims, commercial or artistic; and the modes of representation such as the code of perspective, which governs two-dimensional imitation of deep space. Photography denotes a process of *making meaning* through pictures. By the 1890s, this cultural process had infiltrated the entire society, establishing itself as perhaps the prime arbiter of "reality."

As Lindsay well understood, the infant art of moving pictures drew its lifeblood from photography and the general visual culture in which photography played a leading role. Indeed, as the earliest films often so charmingly and intelligently reveal, a lively symbiosis joined the two media. The industrialized urban societies of the nineteenth century seemed obsessed with visual aids. Binoculars, opera glasses, and scopes of all sorts, as well as devices for specular illusion such as dioramas, panoramas, stereopticon and lantern slide projections, all gained tremendous popularity. Technologies of vision, not confined to photography, provided a matrix for the new moving pictures and animated illusions. Photography itself proved the most consequential of these technologies. It offered a way of seeing and explaining commonplace experiences. In city views and street scenes, everyday life took on a new immediacy, often without the controls and mediations of pictorial composition.

Photography as narrative also anticipated cinema. From the earliest years, photographers sought to combine pictures into sequences for the sake of telling stories. As early as the 1840s, photography's first decade, there were sequences of images, protonarratives of, say, a game of chess or a heated conversation. Staged tableaux vivants, which were standard fare of Victorian photography, developed into the so-called sentimentals. These narrative sequences, often racy and wanton, were produced by the stereocard industry. Yet another popular diversion was the making of photo albums, usually centering on family life, with pictures of places as well as people. The family album invariably told a rambling but coherent story. Albums devoted to special occasions—a tour of the Holy Land, a visit to Rome—were not merely records but also narratives, no matter how naïve and plotless.

Far from naïve, on the other hand, were the fascinating and little-known experiments by Alexander Black in 1894 and 1895, exactly on the threshold of cinema. In what he called "picture plays," sequences of stills were projected on a screen upon a stage. The stills illustrated a story that was simultaneously read aloud from the same stage. In two of his productions, subsequently published as illustrated fictions, Black explored narrative devices such as continuity editing and montage. He took care with staging and lighting, and made a point of including well-known living personages, portraying themselves, along with fictive roles performed by actors, thus "bringing [to life] the living characters of fictitious action against the actual life of the city." Remarkably knowing and articulate, Black explained in prefatory notes that the "effect of reality" could not be achieved by "isolated pictures" but required "the blending of many," which was a protocinematic conception. He described his work as "the art of the tableau vivant plus the science of photography," a staging plus a recording. While art's task was "to translate nature," the "privilege of photography" was to transmit nature. This fusion of science and art was essential for the photoplay, because, he wrote, "the literal is not always the highest truth." He noted "widely divergent ways of transmitting a fact" and sought to create "the illusion that the thing seen is something that is happening or actually has happened in an actual room." Creating "the effect of reality" is paramount: as Black explained, "The photographer is in a disappointing business when he devotes himself to making his very pretty Rhine stone look like a real diamond."

Preferring the rhinestone *as it is*, its real prettiness against a fake brilliance, Black speaks in the language of "realism," a way of thinking about art and life as well as a set of conventions for representing the world. His mode of thought and practice seemed naturally akin to photography. "In recording literal fact the painter cannot draw like the camera," wrote Black, "for no eye has the truth of a good lens." This idea pervaded modern culture by the turn of the century; it was a mode of consciousness founded upon a cultural belief in the mechanical reproducibility of all real things—of reality itself—and in the truth of photographs.

A mere ghost in an emulsion, the photographic image proved capable of adhering to any surface—to glass as easily as wood or paper—and it insinuated itself everywhere. By the 1890s, the term "photographic" implied ease of transfer, interchangeability, as well as mechanical reproduction. A new way of representing what is real, the photograph was itself something new. The emulsified image made an extraordinary difference in how reality was understood; the emulsion was capable of rematerializing as an image, almost instantaneously, in defiance of time, space, and mass. On the threshold of cinematography, then, the realm of photography was already established as the realm of free-floating, emulsified images. Not "pictures," properly speaking, photographs performed their work in society in similar ways, as depictions of the real.

The belief in a pure photographic truth is worse than naïve; photography becomes an instrument of deceptions. Still, taken simply as a kind of communication, a signifying field, the photograph *is* relatively free of overt signs of interference from an editorializing hand. The photograph does compel its viewer to contemplate what seems an authentic token of reality, teaching viewers to read signs of life in black and white. Photography helped engender a new visibility in things and contributed to a rise in visibility itself. A high value was placed upon sight and its uses in modern culture—from surveillance to survey to spectacle to art. More intensely and urgently than in the past, to see became to know—or to hope to know.

And this uniquely modern conflation of vision and knowledge lay at the basis, at least as Vachel Lindsay insisted, of the art of moving pictures. Lindsay wanted "no words" in his ideal film because pictures possessed the voice of "our new picture alphabets." Indeed, long before Roland Barthes's remark that cinema speaks in a "purely gestural vocabulary," Lindsay introduced the notion of "Photoplay Hieroglyphics" as the essential signifying element in film. Such hieroglyphics might well achieve that same precision of meaning found in the ancient Egyptian prototypes. For example, in ancient texts a picture of a window, with closed shutters, is the equivalent of the Latin *P*: a coincidence Lindsay interprets as meaning that the "Intimate Photoplay" itself "is but a window where we open the shutters and peep into someone's cottage." Lindsay employs the term "hieroglyphic" as a trope for visual interpretation, for the deciphering of pictures in general. "A tribe that has thought in words since the days that it worshiped Thor and told legends of the cunning of the tongue of Loki," he wrote, "suddenly begins to think in pictures." Thus the moving picture heralds an altogether new moment in cultural history.

Lindsay's observation that "American civilization grows more and more hieroglyphic every day" might well be confirmed by a close look at the photographic hieroglyphics worked into early films to provide moments of scrutiny and scrutability. Such instances can tell us much about the photography/cinematography symbiosis. Most often the photographs glimpsed in early films are portraits, serving to identify or unmask false identities, as in *The Ranchman's Rival* (Essanay, 1909), in which the already married pretender is undone by an old photograph. In *The Girl of the Golden West* (Lasky, 1915), the question of the identity of Ramerrez is settled by the studio photo that the jilted and vindictive Nina slips to Rance. In this photo the outlaw is intentionally shown posing as a conventional romantic cowboy, a guise that proves almost true at the end, the photograph thereby complicating the question of identity. In *How Men Propose* (Crystal, 1913), the sly young lady gives away her own game, at the expense of her several suitors, by bestowing upon each an identical photograph of herself. In other instances a photograph serves as a surrogate person by which a character, and the viewer, can measure changes in a relationship. In *The Passer-By* (Edison,

1912), a framed photograph of the storyteller's old sweetheart reminds him of the betrayal that launched his decline; the framed portrait of the same lady, now a society matron, looms behind him on the wall of the gentlemen's club where he recounts his pathetic tale, a token for him and for us of the terrible irony of that moment of recognition. An extreme example of a photograph substituting for reality is in *The Dream* (IMP, 1911), where the reformed profligate passionately tears up the picture of his adulterous sweetheart, a symbolic gesture of reformation. Just as extreme, although in a vein of comic foolishness, are the histrionics in the game of exchanging locket tintypes in *A Tin-Type Romance* (Vitagraph, 1910).

Photography uncovers the truth astonishingly in *The Story the Biograph Told* (Biograph, 1903), in which the camera is a moving camera and the picture is not a photograph but a film. The story revolves around the making of a film within the film. An unsuspecting married businessman, unaware that a mischievous office boy is recording his antics with a motion picture camera, flirts with his compliant secretary. Later, the philanderer's wife sees the office boy's film, discovering her husband's infidelity and soon putting a stop to his pleasures. This curiously self-reflexive little film is also the occasion for striking cinematographic innovations: double exposure is used to show both ends of a telephone conversation simultaneously; the main scene is refilmed, this time from behind the couple, to replicate the point of view of the on-screen camera.

On the whole these are fairly simple situations, and the photograph plays an apparently uncomplicated role. People in the films act as though photographs were reliable pieces of evidence, yet in so doing they are interpreting the picture, bringing to life an inert image. Are the pictures in these films reliable and one-dimensionally referential? Does the studio portrait tell the full story about Ramerrez; does it reveal who he is? In fact, a good number of these early films concern themselves with just such disguises, impersonations, deceit, betrayal, trickery, and pretense. Such films depict a comic world in which the acts of unmasking and reestablishing of social order are often central, and the reading of a photograph frequently provides the catalyst for such a corrective act. But reality often remains elusive and appearances ambiguous. Consider *Getting Evidence* (Edison, 1906), in which a gum-shoe is retained, presumably to keep an eye on an errant wife. He decides to use a camera, a decision fraught with danger for himself and laughs for the viewers. In the end, it is a case of mistaken identity, the detective-photographer in pursuit of the wrong party. While the film does not call into question the validity of the camera as an instrument for "getting evidence," it does portray the photographer as a buffoon, whose disguises and gaucheries make him the butt of the joke. It is as if the photographic eye, the prying eye of the surrogate authority figure, undergoes exorcism here. In the mockery, the image itself loses some of its authority, as it also does in the behind-the-scenes view of mug shots being made in *Photographing a Female Crook* (Biograph, 1904). The crook in question resists with all her might, making faces at the studio camera, refusing to allow a clear view of her physiognomy, all the while the movie camera moves steadily toward her in a close-up. The moving picture seems to be wresting authority from the still picture.

The prominence of still photographs and photographers in these early movies may signify a kind of homage from the younger to the older medium, perhaps even a covert acknowledgment that still photographs are at the heart of film. The actual photographs embedded within the mise-en-scène symbolize a visual culture shared by photography and cinema in film's earliest years. For example, the moving-picture street scenes seem at times like Alfred Stieglitz's photographs of such subjects as horse-drawn streetcars in the snow. At other times they call to mind Lewis Hine's scenes of Lower East Side streets brought to life. Such resemblances point to other transactions between the mediums, as when early films appeared as components of variety shows, often sharing the bill with lantern projections of still photographs.

Developing in the shadow of photography, moving pictures defined themselves willy-nilly by reference to their opposite. Indeed it was routine to project the opening shot of a film as a still image, which the film would then bring to life, activated as if by magic. This practice openly declared the symbiosis of still and moving photographs, acknowledging the still as the buried but essential component of film. The germinal image of each cinematic scene is nothing more than a single still photograph from which the whole scene springs. Every scene interprets its own still image—the originating hieroglyph—in an effort to make sense by exploring the still's dynamic implications. As Béla Balázs explained, "Pictures have no tenses. They show only the present—they cannot express either a past or a future tense. In a picture itself there is nothing that would compellingly and precisely indicate the reason for the picture being what it is." Cinema responds to the atemporality of each still picture by supplying narrative flow, embedding individual pictures within an explanatory structure. In short, every still photograph implies both a spatial and temporal edge where what is not depicted in the image becomes present to it. Every still implies motion. The stopped action might continue and the story unfold in any direction.

But it is not motion alone that constitutes the art of moving pictures. Photography reproduces the world by abstracting from it, freezing time and space. Cinematography reconstructs; in Sergei Eisenstein's words, it is "organization by means of the camera." Assembling its lexicon of devices from other media—mise-en-scène from theater, the fade or dissolve from the stereopticon, the cut from albums and from picture stories such as those by Alexander Black—cinematography nevertheless produces a new artifact. Its aim is to create an illusion of total reality—to eliminate all signs of artifice and present a perfectly autonomous and self-generated world. In cinema, viewers are encouraged to leave their critical sense of artifice at the gate, to bring nothing into the darkened chamber with the silver screen but the capacity to surrender and to believe.

Certainly in its role as instrument of realism and arbiter of reality, photography governed cinema's quest for that illusion of reality. ("With the certain perfecting of orthochromatic photography and chronophotography," wrote inventor C. Francis Jenkins in 1898, "the means for recording the physical phenomena of nature and life will be complete.") What photography itself helps us see in the early films is a cinematography still in the grip of older artifices, of modes and styles soon to be surpassed. On the whole, they derive from theater and take the form of painted sets and exaggerated histrionics, both of which are perfectly at home on stage. The proscenium itself declares the rule of pretense: the temporariness of the setting and backdrops, the unreality of role playing on stage. No one confuses the actor with his role, and if so, the confusion is not permitted to survive curtain calls and bows at the end.

Reproduced as moving pictures, such devices seem stilted, incongruous, and exposed as false. Cinematography endows settings as well as persons with the air of immediacy and actuality, and if an actor seems to be a melodramatic character actor, so be it—the rhinestone, not the fake diamond, paint seen as paint. Erwin Panofsky speaks of "that curious consubstantiality that exists between the person of the movie actor and his role," which is precisely the effect of photography within cinematography. It was this power of making an image seem real and present that early cinema impressed upon both its audience and its experimental practitioners at the same time.

Hugo Munsterberg evoked just this capacity when he wrote in 1916 that "the true field for the photoplay is the practical life which surrounds us, as no artistic means of literature or drama can render the details of life with such convincing sincerity and with such realistic power. These are the slums, not seen through the spectacles of a littérateur or the fancy of an outsider but in their whole abhorrent nakedness. These are the dark corners of the metropolis where crime is hidden and where vice grows rankly." We have fleeting but compelling glimpses of such contemporary scenes as these in the early films: in *What Happened on Twenty-Third Street* (Edison, 1901), the camera is stationed on a sidewalk and creates its own subject; in the American Mutoscope and Biograph dramas, *The Skyscrapers of New York* (1906) and *The Tunnel Worker* (1906), there are astonishing scenes of workers at their worksites; and in several early Biograph films, notably *The Black Hand* (1905) and *The Romance of a Jewess* (1908), brief unstaged views of crowded lower Manhattan streets taken with a hidden camera are knit into melodramas otherwise staged upon the usual painted sets.

Such glimpses of a world captured and organized by the camera help to identify cinematographic potentialities in the new medium— what Lindsay meant by "an unbroken sheet of photography." Photography in all its guises helps us see this—photography as technique, theme, trope, and artifact within films. Even what is falsified stands revealed for what it is before the lens. In cinema's earliest decade, as perhaps never again, photography brings incongruity into focus and thereby serves as the perspective in which the future of cinematography becomes clear.

FIFTEEN

THE FSA FILE

From Image to Story

I

IN 1935, early in Roy E. Stryker's career as chief of the Historical Section of the Resettlement Administration, a woman appeared in quest of a photograph made by Walker Evans in Bethlehem, Pennsylvania. Stryker recalled the episode some forty years later in his 1973 book on the Farm Security Administration photographs, *In This Proud Land*. The picture was

> one of a cemetery and a stone cross, with some streets and buildings and steel mills in the background. Months after we'd released that picture a woman came in and asked for a copy of it. We gave it to her and when I asked her what she wanted it for, she said, "I want to give it to my brother who's a steel executive. I want to write on it, '*Your* cemeteries, *your* streets, *your* buildings, *your* steel mills. But *our* souls, God damn you.'"

In Stryker's mind the woman's reaction caught something essential in the project he had just undertaken to direct; it helped him define a

First published in *Documenting America: 1935–1943*, edited by Carl Fleischhauer and Beverly W. Brannan (Berkeley: University of California Press, 1988), pp. 43–71.

goal. "Pictures like these were pretty heady. . . . They gave me the first evidence of what we could do."

The anecdote is slight, but it catches something essential and instructive in our project as well, our own encounter, fifty years after the making of the images, with the formidable Farm Security Administration–Office of War Information (FSA-OWI) file. The file is tangible: actual file cabinets, microfilm readers, card catalogs. It is public property, open to all in the Prints and Photographs Division of the Library of Congress. We are free to visit it, open its drawers, browse among its images and captions; free to request any picture that catches our fancy or fills a need. Preserved here is an unexampled record of social observations, of visual detail awaiting absorption and interpretation. Our own needs may be less fired up than those of the woman in the story and more decorous, less immediate, more critical or aesthetic or historical. But whatever we may think of her particular reading of Evans's great picture or the propriety of even wishing to deface an image by writing upon it, her fervor teaches a vivid lesson. Her wish to put words on the image makes literal a desire to possess it as her own, to put herself into the picture as its active interpreter. However rash she was, however naïve in literalizing a complexly organized picture, her spontaneous participation in the image by remaking its meaning on her own ground (in this case fraught with social, political, and perhaps fratricidal motives) can be nevertheless an inaugural model and exemplum.

There is another lesson here for our own confrontation with the file and its contents. To recognize that an image is a kind of writing prepares us for the larger challenge of reading or making sense of the file as a whole—that is, of the FSA-OWI documentary project itself. The file represents that project, though not as transparently as we might think. The FSA-OWI file did not spring into being all at once; it has its own interesting history, linked to the evolving shape of the project itself but in the end a structure placed upon the project after it had ceased. From the beginning the project and a filing system existed in symbiosis. To assemble a great collection of pictures portraying the nation at the nadir of the Depression emerged as the overriding goal of Stryker's enterprise. "This file," wrote a staff member, "should be considered the thing we are building." The same writer described the goal as "a monumental document comparable to the tombs of the Egyptian Pharaohs or to the Greek Temples, but far more accurate."

The architectural metaphor is not far-fetched. From the birth of the medium in 1839 practitioners encountered unique problems of accumulation, storage, and organization. The problem of filing, although mainly technical, was nonetheless inseparable from questions of meaning and interpretation, of knowledge and use. The present file, built by Paul Vanderbilt beginning in 1942, is one of the most literate, self-conscious, and I think elegant solutions to a problem as old as photography itself. The solution is also complex, and I want to show that its elaborate technical procedures do not exist for their own sake; they are not "neutral" devices. They represent ideas, a distinct view of society and history and human action. The file deserves to be recognized as one of the prime cultural artifacts of the New Deal. As we shall see, it embodies the era's ideology of human history as "universal" and "progressive." The file helps us see through the eyes of that vision. It gives us both the insights and the blind spots, the strengths and limitations of a major American outlook: the liberal view of society as "natural" yet infinitely manipulable. In its cultural ambition the file reaches beyond the particular goals of the FSA and the OWI. It is a view of photography itself, particularly as a medium of cognition and social knowledge. In our approach to the photographs, then, and especially to the use of recombined separate images as stories, we need to consider the file as an intellectual construction, one that stands as a massive presence between the tens of thousands of single images it contains and the meaningful stories those images might tell.

The nexus of images and stories is in fact the main theme of the file, as it was of the FSA-OWI project. Roy Stryker believed he possessed a "master" narrative of the project, and others shared his confidence in a controlling theme. Vanderbilt clarified this master story in the nuanced modulations of his classification system. But the anecdote of the fervent woman and the Bethlehem picture introduces a provocative, skeptical note. To read an image is to write upon it, to incorporate it into a story. This is not to say that an image is a blank writing pad. There is something there to be seen, and we want to see it. We never (or rarely) read nakedly, however, but always through a veil, the screen of previous interpretations, of intervening contexts or discourses, and of our own motives, hidden and known. Even the setting of our encounter leaves its imprint, coloring our perception of the image. Reading, then, often takes deliberate rewriting; we can think of it as a contest, an effort to wrest an image from the grip of previous or contending readings. Arriving at our own vision takes a conscious act of revision. This is true whatever the object of our attention, but it is notably true of photographs, the most written upon, under, above, and around of all visual artifacts.

II

In 1938 a slightly cropped version of the Bethlehem image appeared in Archibald MacLeish's *Land of the Free*—"a book of photographs," explained MacLeish, "illustrated by a poem." Like each of the book's eighty-eight images, drawn mostly from the FSA-OWI file, Walker Evans's photo occupies a glossy page by itself, is bled vertically to the edges, and appears without caption or identification (a list of captions and photographers appears at the end of the book) opposite a page of text.

> We wonder whether the great American dream
> Was the singing of locusts out of the grass to the west and the
> West is behind us now:
>
> The west wind's away from us.

The image takes its place in a sequence of words and images, the governing theme of which is proclaimed in the poem's opening words, "We don't know / We aren't sure," which evoke the dubiousness of the American dream at a time typified by images of gaunt faces, resigned bodies, gnarled hands, ragged children, abandoned farms, police violence, and barbed wire.

Just preceding the Evans picture is photograph of a Congregationalist church and graveyard: "We tell our past by the gravestones and the apple trees." Just following it is a Russell Lee picture of a worried-looking farmer and two children "on cutover land in Wisconsin": "We wonder if the liberty is done: / The dreaming is finished / We can't say / We aren't sure." The three images make up a coherent passage within the argument of the poem, a kind of stanza: the Bethlehem picture with its commanding rusticated cross (implying a Catholic cemetery and immigrants) and its compressed urban-industrial imagery serves as a descending bridge from the pleasantly familiar rural Connecticut scene (all in white, with ancient lichen-covered slabs for grave markers) to the Wisconsin scene of depleted energy and belief. In that movement—from the spire of traditional communal belief, to the cross of stern judgment, to the abandoned farmer and children and the unpainted shack behind them—lies the inscribed meaning of "Bethlehem" in this setting: the alien hell that lies between there and here, between then and now.

Figure 26 Graveyard, houses, and steel mill, Bethlehem, Pennsylvania, November 1935, by Walker Evans. (Library of Congress, Prints & Photographs Division, FSA-OWI Collection)

The following year the Bethlehem picture (Figure 26) appeared in a quite different guise on a two-page spread as the concluding image of a group of forty-one Farm Security Administration pictures presented by Edward Steichen in *U.S. Camera 1939*. The pictures had been shown in an International Photographic Exposition held in New York City to mark the hundredth anniversary of the birth of photography, taking their place thereby in a celebrated history of the medium as, in Steichen's words, "the most remarkable human documents that were ever rendered in pictures." Steichen explained "documentary"—at the time a novel category for a salon exhibition—as pictures that "tell a story": "Have a look into the faces of the men and the women in these pages. Listen to the story they tell." As if to enhance the story, or to provoke the reader, Steichen included on the face of each image (except the first and the last) actual writing culled from the written comments of viewers of the exhibition. The comments display varying degrees of outrage, sympathy, sensitivity, and obtuseness. Their effect as captions is often ironic, at the expense of the anonymous author: "Next time play up the other side" appears on a Russell Lee picture of four children standing at their meager Christmas dinner; "Subversive propaganda" on Dorothea Lange's nursing migrant mother. The irony points the reader in the right direction.

Free of any explicit commentary, the blown-up Evans picture pointedly concludes the section, the hovering angel of the group. "For sheer story telling impact," Steichen wrote, the Bethlehem photograph, "picturing in parallel planes the cemetery, the steel plant and the home, would be hard to beat." Bled to the corners, printed like all the pictures in deeply saturated blacks on heavy pulp stock, and severely cropped at the top and bottom with the ominous foreground cross occupying even more of the picture plane than in the uncropped version, the presentation highlights the iconic message.

Yet another connotative use of the picture appeared in the same year. Roy Stryker and Paul H. Johnstone included it among nine images illustrating a lecture on documentary photographs before the American Historical Association in 1939, identifying it in their text only as "Picture No. 8," which shows "housing and factory construction" and "speaks volumes about the unplanned growth of an industrial city, although the dramatic composition of the photograph makes it an example of a type that is interpretative as well as documentary." Arguing for the value of photographic documents for historians, they explain that in depicting an aspect "of the urban milieu of which the immigrant from a peasant culture has become a part," the picture "has an insistence for the historian that no verbal document can carry."

MacLeish, Steichen, and Stryker: each joins the embattled sister of the steel executive in rewriting Walker Evans's picture, releasing some vibrations, subduing others. This process resembles the capture of an elusive creature in a tightly meshed net. As it takes place, we overhear the bemused voice of the original author, Evans himself: "People often read things into my work, but I did not consciously put these things in the photographs," Stryker and Johnstone quoted him as saying. In an unpublished note written in 1961 for a reissue of *American Photographs*, Evans said of his own work: "The objective picture of America in the 1930's made by Evans was neither journalistic nor political in technique and intention. It was reflective rather than tendentious and, in a certain way, disinterested." Disinterest is exactly what is purged from the image by the readings projected upon it.

Indeed, such representations of FSA pictures in the 1930s and since have made tendentiousness seem the inner motive of the project: the Farm Security Administration had a story to tell about the hardship, and also the hardiness and heroism, of the times. Stryker's project has been severely criticized for promoting New Deal ideology and policies: in a complex process, images that can otherwise be seen as disinterested, objective, and reflective were manipulated in presentation to favor the needs of the Roosevelt administration. However we judge the uses of Evans's picture, we should note that it appears in various contexts not so much as a picture by Walker Evans but as an *FSA* photograph. FSA itself has come to represent a context and to connote a particular story of the Great Depression.

Steichen mentions no photographer by name in his *U.S. Camera* introduction; he subordinates "the work of individual photographers" to "the job as a whole," each image standing for the collective project rather than an individual vision or practice. Curiously, the list of names he includes at the end of the group appears without captions or other information linking the pictures to particular investigations. Presumably the stories are internal, readable (or audible) within the pictures themselves, each self-sufficient, so long as the category FSA appears. The category projects a story or a meaning, and in the absence of captions, a meaning general, nonspecific, and perhaps self-assuring of fortitude and perseverance, those innate and invincible American values. Would particularizing captions have diverted attention, at the international exhibition as well as in the pages of *U.S. Camera*, from the images themselves, compromised their credentials for salon exhibition, cast doubt on their claim to a place within the *art* of photography? In the Steichen presentation the pictures fluctuate indecisively between two worlds: the FSA file and the galleries of fine art.

This indecision reflects the ambiguous status of photography in general, split as its functions have been between utility and aesthetics. This ambiguity in thinking about photography stands guard over any easy access to the FSA-OWI file; we encounter it as soon as we confront the file as a physical entity, in the very form and structure of the collection. Shall we seek, for example, the work of individual photographers, or the totality of pictures on certain subjects, made in certain places?

Two representations of the Bethlehem image dramatize this dilemma rather starkly. Both are uncropped, showing the full image as Evans himself presented it. In a 1971 Museum of Modern Art monograph on the artist, the photograph appears pristine, set alone on a page surrounded by white space, facing a page of white: the form replicates a gallery wall. Here we have the image in the context of the photographer's work, representing his vision, taking its place in his career as a picture maker. It has this place, moreover, through a process of aesthetic selection: it has survived the siftings and exclusions from the entire body of his work. In 1973 the same uncropped version appears in quite another kind of book on Evans's work: a catalog of the photographs he made for the Farm Security Administration, a publication over which he had no control or influence. It appears in two locations: in the opening portfolio of selected images presented one to a page as pictures unto themselves and also as a small catalog image along with other such images of pictures made in Bethlehem and

Pennsylvania on the same FSA trip. In the one case the image testifies to Evans's status as an artist, the maker of single fine pictures, and in the other to his practice as a journeyman photographer creating a cumulative record of social observation. Evans alone is really the context of both, but the presentation makes a difference in our reading of the same image.

Is the lesson of the Bethlehem image that there are no true meanings? Are all photographs vagrant images in search of a context, of readers prepared to write meanings across their face? It is tempting to name what seems the purest, least-written-upon version of the image as the truest: the exhibition version within the mise-en-scène of Evans's 1971 book. But "art" also gives context, a discourse within which we identify and act upon certain experiences. Recognition of this can shelter us from the difficulties associated with trying to imagine an original and essential meaning. Instead of seeking essences, the perfect meaning of single images, or an FSA "style" or "vocabulary," we should focus on the actual work of the photographers, their discoveries, their inventions, their reflections upon their activity. By entering the file and negotiating its intricate passages, we can begin to sort out its implications and impositions, its explicit intentions and those that remain hidden.

III

We start with an image of a horse (Figure 27). The horse appears to be cold; frost gathers at its nostrils. Is it a picture of "a shivering horse" or a photograph of "cold weather"? The present version of the FSA-OWI file was built on the answers to such questions. In a remarkably lucid "Preliminary Report" (1942) on theoretical and practical aspects of the constitution of the file, Paul Vanderbilt cites this dilemma to cut to the bone of the matter. His reasoning invites close attention. He writes, "Objectively, what appears in the photograph, without any whys and wherefores, is the basis for stability in our kind of record. Yet this is far from clear." There is no escaping a "subjective element," no certainty that two people will agree to any single statement of what the

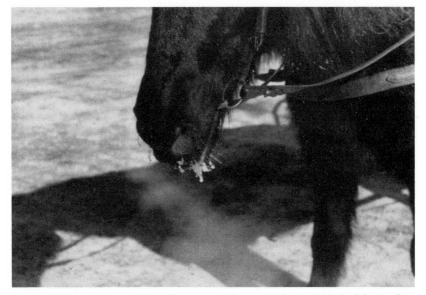

Figure 27 Horse on a cold day, Woodstock, Vermont, March 1940, by Marion Post Wolcott. (Library of Congress, Prints & Photographs Division, FSA-OWI Collection)

photograph actually shows. Should this particular image be filed under "horse" or under "cold weather"? Edwin Rosskam, who had helped contrive the earlier file organization that Vanderbilt's system displaced, and with whom Vanderbilt discussed the matter of the shivering horse, insisted, as Vanderbilt recounts the episode, that the horse best depicts not its own horseness but atmospheric conditions. Vanderbilt agrees: "Since cold must be shown through some objective medium, this is *in a sense* an objective judgment" (my emphasis). A good case could be made for either term, subjective or objective. It is a judgment call. But the categories "horse" and "weather" still do not tell us anything particular about the picture as a picture or what it might mean under all circumstances of its viewing; they tell us only how to *identify* the picture, where in the file to look if we wish to see it again. What we see and how we understand what we see are further matters: here the subjective/objective dance begins again.

The horse is no "Bethlehem" or "Migrant Mother." But commonplace images are more typical of the FSA-OWI file and its problems of readability than is generally acknowledged. The comedy of choosing

to ask, What appears in the photograph? arises as a perfect emblem of
the ambiguity in which most photographs reside—the same ambiguity
that allows one image to serve different masters under different captions on different stages. In his many writings on the file Vanderbilt
often emphasized the inescapable ambiguity of an uncaptioned, free-
floating photograph and the final arbitrariness of declaring, This is
cold weather, not horseness. The making of any file, he realized, is an
exercise in arbitrary judgment. Yet arbitrary does not mean without
reason or intent.

Among Vanderbilt's accomplishments were a number of unpublished essays and lectures explaining the principles of his system. His
chief explanation of the basis of his revision of the older filing system
in place when he arrived on the scene in 1942 is cognitive: the relation
of photographs to knowledge. How do photographs help us know reality? We must learn to see them, he argued, not as "facts so much as
conceptions." In his frequent use of terms drawn from linguistics, like
"denotation" and "connotation," Vanderbilt drew a fundamental analogy between photographs and language. He built into the file the theory that, like words, images can and should be endlessly recombined
into new relations to generate new ideas, new cognitions, new senses of
the world. Though he also designed the file for the single-image needs
of picture editors and historical researchers, he described his primary
goal as facilitating the use of pictures to make new and original "stories." Thus he wrote in 1959 that the task of assembling a file "is to
provide for recombination and reuse. . . . Certainly the provision for location of pictures on call is not to be neglected, but more important is
*the scattering of pictures in the pathways of search, where they may be found unex-
pected as fresh inspirations*" (my emphasis).

The earliest method of organizing the burgeoning number of photographs seems to have been by state and by subject. But sheer accumulation of differing images began to undermine this relatively simple
structure. On August 1, 1939, Stryker's section tried to provide some
guidance to the growing number of users, especially newspapers and
periodicals, by listing "suggestions for picture stories," such as "stories
of groups of people," "crop stories," and "stories of places." In a
memorandum in 1941 Edwin Rosskam exhorted Stryker to introduce

a clear "subject file" so that users could find what they needed with some dispatch. What stood in the way was the "haphazard system" of also filing together all pictures made on specific assignments—what later came to be known as "lots"—without cross-reference. Rosskam said even such unified groups proved to be "thoroughly unreadable" because they ignored the "intentions" of the individual pictures. Thus he titled his memo "Hieroglyphics we call our photographic file and how to decipher them."

"Decipher," "hieroglyphic," "readability": the elementary need of the file, such terms suggest, was the creation of an order like that of language, based on a clear, unequivocal code. One of Vanderbilt's first tasks was to clarify the distinction between groups of pictures that belonged together because they had resulted from a specific assignment and those whose connection with one another could be based on similarity of subject. Such similarities would provide the foundation, eventually, for the highly intricate system of classification now in place. This distinction between two radically different principles of grouping the pictures resulted in two separate physical systems: a microfilm system for the original lots and a vertical file system for the classifications. The bridge between the two is the lot number stamped on the back of each print in the classified file. To be sure, the two systems are not equal in prominence or authority. The vertical files stand in the Prints and Photographs Reading Room; they can be seen; we can open their drawers and touch the prints. Viewing the microfilm images requires special assistance at a mechanical reader. But the relation of the two systems is fundamental; it represents Vanderbilt's wish to keep intact a record of the actual order of pictures as they were produced in the field, even while he systematically dismantled that order for the sake of the larger, more intricate, and intellectually coherent order of the classification system.

No more than a system of convenience, Vanderbilt insisted, the classification categories simply clarify what is already there. The new system revises the old by rearranging it into a logically coded structure of similarities and differences. It replaces what was "linguistically" inchoate ("haphazard") with a lucid outline of nine major headings, or classes (Land, Cities and Towns, People, Homes and Living Conditions, Processing and Manufacturing, etc.), divided into six parallel regional divisions (Northeast, Southeast, etc.). The list of major headings gives no clue to the actual shape of the subject dimension of the file, with its thirteen hundred subheadings and a scheme of descending categories. A portion of "Homes and Living Conditions" illustrates a typical breakdown:

4 Homes and Living Conditions
41–43	Houses, rooms, furniture, people at home, visiting, hobbies
44–447	Life in tents, shacks, rooming houses, hobo jungles
448–46	Personal care and habits, housework, cooking, eating, sewing, sleeping
47–48	Porches, yards, gardens, servants

A more detailed breakdown shows an additional sixteen subheadings under "Permanent Homes" alone, including "Row Houses," "Rammed Earth Houses," "Mansions and Plantations," and "Architectural Details." The placement of images within this elaborate structure depended on just such choices as that about the horse: what is the "objective" content, as best we can say, of this image?

"The theoretical basis of classification," Vanderbilt wrote in 1950, "is the actual literal subject matter of the picture itself, and not its connotation or association." But how is the "literal" to be distinguished from the "associative"? There is "no way," he conceded, "of systematizing subject headings." The success of the file depends entirely on the aptness of countless decisions. No wonder Vanderbilt took such pains to distinguish between "objective" (denotative) and "subjective" (connotative) meanings and to insist that the distinction was always relative and provisional, that the decision to place the horse under cold weather is only "in a sense" an objective judgment. About the actual work of assigning images to classes, he wrote in 1942: "Don't try to systematize it. Get good classifiers, trust their intuitions on what a picture is primarily concerned with, let them make such exceptions and inconsistencies as seem advisable, reverse their decisions and shift photographs when the argument is strong enough." Such remarks help us see the file not as something given by the nature of the material but as something *made*, a vast cellular edifice constructed of distinct human choices. Throughout his "Preliminary Report" Vanderbilt meticulously describes that labor and reiterates his cardinal interest: to *facilitate* access to the pictures for the sake of new combinations, new associations or "subjective" meanings. He is willing to modify headings, invent new ones, shift images from place to place. Not the form of the file matters, he explains, but logical access to the pictures: "I am trying to use classification in a workable plan for the disposition of photographs, not to determine relationships or set a pattern for future use." The file is "no more than a means to an end, and not an end in itself."

Vanderbilt conceived the file as a facilitator, a structure of convenience. His metaphors stress the instrumental relation of means to end: the file was the dictionary to "a forceful, colorful book," "a stock room of parts" to "the assembled useful machine," a menu to the "well-balanced meal." The pictorial richness of the collection lies in "the astounding juxtapositions, the sensitive and subtle details, the significant backgrounds"—connotative features the file makes no effort to reduce to number and class. The file is blind, in short, to *pictures*; it recognizes only subjects, facts, data, assuming (or pretending, in Vanderbilt's metaphors) that a detail in a photograph is indeed a transparent copy of a thing in the world, a veritable fact to be filed away, rather than an image within a larger image that may qualify, modify, contradict, or cancel its presumed status as "fact." The archival file limits itself to this pretense to ease the extraction of exactly those troublesome and complicating connotative values, thus allowing for "infinite variation in combination of photographs and in approach by users." Rather than predetermine combinations that constitute a finished whole, the file traffics in component parts.

To Vanderbilt, his design was a rationalized facility for storage and retrieval, a machine apparently intending no meanings of its own, no interpretations or ideology. Strictly functional, Vanderbilt's classification system aims to neutralize conflict over the meaning of specific images by agreeing to a provisional "objective" or referential meaning *in* the file to allow convenient releasing of single images *out* of the file into contexts of the user's own devising. The file, he writes, allows access to "individual pictures of specific things" as well as to "stories" on general topics. The system accommodates "both approaches (to a specific subject regardless of connections and to a connected story made up of many subjects)." Once retrieved and delivered, the image might serve any purpose. Delivery liberates the image from its categorical confinement. Mere datum in the file, in the world it becomes a picture to be read.

The process has a paradoxical result: it transfers the hieroglyphic effect from the file to the image itself, now rendered dense and opaque by its freedom, its detachment from any determinacy. By first defining the image by an "objective" determination of its subject and then releasing it into indeterminacy, the file affirms rather than subdues the ambiguity it sets out to resolve.

In the descending subheadings and sub-subheadings we catch the full thrust of the structure, the formal elegance of Vanderbilt's solution. We have only to imagine alternative systems to realize the high order of craft of this achievement, the generosity of its pragmatic efficiency. The file's clarity can arouse only respect and gratitude. Yet to imagine alternatives, no matter of what sort, impresses the truth Vanderbilt himself insisted upon: the arbitrariness of the entire vast and intricate structure. Think of a system based instead on categories like conflict, tension, paradox, contradiction. Or emotion: anger, hate, lust, affection, bafflement, wildness. Or spatial forms, ritual gestures, modes of exploitation and cooperation. The collection could have been organized into an unlimited variety of different subjects and subheadings. Vanderbilt admits as much. "There is no such thing as an ideal general sequence of subject matter." He intended an open-ended, ever-changing structure. "The order of classes is neither a very important nor very profound matter," he wrote, and while one might "claim that work, in the class sequence, comes before play, it is not in the spirit of analytical criticism, but merely to facilitate storage and have a place to keep the photograph while endless discussion goes on." "The sequences of classes," he insisted, should not have "a yes-or-no, animal-vegetable-mineral type of rigidity. . . . There should be opportunity to add an infinite number of classes." A breathtaking vision: the FSA-

OWI file as "the nucleus of a great photo documentation of all America, the collective repository for the work of tens of thousands of photographers," a "panoramic central" file.

Contingent, arbitrary, provisional, subject to change, contraction, and expansion: still, as much as Vanderbilt insists on the system's neutrality, it cannot help imposing its own meanings. Its encyclopedic intention alone inscribes a signifying order upon the variegated materials it holds, an order of descriptive classes that the "stuff" of the pictures can then be interpreted as validating, making the file seem permanent and authoritative, a sure guide to reality. The chosen classes and headings thus also represent the FSA-OWI project in a particular way. Vanderbilt's significant and often-overlooked disclaimers aside, the classification system implies an ideal order and a unified purpose: to scan the American world with a neutral photographic lens, picking out details that construct a "panoramic" view of America.

Vanderbilt, however, seems not to have realized that his system harbored an internal contradiction: verbal classes and headings cannot be "neutral"; relations among names cannot be free of associative meanings; a structure of relations cannot avoid interpreting its materials. In short, beneath the "theoretical basis" Vanderbilt developed in his 1942 report was a set of additional assumptions that shaped the file into these particular classifications, these terms and categories and names. For example, Vanderbilt's occasional remarks about the "universality" of the total effect of the collection imply an ambition to tie the "panorama" of America to categories of existence true for all times and places. "The classification should be based on the history of man," he noted in an untitled, undated memorandum, and in a "Memorandum on the Photography of America" written in 1963, he spoke retrospectively of the collection as "a kind of timeless life panorama of great dramatic richness," something "contemplative and almost philosophical, something essentially Christian about man's concern for his fellows and the fabric and texture of our country."

The Christian allusion suggests, of course, a particular source for the "universal": the Western tradition and its Bible. Furthermore, the specific categories employed in the file indicate social science as another source of universalism. Vanderbilt explained in 1950 that his use

of "the geographical basis with subject divisions" drew on the model
of "the cross cultural survey of the Institute of Human Relations at
Yale University" along with principles of geographical classification
developed by the sociologist Howard W. Odum at the University of
North Carolina. The conjunction of biblical and social-science notions
of universality creates a powerful impression of authority, powerful
enough to make us see the natural, self-evident form of the "history of
man." In a revealing passage in the 1950 draft Vanderbilt makes explicit another controlling idea, one that fuses biblical and sociological
categories into a literary form:

> The best conceptual picture of the history of mankind which
> we have been able to devise was that of a drama in which the
> world is a stage, people the actors, and the struggle for existence
> or survival, the plot. We imagine the history of mankind as a
> play presented before our eyes in which we would see actors ap-
> pear within a setting and identify themselves, establish relation-
> ships one with another, evolve a capacity for action, face the
> realities and necessities of making a living, form associations for
> their mutual benefit, engage in mighty conflicts between larger
> and larger groups, achieve through their efforts a high symbolic
> degree of spiritual, intellectual and technological satisfactions.
> The climax of our drama seeks relief and recuperation in rest
> and amusement and yields in the end to human weakness in the
> debasement of ideals for personal advantage.

Two aspects of this extended and revealing analogy stand out: the file
is like a book in that "dramatic events are then *made to* follow one another in a printed version of a similar drama in book form" (my emphasis); and the story of the drama is essentially evolutionary, a biblical
story with God left out. A further aspect of the Christian element is the
hint of a jeremiad in the final detail: "and yields in the end to human
weakness in the debasement of ideals for personal advantage."

In the same essay Vanderbilt describes the file as "a functional
arrangement neutral in its character founded upon evolution and actual relationships." But is "evolution" applied to social history really a

"neutral" concept? Are "actual relationships" conceived as a drama or book really "objective" or scientific? In fact, the file embodies the familiar idea of history as "progress," history ordered according to climaxes and resolutions as well as the moral imperatives of a Judeo-Christian ethic. It is "progressivist," essentially optimistic about solutions to conflicts and about its own universality. In its very form, its relations of headings and subheadings, its categorical progressions, the file represents diagrammatically a grand master story, a generative cultural myth: civilization begins in a relation to "land" and proceeds to build an increasingly complex society. Deeply rooted in the national culture, this "liberal" myth remains strong, if not dominant, in many realms of American life. It views conflicts as archetypal rather than specific to social circumstances, arising from the hearts of men, from selfishness and weakness rather than from irreconcilable needs and interests of antagonistic economic groups or social classes. In short, the file tells a story of its own, and its photographs serve as much to illustrate and validate that story as the file serves to facilitate access to those images. Thus the irony of its magnificent achievement: by its very success it enacts the problem it sets out to solve. The shape of the file predetermines "objective" categorical descriptions of each image, descriptions it claims are arbitrary, provisional, disposable. But the arbitrary splitting of each image into "objective" and "subjective" aspects—stable "literal" meanings and unstable associative meanings—endows the master story with a power beyond that of a mere filing device. Such is the power of cultural myth, of ideology, that the master story seems not a story at all but a neutral "arrangement."

IV

If the file contains an unresolved tension between "objectivity" and "subjectivity," so the project had tensions and contradictions of its own. There are many ways to describe and evaluate the FSA-OWI project: from the perspectives of New Deal politics, of "documentary" photography, of new modes of photojournalism in the mass media of the 1930s and 1940s. When viewed from the perspective of the file, however, the project presents the dilemma of representing society, of telling stories about American life, through photographs. Apart from its political motives and imperatives, its personality conflicts, its inner chain of command, the FSA-OWI project brought into focus large questions about American social reality and how it might be formulated and communicated in pictures. The project was perhaps the greatest collective effort (though not the first) in the history of photography to mobilize resources to create a cumulative picture of a place and time: in Roy Stryker's words, "to portray America." In the process, it encountered significant problems of depiction latent in the medium but also arising from the severe crisis (social, economic, cultural) of American society in the throes of the Great Depression. A mass of memoranda and drafts of essays and lectures stored in the Stryker and Vanderbilt archives discloses a remarkable effort among the staff to clarify goals and formulate theories of photography and society. These, together with Vanderbilt's file, can help us identify hidden issues of the FSA-OWI enterprise itself.

It is enlightening to learn how indistinct was the plan Stryker brought with him to Washington in 1935, how much in the early days he took his cues from his photographers and their work. Nothing in Stryker's original charge as chief of the Historical Section—to "direct the activities of investigators, photographers, economists, sociologists and statisticians engaged in the accumulation and compilations of reports"—anticipates the goal of portraying a whole society, an act of documentation for its own (or for the file's) sake. But the First Annual Report of the Resettlement Administration in 1935 notes that the goal of the Historical Section would be reached "not only in keeping a record of the administration's projects, but also in perpetuating photographically certain aspects of the American scene which may prove incalculably valuable in time to come."

Whatever its sources, Stryker adopted the idea of a historical record with evangelical fervor, which explains the remarkable latitude he afforded his corps of predominantly young, middle-class photographers. Arthur Rothstein writes that "the Farm Security file would never have been created if we hadn't the freedom to photograph anything, anywhere in the United States—anything that we came across that seemed interesting, and vital." John Vachon agrees:

Through some sublime extension of logic which has never been satisfactorily explained to anyone, Stryker believed that while documenting these mundane activities [routine pictures of housing projects, farmers on federal aid, and so forth], his photographers should, along the way, photograph whatever they saw, really saw: people, towns, road signs, railroad stations, barber shops, the weather, or the objects on top of a chest of drawers in Grundy Co., Iowa.

In his eight years as chief of the unit Stryker cast an ever-widening net, seeking from his photographers an expanding horizon of scenes, things, faces, places—an epic ambition resulting, as he put it in *In This Proud Land*, in "the great number of photographs that got into the collection which had nothing to with official business."

Was there a single coherent idea or theory guiding Stryker in his

Figure 28 Walker Evans, "Railroad Station, Edwards, Mississippi," February 1936. (Library of Congress, Prints & Photographs Division, FSA-OWI Collection)

expanded intention? The extraordinary leap beyond the routine official purposes of his office is not easily accounted for. Stryker attributed the birth of the larger project to a "personal dream" of "a pictorial encyclopedia of American agriculture." We can understand "dream" in two senses, not only as an ambition but also as a wish fulfillment. American agriculture and small-town life had already changed in profound ways. Stryker wished to preserve what was already lost. "Through the pictures," he recalled, "the small town emerged as a thing possessing emotional and esthetic advantages: kinship with nature and the seasons, neighborliness, kindliness, spaciousness." And in a passage of remarkable pathos:

> I remember Walker Evans' picture [Figure 28] of the train tracks in a small town, like Montrose [Stryker's hometown in Colorado]. The empty station platform, the station thermometer, the idle baggage carts, the quiet stores, the people talking together, and beyond them, the weather-beaten houses where they lived, all this reminded me of the town where I had grown up. I would look at pictures like that and long for a time when the world was safer and more peaceful. I'd think back to the days before radio and television when all there was to do was go down to the tracks and watch the flyer go through. That was the nostalgic way in which those town pictures hit me.*

The chord struck here betrays one source of Stryker's encyclopedic ambition: the dream of translating what was no longer a vital culture into an abstract and timeless "value."

The hold of this lost vision on Stryker and many other Americans cannot be exaggerated. The specific form it would take in the FSA-

---

*In a review of Sherwood Anderson's *Home Town* published in the October 13, 1940, issue of the New York newspaper *PM*, Evans's picture appeared over the following caption written by Ralph Steiner, editor of the newspaper's photography department: "Walker Evans likes scenes which bring back memories of the turn of the century. The empty station platform, the waiting baggage trucks, the station thermometer, the small, dead stores, the quiet knot of townspeople remind you of the town you came from or visited as a youth when the world was slower, safer, more peaceful. This is just the sort of place where the evening diversion was to go down to the tracks and watch the 'flyer' go through. Today many a small town looks about the way it did in '99. Had Evans taken more photographs he would have shown how the town has changed."

OWI project began to emerge in 1935, paradoxically, with the enlistment of the urbane Walker Evans. Beyond doubt Evans was the most decisive figure in the early years of the project. "I saw his pictures," recalled Stryker. "I walked at night with him and I talked to him. He told me about what the photographer was for, what a photographer should do, and he gave me his rationale for pictures. It was extremely interesting because it was opening up a whole new field of ideas." Evans joined the Resettlement Administration with an already mature view of his intentions in photography. "I am exceedingly interested in the undertaking," Evans wrote about a month before his initial appointment as an Assistant Specialist in Information, "which seems to me to have enormous possibilities, of precisely the sort that interest me." As early as 1931 he had written in a *Hound & Horn* essay archly titled "The Reappearance of Photography" that "the real significance of photography was submerged soon after its discovery." Fakery, pretension, and commercial slickness had prevailed over the kinds of direct, honest records foretold by Louis-Jacques Daguerre and other pioneers. In the work of Eugène Atget and of August Sander, however, the young Evans recognized "one of the futures of photography. . . . It is a photographic editing of society, a clinical process; even enough of a cultural necessity to make one wonder why other so-called advanced countries of the world have not also been examined and recorded." In a 1934 letter to Ernestine Evans (also an acquaintance of Stryker's and no relation to Walker Evans), Evans sketched what may be the earliest model for Stryker's famous shooting scripts:

> People, all classes, surrounded by bunches of the new down-and-out.
> Automobiles and the automobile landscape.
> Architecture, American urban taste, commerce, small scale, large scale, the city street atmosphere, the street smell, the hateful stuff, women's clubs, fake culture, bad education, religion in decay.
> The movies.
> Evidence of what the people of the city read, eat, see for amusement, do for relaxation and not get it.

In the "Outline Memorandum" he wrote for Stryker about his first trip for the unit through Pennsylvania, the Ohio Valley, and the southeastern states, Evans described his general intention as "still photography, of a general sociological nature," and his "first objective" in the Pittsburgh vicinity as "photography, documentary in style, of industrial subjects, emphasis on housing and home-life of working-class people. Graphic record of a complete, complex, pictorially rich modern industrial center."

Evans provided a theory and an exemplary practice for the project in its early days, one that it could not effectively sustain. Whatever the intentions of a "pure" record, government sponsorship imposed its own needs and demands. In its effort to bolster a stricken economic system without abandoning the basic forms of private ownership and capitalist enterprise, the New Deal sought to employ all the technologies of communication to foster its authority and to win support for its programs on behalf of a liberal, progressivist idea of America. Evans had proclaimed the credo of the "pure" record maker even before joining the project. "Never make photographic statements for the government or do photographic chores for gov or anyone in gov, no matter how powerful," he wrote in a draft for the memorandum before he accepted the government position. "This is pure record not propaganda. The value and, if you like, even the propaganda value for the government lies in the record itself which in the long run will prove an intelligent and farsighted thing to have done. NO POLITICS whatever."

Significantly, Evans's insistence on independence had more to do with politics than with the notion of photographs as *social* knowledge. His mention of the "general sociological nature" of his pictures accorded at least in principle with Stryker's social-science outlook. Indeed, rapport between photographer and social scientist would emerge as a key motif in the project, an explicit part of its developing rationale and a theme repeated often in memoranda. Stryker conceived of that rapport as a two-way street: the photographers "must be something of sociologists, economists, historians," and "the student of social structure needs to know what the photographer is prepared to reveal." If the aim was "to bring the photographer together with the social scientist and historian," Stryker's means included requiring the photographers to prepare for their fieldwork through systematic, close study of local conditions: "geography, the agricultural system, the crops grown, the dominant industries, the living habits of the people." This entailed two essential obligations on the part of the photographer: to prepare a "shooting script" beforehand (usually in cooperation with the Washington staff) and to accompany each print with a report and caption.

Stryker schooled his photographers in both tasks. Of key importance is the fact that the *words* of scripts and captions played a central role in shaping the preliminary file before 1942, providing the raw stuff that Vanderbilt molded into the liberal-humanist vision of the completed file. Vanderbilt's subject headings correspond roughly to the less systematic ethnographic and geopolitical categories included in Stryker's shooting scripts. After a meeting in 1936 with the sociologist Robert S. Lynd, Stryker jotted down what became the first script sent out to all his photographers:

> Home in the evening
> > Photographs showing the various ways that different income groups spend their evenings, for example:
> Informal clothes
> Listening to the radio
> Bridge
> More precise dress
> Guests.

The following excerpt from a letter of October 17, 1938, to Sheldon Dick before his assignment to a Pennsylvania coal town expresses more eloquently Stryker's idea of social depiction:

> The specific things I noted when I was there were that the town dropped down into a Pennsylvania mountain valley. Everywhere you look is man-made desolation, waste piles, bare hills, dirty streets. It is terribly important that you in some way try to show the town against this background of waste piles and coal tipples. In other words, it is a coal town and your pictures must tell it. It

is a church dominated place. . . . The place is not prosperous, people are loafing in saloons and around the streets. You must get this feeling of unemployment. There are many unpaved streets. . . . The houses are old and rundown. The place is devoid of paint. I am sure lots of cheap liquor is consumed for no other reason than in an attempt to blot out the drabness of the place. When you are ready to shoot people try to pick up something of the feeling on the side of youth. Try to portray the hopelessness of their position . . . youth's confusions—liquor, swing, sex, and more liquor. The actual details will have to be worked out by yourself.

An amalgam of social science (geography, ethnography, sociology), New Deal politics, and liberal reformism, the passage is a virtual scenario; it implies a narrative, a chapter in that master story of the "history of mankind" that Vanderbilt would inscribe as the "neutral" shape of the file. To separate the strands of social-science assumptions, political agenda, and moral attitude is impossible; all are fused indivisibly into a single vision. It is not to demean the vision or to question its sincerity or even validity as a program of representation to say that it bears the mark of cultural myth or wields the invisible power of ideology: it tells a story even before the making of the pictures.

V

"A 'story,' " wrote Vanderbilt, "is what any man thinks it is, in the light of his ignorance, knowledge, prejudice or imagination." It is a fabrication, something imagined, made up. The "author" of the file never wants us to forget this fundamental premise of his own construction: the role of the arbitrary at every turn. In Vanderbilt's terminology stories are "subjective," a product of "ignorance, knowledge, prejudice or imagination." Because stories might cut across all possible "objective" designations of subject, region, or photographer, better, he explained in his "Preliminary Report," that "story" signify "known photographer's assignments, one of the few more or less controllable factors we have." Thus the lot, the basic unit of the file, consists (more or less) of pictures made on a single assignment. The system of subject classification and cross-referencing facilitates that "infinite variety" Vanderbilt imagined; the lots give us stories already constructed, from pictures made by the same photographer at a given place and time (during periods ranging from an hour or two to, more rarely, several days).

Is the master story, the universal "history of mankind," that runs through and organizes the "objective" categories also arbitrary, a fabrication? What role does it play in saying what kinds of stories the file makes available in its role as facilitator? The question is more easily stated than answered, more readily explored than laid to rest, but must be kept in mind.

The unity of time and place found in the microfilmed lots does not suffice as a story; we need an action, a happening in space and time, and a teller, someone responsible for the order in which the action is recounted in voice, writing, or image. In a photographic sequence of an ongoing or unfolding event, such as a baseball player rounding first base in an effort to stretch a single into a double or a presidential press conference or an assassination, the aptness of the term "story" is unmistakable: something happening, even if not particularly complex or interesting, is being reported. Pictures can infuse a dry verbal account of phases of an action with the illusion of life. Most often "story" is loosely applied to groups of photographs in the sense of "news story"—a presentation of facts regarding an event or occasion or character, but not necessarily with a distinct narrator or even a distinct plot. In many instances of static, descriptive photographs, the happening is the actual making of the photograph, which is inscribed in the image and is an essential even if hidden element in the content of any "photostory."

Like other visual forms with inscribed narratives, from carved burial urns to stained-glass windows, comic strips, and movies, photographs seem to make do without an overt narrator; their fiction is that the world tells or writes about itself through images, that in photographs we see not the view of a "narrator" but the world itself— people, rocks, fences, clouds. No teller tells (or writes) these stories; they happen by themselves. Thus Steichen imitating a circus barker in his essay "The F.S.A. Photographers" in *U.S. Camera 1939*:

"Now step up folks, and look this way!" Have a look into these faces of the men and women in these pages. Listen to the story they tell and they will leave you with a feeling of a living experience you won't forget; and the babies, and the children; weird, hungry, dirty, lovable, heart-breaking images; and then there are the fierce stories of strong, gaunt men and women in time of flood and drought. If you are the kind of rugged individualist who likes to say "Am I my brother's keeper?", don't look at these pictures—they may change your mind.

Steichen's response to the Farm Security Administration photos was and is still the most common. We want to understand the source of that response: does it come from the pictures themselves or from the way he views them?

Steichen's way of viewing the images can be discerned in the kind of story he "hears." "Fierce stories of strong, gaunt men and women in time of flood and drought" are presumably the stories of the Depression, the monumental economic collapse and consequent social distress that constitute the major "stuff" of the FSA-OWI Collection. Steichen's response places the crises elsewhere, somewhere we are not, yet can view, thanks to the photographs. The pictures transport us as disembodied, even voyeuristic eyes to the Southern countryside and small towns, to shantytowns on the edge of California's fruit fields, to the interiors of sharecroppers' shacks and the dark doorways of the poor, to the roads trod by migrant laborers, to the dole lines with the great army of the unemployed. The photographs did not invent these unpretty scenes, but our reading of the images makes them seem *real* in this particular way. In Steichen's version the pictures are transparent communications of the story of those who suffer. The sympathy and pity and perhaps guilt we feel confirm for us that we have indeed heard a story, have had "a living experience." We ourselves, this very publication of the pictures in *U.S. Camera* assures us, are not among the afflicted; the crisis is felt only among the "lower orders," that is, the uneducated, chronically poor blacks and whites, the drifting migrant families, whom we can look "down" on in an act of self-ennoblement. The story we hear is a "pastoral," a story in which the lowly "shepherd" characters—the ignorant, dirty, and hungry but wise and just country folk—instruct us in dignity, humility, sorrow, transcendence, or whatever we clean urban people (perhaps just beginning to feel the crunch ourselves) might wish to hear from such imagined characters. We have become *their* narrators, the tellers of *their* story; that we are merely listening to a tale told by a picture is only an illusion fostered by a certain way of thinking about these pictures.

The most common way of thinking about these and any self-declared "documentary" photographs is that they are "realistic." A very loosely used term, "realism" most often means that such pictures have a strict reference to subject, time, and place and cannot legitimately be understood in any other way. Beaumont Newhall in "The Documentary Approach to Photography" (1938) addressed the problem of how to see the images as both social science and art, as factual document and imaginative expression—the same ambiguity systematized in Vanderbilt's conception of the file. Newhall insisted that Stryker's photographers, while "never losing sight of the primary sociological purpose of their survey," nevertheless produce "photographs which deserve the consideration of all who appreciate art in its richest and fullest meaning." But because of their origin as documentary, referential images, such photographs cannot be taken as pictures alone. "The photograph is not valid as a document," wrote Newhall, "until it is placed in relationship to the beholder's experience." An identifying caption naming a place and time may suffice, "but more extended captions enable the beholder to orientate himself." "A series of photographs" is even better, "the richest manner of giving photographs significance, for each picture reinforces the other." Of course, true works of photographic art can stand on their own. Thus the dilemma of making "art" out of social observation remains unsolved; even as art, social documentary photographs are considered intrinsically different. Such pictures demand a "relationship to the beholder's experience" presented clearly and unambiguously.

The concept of pictorial realism provides a key to that relationship, the link between the picture and the world. As a concept realism signifies not only the appearance of actuality within a picture but also a moral outlook. "Certainly the documentary photographer is a realist rather than an escapist by the very fact that he accepts his environment," Stryker wrote in his essay "Documentary Photography," in 1939. He goes on to define realism as a moral stance, "a deep respect for human beings." "The 'documentarians' differ from strictly pictorial photographers chiefly in the degree and quality of their love for life. They insist that life is so exciting that it needs no embellishment." To define a pictorial system as a function of a "love for life" may seem a confusion of genres. But few words are as tainted by promiscuous crossings of boundaries as this honorific label, "realism." Stryker and Steichen both assume that the term connotes a positive, cheerful, hopeful, and uplifting view of things. "An affirmation, not a negation," as Stryker puts it, as if abstractions like goodness, dignity, and endurance rather than the particularities of time and place constituted the reality captured and classified in the FSA-OWI file as a whole. "There's honesty there, and compassion, and a natural regard for individual dignity," wrote Stryker. "These are the things that, in my opinion, give the collection its special appeal." Such terms distract us from the particular to the universal; to put it strongly, they drain the image of exactly what gives it its photographic power: particularities of place and person, costume and texture, hour and minute of day or night.

Ben Shahn recalled that "we tried to present the ordinary in an extraordinary manner. . . . We just took pictures that cried out to be taken." That cry belonged to the decade; a hunger for "the real thing," for the true and enduring *American* values, appeared in the arts, theater, cinema, design, fiction, popular song and dance and speech—hardly a surprising response to the often shattering breakdowns, the social and personal traumas of the period. A quest for "the real" had another significance in this decade of exodus, of uprootedness and movement: it was also a quest for place, a desire for images of rooted settlements and familiar landmarks. This collective wish, if we can read retrospectively from images consumed to images desired, arose in reaction to the great changes in relation to place and to "cultural space" represented by the destruction of rural culture. If there is a great overarching theme of the FSA-OWI file, it is surely the end of rural America and its displacement by a commercial, urban culture with its marketplace relationships. Automobiles, movies, telephone poles, billboards, canned food, ready-made clothing: these familiar icons from the file bespeak a vast upheaval—Edmund Wilson called it an earthquake—a profound breach in the relation of American society to its "nature" and to the production of sustenance from the land. Throughout the file we observe the machine as the agent of change and particularly of the impoverishment of displaced, not to say annihilated, rural workers. The replacement of handmade signs by printed signs and billboards and the extrusion of handcrafts to the margin known as "folk culture" reflect deeper displacements.

Under the heading of realism the pictures are assumed to be statements already complete and self-sustaining, statements moreover of general and typical rather than particular meanings. So deeply ingrained that it seemed "natural," the theory of photographic "realism" implied by words like "look" and "listen" hardly needed explicit statement and defense. Indeed in their sundry uses in the 1930s the Farm Security Administration pictures helped define and confirm realism as the medium's normative aesthetic standard. Through Stryker's efforts certain images appeared regularly in a variety of media—newspapers, magazines, government reports, scholarly works, exhibitions, photographic books—creating an impression of a "new FSA vocabulary in photography," a distinct mode of picture making and storytelling. Whether in the press or in the newly established photographic magazines (*Life, Look, Fortune*) or in texts such as Herman Clarence Nixon's *Forty Acres and Steel Mules* (1938), the pictures are typically captioned, framed in words that focus each image on a central theme. In the two books for which Edwin Rosskam selected and edited FSA pictures, Sherwood Anderson's *Home Town* (1940) and Richard Wright and Rosskam's *Twelve Million Black Voices* (1941), the images are embedded within a text, not as illustrations but as illuminations, pictorial correlatives, parallel visual texts. In all cases, although the images appear in groups, the burden of communication rests on the cumulative effect of *individual* images, not on interactive relations, juxtapositions, or serial progressions. The pictures are assumed to be self-explanatory, yet they are ringed and focused by words, securely held in check by a textual frame that ensures that they will be understood as "realistic."

Taken alone, Dorothea Lange's famous "Migrant Mother" (Fig-

ure 29) is a timeless madonna. The "holy mother" theme captions the
image, placing it so that we apprehend the universal in the guise of the
immediate, the sacred incarnate as the humble. In the same act of
recognition we note pathetic differences: a worried rather than beatific
look, children clinging for protection rather than lolling in bliss. The
differences produce an ironic effect: how worn and beaten, how sor-
rowful this holy mother, who takes upon herself the entire spiritual

Figure 29 Dorothea Lange, "Migrant Mother," Nipoma, California, February
1936. (Library of Congress, Prints & Photographs Division, FSA-OWI Collection)

trauma of the times—the social destitution of the poor and outcast. If there is redemptive power here—the extraordinary fame of the image suggests so—one of its sources is the particularizing power of the camera, which makes the madonna seem a real creature of here and now, as frail against the storm as you and I. But that is as far as the "madonna" interpretation goes toward acknowledging the particularities of the image. The story proper to the actual woman and children and to the photograph itself remains outside the frame of the universal. While elevating the image to sacral heights, the abstract theme threatens to dissolve the photograph's thisness of time and place into a whatness of pious emotion. Thus "humanitarian realism" captures and binds the fleeting image to an abstraction, completes its meaning at the expense of particularity. Because we are unable or unwilling to see what is there—the blank future in the woman's squinting eyes—we confess ourselves haunted. The abstraction allays our fears and gives us "art" besides.

"Madonna of the Migrants" is one thing; the same picture set within the sequence of six exposures made by Lange on that gray afternoon near Nipomo, California, and read with Lange's own commentary in mind is quite another. We can take this group as a unit in itself, several perspectives of a single scene, Lange's camera selecting and excluding details and personae as it changes position. The mother remains the central point of interest in each, but less dominating in some than in others. The group of pictures can be read also as a sequence of "trial" takes leading up to the final image, as if the setting were a studio, Lange a director seeking a certain image, a special effect—and, of course, we ourselves the narrator of the story as revealed by the sequence of images. Whether we read the group as a multiperspective account of a scene, one of whose images stands out in pictorial strength, or as a pyramidal process culminating in a masterpiece of direction and manipulation, the meaning of the madonna has been altered for us; it is no longer the Virgin in humble earthly guise but a photograph and thus capable of serving more than one meaning. The sequence compels a different view of the image, but even sequences are subject to alterability, capable of more than one reading, of telling more than one story.

There are dangers in rejecting abstract categories altogether—one is a radical nominalism that would have us attend to only the surface, to proper names, to individual life histories. This would be too unsparing, leaving us with fragments and shards. The caption "Migrant Mother" may say too much and too little about the case at hand, but the woman's proper name by itself tells us even less. We need a balance: enough categorization (such as social class) to connect the individual with others living the same history, yet not enough to hide the individual in a cloud of global categories. The terms "mother" and "migrant" each imply a social setting that might explicate this image in relation to others. In contrast, a different reading emerges when we see the image within a setting of other photographs made on the same occasion—in the context of a shooting sequence or assignment.

The FSA-OWI photographs tell not a single "story" but a multitude of stories. Images deposited in the lots are raw material, not yet ordered, not yet inflected into distinct relationships or sequences. They await another editorial act, a more focused construction: the invention of a "story" in which each image has its say. The most telling lesson to be learned in the process of recombining and reordering images is that rather than providing objective facts of time and place, photographs place us in someone else's point of view. The series presented here, composed of the work of single photographers on specific assignments, allow us to examine and explore different perspectives. What habits and qualities of seeing account for an individual point of view? What makes one photographer's work more or less intelligent, acute, knowing, persuasive? Such differences may seem obvious in some cases—one cannot mistake a typical picture by Ben Shahn for one by Dorothea Lange—but in most cases discrimination takes careful scrutiny and judgment.

The point is simple and commonplace but still worth noting: differences in point of view, or in what is loosely called "style," produce different versions of reality. Rather than as a measure of an objective reality, indicating what exists in the world, photographs are better thought of as a means of representation. In regard to photostories, unity of place and time give us no particular assurance of the truth of time and place. Such unities are just as arbitrary as other categories.

This is not to doubt "objective" reality but to say that in opening us to the world, these photographic series help us understand that what we call reality rests on certain chosen ordering principles, such as causality, chronology, similarity and difference, echo and dissonance, unfoldings and regressions. As fictions, as stories, the photoseries show us that versions of the past are indeed made up. That recognition can free us from the tyranny of any fixed version, permitting critical historical judgment.

The final danger is to see any photograph as fixed and final, either in order, meaning, or time and place. The FSA-OWI file itself seems a monumental fixity, though in the spirit of its liberalism it makes pragmatic provision for change, for construction of countless versions of the America it portrays. This fluid openness within the boundaries of its master story makes the file less a solution than an opportunity. Vanderbilt encourages us to repeat his own act of myth making, of finding or inventing lines of force and resistance, patterns of order among discrete images. The opportunity has its treacherous passages, and we need an abundance of skepticism about the order already imposed. In the end we do well to approach the file in the spirit of the impulsive woman who wished to scrawl her message across the face of Evans's Bethlehem picture. The file becomes our history only by our acting upon it, deciphering its portent in light of our own view of the times and its anguishes, triumphs, conflicts, and resolutions. We might thereby discover a point of view, revise a received opinion. The stories presented here are exercises, in the noble sense of disciplined praxis, in making history. They point us in the right direction, toward our own innumerable everyday acts as unconscious historians. The file invites us to make such acts conscious and knowing.

SIXTEEN

WALKER EVANS'S FICTIONS
OF THE SOUTH

IT'S been said that we cannot know for sure whether Walker Evans recorded the America of the 1930s or invented it. "Beyond doubt," wrote John Szarkowski, "the accepted myth of our recent past is in some measure the creation of this photographer." Record or invention, transcription or mythic fiction, the coy "beyond doubt" points to the putatively irresistible persuasiveness of Walker Evans's photographs. A consensus of several generations of viewers agrees that his pictures go beyond literal photographic truth toward deeper truths about the spirit of the times. It's a way of claiming near-mystical powers of perception, that Evans captures revelations, invisible truths embodied in certain objects in certain places. It's what is meant by genius in photography. In concert with a historian's eye for telling detail, Evans photographed with a novelist's eye for hidden nuances of form and meaning and a poet's eye and ear for the lyricism of things. The apparent magic of his pictures is that he makes historical record and poetic invention seem one and inseparable, what can be called lyric history or fictions of fact.

Early reviews of his first book, *American Photographs* (1938), registered just this sense of uncanny preternatural reality. "I got a strange feeling of wandering through America," Gilbert Seldes wrote in *Esquire*. "The photographer has put us on record," wrote the filmmaker Pare Lorenz in the *Saturday Review*. And William Carlos Williams, in *The Nation*: "It is ourselves we see, ourselves lifted from a parochial setting." It's as if Evans's pictures put contemporary history on the table, Lincoln Kirstein added, helping his contemporaries see themselves, their times and places, as already historical, fixed in the stillness of photographs and laid out for contemplation, study, and sheer pleasure of recognition. And since their initial publication, audiences have taken Evans's pictures not just as the look of the 1930s but also as the palpable inner life of the times.

Evans called his book *American Photographs* not out of flag-waving patriotism but to acknowledge that the book had something to show and to say about the idea of America. The book tells a national story, at least as much of the nation as the eastern seaboard and sections of the Midwest can be said to constitute (a handful of pictures from Cuba insinuate additional transnational meanings). The aim decidedly is not to represent the nation in the mode of photojournalism popularized by the new picture magazines of the decade, a mode Evans scorned, although he would spend a significant piece of time working on special assignment for *Fortune* from the 1940s through the middle 1960s. The book has nothing to do with news or current events; it juxtaposes pictures in sequences without regard for the unities of time and geographical space, as if regions named after points of the compass—north, south, east, west—were an arbitrary category inessential to the meaning of America.

Considering how prominent his pictures taken in the South seem in retrospect, it's interesting to learn that only about one-third of the eighty-seven pictures in *American Photographs* are identified as made somewhere below the Mason-Dixon line. *Let Us Now Praise Famous Men* (1941), on the other hand, is entirely a Southern book, and not simply because all the pictures are made in the South, primarily in Hale County, Alabama. In both books, we have to distinguish between "Southern" as a regional or geographical term and "the South" as a cultural and ideological term. In the first book the distinction is muted, but it is very much in evidence in the second book, in the actual pictures and in Evans's arrangement of the pictures into the portfolio that precedes the text written by James Agee. Pictures that Evans added in the second edition of the book in 1960, after Agee's death, expand his pictorial exploration of cultural meanings of the term "South."

To see how a symbolic meaning of "South" helped shape and focus Walker Evans's contribution to *Let Us Now Praise Famous Men*, we need to take measure of the complicated American history of that word "South," especially of its status in the 1930s. Few American terms have been as charged as "the South," as contested in meaning and as provocative of fierce loyalties and antagonisms. As historians have shown, its meanings have been as much a product of Northern desires and imagination as of Southern efforts to explain and defend the region's uniqueness. In the 1930s, by virtue of the tenant lien system and the visual evidence it produced of backwardness and hardship, of hard-core class and racial injustice, to Northerners the South seemed an inert social and economic system. Yet the same visual images struck certain Northern artists and intellectuals as evidence of paradoxically worthy and attractive values. The idea and image of "the South" that emerged in the 1930s fell into an old tradition of Northern fascination and ambivalence, an idealization sitting uneasily on the edge of moral disapproval that reached back to the years before the Civil War.

A transplanted Midwesterner who lived most of his life in New York City and vicinity, Evans first went south in the winter of 1934 on a "picture job" in Florida. "I motored down," he wrote in a letter, "Carolina & Georgia, a revelation." A year later he was in New Orleans with plans for a book on antebellum classical revival houses. The plan fell apart, but he stayed on, photographed houses and people in the city and along the River Road, and later that year took a position as Information Specialist with the Resettlement Administration (later the Farm Security Administration), and more Southern revelations came his way. From the spring of 1935, when he embarked on an eight-week automobile trip for the FSA through the southeastern states, until he left the FSA in 1937, Evans toured the South under the ensign of government photographer. In the summer of 1936 he was in Hale County, Alabama, to collaborate with his friend James Agee on an article for *Fortune* on the lien tenancy, or sharecropping, system. In later years Evans went south on brief trips, including a visit to Mississippi in 1948 to make pictures for an article in *Vogue* on "Faulkner's Mississippi."

An occasional visitor, an outsider usually working on a commission or an assignment or in the employ of an agency of the federal government,

Evans gave what many consider the definitive pictorial account of a place called "the South" at that time, a vision apparently transparent enough to have lost the signature of an individual artist: unpainted shacks, ragged but stalwart sharecroppers, old plantation mansions in disrepair—a region under duress, depleted, haunted by ghosts and by something else, with an aura perhaps only a stranger could detect, an air of propriety and decorum that refused pity and resisted condescension.

The test of the revelatory power of Evans's Southern pictures is that Southerners accept them as true as much as others do. Being an outsider has never been held to disqualify his portrayal. Still, the case of Walker Evans in the South poses some interesting conundrums. He came from far away and had no personal ties to Hale County. He spent several weeks there in 1936, didn't return until the 1970s and then very briefly. Yet if Hale County now enjoys the status of *place* in American art and imagination, it's largely because of this stranger with a camera and his collaborator, also an alien to the place, a Southern-born but New York–based writer. A product of Agee's tense, rhapsodic, sometimes overblown prose and Evans's cool, spare pictures, both examples of cosmopolitan sensibilities, *Let Us Now Praise Famous Men* is often cited incongruously as a "Southern" work, part of what has been called the "cultural awakening of the American South" in the 1930s. Yet to say so brings us up against an inescapable paradox that comes into play when we speak of "South" or "Southern" as an identity.

The question arises: if to be a Southerner means, as many have believed, to have a unique regional attachment to the South as a place of enduring local value, where does this leave the stranger, the outsider, the visitor passing through? Can an outsider, according to this scheme, come to know a Southern place intrinsically enough to give a reliable account of it? Place suggests the idea of belonging, feeling at home, part of a tradition, rooted, as in the expression "in place." Eudora Welty, the great Mississippi writer and storyteller (and gifted photographer as well), offered the following in explanation and in honor of the presumably core Southern value of place:

> A place that ever was lived in is like a fire that never goes out. It flares up, it smolders for a time, it is fanned or smothered by cir-

cumstance, but its being is intact, forever fluttering within it, the result of some original ignition. Sometimes it gives out glory, sometimes its little light must be sought out to be seen, small and tender as a candle flame, but as certain.

This is from Welty's tribute to the Natchez Trace in her essay "Some Notes on River Country." In another essay, "Place in Fiction," she says about the writer that "place is where he has his roots, place is where he stands; in his experience out of which he writes, it provides the base of reference; in his work, the point of view." For Welty, reciprocity between place and consciousness not only assures the integrity of persons but also makes art possible. Place gives the artist the sense of integral identity indispensable to the making of art.

This view of place is hardly unique to the South or North or West; it's a global concept that gained force in modern times during the Romantic movement that started in northern Europe in the late eighteenth century, when local communities underwent decisive change under pressure from forces beyond their borders—steam-powered transportation, mass-produced goods and newspapers circulating from urban centers, and expanding market systems. The idea of place, associated with the belief that life on the farm was better and happier than life in the city, and tied to a distinct region of earth, expressed discontent with the fast-changing forms of modern urban-industrial life. When in ancient Greece and Rome the pastoral emerged as a poetic genre, it arose not as a folk art of shepherds and farmers but as an urban art form in which imaginary shepherds offered an alternative to the artificiality and corruptions of city life. "You miss that in our urban life," Eudora Welty remarked about the value of "place," which, in her account, sums up the major meaning of "South" within a nation suffering in the 1930s from social and economic distress and profound dislocation of local communities.

A traveling photographer might seem exactly the wrong person from whom to expect a satisfying account of place. The medium of photography calls for speed of perception, swiftness of mental action, a strong degree of detachment. "With the camera," Evans said in an interview in 1971, "it's all or nothing. You either get what you're after at once, or what you do has to be worthless. . . . The essence is done with a flash of the mind, and with a machine." On the other hand, the very detachment and need for quick eyes might give the photographer an edge when it comes to registering what is there. "It's as though there's a wonderful secret in a certain place and I can capture it," Evans said. "Only I can do it at this moment, only this moment and only me. That's a hell of a thing to believe, but I believe it or I couldn't act." Asked in an interview in 1974 what he was looking for in the South, he replied, "I wasn't looking for anything; things were looking for me, I felt—just calling to me. I had an eye and a sense of regional atmosphere, and I automatically recorded it."

Evans's words bring to mind a passage in one of Welty's essays that might have been written out of her own experience as a photographer. She asks:

> If place does work upon genius, how does it? It may be that place can focus the gigantic, voracious eye of genius and bring its gaze to point. Focus then means awareness, discernment, order, clarity, insight—they are like attributes of love. The act of focusing itself has beauty and meaning; it is the act that, continued in, turns into meditation, into poetry. Indeed, as soon as the least of us stands still, that is the moment something extraordinary is seen to be going on in the world.

Perhaps the act of focusing, of standing still, makes the camera, even in its impersonality and objectivity, the perfect instrument (paradoxically as it may seem) for imagining and picturing place. Henry James might be speaking directly to Walker Evans's art of photography when he writes that "things . . . objects and places, coherently grouped, disposed for human use and addressed to it, must have a sense of their own, a mystic meaning proper to themselves to give out: to give out, that is, to the participant at once so interested and so detached as to be moved to a report of the matter." To Welty's stillness and focus James adds the explicit paradox of simultaneous participation and detachment, a doubleness that well describes the photographer's craft.

Evans's relation to the changing discourse of "South" during the

Depression years itself changed. In interviews in the 1970s, Evans often spoke about his Southern experiences in ways suggesting that to him the South was a region of mind and imagination as much as a geographical section of the national map. An interviewer in 1974 asked him, "Why do you think you were attracted to the South, Walker? What attracted you?"

> I don't know, really, how to put that in words. I guess its romanticism and history and heritage. It has to do with the romantic instinct, really. After all, we used to call it the Civil War, and it was a great sort of trauma and historic shock to this country. But it had its romantic side, too. Even the music that went with it, and the whole horror of those men fighting each other, cousin to cousin . . .

About his time in Hale County, Alabama, forty years earlier, he remarked:

> Well, I felt pretty much at home there; perhaps not as much as Agee did, because he came from Tennessee stock, with a rural background. I don't know much about my forebears, but there was a combination of old Massachusetts and, I guess, Virginia gone west into a place like Missouri. I think some of them must have been dirt farmers even. They had an attachment to the land. I was divorced from it by then. I was a suburban-city son of a Chicago businessman, so I didn't really know a hell of a lot about what was there. But I had almost a blood relation to what was going on in those people, and an understanding and love for that kind of old, hardworking, rural, southern human being. They appeal to me enormously from the heart and the brain.

It's as if what he was looking for in the South was himself, himself as Southerner, recovered in the pale light of mythical dirt farmers flickering in his past. But mainly what he affirms here is an idea of an *American* identity brought home to him in Hale County.

I saw old America again, which goes so far back that some of
the people still speak with something reminiscent of the Eliza-
bethan Age. And their faces are like that, too. That sharecrop-
per's wife is a classic portrait of a real, old pioneering, American
woman of English stock, and pure, too. . . . The unpainted
wood is very attractive to me. It's hard to say why. Well, that's
America, of course, and I guess I'm deeply in love with America
anyway.

"Agee and I," he said earlier in the same interview, "were both old
Americans."

Evans took quite seriously this idea of an "old America" kept alive
in and by "the South." There is an autobiography buried alive within
his pictures of the 1930s, a gathering of personal experience and, in
his books and sequences of images, a studied reflection on that experience. Interestingly, Evans's capsule view of himself as an embattled
and possibly Southern "old American" echoes a view of the South
shared by a diverse group of Southern writers, artists, critics, and aca-
demics during the 1930s and since—a view, in C. Vann Woodward's
words, that there was "a Southern way of life against what might be
called the American or prevailing way," and that "the best terms in
which to represent the distinction are contained in the phrase, Agrarian *versus* Industrial."

The idea lay at the heart of a book published in 1930, *I'll Take My
Stand*, the manifesto of a group of Vanderbilt University writers and
critics who called themselves Southern Agrarians or Fugitives. They
believed that the South, a homogeneous region of farmland and traditional cultures, should resist the temptation to take up the modern
industrial and urban ideal of "progress." They proposed resistance
to preserve traditional values, a Southern way of life unified by religion, community, family, and respect for tradition and hierarchy. A
revival of the pre–Civil War self-image of Southern aristocrats as
"Cavaliers" holding the line against "Yankee" upstarts had already
become anachronistic, since by the 1930s the South was well on the
path of economic integration with the national system of industrial
capitalism. As the historian Pete Daniel has put it, "In those years [of

the Vanderbilt Agrarians] one could hear the death rattle of the old culture."

Still, the vision of *I'll Take My Stand* proved astonishingly resilient and attractive to many Northern intellectuals. There was a need to believe in a continuing Southern identity, a folk identity linked to place and to traditional ways of life, something different from and, in spite of the cruelties of racism, more appealing than standard middle-class Americanism. A familiar picture emerged: the South as backward, underdeveloped, provincial, violent, but nevertheless proud, reverential toward the past, devout toward a sense of honor, respectful of good manners and honest work—perfect antithesis to the alienated life of big cities, capitalism, and modernity in all its guises. The South's backwardness became its virtue, and its peasants, as in *Let Us Now Praise Famous Men*, emerged as potentially redemptive figures for the nation—"famous men" deserving praise.

The South as a ground of dissent from a nationality wedded to modernity, corporate capitalism, metropolitanism, and centralized nationalism became a metaphor of difference and otherness. Evans in the 1930s was often an angry young man, filled with hatred of big business and suspicious of big government, troubled by the absence of support for artists and by popular contempt for and ignorance of serious art. "When you stop to think about what an artist is doing," he said in 1971, "one question is, what is the driving force, the motive? In this country it is rather obvious; different, say, from European culture. The artist here is very angry and fighting. Everything makes him angry: the local style of living, and one's competitors."

Evans's ventures into the South, into such a South as the antimodern myth prepared him to find, may have felt like a personal quest, a quest for an identity as an American, an artist, and a photographer. From the late 1920s until the end of his life in 1975, Evans was preoccupied with the problem of the photographer as artist. He had rejected Alfred Stieglitz's "artiness," as he called the older man's tendency toward bombast as well as all forms of pictorialism. His interest lay in straightforward picture making of a personal, lyrical sort. In his interviews in the 1970s he ardently denied that his pictures in the 1930s were driven by political motives. "The secret of photography," he explained, "is, the camera takes on the character and the personality of the handler." For Evans the two secrets fuse, the wonderful secret of place and the secret of photography; he described his 1930s photographs not primarily as documents or pictures of social crisis, but as lyrical moments of self-discovery in and through the world that his camera made visible.

Evans's photographs might better be called fictions, then, documentary fictions in that his mode of self-presentation is the mode of self-abnegation or the participation by detachment that he learned from his cherished masters of modern writing, Flaubert and Henry James and others. Evans called his method "documentary style," to distinguish it from literal and instrumental documentation; he means he is after the *look* of objectivity, of vernacular directness and simplicity. It's this look that gives his pictures their illusion of being merely transcriptive records of a given time and place. That look is as much a pose as any fiction, a fiction of literal fact that disguises the artist's more complex purposes of interpretation. Intentions beyond literal documentation show up in how Evans typically presented his 1930s pictures in sequences, neither chronological narratives nor thematic clusters but as dialogic interactions of images in conversation with each other.

His best achievement of constructive sequencing occurs in the contrapuntal form of *American Photographs*. Here the pictured world is made up of things, people, signs, and pictures themselves, traces of a pervasive impulse toward imitation that gives the Evans universe its distinctive character. The book's subject matter mimics the book's own activity of photographic representation. It is a book about art and artifact, the countless activities of making and shaping that represent the tangible America of the title.

While also presented as sequences, the photographs in *Let Us Now Praise Famous Men* play a quite different role. They are set apart as "Book One," a sly, self-mocking device in which the photographs appear in a self-contained portfolio preceding the title page: they are "Book One" even while having a place, indeterminate as it may be, within or beside the larger book authored jointly though unequally by "James Agee and Walker Evans." The first edition of the book in 1941 thus presents thirty-one photographs in a continuous, unbroken flow—

one exception is a blank page between the Gudger and Woods families (the names are fictional)—in which, after an opening picture of the landlord standing in a rumpled summer suit and a rumpled expression on his face, three separate tenant-farmer families are grouped together in pages of portraits and interior and exterior shots, family members alone and together within their settings; each group opens with a portrait of the father or head of the family, which may or may not echo the inaugurating image of the male authority figure of the landlord; without breaking the flow, the sequence ends by leaving the family compounds for three images of the local town, the main street with its parked cars, a row of shops with unpainted wooden porticoes supported by thin, rickety posts, and the mayor's two-story office across a puddle of standing water.

A second edition published in 1960, after Agee's death in 1956, has become the text most familiar to readers. It retains the fiction of the photographs being "Book One," but Evans made extensive and consequential revisions, doubling the number of pictures to sixty-two, changing the size and cropping of some images, and altering the order of the family sections. The changes sacrifice tightness, intensity, and intimacy for a widening of the horizon. The landlord again opens the sequence, the male head of each family again begins each family group, a blank page now separates each family sequence from the next and from a large concluding section—the last three images of the local town expanded to nineteen photographs of the town and its surrounding region. This new fourth sequence enhances the portfolio in several ways: territorially, reaching beyond Hale County as far away, in at least one image, as Birmingham; and thematically, beyond the suffocating constriction of the rude cabins and outbuildings that form the domain of the three tenant families. This tightly sequenced fourth section is a major revision in the role of the photographs vis-à-vis the text, adding social and historical context as well as a number of memorable lyrical pictures of a "South" to which the predicament of the tenant families belongs.

A key element of the popular myth of the South was the idea that its farmers were independent yeoman, tillers of the soil to whom nature and a benign government allowed appropriate rewards of middling prosperity and happiness. They stood, in the myth, for the virtue that comes with closeness to the soil; they assured the health and continuity of the republic. The tenant lien system flew in the face of this Jeffersonian myth, and the FSA project exposed the system as a form of peonage all the more cruel for its mockery of the early dreams of the United States as an agrarian republic. The sharecropping system kept its white and black victims in terrible, unremitting poverty. Neither Agee nor Evans wishes merely to expose the wickedness of the system, or further to diminish the humanity of the subjects by reducing them to the status of pathetic victims. While Agee struggles openly with the problem of an appropriate point of view toward the tenant families, Evans's pictures perform a near miracle of balance: poverty made painfully visible but pride and grace rising in counterpoint to the hardscrabble daily difficulties depicted in both pictures and prose.

The method is to show that these dispossessed families possess something of their own; there is the world given them, a world of deprivation, which they repossess by means of gestures such as pinning their snapshots on the walls of their homes or placing their crockery pots where they look best. They make of someone else's property something of their own. Each of the three family sections includes single and group portraits set within expanding spheres of daily life and work: the cabins, their furnishings, the surrounding yards and fields. The mode of each picture is exactitude of observation. The first sequence, opening with the standing portrait of the landlord, introduces the tenant-farming system the families live in as represented by the figure who fills the entire frame: large, rumpled, shrewd, a perfect emblem of the invisible system of absentee ownership, a figure whose afterimage hangs over the sequence like a restless reminder of the weight and insistence of private property in land. Each family sequence shows individuals alone and grouped together. Not unmarked by tensions and complications in their familial relations, they take possession of each other and of their physical spaces; the walls, the floors, the bed and tables and cooking utensils, all express daily use and patterns of family life, relations between man and wife, between parents and children, between individual and family and the wider unseen but impinging world.

Figure 30 Walker Evans, "Mule Team and Poster," Alabama, 1936. (Library of Congress, Prints & Photographs Division, FSA-OWI Collection)

The fourth section, added in 1960, opens with an unexpected shift of location and perspective, from the cloisterlike confines of the family cabins and outbuildings to the main street of the local market town. The final image of the preceding section is a transition: a view from behind a tenant farmer with some of his family in a wagon pulled by a pair of mules, probably off to town with a load of freshly picked cotton. Suddenly we are in what seems another world—with a paved street, automobiles and pickup trucks slanted diagonally at the curb, shops, stores, pedestrians with shoes and clean clothes, and we realize that Walker Evans now tells more of the story of the three tenant families than in the first edition, an expanded story in which contrast and connection with outside institutions and forces become visible and palpable. The sequence of nineteen images gives an inventory of the town and county and beyond—the South—and the stories of the three families are told again with greater social nuance. We see signs of social life, the mayor's office, schools, fire hydrants, a post office, a railroad station in Mississippi, a boardinghouse in Birmingham, a ruined plantation house in Louisiana, all representing the regional setting of "the South" that bears on the lives of the three families. And we see black-skinned Southerners, segregated but part of the same scene, the same streets and shops. The presence of blacks in the mind and imagination of what Evans designates as "South" appears in a stunning picture (Figure 30) that follows directly after the image of a down-at-the-heels plantation house, a picture in which Evans confronts myth and fiction with fact, a quiet event in the shimmering heat of a high noon sun.

The poet Donald Justice, himself a Southerner from Florida, was once stopped cold by this picture and wrote a poem about it that he later placed within a sequence he called "My South." He might well be speaking for Walker Evans.

Mule Team and Poster

Two mules stand waiting in front of the brick wall of a warehouse,
    hitched to a shabby flatbed wagon.
Its spoked wheels resemble crude wooden flowers
    pulled recently from a deep and stubborn mud.

The rains have passed over for now,
    and the sun is back,
Invisible, but everywhere present,
    and of a special brightness, like God.

The way the poster for the traveling show
    still clings to its section of the wall
It looks as though a huge door stood open
    or a terrible flap of brain had been peeled back, revealing

Someone's idea of heaven:
    seven dancing-girls, caught on the upkick,
All in fringed dresses and bobbed hair.
    One wears a Spanish comb and has an escort . . .

Meanwhile the mules crunch patiently the few corn shucks
    someone has patiently scattered for them.
The poster is torn in places, slightly crumpled;
    a few bricks, here and there, show through.

And a long shadow—
    the last shade perhaps in all of Alabama—
Stretches beneath the wagon, crookedly,
    like a great scythe laid down there and forgotten.

on a photograph by Walker Evans (Alabama, 1936)

Poem and photograph both hinge on the relation between the commonplace world represented by the mule and the world of romantic fantasy of the minstrel poster. These are separate but joined perspectives by which, as the poem leads us to recognize, the photograph composes its own fiction. The fantasy performed behind the back of the mule munching its meal tells the whole story. Justice's poem helps us to see how Evans sees, the way his photographic eye works, how it creates the fiction of a place by giving the viewer things in space, in time, and in the imagination at once and together. People are absent but the poem traces their presence: the someone who scattered corn shucks for the mules, the someone who had an idea of heaven and made a minstrel poster out of it, and the someone who owns the mules and wagons and the labor they perform, the warehouse in which the products of that labor—probably bales of cotton—are stored until taken to market and exchanged for cash. A tense balance of opposites, then: dreams and realities, minstrel poster and brick wall, unseen laborers and owners, mules, wagon, pavement and street, all perceived by photograph and poem as a unified whole, a harmony of parts yoked together by someone's eye for the beauty that is truth on a hot, still summer day in Alabama.

    The noon sun drops a shadow beneath the wagon, a meager bit of shade in the shape of a scythe, sign of the grim reaper, emblem of time and death, of things passing away. The poem glosses the photograph as if it were a constructed or invented fiction, fiction of a "South" where eloquent brick walls sing erotic dreams of a heaven where racial boundaries invite transgression, while shadows proclaim that nothing lasts forever.

Put the three families back into the picture, imagine them as part of the same fiction the South projects of itself, and we can see why one would wonder whether Walker Evans found it this way or made it up. In his pictures ordinary things glow with the revelation of historical-poetical truth. In that sense they are among the twentieth century's most persuasive revelations of photography itself, its power to expand and discipline while inventing visions of the real.

SEVENTEEN

W. EUGENE SMITH'S
PITTSBURGH

Rumors of a City

Every one will agree that a city is a material and social organization which derives its reality from the ubiquity of its absence. It is present in each of its streets in so far as it's always elsewhere. —Jean-Paul Sartre

To portray a city is beyond ending; to begin such an effort is in itself a grave conceit. For though the portrayal may achieve its own measure of truth, it still will be no more than a rumor of the city—no more meaningful, and no more permanent. —W. Eugene Smith

WHAT brought W. Eugene Smith to Pittsburgh in April 1955, at age thirty-seven, was a piece of work he might have completed in a few weeks. What kept him there off and on for about two years, and another two years printing, selecting, and devising endless variations of layout of images and poetic text, was a fierce desire to break free of all external editorial constraints, to develop an alternative way of working as an independent "photo historian or journalist," and to produce an "essay" true to his imperious vision. "Let it be clear," he wrote in a letter early in 1956, "that from

First published in *W. Eugene Smith: Photographs 1934–1975*, edited by Gilles Mora and John T. Hill (New York: Harry N. Abrams, 1998), pp. 174–83.

[the first] I had an essay—for itself and as a tool against *Life*—as my driving ends."

Smith's lucidity about his ends made them no less compulsive, no less grandiose. In notes published with the photographs in 1969 he explained: "Began most ambitious effort to date in medium of photographic essay, study of the city of Pittsburgh. Predominantly self-financed, hoped to establish precedent of photographer's control over usage of work, text, and layout; to encourage magazines toward real-ization of greater flexibility in approach to photographic essay." The Pittsburgh assignment became a heroic, eventually lopsided act of re-venge against the commercial system that had nurtured his career and his worldly fame.

From a straightforward assignment Pittsburgh became an obses-sion, a personal challenge whose gargantuan impossibility, as he per-sistently reset its horizons, proved a perversely irrefusable necessity. Eventually the entire tortured experience seemed to him a fateful para-ble: the angelic artist doomed to suffer misunderstanding and defeat. "Mine would not be the first wings to melt near the sun." In the excru-ciating four years of shooting, printing, struggling to resolve thousands of images into one perfect and unchangeable design of image and text, Smith often likened himself to Icarus, son of Daedalus, a mythic role that would turn bitterly ironic as one publisher after another refused him the autonomy he demanded. Pittsburgh came to mean poverty, horrible indebtedness, recurrence of old self-destructive habits, am-phetamine addiction, the wreckage of his already fragile family life, sickness of body and spirit. In the end, after the publication of a flawed version of his grandiose essay in the *1959 Photography Annual*, Smith be-lieved that Pittsburgh was a "debacle" and his obsession a "wry and tragi-comic satire of my whole intent." "Other than that, Icarus," he mordantly quipped, "how was the flight?" Perhaps fear of failure drove him to longer and more anxious labors, more exposures, more images, more proof prints and trial layouts, more Benzedrine, more scotch, more binges of work without sleep. Pittsburgh transmuted itself into a site smouldering in Smith's imagination, a promise of transcendence and salvation, or, equally self-exalting, a personal hell. But if Pittsburgh was in part a pathology, in another part it was a quest, the pursuit of an artistic vision—not always distinct, but enough of an idea to make sense of the apparent anarchy of his Pittsburgh frenzy. Through all the agony he preserved an extraordinary confidence in his vision, in the power of his immanent "essay."

In November 1954 he had quarreled with the editors at *Life* over their treatment, which he decried as simplifying and reductive, of his Albert Schweitzer story, "A Man of Mercy"; he resigned in anger, then offered to return if certain conditions were met. *Life* refused, and when his contract expired on December 31, 1954, Smith found himself on the street. By February 1955 he had joined Magnum, the famous cooperative agency founded by Robert Capa, Henri Cartier-Bresson, and others, and within the month Magnum had secured him an assignment he readily accepted. Stefan Lorant, a Hungarian journalist, photographer, and art editor who had immigrated to the United States in 1940, was commissioned early in 1955 to produce a deluxe bicentennial volume of texts and pictures on Pittsburgh, to chronicle and illustrate the growth and recent transformation of the old "smoky city" into "one of the most beautiful cities in America." Smith's job was "to show life at present" in about a hundred prints—landmarks, buildings, notable persons—for a chapter on the city's "rebirth." It became clear at once, as Smith put it in a letter shortly after arriving in Pittsburgh, that "Lorant and I are with differences in direction and intent." Cut loose from *Life* and the system of rewards and routine that had nurtured his career and bestowed prestige and esteem, Smith sought nothing less than a rebirth of his own, into an absolute freedom (the sort of angelic freedom dreamt of perhaps only by true narcissists) to choose his own work, his own conditions, his own "essay."

Pittsburgh was an ironically apt site for the personal renewal of an artist angry at the commercial system in the 1950s. Since the late nineteenth century, it had been the country's leading symbol of a raw, brutal industrial system, Vulcan's city of blast furnaces and Bessemer ovens, of immigrant workers paid starvation wages while the private wealth of capitalists like Carnegie, Mellon, Frick, and Heinz reached dire heights. Pittsburgh stood for America's dark Satanic mills, the heavy industries that produced the great war machines of 1917 and the 1940s, and polluted not only the air but also the spirit. Pittsburgh represented a provincial hell, crude, ruthless, a fiefdom in the hands of a cabal of smug capitalists, and without the amenities of either high culture or clean air. Now, in the mid-1950s, an apparently new Pittsburgh had appeared. A regional improvement plan was put into effect, fostered by the same magnates (or their children) who still controlled the city. Rivers and air were cleansed, buildings scrubbed clean, highways constructed, and the Point that defined the downtown area was adorned with crisp straight-edged buildings of steel and glass and, in Mellon Square Park, with real trees and flowers. The "Golden Triangle" replaced the fearsome steel mills along the Monongahela River as the city's logo, a cool corporate "international style" replacing the rough baronial manors and haughty ostentatious estates of the old ruling elite. Pittsburgh, wrote Lorant, was "on the march." And his volume was meant to contribute to the renewal of the city's reputation.

Smith could hardly have been pleased at the prospect of celebrating politicians or businessmen (his portrait of Mayor David L. Lawrence, the political force behind the "renaissance" and author of the chapter on "Rebirth," is compelling [Figure 31]). From the beginning, Smith realized that his motives were incompatible with Lorant's, indeed openly subversive of any commemoration, and this knowledge must have both clarified and complicated his own intentions. At one point he noted, "One morning, looking out of a window, I wondered what the hell I was doing in Pittsburgh. Mine was no love affair with this city, and I felt no crusade for the Mellons." What, then, did he have in mind as a focus for his essay?

A core idea appears in his first letter to Lorant in February 1955. Smith explained what appealed to him: "The relationship of industrial [*sic*] to man, theme and counter-theme through the history of such a city, can be a wonderful challenge." Piecing together several fragmentary statements of intention from letters, notes to himself, and his Guggenheim application in 1955 (he would win two Guggenheim Fellowships, in 1956 and 1957, for the project), we can surmise the shape of an intention: to portray the city as a "living entity," a totality in its own right, virtually a character in a fiction, self-sufficient, either heroic or villainous or both, and ever-present. "I will not search to know any individual as a complete person," he wrote at the outset. "For the indi-

Figure 31 W. Eugene Smith, "Mayor David L. Lawrence," 1955. (Black Star, Inc.)

vidual, in the present essay, is a part of the teaming into the whole that becomes a city, singular—and Pittsburgh, the City of, is my project and is the individual to be known." He also speaks of "the people who give the structural image of static stone and bracing steel the facts of heart and pulse." Like Lewis Hine, who preceded him in the mills and streets of Pittsburgh by almost fifty years, Smith kept an eye on labor, the "pulse" that brings the city's stone and steel to life.

Unlike Hine, however, Smith purposefully diminishes the role of people as individuals. With few exceptions, he portrays his workers not as persons but as laboring bodies; in his magnificent, demonic pictures of steel making, for example, workers are abstract figures rather than individuals, swathed in darkness, silhouetted against hearth flames and smoke, their faces averted. The virtual absence of eyes caught noticing the camera or responding to it adds to the sense of inwardness touched with gloom in many of the pictures. Or is it the aversion of the photographer for a place he does not love? Smith's decision to seek knowledge of the city itself rather than of its individuals comes from his guiding insight: that to know a city means to take its people as integers or emblems, performers in the larger drama of his own experience. "A City Experienced; Pittsburgh, Pa." he titled a collection of his proof sheets submitted for copyright in 1956. "In this essay (photographically, that is)," he wrote, "and unlike other essays of mine (such as the Nurse Midwife), I will not search to know any individual as a complete person." The city itself "is the individual to be known."

Did Smith intend the subordination of persons to the larger design as a commentary on the new impersonal order of the corporate city and the society it represented, a version of the critique heard frequently in postwar America in sociological tags such as "age of conformity" and "lonely crowd"? Would allowing "complete person[s]" on to the stage have risked sentimentality in place of critique and, more important, have distracted from the *personal* experience he was moved to convey? There is an important insight in Jim Hughes's remark about the 1959 publication, which Smith subtitled "A Labyrinthian Walk": "While the Pittsburgh essay was a powerful and accurate visual portrait of an industrial city in the throes of change, its greater significance lies in its being a symbolic rendering of the artist himself."

Did Smith prowl through Pittsburgh like Baudelaire in Paris, seeking semblances of himself? To say that he is not interested in knowing people but in knowing the city itself as an individual is to say that his subject is always finally *himself* in quest of an impossible knowledge. His pictures communicate a quest, though he seems often at a distance, drawn to tableaux rather than persons, to silhouettes, to spaces broken and fragmented into parts that do not communicate with or know each other. Against the monumental he shows the drab, the dark, the rundown, with human persistence registered most movingly in the spontaneity of children at play and most stoically in the grim faces of his steelworkers. His many images of black faces and bodies, children, workers, women in slum neighborhoods, stand out as figures of both resignation and aspiration, semblances of the artist's own sense of difference, exclusion, and determination (comparable to the role blacks play in Robert Frank's *The Americans*, which appeared in 1958). Social distance, a pattern of inclusion and exclusion, endangers the sense of the city as a whole place. Thus "A Labyrinthian Walk," a journey without end, a walk in search of the "elsewhere" that Jean-Paul Sartre names as that which is always absent yet always present: a sense of the city as a whole in each of its particulars. A recurring image throughout his career, as Jim Hughes has shown, "labyrinth" can stand as Smith's summary trope both for his experience of Pittsburgh and for his efforts to find his way toward a formal expression of that experience.

That Smith intended a *personal* essay, a work of art in the guise of a work of photohistory, was evident from the start. He spoke often of "photographing with an awareness of the relations . . . something that is optical and mental at once." How do images cohere, if not through the eye and mind of the artist? As against the literalness and "objectivity" that are journalism's delusion, Smith wanted to communicate the fact that Pittsburgh was *his* experience, not his camera's (he once remarked that cameras can do so much, except think). His comments in letters and notes to himself, together with the metaphoric structure of the 1959 sequence, foreground the photographer's activity, *his* experience (not only shooting and printing but organizing the essay) of inventing order out of the things at hand.

Smith understood this, especially in Pittsburgh, as a dialectical process and a process of art. He spoke of "interweaving many photographic themes," each of which "could be individual photographic stories" but, woven together, would project an epic totality, "gigantic and complex." In other random notes he reached for literary analogies: in a letter to Minor White in 1956 he wrote, "Pittsburgh, in a special way—perhaps a Thomas Wolfe way . . . is the most complex photographic literature, and the richest in scope and depth of theme and characterization I have ever . . . well, wrought." He compared his work not only to the literary personal essay but also to drama: "A comparison to the playwright probably comes closest to illustrating the way of my thinking in building a work," and claimed literary more than photographic precedents for his Pittsburgh ambition: "Photographic essays must reach beyond their realization as now achieved—it is imperative." And music was a constant source for him of musings about composition.

The analogies—woven tapestry, novel, drama, musical statement of theme and countertheme—all suggest a groping toward a new comprehensive form, dialectical in character, lyrical and epic in execution. Smith sought a new form appropriate to a new age, a new moment in the nation's history. By combining image and text in new ways, he hoped to construct a new "whole as a third medium." Bringing to mind Eisenstein's theory of "montage," the words "third medium" suggest that at some level Smith may have understood—yet another analogy—that his goals were cinematic. But a printed spread of images and text on facing pages defined the only mode in which he felt competent to work, that of "essay." The opportunity allowed him by the *1959 Photography Annual* was exactly what he had quit *Life* to achieve: a chance to compose an essay entirely on his own. The space was less than he felt he needed, the page size too small, the quality of the paper and printing inadequate for the tonal range his pictures required. But the chief failure, Smith himself painfully recognized, lay in the text itself, in his labored, unmusical prose, which fell sadly flat as either poetry or argument. Whatever the explanations in Smith's turbulence in this period, he proved to himself that he was not up to the task he dreamed of. In the light of his high ambition, the result felt like a world-shaking defeat: "the final failure, the debacle of Pittsburgh as printed."

Still, it was not a complete loss. Close attention uncovers hints of a difficult formal coherence in the undertones of its tortured prose poetry, the nuances of the photographic sequences, the tremulous rapport often struck among linked pictures. The opening paragraph declares itself, and what follows, as "a personal interpretation." It announces "debate" and "paradox" as keynotes, and Smith announces *impossibility* as the ultimate theme, what the entire "Labyrinthian Walk" is finally about: "To portray a city is beyond ending; to begin such an effort is in itself a grave conceit. For though the portrayal may achieve its own measure of truth, it still will be no more than a rumor of the city—no more meaningful, and no more permanent."

The absence of closure, Smith's romanticism would insist, is the mark of authenticity, the sign that this essay makes no dubious claims to a positivist notion of "truth." We have not "Pittsburgh" but the artist's "labyrinthian walk" in search of a Pittsburgh, a sequence of images and text, a coherent form of relationships commensurate with Smith's experience of paradox, of the coexistence, as in the opening triad of images, of war (Reserve Officers' Training Corps troops parading in a park), love (a shadowy street sign so inscribed [Figure 32]), and the figure of paradox itself, a tightly framed close-up of the head of a steelworker, his helmet a black halo, his goggles reflecting (and doubling) the explosive burst of fire from a furnace, with his eyes, and thus his identity, occluded (Figure 33).

An image of blindness, or of preternatural vision? Hell or redemp-

Figure 32 W. Eugene Smith, untitled (street sign, Pittsburgh), 1956. (Black Star, Inc.)

Figure 33 W. Eugene
Smith, "Steelworker
with Goggles," 1955.
(Black Star, Inc.)

tion? In an interview late in his life Smith said of this ambiguous opening image, "I wanted to show that the worker was fairly well submerged beneath the weight of industry; the anonymity of the worker's goggles and factory behind him told the story. Still, I did not want the worker to be entirely lost as a human being." Triangulated with the ROTC students at their drill, signifying the conspiracy of education with war (yet the student soldiers look distracted and lackadaisical, and the chess players undisturbed by their presence), and "Love" in the shadows, the worker is placed within a dialectical structure that offers hope he will not always "be lost as a human being." The three opening images, Smith explained, establish themes that play together in counterpoint in the rest of the essay. And the opening figure suggests yet another supplemental reading. The worker's Daedalian character, an artificer whose medium is molten metal, suggests an identity with the artist himself, who also deals in fire (light), whose eyes burn furnacelike, whose lenses cannot but reflect that toward which they are directed.

And Daedalus's most famous artifice was, of course, the labyrinth, a maze of blind alleys.

Smith's conceit was to make of Pittsburgh a composite subject whose ultimate theme concerned art and modernity, fusing the experience of an individual artist with the moral condition of humanity in an ambiguously new urban world rising within the framework of the old in 1950s America. "You should think not only of photography," he said in a late interview, "but what is going on in the world." Striving to be one of those photographers of whom Walter Benjamin speaks as knowing enough about the world to write their own captions, he struggled as intensely to find an adequate verbal language as he did to invent a perfect layout.

Did Smith have in some corner of his mind a political agenda, a jeremiad against the changing face but persisting inequities of American capitalism? Not likely; his goals seem more private than political, the apocalypse he tempted more personal than social. Still at work on his "long poem," the Pittsburgh essay, he began just as obsessively to photograph New York from his studio window on Sixth Avenue and then, turning even more inward, the brooding interior life of the studio itself, the painters and musicians (mostly black artists) who shared his space. In love with paradox, Smith had contrived failure and impossibility as the enabling presumptions of his work in Pittsburgh, clutching the heart of the project, its definitive feature. Expectation of defeat underwrote his aspirations toward greatness. Thus his pathology. Thus what Lincoln Kirstein must have meant by the "hysteria" of his best pictures, "a brooding calm before a presumed, inevitable explosion." And thus "Pittsburgh," an archive of stunning pictures, and an essay yet to be achieved.

EIGHTEEN

REALMS OF SHADOW

Film Noir and the City

FILM noir, as the film historian James Naremore has put it
nicely, is easier to describe than to define. "Dark slithery films,"
we read in *The New York Times*, "peopled with the desperate and
the depraved." Casting a somewhat skeptical eye over the recent crowd
of claimants to the honor of the tag "film noir," the *Times* reviewer offers a potted version of a definition:

> We all know the standard film-noir ingredients. A world-weary
> private eye, following a trail of increasingly sordid clues, winds
> up gazing into a bottomless pit of corruption and evil. The cast
> of players usually includes at least one femme fatale and any
> number of murderous fat cats chortling behind the scenes as
> they pull the strings. Even after the ugly truth spills out on the
> bathroom floor, good doesn't necessarily triumph over evil. The
> evil is simply mopped up and flushed back where it came from
> in the hope that on its return trip the pipes don't clog.

It's true that many films listed as noir, especially those featuring tough-
guy detectives, display some of these ingredients. But not all do. *Gun*

This material was first presented as a lecture at the University of Oklahoma in March 1998. An-
other version was published as "The Modernist City of Film Noir: The Case of *Murder, My
Sweet*," in Jay Bochner and Justin D. Edwards (eds.), *American Modernism Across the Arts* (New York:
Peter Lang, 1999), 284–302.

Crazy (1950), originally titled "Deadly Is the Female," for example, one
of the very best noirs from the 1940s and 1950s, when such movies began to appear regularly, and films adapted from novels by James M.
Cain—the great *Double Indemnity, Mildred Pierce,* and *The Postman Always
Rings Twice*—none of these have private eyes, chortling fat cats, or
black pits.

Even the dating of film noir is open to controversy. Does it start
with *The Maltese Falcon* in 1941, or perhaps *Citizen Kane* the same year,
and go through the 1950s until it ends apocalyptically with *Kiss Me
Deadly* in 1955, or perhaps Orson Welles's *Touch of Evil* in 1958? How
one periodizes the phenomenon of dark, brooding thrillers depends on
how one defines what comprises the artifact: a system of lighting? a
convoluted plot? a female seductress and vulnerable hero? an ambiguous outcome? Is film noir a genre, a style, a mood, an outlook, perhaps
an ideology? Is it the camera that makes for noir, lots of shadows, low-
key lighting, low-angle shots mixed with ominous close-ups and many
diagonals? Is it a kind of plot, one unsolved crime leading to another, a
devious, wicked, irresistible woman at the center, an investigation, a
mind-bending tangle of circumstances, a dispersal of guilt across the
board? One scholar has proposed a "family tree" of film noir, with
various branches such as "crime as social criticism," with further sub-
branches of "the fight game" and "juvenile delinquency," also "under-
world" films, "on the run" films, films based on "private eyes and
adventurers," "sexual pathology," and "pyschopaths."

Then, too, as Naremore points out, "We need to recognize that film
noir belongs to the history of ideas as much as to the history of cinema; it has less to do with a group of artifacts than with a discourse—
a loose, evolving system of arguments and readings, helping to shape
commercial strategies and aesthetic ideologies." Scholars make the
same sensible point: to tag a movie as film noir may obscure more than
it illuminates. True, it is difficult to see a film without wanting to type it
as being of a certain kind; certainly Hollywood, like all nervous manufacturers, promotes its products in this way, and "film noir" or "neo-
noir" are advertising taglines as much as they are, perhaps even before
they are, critical categories.

Its history further erodes confidence in our casual use of the term.
The makers of what we now call film noir had no idea they were in-

venting a new genre or were part of a movement or school. Edward
Dmytryk recalled lecturing at a school after he had stopped directing.
The students asked him about film noir. He asked them what film noir
was, and they replied that *he* had helped to invent it. The term came
not from Hollywood but from France, appearing first in an article in
1946, then in a book published in 1955 by the film critics Raymond
Borde and Étienne Chaumeton, who write that in the summer of 1946
French moviegoers saw five American films that "shared a strange and
violent tone, tinged with a unique kind of eroticism": *The Maltese Falcon*; *Laura*; *Murder, My Sweet*; *Double Indemnity*; and *The Woman in the Window*, followed a few weeks later by *The Killers*, *Gilda*, and *The Big Sleep*.
They concluded that "a new 'series' had emerged in the history of
film," "nightmarish, weird, erotic, ambivalent, and cruel."

Film noir then rather slowly entered the lexicon of American
cineastes as a key formative concept in the emerging academic field of
cinema studies, leading to the construction of genealogies, an evolutionary theory of genre production, a historiography of the study of
film styles, and countless quarrels small and large about definition, pe-
riodization, and historicization. Why did such films appear at this time?
How much is owed to the economics of film production, the B-film
units of the 1940s, which made the best of limited budgets, means, and
time to experiment with location and available light, melodramatic
lighting techniques, and swiftly told stories? How much is owed to the
expressionistic styles brought to Hollywood by that extraordinary
group of emigré directors in flight from Nazi Germany who found
refuge and new careers in Hollywood: Billy Wilder, Fritz Lang, Otto
Preminger, Robert Siodmack, and others? How much is owed to the
temper of the times, the postwar malaise, uncertainty, alienation, cynicism about the new direction in Cold War America toward suburbia,
shallow prosperity, a wallowing in material goods, loyalty oaths, paranoia about enemies without and within, and anxiety about "the
bomb"? And how do we fit the notion that film noir arises in part from
the culture of the times with the fact that none of these films was notably successful at the box office or won an Academy Award (though
several were nominated)? These questions have no definitive answers.
Is film noir, indeed, more properly understood as an artifact of critics

and historians, a construction that lends weight to a new, somewhat insecure academic field?

Still, the term "film noir" is too ingrained to be dispensed with altogether. Perhaps its usefulness lies precisely in its open-endedness, in the fact that it is not only filled with questions but is itself a huge question: film noir, what is it? I am not interested in proposing answers here, definitive or otherwise, but in looking closely at one particular issue, theme, or set of circumstances associated with the term "the city"—the urban landscape and urban experience—as it affects the delineation of the figure often taken as the essential ingredient of film noir, the private eye, the hard-boiled detective.

For most moviegoers the "tough, cynical Hammett-Chandler thriller" probably remains at the heart of film noir, and indeed the hard-boiled school of detective fiction associated with the 1920s magazine *Black Mask*, where Hammett got his start as a writer, is widely accepted as a source of the postwar eruption of crime films made in the noir manner. But it is clear that the fiction alone was not the determining factor; novels like Hammett's *The Maltese Falcon* and Chandler's *Farewell, My Lovely* were filmed several times in the 1930s and 1940s in a manner neither hard-boiled nor noir, before John Huston's version of the Hammett masterpiece in 1941 and Edward Dmytryk's treatment of the Chandler novel, renamed *Murder, My Sweet*, in 1944. More important than the emplotments and characterizations derived from the fiction are the cinematic devices that converted these fictions into urban dramas of a very particular sort.

Take the opening of *Murder, My Sweet*, perhaps the very first movie to transform a hard-boiled detective fiction (discounting for the moment *The Maltese Falcon*, arguably proto-noir) into an idiom unmistakably that of whatever we mean by film noir. Even before the title and credits appear and the scene unfolds beneath them, we may not know exactly where we are but we know it is somewhere in the realm of film noir; the dark snap-brim hat seen from above on the right, the naked hand extended in a gesture of determined patience and potential violence on the left suggest a place of threat, menace, intimidation. We may guess it is the scene of a police procedure, but before anything else we know it is a place of unbearably intense light piercing inscrutable darkness. The contrast, we can call it the paradox, of coexisting and mutually dependent light and dark, of brightness and blackness, of visibility and blindness, immediately engages us; slowly the scene becomes familiar after the initial disorientation: the camera relents in its tracking toward the source of light (or is it toward the reflection of the light source on the white tabletop?), pulls back, shows us more of what the opening intensity had obscured. Now we confidently recognize, from other movies we've seen, a police interrogation room.

This scene, including Marlowe's bandaged eyes, does not appear in the novel. It's a contrivance, one of several deviations from the novel which, while heightening the noir effect, dilute its social detail. The film changes a character or two and eliminates one large section featuring an offshore gambling casino and a new breed of racketeer who manages his criminal enterprises in the style of a respectable businessman with the help of corrupt police officials. Also gone are all mention of blacks, prominent in the novel's opening scene, which takes place on a street and in a black bar and a black hotel lobby in a neighborhood on Central Avenue that is "not yet all Negro." Much of the novel's important social detail and social meaning, its corrosive view of the complicity of wealth and power and its sympathy with victims of the city's inequalities, is subordinated to the cinematic telling of a tight, trimmed-down, dramatic story of greed, lust, and fear. (Chandler seemed to approve of this shift; he reportedly admired this film very much.) The relative absence of blacks from film noir of this era, except for entertainers and menials (*Murder, My Sweet* has an Asian nightclub dancer, in a teasing touch of Orientalism), poses—and begs—another question about film noir, black film.

Why does the film begin by denying us, even momentarily, a sense of place, withholding our access to fixed spatial markers indicating up and down, and then, once we gain our bearings, to sufficient information to explain why we are there, and especially why the figure seated under the glare of the light is blindfolded? The film begins, in this extraordinary construction, by entangling the viewer, as it were kinetically, in a number of questions. Why are we here? What's going on? What lies behind this scene? What's the story?

The story unfolds in Marlowe's flashback, a confused, murky account of false identity, deception, murder, and a final shootout that leaves several corpses and Marlowe's eyes scorched from a gunshot close to his face. In Chandler's novel the intrigue is even more convoluted; the film simplifies, though not much. The problem for the detective is to sort out the connections between two jobs: a missing woman, Moose Malloy's old girlfriend Velma; and a missing string of jade beads that had belonged to a Mrs. Grayle, a very sexy blonde married to an aging aristocrat who lavishes such gifts on her. Stymied in his search for Velma, Marlowe is engaged next by a Mr. Marriot to accompany him while he delivers an envelope of cash to buy back the jade for Mrs. Grayle, which he says (and probably believes) has been stolen. Marlowe ends up unconscious from a blow to the head; he awakes to find Marriot beaten savagely to death in the car. Why? Who did it? His next visitor, Mr. Grayle's daughter, leads him to the Grayle mansion and to Mrs. Grayle, who entices Marlowe to a nightclub and then disappears; Malloy now appears and brings Marlowe to the slick apartment of a self-confessed quack doctor, Amthor, who also has Marlowe knocked out and drugged, in an effort to get information about the jade. What is Moose Malloy, still panting after Velma, doing in this scene? After a surreal drugged-dream scene, Marlowe escapes, begins to piece things together, agrees to meet Mrs. Grayle at her beach house, where he finally puts everything together: the well-heeled Mrs. Grayle is in fact the former low-class singer Velma, a false identity she must protect in order to keep her high-class marriage. Malloy had taken some sort of fall for her eight years ago; his recent release from jail now threatens the whole setup. A Mrs. Florian, in the pay of Velma-Grayle, tells her about Marlowe's search; she sets up Marriot in a plot that will kill him and frame Marlowe, who inconveniently survives. Knowing about Malloy's release from jail, Amthor is blackmailing Mrs. Grayle and trying to seduce Marlowe into killing Malloy—though Malloy self-destructs first, breaking Amthor's neck out of frustration about the still-missing Velma. In the beach house, Velma turns a gun on Marlowe, but before she can pull the trigger she is gunned down herself by the despairing Mr. Grayle, who also shoots Moose, and is killed in return in a fight for the loose gun with the wounded Malloy, before Moose himself dies. All this—a story marked with Raymond Chandler's typical twists and turns and revelations of pervasive criminality—the blindfolded Marlowe recounts to the police in an order that first mystifies, then clarifies, in the deep shadows of the love nest beach house turned killing field.

Back, then, to the opening sequence of shots. We only then get the picture when the camera moves from its overhead perspective to an eye-level position, disclosing the three grim knifelike faces we recognize at once as belonging not to the legendary Fates but to plainclothes detectives. Marlowe, whom we already know from the novel and/or from the advertisements that lured us to the movie house, is a private eye, the hard-boiled sort whom the police always enjoy persecuting. Does he really face a triple murder rap? Or, as we can guess from the look of exasperated resignation rather than determination on the face of Randall, the homicide lieutenant, are the police putting him through this ordeal in order to pry information from him about killings that they, with their usual flatfooted routine, failed to solve? Once Marlowe agrees to talk and the stenographer begins to type, and the camera moves us out of the window of the police room into the nighttime city and up to Marlowe's office, a temporal as well as spatial movement, a flashback synchronized with the onset of his voice-over story, we are certain that's the case. From being a figure under the lamp facing a deadly accusation, Marlowe segues into being a figure of authority, the storyteller who possesses truth, some kind of truth, even in his blindfolded state.

The ending of the film, which returns to the scene in the police room, the "present" of the movie and the site of the storytelling, reveals that Marlowe's blindfold has remained in place throughout the recitation of his tale: a crucial foregrounded feature of the movie's thematic treatment of perception, which includes several instances of beams of light penetrating dark spaces in search of secrets, of matches struck in the dark, and on two notable occasions when Marlowe is slugged into unconsciousness, of pits of blackness rising up to swallow and erase the screen itself. As a private detective Marlowe sees not only what there is to be seen but also what dark secrets lie dangerously hidden in shadow. The white blindfold, which restates the opening paradox of light coexisting with darkness, may be Marlowe's emblem of just how the "private eye" manages to see what the police, despite their interrogation lamp, cannot. And the blindfold is also an emblem of Marlowe's irregular methods as an investigator, following his hunches, putting himself, his body, at risk: a signature of the tough-guy style of detective fiction. The Marlowe we meet in the interrogation room has survived criminals who use drugs as well as brute force, and a truly slithering femme fatale who also has designs on his body, or at least plots to use his body to confuse his senses, perhaps to eliminate him altogether; it is she, after all, who zaps him from behind into his first blackout early on. It's by means of his scrappy, vulnerable body as much as his private "eye" that Marlowe manages to pierce the web of deceit, to see the entire story in a blinding insight. What begins as two separate cases of a missing woman and a stolen string of jade ends in a tangle of greed, vanity, lust, and murder. His bandaged eyes represent the expense of Marlowe's final cumulative insight, the price he pays for what he comes to know and the condition of his knowing.

None of this we yet know. The camera takes its cues from Marlowe's voice-over narrative as the opening interrogation scene beautifully flows into the pulsing city street like a gesture in a dream, and then an exquisitely measured montage of city images—the location not specified but probably in the Los Angeles area—brings us to that moment in the past when the formidable Moose Malloy appears as a reflection in Marlowe's office window. Before that apparition disrupts the mood, we see Marlowe seated by the window, a sedentary flaneur enjoying the city view in comfortable detachment, awaiting the return call of "soft-shoulders" and her promise of an evening of relief from the squalid missing-person job that had given him sore feet earlier that day. Once we cut from the shot looking into Marlowe's window from the street outside Marlowe's view of that street, with its flashing neon signs, the camera has established itself as the equivalent (more or less) of Marlowe's own eye.

The slow tracking shot out of the police window and the four dissolves that comprise the transition to another interior space in another time give us a perfect sense that this is just what is happening: a movement from one spatial-temporal location to another, from one perspective (we can call it an omniscient third-person point of view) to another

(Marlowe's first-person subjective point of view). But by making the transition evident by means of the montage—instead, say, of an abrupt cut—the camera actually concedes that final authority remains with the omniscient third-person perspective: this is where we begin, it is to this we will return. Everything in between may seem to belong to Marlowe's eye, as he in blindness relates his tale, but Marlowe's eye is always contained by the objective eye that launches the film. We continue to see Marlowe himself, his body, even while we see through his eyes; Marlowe himself always remains in sight; he is always seen objectively by us and by others in the film; that is, he is always under scrutiny, even as he scrutinizes the illusionary world before him. In the end, convinced of his innocence, the police let Marlowe go. By releasing him the police confirm his tale, legitimate it, and thereby also legitimate the omniscience that the objective camera had never abandoned. Marlowe himself has never been beyond the reach of third-person observation; someone else has always had an eye on him, controlling and manipulating him by a gaze just as he controls the inner narrative by his dangerously inquisitive eye: Moose Malloy, for example, whose blank, perhaps crazed eye Marlowe is startled to discover fixed on him when the flashing neon light from the street makes an intermittent mirror of the inside surface of the window onto the street.

That Moose appears on a mirrorlike surface, as if from inside Marlowe himself, is one significance; that he appears as if an emanation from the street, an image disclosed by the city outside the window and superimposed on it, is another cognate significance. The montage of four nocturnal city images that effect the transition to Marlowe's own story does more than simply establish the city as the indigenous terrain of the movie; it also reveals a deeper nexus, a formative link, between Marlowe and the street toward which he appears at first as a passive flaneur. The montage conveys a flowing, directionless movement through downtown city space: a main street viewed from above, with its traffic, hotels, bars, and office buildings, all emblems of nightlife, of the transient, chintzy glitter of the postwar city (already in transition, we should note, toward that abandonment of the center that would soon become evident across the country as a consequence of suburbanization); a street-level pedestrian view of the same; another with the bright headlights of a sleek automobile bearing down on us; the next a high-angled shot showing yet another neon sign of a cheap hotel; and another looking up at the converging tops of tall buildings. The police, with their own window above the city, which Marlowe's window will parallel but not exactly replicate, are situated directly within the city and at an angle above it: an angle of routine surveillance. The opening moments in Marlowe's office showing his exhaustion and disgust after a penny-ante job gone sour, the appearance of Moose Malloy just out of jail and his engagement of Marlowe by means of ready cash, help us to distinguish the private eye's function, and his relation to the city, from that of the police. This is a crucial moment in the film's unfolding not only of the story but of the private eye who relates it.

In a resonant passage in his *Theory of Film* (1960), Siegfried Kracauer might be speaking of Marlowe's state of mind at the moment before Malloy appears. About the "city street with its ever-moving anonymous crowds," Kracauer writes:

> The kaleidoscopic sights mingle with unidentified shapes and fragmentary visual complexes and cancel each other out, thereby preventing the on-looker from following up any of the innumerable suggestions they offer. What appears to him are not so much sharp-contoured individuals engaged in this or that definable pursuit as loose throngs of sketchy, completely indeterminate figures. Each has a story yet the story is not given. Instead, an incessant flow of possibilities and near-intangible meanings appear. The flow casts its spell over the flaneur or even creates him. The flaneur is intoxicated with life in the street—life eternally dissolving the patterns which it is about to form.

Malloy interrupts Marlowe's reverielike absorption in the "unfixable flow" of lights and movements in the street below him, and the interruption mobilizes Marlowe into action, into his work of detection.

In picturing the experience of the private eye, what is at stake is not just to show the difference between methods of investigation but, more deeply, to explore the problem of perception and comprehension posed by the city itself. Malloy appears from the street at a moment of particular irreality for Marlowe: "There's something about the dead silence of an office building at night—not quite real. The traffic down below was something that didn't have anything to do with me." In the novel Chandler has Marlowe at one point describe traffic as a wave of nausea. Malloy's two twenty-dollar bills snap Marlowe back to the reality of his empty bank account and his dependency on clients as sordid as Malloy, often themselves part of the criminal system, like Malloy, or seeking a cover-up or fall guy. Taking on a client, the condition of Marlowe's economic labor, inevitably results in involvement, entanglement, and threats to his clarity of mind and to his life. Throughout the film Marlowe struggles for clarity: he strikes matches, he shines flashlight beams; twice he is knocked unconscious and the screen fills with blackness, obliterating for the moment even the screen; he is drugged and struggles to free himself from the effects; he is blinded and knocked out by a gunshot at the end. At stake in perception is consciousness itself. In the plot, the threats to vision and consciousness arise from the pervasive villainy of the drama. But the plot belongs to a larger story about the city itself, and it is there, even more than in the villainy, that serious cultural implications lie.

To put it differently: the issue, or process, in this film, as in hardboiled detective fictions and films in general, is not so much to establish who is guilty but to uncover crime and guilt in all its ramifications. This process is inseparable from the simultaneous uncovering, or discovery, of the city. Rarely in noir fiction or film is there a single mastermind, an incarnation of evil like Dr. Moriarty with Sherlock Holmes. Noir crime belongs to a system; isolated events, deceits, thuggery, and seductions pose problems of decipherment from within an interlocking network of dependency and control in which all participants are in some measure guilty (thus the pervasive noir theme of blackmail). And the pattern that eventually comes clear thanks to the hero's physical efforts and, in this film, at the expense of his vision, is also the pattern of interdependencies and covert relations in the city spaces and population.

The urban setting characteristic of film noir is more than just a terrain in which crime occurs, as tends to be the case in the gangster films of the 1930s. Crime is integral to the noir city, as it often seemed to be in actual cities in the postwar years, a time of heightened alarm about the reach of organized crime and its syndicates. The film noir city is constructed of illusions, deceptions, unreliable or indecipherable images. Films such as *Murder, My Sweet* revive an old convention from early nineteenth-century popular literature, which arose as industrial capitalism was reorganizing city spaces: the city as a mysterious, dense, unfathomable reality exceeding any perception of it, a place of disguise and impenetrable surfaces as much as of wickedness and social cruelty. Poe's great story "The Man of the Crowd" presents the modern city—literally London, figuratively also New York or any modern metropolis—as a place that cannot be read, that defies comprehension even as it excites obsessive exploration, a place that produces a desire in certain of its inhabitants to roam its streets and experience its separate parts and regions with a fierce need for comprehension. The city produces this generalized desire and need for detection, and the need is particularized in the police pursuit of solutions to crime.

Poe and other writers of the "city mystery" school remarked on the incapacity of the legitimate police and their traditional rule-bound routines to fathom the irrationality of modern crime: random animalistic brutality on one hand, elaborate conspiratorial schemes driven by greed and lust for power (including sexual power) on the other. Noir fiction and film of the mid-twentieth century confronted a new stage in the mystification of city spaces and urban social relations. In the fiction of Hammett and Chandler and Cornell Woolrich, whose stories of urban terror probably influenced the threatening, alienating way the city appears in many thrillers in this period as much as or more than hardboiled detective stories, the city loses that air of excitement, fascination, and desire that so intrigued Dreiser and Dos Passos. More somber, sullen, wary, resigned, frustrated, the film noir city bears signs of the Great Depression, as if loss of bearings after the trauma of world war remains. And with new threats lurking in its deepened shadows—criminals in business suits, crooked cops, tainted politicians, sleazy nightclubs, devious women on the make, sly, manipulative men, ambiguous sexuality, an air of menacing bewilderment—the postwar city represented in these films sends up signals of danger and alarm.

That the modern city is alienated from itself is a powerful idea shown in the opening of another film from the film noir period, though it is probably better described as a semidocumentary police procedural movie, shot entirely on location in New York City, its density offering a different challenge from that of the dispersed spaces of Marlowe's Los Angeles. *The Naked City* (1948) opens on a panoramic aerial view, as if only in this perspective, unavailable to the pedestrian, can New York be apprehended as a whole place in a single act of perception.

The film plants its action within the ongoing life of the city's streets and buildings, and the sudden intrusion of the murder silhouetted against a window shade—as if on a movie screen?—launches the police investigation that eventually uncovers an unsavory nest of jewel thieves who use sex, charm, and drugs to fuel their desire and brutal thugs to do their dirty work. The film traverses a variety of urban locations: several uptown and downtown flats of different social class, police headquarters, the homicide office, a crooked doctor's office in an upscale building, numerous shops and streets in different parts of New York. The investigation results, then, in a social panorama consistent with the opening aerial shot: an attempt to see the city's fragmented and socially disjunctive urban spaces as a single whole. The film closes with a manhunt and chase through the streets of the Lower East Side and onto the Williamsburg Bridge; as he mounts the bridge the fleeing murderer crashes into a blind man, shoots his Seeing Eye dog, and seals his own fate.

Rather than the documentary style of *Naked City* the hard-boiled private eye thrillers usually employed expressionistic techniques of visualization that make the city's material surfaces into subjective experiences and signs of interior life. In film noir the object life of the city, its buildings, walls, staircases, traffic, signs, and crowds, become expressions of states of mind and feeling. The realm of shadow joins the self to its surroundings; self and place seem continuous. The noir camera constructs and then assumes an internalization of the dark, mysterious, crime-ridden places of the city—thus the appearance of Malloy when Marlowe faces his mirrored window on the street, the "unreal" erupting from the streets as a haunting presence. This does not mean that the detective enjoys an integrated relation to the city, as if it were a

meaningful home for him. Everything about him bespeaks his alienation: his rather bare office with its window above the street, the bachelor apartment where he lives an undomestic existence (we see a
delivery boy at one point picking up Marlowe's laundry), his tough-guy
stance, his gun, the cynicism and suspicion with which he confronts the
world. To say that the film reveals his internalization of the city is to
say that the city itself as visualized in the film is both the source and
the form of his alienation.

The unexpected intrusion of the mystery of the city in the person
of Malloy launches the private eye's journey down mean streets and
into the city's estranged spaces in search of an elusive truth. Working
outside the domain of the police, Marlowe's methods assume sufficient
familiarity and empathy with criminality to give him access to crime
milieux. The complications, deceptions, and violence that follow from
his unexpected journey take him (and us) deeper into the mystery of
the city's own spatial alienation, the apparent isolation, difference, and
autonomy of its separate regions and habitations: Florian's sleazy bar,
a "second floor dine and dice emporium" in the novel; the shabby living room of Mrs. Florian's run-down bungalow on a seedy residential
street; a dead-end canyon road shrouded in fog (a buck deer—or is
it a moose?—appears at one point, his horns suggesting something
primeval, indifferent, and menacing directly within the city limits); an
ostentatiously genteel mansion; Marlowe's own bachelor pad; a plush
nightclub decked out in tropical decor; a very moderne penthouse
apartment; an old Victorian Gothic house where Marlowe is drugged
and held prisoner; the cozy flat where Marlowe's love interest lives (a
genuine relief); and, completing the diagnostic traversal of city space
that tracks Marlowe's story, the dark and sensuous beach house in
whose shadowed bedroom the final confrontation occurs, which produces three corpses, Marlowe's scorched eyes, and a solution to the
story. Just as he disentangles the knotted threads of the plot and reknits
them into a coherent narrative of crime, so Marlowe exposes the links
of crime that tie the city's separate social regions into one conceptual
unit. The gunshot that deprives him of sight marks the exact moment
of revelation, when all (almost all: he still doesn't know whether his
girlfriend survived the crash of bullets) becomes clear to him (and to

us). The topography of Marlowe's near-fatal investigation has produced a kind of urban geography, not the sort found in official guidebooks. All of this is revealed, recall, under the unblinking glare of a police lamp.

The films of the so-called film noir period typically skirt the margin of respectable or official views of how things are. As a representation of the new postwar urban condition, *Murder, My Sweet* opposes optimism with cynicism, hope with resignation, conformity and orthodoxy of belief with subversive disbelief. Its director, Edward Dmytryk, and producer, Adrian Scott, would shortly find themselves in jail for resisting the House Un-American Activities Committee, along with Albert Maltz, one of the writers of *Naked City*, whose director, Jules Dassin, was blacklisted and made most of his films abroad during the 1950s. It helps to understand at least one source of the air of paranoia and fear in many film noirs to know that they were made under the pall of the loyalty oath. If you take Marlowe as a guide, your first lesson is to abandon the beliefs about goodness and justice that you have imbibed from America's major institutions of government, religion, education, and, especially, advertising, beliefs that supposedly measured American loyalty. Marlowe is the anticonsumer par excellence. The string of jewels at the heart of much of the fuss that leaves several corpses by the end of the film means nothing to him; he declines with a tired wave of the hand when the lieutenant offers it to him. What drives Marlowe is the need to finish honorably the job for which he is hired, and to do it so as to bring the facts to light. His experiences reveal the facts of American life, of the city, hidden behind respectable façades and lost to normal everyday perception in a realm of shadow. It takes the glare of the police lamp and its suspicion of guilt to bring them forth.

Like Marlowe, we too have undertaken an investigation, have performed an act analogous to his, as viewers of the film privileged with a double point of view: that of Marlowe's voice-over narration and that of the objective camera, which never relinquishes its authority to track the detective even as he detects the urban scene of the crime. The hard-boiled noir detective serves as our surrogate in negotiating the city's duplicitous face and its shadowed spaces, which at least partly explains the enduring appeal of this movie-made figure; he stands in for us.

The film initiates its audience into a way of seeing that begins in suspicion, proceeds through disbelief, and ends not in confidence that the world has been set right but in relief that the job has been done and we are still alive. This hard-boiled perspective is a truly critical perspective; it probes, it refuses glib explanations, it digs beneath the surface of wealth and social power to expose the rottenness within. It offers a commentary on the disjunction in the American belief system between appearances ruled by the icons of social success and the realities steeped in greed, lust, and criminal violence. The kind of city encountered in these films presents challenges never fully overcome. Certainly Marlowe's solutions give pleasure, but we should not fool ourselves into thinking that the private eye has made the city world transparent again, open and self-revealing to our gaze. Some sort of order may be restored in the bittersweet ending of *Murder, My Sweet*, but enough ambiguity remains to dampen any celebration. We have seen enough to know that Marlowe knows that any wrapping up of the case can be only a momentary stay against confusion. The shadows remain, and seem only to have deepened since.

NINETEEN

THINGS ON FILM

Wright Morris's Fields of Vision

Leon Battista Alberti says,
Some lights are from stars, some from the sun
And moon, and other lights are from fires.
The light from the stars makes the shadow equal to the body.
Light from fire makes it greater,
there, under the tongue, there, under the utterance.
—Charles Wright, "A Short History of the Shadow"

W RIGHT Morris's photographs abound in things seen, standing or lying there for the eye's attention and the mind's endless play of seeking and inventing meanings. About his early camera work Morris wrote: "Apparently I had more than texture in mind on the evidence of the subjects I assembled. Doors and windows, gates, stoops, samples of litter, assorted junk, anything that appeared to have served its purpose. . . . Expressive fragments that managed to speak for the whole." We begin with artifacts, inert, well-worn things that reflect light and project shade—objects chiefly of ordinary life on farms and in towns of the rural Midwest of

First published in *Things*, edited by Bill Brown (Chicago: University of Chicago Press, 2004), pp. 431–56.

the United States in the 1930s and 1940s, the homely world of farm-houses, furniture, tools and implements, and signs that mark everyday existence in that place at that time. Practical objects unmistakable, yes, but meanings ambiguous, imprecise, inciting the imagination to flights of memory, dreams, and wonder. The field of vision, the field of things, the field of reverie: Morris has made the convergence of these territories his own fictive domain. A Morris photograph is less a specific place than an idea of place arising from acts of creative imagining. To imagine means, according to the OED, "to picture to oneself" with imagination, that faculty of mind by which we conceive the absent as if it were present. It's the means by which we make what is not present to the senses, what's *in*visible, seem as if it were present, there to touch as if it were real. It is the way of dreaming, making the unreal seem real enough to entice us, frighten us, move us with passion or hatred, perhaps awaken us in a sweat. The power of things in Morris's field of vision lies in how they simultaneously invite and elude us, how they incite and excite desire and need for certainty even as they flit away into shadowed uncertainty.

There's an excess of attention to things, an excess beyond what's needed to say what the objects are, what their uses might be for the people we don't see and can only imagine. While referentiality or identity—this is a house or a chair or a barber pole—may be their first effect, the pictures draw us farther, beyond mere designation. Why are we given such things to see in just this way, from this perspective, in this light? Perspectives vary and multiply: we see buildings directly fronting the eye, erect and decorous and often mysterious; there are varying degrees of closeness in views of mundane things; textures seem to detach themselves from surfaces, a jarring effect that raises questions about how we might understand what makes up a thing. Morris gives us a world that catches and holds our attention not by dramatic or quirky displays of human behavior—his pictures are almost entirely unpeopled—but by the attention of his roaming eye. "Anything that appeared to have served its purpose," Morris notes, "except people. Only in their absence will the observer intuit, in full measure, their presence in the object."

There's a resemblance here to both visual ethnography and 1930s documentary photography, but both categories come up short in accounting for the effect of these pictures. Morris's photographs provoke us to put questions to and to think critically about photography itself, about the medium's implication in the way it pictures the world's physical body. What can the camera give us to see, for example, from a corner of one room into a corner of another, or through an intervening scrim curtain, or as reflected in mirrors set at oblique angles to the objects registered there? What comes into the camera's view when we open a drawer and linger closely, looking down on objects we normally pass without further thought? What does it mean to look down rather than up or sideways or straight ahead? Consider the presence of photographs and other pictures: displayed on tables, hung on walls—things picturing other things, incorporated into the world's body. Morris sees pictures and picturing as integral to ordinary life: window frames, doorways; any opening through which the world frames itself; any mirror in a room apparently giving the place back to itself in exact and precise reversal (Figure 34).

Photographers are drawn to mirrors for many reasons: they can show what's behind the camera as well as what is in front of it; often they are interesting objects in their own right, coming in different sizes and shapes, framed in carved wood or unframed, inscribed with etched patterns. And a mirror can seem an emblem of photography itself, its glass surface reminding us of the glass eye of the camera (lens), and the reflection on the surface of the mirrored glass can stand for or even anticipate the picture that will eventually come out of the camera. We can put it this way: what the photographed mirror shows is not exactly what the photograph itself shows, but is like it: an image fixed in time and space yet not dependent, as the mirror image is, on that time and space it depicts. The image in the mirror changes as we pass in front of it, come closer, or back up. The mirror image depends on its immediate instrumental cause, what lies before it at whatever angle. The mirror image anticipates the photograph but is not identical to it. Once fixed on paper, the final photographic image is free to roam anywhere and nowhere; it's no longer dependent on what, in the real world, caused it to come into being.

We have a mirror in a room. Also in that room, visible neither in the photograph nor in the mirror, is a camera. Mirrors and cameras have this in common: they are both instruments for the making of apparently exact and true images. Mirroring means exactitude, like the camera's vision. But the mirror's lateral reversal of the world it gives back plants a doubt. Is the image on the surface of the mirrored glass really a seamless transcription, or is it a transfiguration? We see here, too, mirrored pictures thrice removed, from original to mirror to photograph. The bow and vine and leaves engraved on the mirror's own surface tell us we are looking at both a flat, tangible surface and a fluid reflection on it that gives back the illusion of three-dimensional space. Everything seems fixed and still, yet we know, knowing how mirrors

Figure 34 "Front Room Reflected in Mirror" (from *The Home Place*, 1947). (Collection Center for Creative Photography; © 2003 Arizona Board of Regents)

work, that if we take a step in any direction, everything will change. We know that the mirror cannot help but mirror, but also that what it mirrors counts as much on us, where we stand, as it does on what's there to be mirrored—the way, for example, this mirror shows a reversed image of what's behind us, things not present to us except as reflections. The door standing there materializes the doubt, its solidity as a substance giving way before our eyes into something unsteady, wavering, insubstantial, perhaps an effect of flaws on the mirror's surface—a standing door, unattached, simply there, its blank panels like picture frames waiting to be filled in. The entire mystery of things and their images flashes up before us in all their ambiguity.

Morris's work has often been compared with 1930s "documentary" photographs, Walker Evans's pictures especially, of weather-beaten shacks, country churches rising in elegance, furnishings giving off the dignity of honest purpose and use. It's right to note these resemblances, but it's mistaken to assume that resemblance means sameness. His pictures go toward different ends. He depicts many of the same sights, but with the difference (among others) that he calls heightened attention to the medium, to the act of seeing with the camera. Self-consciousness about perspective and angle of vision, moreover, goes along with an entirely different idea of the use of the photograph: not simply to show what's there but to elicit from the image something "hidden" or "concealed," as he often put it, something not immediately visible or legible. This intention to uncover what's concealed appears in Morris's experimental publications in the 1940s of images together with texts, "phototexts." Another sign of a counterdocumentary motive is his omission of dates and places in the phototexts, denying usual documentary reference. He has a different kind of work in mind for his pictures.

On one of his earliest photographic trips across country, in 1938, Morris witnessed, as he recalled, "the American landscape crowded with ruins I wanted to salvage. The depression created a world of objects toward which I felt affectionate and possessive." "Ruins" and "salvage," words he uses repeatedly about his pictures, are double-edged terms: "salvage" in the sense of recover as well as preserve (recover from where? for what purposes?); "ruin" in the sense of runic as well as vestige or trace, a fragment, a riddle, something concealed in something revealed—as in an extraordinary close view from above, looking down upon an irreparably broken comb on a covered table next to a sewing kit, personal tools of self-mending in an oddly incongruent juxtaposition, the missing teeth seeming to mock any pretension toward restored or mended wholeness (Figure 35). Each thing disrupts the apparent meaning of the other.

Can we take this as a comment on the other baffling remark, that "the depression created a world of objects"? In what sense "created a world"? A destructive event characterized by dispossession of property, of work, of place, of attachments, depression creates a "world" by

Figure 35 "Comb on a Dresser" (from *The Home Place*, 1947). (Collection Center for Creative Photography; © 2003 Arizona Board of Regents)

these very forces, a world that elicits in Morris a sense of affectionate attachment and belonging: dispossession bringing possession. Is there an implication that photography, his photography—a medium for re-attachment and repossession of the world—was also created by depression, brought about, provoked into being by the systemic collapse of the 1930s, photography as his way (like and unlike the New Deal) toward recovery by the salvaging of ruins? If by the effacement of date and place and the fictionalizing of the voice he attached to images in the phototexts Morris seems to remove his pictures from historical reference, does this retrospective remark open a rift through which we can perceive a kind of historicity? Are his photographs made mostly in the late 1930s and the 1940s in some concealed but pervasive sense depression pictures after all?

"Vernacular as such is not concerned," Morris warned in 1940. "Vernacular" implies the documenting of a culture, a pigeonhole (like ethnography) too cramped for "provocation," a word that denotes an action of inciting, calling or drawing forth, an invitation, a summons. We are taken by the plain ordinariness of what Morris's pictures adduce, a world of things and their shadows, what John Crowe Ransom means by the "homely fulness of the world." We are also taken by *how* he sees, his way of seeing that makes ruins or runic poems of things, that recovers as it uncovers, reveals as it conceals. Asking what the things in Morris's pictures provoke or summon us to is to ask about his conception and his personal, contingent uses of the medium of the provocation, photography.

What does it mean to say that photographs capture and mediate the world? Putting such a question risks claiming a privileged ontological status and function for the medium, as if there is a uniquely photographic way of standing toward the world. But if there were, and Morris (like all modernist photographers) was one who believed there is, how might we describe it? In his essay "What Photography Calls Thinking," Stanley Cavell wrote about "how little we know about what the photographic reveals," about the specific "transformative powers of the camera," what he calls "its original violence." In an earlier essay, "What Becomes of Things on Film?" from which I draw the first part of my title, Cavell puts this question to cinema; his film, what passes through the projector on its way toward an image on the screen, is a positive version of a negative—a print on celluloid. Cavell speaks of cinema, but we might extend the trope to still photographs. Are they also acts of disruption? Cavell draws on Heidegger's notion that picturing "interrupts" the normal flow of work or play, turns attention elsewhere, hence disruption as the condition of picturing, enabling it. Things stand forth within sight, in Heidegger's words, paraphrased by Cavell, in "their conspicuousness, their obtrusiveness, and their obstinacy," insistent in the way they penetrate our field of vision. At the same time and by the same act of presenting themselves to our eyes, things captured in light give us a doubled experience and a thought of doubleness; images of things on film are taken from things that remain behind. Left behind, they are irretrievably lost to our present tense, but remaining behind in actuality as a pastness they provoke a thought of their future. Will they change location, pass away, alter in small or large degree? Hence it is said that every photograph gives us a thought of what has been (as Roland Barthes famously put it) and what will yet be for that having been, something we cannot perfectly know: a future without a horizon, Barthes's "*without future*." For reasons such as these, Cavell's idea that we worry or at least wonder about what happens to things on film wins assent.

I take "things on film" as apt for a discussion of still photographs for another reason. The phrase denotes the existence of a negative prior to the making of a positive image. In still photography what happens to things on film in the first instance is that they reappear on paper as positive images; their presence on film means they have undergone a process of negation, of reversal, as the condition for their reappearance in the recognizable form of a photographic picture. They are a negation of a negation, right side up, top to bottom, right to left, values matching those of normal vision. Photography negates or cancels the world in order to reproduce it, to present it as a *re-presentation*. And this process itself reproduces the most obvious observation to make about things in photographs: that they exist, as they do in the real world, as surfaces on which light falls; they reflect light but also block light from passing through, producing shadow, the negation of light. Things on film declare their source in real-world space and time by the shadows they cast, negatives of themselves, producing the effect of three-dimensional volume. The mutually constitutive relations between a photographic negative and a photographic print are already signified in any real-world photograph by shadows falling beneath where light falls. The dance of light and dark tells us we are in the presence of things on film.

Light produces shadow—a truism first put into elegant theory in the late fifteenth century by Leonardo da Vinci. Light, he wrote (as paraphrased by Michael Baxandall), is "always accompanied by shadow." Just as there are luminous bodies that emit luminous rays, so there are "umbrous" bodies that emit shadowing rays. An umbrous body is something solid and dense that blocks and creates (casts or projects) shadow, an impenetrability we can perceive only because there is light. "Being dense," wrote Leonardo, "is the opponent of being luminous." The shadow, in Leonardo's studies, is the definitive mark or sign of light; without light, we cannot see; but darkness also enables sight. Light makes dark, and dark makes possible knowledge of a three-dimensional world. Light and dark are, in Barthes's words in another connection, each other's "constitutive negativity." Light brings shadow, shadow reveals light. By its automatic operations photography gives testimony to this plain yet unfathomable truth.

The play of opposites is immediately apparent in Morris's work: heavy projected shadows falling within intense areas of light, marking off edges, shadows that cling to their objects, the kind of shade sciagraphers call self-shadows; objects projecting negative pictures of themselves on other surfaces in the form of silhouetted shadows. A ladder against a wall was one of the commonest visual devices in eighteenth-century drawings of perspective and painting and architecture, an empirical illustration. The same trope appeared in one of the earliest photographs produced in the negative-positive process, "The Haystack" by William Henry Fox Talbot (inventor of the negative-positive process), from his *The Pencil of Nature* (1844), the first publication of photographs in book form, moreover with verbal commentary attached to each image—making Talbot, then, progenitor of Morris's phototexts, as well as Morris's precursor in the photography of objects seen closely in bright light (including printed pages and bindings of books, pictures, and buildings). Shadows tell the life of things in photographs as in reality; by fixing shadows in place the photograph makes possible contemplation of the act of seeing, the simultaneity in perception of the light and the dark of things. Talbot wrote of "The Haystack": "One advantage of the discovery of the Photographic Art will be, that it will enable us to introduce into our pictures a multitude of minute details [such as every accident of light and shade] which add to the truth and reality of the representation, but which no artist would take the trouble to copy faithfully from nature." In the early days of the medium, "shadow" as in "fix the shadow ere the substance fade" or "fixing the shadow" means likeness, the image cast off or projected from dense light-reflecting and light-blocking things of the world. The coexistence of objects and their shadows in photographs such as Talbot's and Morris's can be taken as a self-reflective recognition that the medium defines itself within itself by its capture of the dual modality of objects in light and shade.

What does it mean to picture things on film, then, to picture things in a manner of picturing that is one of photography's capabilities? In painting or drawing, things appear as mimesis, handmade copies or imitations of things according to rules and systems (such as evolved, as Baxandall shows, in eighteenth-century rococo art) for creating on a flat surface the illusion of spatiality and, by use of shadow (along with color filtered with shade), of volume within space, as in Jean-Baptiste Oudry's painting *Hare, Sheldrake, Bottles, Bread and Cheese*. As Baxandall puts it, pictorial knowledge is itself an issue in this familiar kind of painting derived from seventeenth-century Dutch still life. Reflections of the main light source (the window above and to the left) in the bottles on the shelf and caught in the drop of blood dripping from the hare's nose place the subjects in a space filled with light from a designated source. And shadows falling on lit surfaces—the hare's on the wall, a bottle's on the loaf of bread, the bread's on the shelf or table, the cheese on the crumpled paper wrapper—bring these surfaces in relation to the main objects on display, the unfortunate hare and its hanging companion, the duck killed in the act of lifting off. The whole performs an exercise in mimesis; we're not proffered food for nourishment or drink to quench thirst but an example of painterly representation. It is an empiricist abstraction from the work of light and shadow in real space.

Mimesis means the copying of the visible world, the world of things in light. It does not imply that the maker was necessarily present to that world at the time of the mimetic performance. Nor does it mean that the object represented in any physical sense played a role in its own presentation, except, in Leonardo's trope, in that the rays of likeness given off by an object's surface in the "radiant pyramid" of perception can be said to be a "cause." Photographs that capture those rays in an unconditionally physical act (chemical and mechanical) allow us to say that objects *present themselves* to the eye of the camera. Cavell puts it more succinctly: "A representation emphasizes the identity of its subject, hence it may be called a likeness; a photograph emphasizes the existence of its subject, hence it is that it may be called a transcription. One may also think of it as a transfiguration."

All this goes almost without saying in discussions that assume that photography has a character unique to itself. Nothing in a painting requires us to believe that the artist was there where his or her depicted objects were at that very moment, not in the way that it has seemed (pre–digital cameras) a necessity communicated by every unmodified photograph that the things in a photograph were once present to the recording lens, present in space and present in time. This is what we most commonly mean when we say *photograph*, an act of transcription so automatic, so self-performing, that what we see in a photographic picture, what we understand ourselves as seeing, is what the camera cannot help but see once the mechanism has been set in motion (the setup gives us the margin of human will and choice). This is what we ordinarily believe every photograph wants us to know about itself, not as picture (that's something else) but as *photograph*. The powerful corollary of this knowledge is that the things displayed remain behind, outside the transcribed image; by the time we hold and view the image, the thing photographed may have become already something different. This is what we say about every real-life photograph: the thing was once there and now it is not, not precisely the same thing, not precisely in the same way; the picture saves it, salvages it—salvages it from the fate of what once stood before the lens: change of location, decay, decomposition, disappearance, ruination by depression. Every real-life photograph delivers itself as a past tense—a complication for the viewer, who stands then in a doubled relation to the pictured thing. We see it as something absent to us as we are absent to it; its presence now, in the picture, claims mutual absence, including absence from the future of the thing, as the defining condition of our role as viewers. This is what it most commonly means to look at photographs.

It's by subtraction, then, that such photographs put us in the presence of a real world. For Morris, pictures, whether actual photographs or mental images in the mind's eye of characters in his novels and stories, are always something salvaged from the flux of time, from the past and from their own condition of being past; they are always of the *present* even as they deliver traces of their past in signs of use and wear. In his photographs Morris looks at things as if they were already ruins, what's left over, and if they succeed as pictures they become "imaginary gains" recovered from "real losses," what remains and persists in the face of death. "Let me try and explain," Morris quotes Samuel Beckett. "From things about to disappear I turn away in time. To watch them out of sight, no, I can't do it." It's the paradox of things appearing while disappearing, apprehended just in time, and *in* time.

It's in the space (a temporal zone) between what is found, what is salvaged, and what remains behind that Morris undertook his provocative experiment of phototext, philosophically provocative in that it raises questions about itself. Linking image and words, his phototexts are examples of how from the homely world of things sense can be derived—how the hidden, secret life of things can be enhanced in such a way that the thing seen can be seen as if it were encountering us, eliciting our sight by looking back at us. Morris speaks of his photography as sacramental seeing; he speaks, quoting Henry James, of "mystic meanings" that things have "to give out." The phototext emerged for him as a way to summon from the image what is not entirely visible within it. Just as we can say that the photograph cancels or negates the world it envisions in order to make it visible, so the text cancels the photo in order to bring it into clearer, sharper focus, a focus legible enough to be articulated. He conceived of the form as a particular kind of labor, a labor of reading and refocusing.

This material permits no compromise. It demands the legitimate range of both to communicate the full experience—what there is to be seen must be seen—to say must be said. Two separate mediums are employed for two distinct views. Only when refocused in the mind's eye will the third view result. The burden of *technique* is the reader's alone. His willingness to participate—rather than spectate—will determine his range. It makes no demands beyond a suspension of old formula.

This is from Morris's note to a group of such texts that appeared under the title "The Inhabitants: An Aspect of American Folkways" in the 1940 number of James Laughlin's *New Directions*, in a section titled "The American Scene"; the same section included a selection of text and four photographs from James Agee and Walker Evans's *Let Us Now Praise Famous Men*. The date, the juxtaposition, and the reference to "American Folkways" show that Morris's experiments belong to the same modernist literary and photographic culture of the 1930s in which Agee and Evans worked.

Morris sought a presence in image to reverberate in conversation with someone's voice. "Have a good long look at *Kirby Lee* as you lend him your ears," he wrote in the introductory note. "The result is not a matter of invention, the element of technique is negligible—behind the novelty the *idea* is inherent, the two are the same." The voice invites us to think not just about the adjoining picture but also about photography itself; it makes the revelation of photography within the picture audible and legible at once, but there is nothing in the picture we can point to as the revelation (Figure 36).

Kirby Lee
Sittin here I'll just be looking at the cars when somethin turns my mind to somethin past. A street somewhere or bright lights in a store, or music comin from a phonograph. An I'll be there and not there, funny like. An it will be somethin common, somethin anybody's seen—a couple girls laughin or people millin in the square—or maybe just a light showin through a blind. But it ain't the thing, its what comes over it. Its like a no account scene

just before somethin happens when you know somethin is
bound to happen there. An yet nothin happens after all. Just
people doin nothin, walkin around. Sometimes its Saturday
night an there's a kind of quiet razzle, wimmen sittin in the bug-
gies starin at the barber pole an the popcorn burner sparkin in
their eyes. An yet its like people passin on a stage. Movin around

Figure 36 "Meeting House, Southbury, Connecticut," 1938. (Collection
Center for Creative Photography; © 2003 Arizona Board of Regents)

before the curtain waitin for the thing to rise an the hero or the shero to come on. Only they don't an the millin just goes on. An yet I sit like a man caught in a spell. Like I was seein what nobody'd seen before an was a thing like the burnin of the bush—only I aint Moses an nobody calls. An yet in my own way I seen the light. I aint liked many an there aint many favored me. But I loved a thing an I know how it feels. An there's somethin over people that can touch a man deep, not just them you like through knowin, but the rest. There's somethin over people I can love. Seems they're just the same people but there's somethin in the air, softer kindof, like a secret was around. As if what I was seein was bigger than it was. Like what an Injun summer haze does to the moon.

As revealed in the voice text, the photograph has become a scene of consciousness. The scene opens with a disruption in the present tense; the mind turns from looking at cars, things passing, toward "somethin past" already in the mind: an image like a photograph, which is always "past," a present pastness. The effect is a strange placelessness: "An I'll be there an not there," pastness and presentness fused in a single act. It's a past with a future yet unknown: "a no account scene just before somethin happens when you know somethin is bound to happen there. An yet nothin happens after all." Nothing happens but always something is about to happen—exactly the sense one gets in looking at photographs under the spell they cast.

In Morris's phototexts voice and image stand in no definitive relation to each other; he often shuffled photos and texts, applying different voices to the same image and different images to the same voice, just as he often flipped the negative while printing to produce reversed images. The same picture often appeared on different occasions as a kind of positive-negative of each other—small but telling ways to unfix the apparent fixity of the photographed image. The relation of text to photo is contingent; one does not illustrate or authenticate the other; they are in fact disjunctive, and it's in the jolt that the attentive reader will find delight in having to *imagine* for oneself invisible connections, to seek associations within the image that give plausibility to the linkage.

Figure 37 "Rural Schoolhouse, Eastern Kansas," 1939. (Collection Center for Creative Photography; © 2003 Arizona Board of Regents)

Each of two materialities, image and word, remains self-sufficient; paired together, they gain more than they lose. Each is, as Morris says, *enhanced.*

By 1946 the sequence of fifteen phototexts had expanded to fifty-two in the book *The Inhabitants*, which retains some of the original texts, alters others, drops the introductory note, and adds a new textual frame. In both publications—and in the extraordinary *The Home Place* (1948), an extension of phototext to the scale of a novel—all of Morris's photographs appeared untitled and undated, which is how they remained until republication in the catalogs of 1982 and 1992. "Rural Schoolhouse, Eastern Kansas, 1939" appeared in *The Inhabitants* (1946) and reappeared in *God's Country and My People* (1968) with a different text. Here is the 1946 photo and text (Figure 37):

> Shadows are the way things lay-me-down. Daddy can lay-me-down across the street. Mr. Clark's store can lay-me-down on the barn and the barn can lay-me-down on Mr. Clark. Everything that stands must lay-me-down. The fence, tracks in the

road, birds that fly low, poles, trees, myself. Everything tall must lay-me-down like everything short. Everything hard as flat as everything soft. Everything as quiet as everything still. Even birds know why and have to lay-me-down too. Even the night must come and lay-me-down to sleep.

A leafy field of play raked by low-falling shadows of trees lies between us and the austere pattern of whites and blacks on the elegantly plain structure in the upper half of the image. The spellbinding shadow of the pump handle makes a timepiece of the white, one-windowed, shingled wall, joining the shadows falling from the eaves and the invisible trees, the cast shadow of the post on the right, and the rectilinear self-shadows by which the clapboards define themselves. It's a moment in the sun before all goes dark (the long shadows imply dusk, though perhaps dawn), the teasing repetition of the old Puritan children's prayer echoing with thoughts, fears, certainties, and uncertainties of death: "Now I lay me down to sleep, I pray the Lord my soul to keep. If I should die before I wake, I pray the Lord my soul to take."

Morris's kind of photography reveals itself here as another laying-me-down of things of the world in a stillness evoking death but within which things can come to life again in the voices they summon. And the foregrounding in both text and image of shadow suggests quite powerfully that Morris's treatment of the trope (verbal and visual) verges toward an allegory for his entire project: shadows doubling things in real light; things and their shadows redoubled in pictures; a redoubling again of picture by words, by phototext and yet again by sequences of phototexts. By now the object-in-the-world and the picture-in-the-world each lose any privileged ontological status; separately and together they are given over to the utter contingency of perspective.

Derived in part from the "Camera Eye" sections of *USA*, John Dos Passos's great experimental trilogy of the 1930s, the subjectivism of phototext similarly declines the easy looking at photographs that are buttressed by textual translation (caption or gloss), replaces ease with difficulty for the sake of heightening the experience of the associative dimensions of things. Phototext enacts a relation between eye and mind, photography and consciousness, a relation about which Morris

writes at length in a remarkable group of some dozen essays and interviews on photography, collected in 1999 in a volume titled *Time Pieces:
Photographs, Writing, and Memory*. He repeatedly makes the point that
photography gives access to the world, a way of connecting mind and
matter, of affirming the real world toward which we stand as sensing,
seeing creatures. Eyesight attaches us to things, the world's body, as if it
were a kind of touch; seeing is the first step in the penetration of matter by mind, a way provisionally, momentarily, to overcome the alien-

Figure 38 "Starfish and Portrait, Cleveland, Ohio," 1940s. (Collection
Center for Creative Photography; © 2003 Arizona Board of Regents)

ation Emerson and other romantic thinkers attributed to consciousness itself—a way to join self to world in a "third view." Morris's "third view" that results from refocusing "in the mind's eye" the two "distinct views" of photo and text stands close to what Roland Barthes calls, in a reading of stills from films by Sergei Eisenstein, "the third meaning." Barthes talks about something left over in still photographs, something "evident, erratic, obstinate." The third meaning follows from a first informational or communicative meaning, what the sign refers to, and the second or symbolic meaning. Analogous to the act of listening—of the classical five senses hearing is listed third—apprehension of the third meaning, Barthes writes, "compels an interrogative reading." In *Camera Lucida* he calls this a "punctum," that wounding mark in a picture that compels attention beyond the "studium," what the picture's communication and signification make *obvious*. The third meaning lies beyond the reach of intellection, a supplement in the form of something "fleeting, smooth and elusive." Barthes calls this "the obtuse meaning," "a meaning which seeks me out, me, the recipient of the message, the subject of the reading."

The fit may not be exact, but I think Barthes's "third meaning" helps us see what's up in Wright Morris's phototexts. What Barthes calls a "mutation of reading" results, in which photo and text cancel or negate each other in order to make visible and audible a third thing, a new "view" in the mode of a voice, a view in which text and image become each other's "constitutive negativity." Morris distinguishes between his phototexts and typical word and image links in the daily press and most picture books; they show "a *technique* of translation," he writes, in which "the picture leans on the prose, the prose stiffens gallantly." Phototext abandons "the lean-to picture, the translated prose" for the sake of a new "quality of experience."

A gloss of these relations appears in an early picture never before exhibited or published (as far as I know), "Starfish and Portrait, Cleveland, Ohio," and presumably never linked with a text—yet a picture that lends itself to a near diagrammatic interpretation of the relations embodied in phototexts (Figure 38). A small framed portrait sits on one side of a table, just under a milk-glass vase whose stamped floral pattern echoes the leaves and flowers on the wallpaper behind the table.

Neatly covering the table, its folds or ridges defined by self-shadows from an overhead source of light to the left, a white cloth lays down square frames on the surface of the table; pen and pencil in a stamped-glass goblet stand opposite, alone in one of those frames. In front of the portrait, three stamped and postmarked and apparently unsealed letters lie as if casually dropped, forming an ensemble of rectangulars; they may await reading or reply. In any case, they bring into the picture signs of an elsewhere (and the possibility of a message) to which the things in the picture bear some unarticulated relation. And we see, propped against the floral-patterned papered wall, the glorious five-pointed starfish. Reticulated veins or ridges on its surface form into a pattern of rays flowing as if by electrical energy toward each of the tips of the five points, emanating from the circle at the center of its surface. Something salvaged from a beach and placed as memento, an obdurate thing, once quick with life, now stiff in its afterlife as keepsake or souvenir, the starfish has been placed (we can imagine it only as intentionally placed, propped up as a standing object, though the decorative intention may not exhaust all the implications of the placement) in such a way that its two bottom legs triangulate the pictured photograph and the writing tools. Everything in the picture casts a shadow, on the table, on the wall, on itself.

A corner in a modest home transcribed by the camera reveals objects and an idea: photograph, personal letters (standing in for writing as such), and writing tools stand to each other in the form of a starfish, as if they form a third thing, something simple yet inexpressibly elegant, reminding us of the pleasure and thrill of a find, something rescued from tides and time, its name a metaphor yoking together two elements, star and fish, sky and sea, opposites yet similar in a way that signifies profundity (literally and figuratively: a vast depth). Tightly focused, severely cropped or quoted from the space it shares with the camera, Morris's photograph gives the starfish a monumental scale. Standing between writing and picturing (the floral patterns of vase and wallpaper are also a form of picturing), this thing of nature, made into something supplemental by its capture on a beach and its transmutation into metaphor, points toward further possibilities of meaning, the cognition implied by the joining of photograph and writing. The starfish stands for that cognition, but in no obvious way. It's a gratuity, a mere compositional element (on the level of information); as a symbol we may take it to signify something found or salvaged from nature, cognate to the originals from which the floral wallpaper patterns were drawn and to this scene itself found by Morris's camera. Its five points might take us symbolically toward the five senses, but that's a stretch. Or we can see it as the sign of a rough kind of beauty cherished in this modest home where more lavish signs of beauty are likely very sparse. Everything else in the picture speaks of human history, including the cloth, probably retrieved from storage in a chest where its folds became as natural a deformation as the ridges of the starfish. The starfish too, in a sense, belongs to human history; it was brought here from somewhere else, a beach, a rocky shore, perhaps purchased in a gift shop. Its upright position stands for nature or the feral overcome by human will; it stands for death, the laying-me-down of something once alive and prone in the sea, facing up toward the sky; and its name bespeaks the human heritage of language and metaphoric naming. But something survives this humanizing of the object, something excessive beyond and outside what makes everything else in the picture signs within a signifying system: a third meaning. The dead thing awaits resurgence into new life, resurrection into unexpected and unspecified meaning.

What becomes of things in photographs, then, is that they expire into new life. They issue into a transfiguring voice, actual or imaginary, a voice that triangulates image and viewer. In the third view, pictured things become sites of consciousness registered in speech. Like the starfish, photography joins opposites: *photo* and *grapheis*, light and writing, shadow and word. Yet the act of joining in metaphor has its own negative moment: what can be joined can also be disjoined; the hinge marks a rift as well as a joint, difference can insist upon itself even as it seems to be overcome. Photography makes its appearance at the hinge—a device that holds separate what it joins—between image and speech. It is an agent of a visibility that destabilizes by provocation. What happens to things on film is that they provoke and summon their opposite—shadow, word—in order to realize themselves as human experience. Photography shows that the quest for understanding is a dance of negativity. It is not so much a guide to reality as it is a uniquely modern means of questioning reality, helping us sort out what belongs to vision and what to mind and speech. It's an elusive visibility the camera lends to the world's body. As Wright Morris's pictures teach, it takes more than an eye to see what's there.

ACKNOWLEDGMENTS

Leo Marx kindly read a draft of the Preface and offered cogent suggestions. I am grateful to him, too, for extended conversations over the years, including exchanges on topics related to these essays. John Hill has been extremely kind in helping me locate images for this book and in offering advice about the selection of texts.

I am indebted to the Andrew W. Mellon Foundation for assistance in securing images and permissions for this volume.

Many of these essays first saw the light in response to invitations to lecture, to contribute to a collection, or to write an introduction to a catalog essay. I acknowledge and thank for their kindness John Wood, Richard Stein, Larry Reynolds, Arien Mack, André Schiffrin, Betsy Erkkila, Jay Grossman, Theodore L. Gross, the late Jay Leyda, Charles Musser, Gilles Mora, Jay Bochner, and Bill Brown.

To Elisabeth Sifton, creative editor par excellence, the book owes its very existence. She saw the possibility and proceeded to realize it, with conviction and grace. I am deeply grateful to her and to her stalwart assistant, Charles Battle.

My greatest debt is to my family: Betty, Zev, and Tina; Lissy, Julie, Naomi, Ben, Anna, and Isaac; and my late brother, William. This book, a gathering of work over forty years, is in the fullest sense for them.

INDEX

Page numbers in *italics* refer to illustrations.